ARKANA

# HIDDEN WISDOM

Richard Smoley was born in Waterbury, Connecticut, in 1956. He was educated at Harvard and Oxford universities. Since 1990 he has been editor of *Gnosis: A Journal of the Western Inner Traditions* in San Francisco.

Jay Kinney was born in Cleveland, Ohio, in 1950. His writings and art have appeared in *Wired, Whole Earth Review, In These Times,* and many alternative publications. He has been publisher and editor-in-chief of *Gnosis* since its inception in 1985.

Further information about *Gnosis* magazine is available from: GNOSIS, P.O. Box 14820, San Francisco, CA 94114 or at www.gnosismagazine.com.

PENGUIN

ARKANA

# HIDDEN WISDOM

## A Guide to the
## Western Inner Traditions

### RICHARD SMOLEY AND
### JAY KINNEY

Penguin/Arkana

17775

ARKANA
Published by the Penguin Group
Penguin Putnam Inc., 375 Hudson Street,
New York, New York 10014, U.S.A.
Penguin Books Ltd, 27 Wrights Lane, London W8 5TZ, England
Penguin Books Australia Ltd, Ringwood, Victoria, Australia
Penguin Books Canada Ltd, 10 Alcorn Avenue,
Toronto, Ontario, Canada M4V 3B2
Penguin Books (N.Z.) Ltd, 182–190 Wairau Road,
Auckland 10, New Zealand

Penguin Books Ltd, Registered Offices:
Harmondsworth, Middlesex, England

First published in Arkana 1999

1 3 5 7 9 10 8 6 4 2

LIBRARY OF CONGRESS CATALOGING IN PUBLICATION DATA
Smoley, Richard, 1956–
Hidden wisdom: a guide to the western inner traditions /
Richard Smoley and Jay Kinney.
p.   cm.
Includes bibliographical references.
ISBN 0 14 01.9582 3
1. Occultism.   I. Kinney, Jay, 1950– .   II. Title.
BF1411.S665   1999
135´.4—dc21       98–42295

Printed in the United States of America
Set in Bembo
Designed by Kathryn Parise

# Foreword

In today's spirituality the depth of longing seems to be matched only by the depth of confusion. When traditional forms of religion lose their sway, people often turn to alternative forms of belief and practice. A generation ago, most such seekers were directing their aspirations toward the religions of Asia; today more and more are looking for something closer to home. Many are trying to rediscover the hidden wisdom of the teachings of the West.

This book is meant to help meet this need. It is chiefly directed at two types of readers. The first consists of those who hope to find some form of spiritual practice rooted in Western tradition, but who may have little idea of where to start or which approaches might appeal to them. The second consists of general readers who repeatedly encounter names and terms such as "Jung," "Kabbalah," "Gnosticism," and "New Age" in the media and in bookshops and want to know what lies behind these words. (Of course these two categories aren't mutually exclusive, and many have found that a mild curiosity can blossom into the central focus of their lives.)

It is true, of course, that in our past lies our present: each of these traditions has long antecedents in our civilization, so much so that understanding them may clarify much of what otherwise seems obscure in Western history. On the other hand, we have not attempted to furnish an exhaustive historical perspective, but rather have concentrated on what these teachings offer to the seeker today. We have also tried to steer a middle course between unthinking credulity and unthinking skepticism and to offer a perspective that is respectful but not servile.

Some readers may be disappointed to find that we have not supplied "how-to" information on techniques and practices here. Again, that is not our intention. In the first place, many books are available today that offer such techniques in great detail. In the second place, written directions can only go so far in conveying techniques. Spiritual instruction is not simply a matter of relaying information; something else is imparted through contact with other people, a subtle quality of being that conveys the essence of the teaching. Books cannot do this.

All the same, much can be learned from reading, and for those who want to pursue certain paths of inquiry, we have added a list of suggested readings at the end of each chapter, chosen according to three criteria: excellence, accessibility, and availability. We have not rigorously applied these criteria across the board, so the reader will occasionally find books listed that are of superior quality but which may be comparatively difficult to locate or may even be out of print. Those who want to go still deeper into any subject are referred to the footnotes and bibliography.

# Acknowledgments

Even the most solitary authors must admit that theirs is a collective undertaking, and every book rests upon the collaboration, witting and unwitting, of the writers its author has read and the people he has known. Such is even more the case with this work, itself a collaboration. Jay Kinney has written the chapters on Gnosticism and Sufism as well as the Afterword; Richard Smoley has written the others, though all the chapters have gone through a fine mesh of mutual comments and discussions.

There are many others whose help we must gratefully acknowledge. First among these is our agent, Katie Boyle, who initially suggested this idea to us and helped us refine and polish it; to her and to Leslie Keenan we are indebted for their insights and for guiding us through the submission process.

For many helpful comments on drafts of the manuscript, we would like to thank Refik Algan, Cheryll Aimée Barron, Cynthia Bourgeault, Chas S. Clifton, Cherry Gilchrist, Joscelyn Godwin, Sam Goldberger, John Michael Greer, Kabir Helminski, Heidi Hohener, Brian Lancaster, Rosamonde Miller, Jacob Needleman, Robin Robertson, John Shirley, Yannis Toussulis, and Timothy White. We are also grateful to David Stanford, Robin Waterfield, and Paul Morris of Penguin Putnam and to Karen Reade for their careful reading and valuable suggestions.

For personal help and guidance in the areas covered by this work, Richard would like to thank Glyn Davies, Warren Kenton, Jacob Needleman, Jo-Anne Hahn, Jack Downing, and Frederic Spiegelberg, among many others.

Jay would like to thank, first and foremost, his wife, Dixie, for her support and love both while this book was being written and while it was being lived. He would also like to acknowledge the guidance and friendship of Refik Algan, Metin Bobaroğlu, Ihsan Döst, Sam Goldberger, Kabir Helminski, Rosamonde Miller, Francis Rath, Ivan St. John, and Yannis Toussulis, among many others.

*San Francisco*
*March 1998*

# Contents

# Introduction

Man is the animal that believes something is wrong.

This "something wrong," whatever it is, dogs us in our daily lives, troubles our sleep, and sours our entertainments. Each morning, picking up the newspaper or turning on the television, we blame it on something new. Deep down inside, however, we aren't fooled: we know that if the current crises or our favorite villains suddenly vanished, this "something wrong" would still be nagging at us.

We decide that the fault lies in our circumstances, so we change jobs or houses or families, only to discover that the problem has come along. We make money or pursue pleasures, but these too turn out to be vanity and vexation of spirit. Fearing that we may be emotionally ill, we pursue the consolations of psychotherapy, only to find that even if therapy does help us function better in daily life, in the long run it fails to strike at the heart of this deeper anxiety.

Casting our gaze wider, we may seek the cause of our discomfort in the social order, but if we look across the span of history, we see that practically all possible social and political systems have been tried. Some are certainly better or worse than others, yet none in itself seems to be capable of curing this unease at the center of the human heart. Turning our backs on modern civilization itself, if need be, to escape our discomfort, we may long for the simpler ways of primitive peoples—and then discover that their anxieties and distresses bear a suspicious resemblance to our own.

Finally, there is religion. Here we find at least some acknowledgment of the problem, for all the great religions have this in common: they view the world as deeply flawed, and they see this flaw as lying at the center of the human condition. Some regard the issue as a moral one, saying we have sinned against God. Others use cognitive terms, telling us, as both Socrates and the Buddha did, that all evil is merely ignorance. And each of the great faiths offers its own form of salvation.

Yet even here, within the sacred precincts of religion, the matter is not so simple. In search of lost certainties, we may return to the religions we knew in youth. Although the death knell has often been sounded for conventional religion, it persists and provides consolation for many. How can we say that Christianity is dead when the Christian denominations alone boast approximately two billion adherents worldwide? Nor is this kind of faith inevitably hollow. Educated skeptics who mock "fundamentalists" or "bornagain" types frequently discover that such people have an inner strength and peace that even the cleverest sophisticates may lack.

We must indeed be cautious about dismissing the answers others have found. On the other hand we may not be able to force ourselves to accept these answers. Perhaps we have, as true believers sometimes charge, talked to too many people or read too many books. Our lives can't be undone; we can't unlearn what we have learned. But if we turn to conventional religion, we often find either that it asks us to do exactly this or, in the case of more liberal creeds, that they share our own uncertainties too fully to offer much help.

There's one more thing to consider. The conceptual world we inhabit is in its way as rigid and constrained as that of medieval Europe. What constrains us today, though, is science. The only reality is what can be proved empirically. All authority—often including that of science itself—must constantly be challenged to make sure it is true. Yet the triumph of empiricism has had an unintended consequence. Although for many people it has driven away any hope of taking comfort in venerable creeds, it has by no means led us to abandon the quest for meaning in our lives. Instead it has made us want to test religious dogmas for ourselves. We read of the enlightenment of Buddhist sages or the wonders worked by tribal shamans, and we wonder if such miracles aren't somehow possible for us too.

Hence today's unslakable thirst for the mystical, the occult, the paranormal, for "channeled entities" and living masters from the East. It's true that such manifestations often seem improbable if not comic, better suited to the extravagances of tabloid journalism than to the sober pursuit of a spiritual discipline. What are we to make, after all, of this jumble of crystal skulls, interminable New Age scriptures, and messages from outer space?

We laugh, but there's a hint of discomfort in our laughter, for even the wilder fringes of "alternative spirituality" are marked by a strange integrity. They seem to be urging us to find our own way, even at the risk of making ridiculous mistakes, instead of trusting in worn-out truths and secondhand beliefs.

One of the central concepts in human religious experience is the idea of *gnosis*. *Gnosis* is Greek for "knowledge," but it is knowledge of a very specific kind, neither "knowing about" nor "knowing how." Rather it is something more direct, more immediate, "when not so much as a thought comes between you and what you know," as a character says in *Meetings with Remarkable Men*, Peter Brook's film of the life of G. I. Gurdjieff. Gnosis enables us not only to experience higher realities but also to see more deeply into ordinary reality. Moreover it transforms us, changing our essential nature as yeast changes flour into bread.

Knowledge of this kind is often described as *esoteric*.[1] Usually we associate the word *esoteric* with some abstruse subject, like the neurochemical responses of invertebrates or the grammar of extinct Anatolian languages. The esoteric often seems "far out." But its original meaning is just the opposite, for it comes from the Greek *esotero,* which means "further in." Thus we have to go "further in," into ourselves, to catch a glimpse of what gnosis is.

Esoteric spirituality is often contrasted with *exoteric* spirituality or *religion,* which constitutes the more outward forms of belief and practice. The relationship between exoteric and esoteric spirituality is a subtle and complex one. (As their names imply, esotericism is often viewed as being an "inner circle" to which religion serves as an "outer court.") One important difference between the two has to do with their respective roles in the social order. Part of religion's function is to regulate human life and behavior. It tells us that people have certain responsibilities to God and to one another, and it tries to offer some guidance for these relations.

Esoteric spirituality is less concerned with such issues.[2] Although its ethical principles are at least as stringent as those of conventional religion, it is less preoccupied with setting rules and regulations for society, especially since it usually commands the interest of only a tiny fraction of the population. Esotericism does care about changing society, but exerts a subtler influence, with effects that are felt mainly over the long term. The fruits of esoteric work in a culture may not become apparent till one or two centuries later, or longer.

On a personal level, exoteric spirituality, or religion, is mainly concerned with *salvation.* Nearly all religions teach that the individual soul survives in some fashion after death, but suffers a great trauma in being dislocated from the physical body. Though it has the possibility of reaching God at this point, it may not know this or may have forgotten it, and may wander off into regions of darkness. (Often this process is viewed in terms of sin and damnation.) Exoteric religion is meant to help the individual overcome this danger and win a favorable life in the hereafter.

Esoteric traditions are concerned with *transcendence,* chiefly of oneself. Hence esotericism is closely tied to the idea of perfection. (The goal of Sufi practice is to become *insan al-kamil,* or "perfected man," for example.) Esotericists don't necessarily deny the need for salvation, but they seek to go beyond it. They say it may be possible not only to reach God in the next life, but to experience him in this one. Someone who becomes adept in this kind of realization transcends her own ordinary being. Reaching "perfection," she becomes a god in her own right. She is not only "saved" but has attained everything a human being can attain.[3]

Clearly such a goal is beyond the ability of most people, if only because they're not interested. As a result esoteric teachings don't claim to be the only way to salvation. Some, like esoteric Islam, regard their work as "supererogatory"—something not demanded of the common run of believers. Others say that perfection is indeed the goal of every human life but that it may take many lifetimes to achieve. This explains why reincarnation is such a common teaching among esoteric traditions, both Eastern and Western: failing to reach full realization in this life doesn't damn you to perdition; it simply means you'll have to come back again and again until you get it right.

Yet esoteric traditions say we all have the capacity for perfection, for self-transcendence. Perfection is not only our birthright but part of our duty to God and the universe. By this view, the "something wrong" that nags us in our daily lives arises from a failure to perfect ourselves in this way. It's not that we're missing some piece of information, but that we've forgotten how to "know" the visible and invisible worlds in a deeper, more immediate fashion. As a result we feel cut off from a larger life, and the world seems to suffer with us, growing colder, more sterile, more estranged.

Finally—and this may be the most perplexing characteristic of esotericism—there is the notion of secrecy. Unlike conventional religions, esoteric teachings don't lay their truths on the table for all to see. Even the most public of them seem to have inner dimensions that are withheld from general consumption. We sometimes even hear allusions to "secret brotherhoods" that unite their members in a bond that transcends all others. What are these rumors about? What is the "secret of the brotherhood"?

In the course of this book we will attempt to unravel at least a few strands of these mysteries. For now we will content ourselves with saying that esoteric teachings speak to hidden levels *within ourselves.* Our ordinary minds can understand no more than parts of these teachings; we can gain access to them only by awakening our own inner dimensions. When one has done this, symbols, myths, and ideas that formerly seemed obscure may gain a sharp, sudden clarity. Again, it's not a matter of information as such, but of higher knowledge—gnosis.

The notion of *Western* esoteric traditions is a comparatively new one. To Westerners two or three centuries ago, the term would have been meaningless. For religious believers, the world was rigidly divided into two spheres: Christendom and heathendom. One part was illumined by the light of the Gospel, the other still lost in darkness, in the clutches of the infernal powers, worshiping false and outlandish gods.

During the eighteenth and nineteenth centuries this picture began to change. In the first place, Westerners began to lose faith in their own creeds. Scientific advances cast doubt on the literal truth of Genesis, for example, while historical-critical theory led scholars to believe that much of the canonical life of Christ was mere legend. "Gospel truth" suddenly started to seem not so true after all.

In the second place, the West began to encounter other civilizations more directly and in more depth. As the European nations conquered much of the planet, they were confronted with the need to understand this world they now ruled. Travelers, missionaries, and explorers brought back tales of the mysterious East, while works like the Qur'an and the *Bhagavad Gita* began to be translated into European languages. And, strangely enough, thoughtful Westerners found much wisdom in these exotic scriptures. Philosophers like Schopenhauer and Emerson were influenced by their teachings, while those disposed toward the occult saw in Eastern mysticism the possibilities of attaining states of being that the West had forgotten, if it had ever known. Organizations like H. P. Blavatsky's Theosophical Society arose as conduits for transmitting Eastern knowledge to the Occident.

By the early twentieth century the picture was almost inverted: seekers in America and Europe were seized with passion for the lore of mystic Asia. Swamis and gurus from India with names like Vivekananda, Yogananda, and Krishnamurti found eager audiences, while Sanskrit words like *karma, yoga,* and *nirvana* began to permeate Western writing. Eventually knowledgeable observers like the great Swiss psychiatrist Carl Gustav Jung felt the need to push the rudder in the opposite direction. In 1929, in a commentary to a Chinese alchemical text, Jung wrote:

> It is . . . lamentable indeed when the European is false to himself and imitates the East or "affects" it in any way. He would have so much greater possibilities if he would remain true to himself and develop out of his own nature all that the East has brought forth from its inner being in the course of the centuries.[4]

Well, then, we may ask, what are we to "bring forth"? Do we have to start from scratch, or is there anything in our heritage we can build on?

In the first chapter of this book we'll discuss Jung's answer to these questions. We start this book with Jung, not only because he stated the predicament of modern humanity with unusual force and clarity, but because his ideas are a common entry-point for many people interested in spirituality today. Jung recognized that our own civilization has always had esoteric traditions of its own. Some of them, like alchemy and Gnosticism, even inspired and informed Jung's work. He believed that such traditions formed a much more promising base for fostering the inner life of Westerners than Eastern approaches like yoga.

While esoteric traditions do indeed differ from each other in theory and practice, their differences aren't quite the same as those among exoteric religions. Each of the latter tend to see its own system as the absolute truth, regarding other faiths, at best, as partial and defective, or, at worst, as roads to damnation. As the old Roman Catholic formula put it, *extra ecclesiam nulla salus:* "No salvation outside the Church."

Esoteric traditions see things from another angle. They generally regard the ultimate truth as ineffable and incomprehensible; religious teachings (exoteric and esoteric) may provide access to this truth, but no one teaching has a monopoly on it. Knowledge will be expressed in quite varied and sometimes apparently contradictory ways, depending upon the needs of the time and place. Hence it is not so much that Western esoteric teachings are right while those of the East are wrong; it's simply that Western traditions may speak to our needs more directly and fully.

We must also add that rigid distinctions between East and West are much harder to make today than they were in Jung's time. Today Americans do T'ai Chi and twist themselves into yogic *asanas,* while once-exotic words such as *Zen, karma,* and *mantra* have become part of our slang. The traditions of the West have been affected in their own way: today you may come across a book on "Christian yoga" or "the Tao of Jung," or you may meet a Jewish Kabbalist who practices Buddhist meditation or a Western magician who uses Hindu Tantric techniques.

Nonetheless it is still meaningful to speak of Western esoteric traditions, which have very much their own flavor and which may speak to those who find Taoism or Zen Buddhism alien to their needs. Because Eastern mysticism has received so much attention over the past few decades, it may be useful to discuss some of the differences between Eastern and Western approaches.

**The place of the ego.** It's often been said that the West emphasizes the individual, whereas the East emphasizes the group. The West is the individualist's culture *par excellence.* What this means in terms of spiritual development is that in the West, the conscious ego, the street-level self that takes us through our daily lives, is not necessarily regarded as something to be denied or annihilated. Many Asian traditions tend to speak of "extinguishing" the ego—indeed, this is the root meaning of *nirvana,* the Buddhist term for supreme enlightenment—whereas Western traditions tend to see the ego as an essential element in the human character. Although it can rage out of control, it is not inherently bad. Ideally the ego is a useful servant, firmly under the guidance of the master, the higher Self. (This idea helps us understand Christ's parables that speak of a "faithful and wise servant" or of servants who get out of hand when the master is away.)

**The personal versus the impersonal.** One reason Eastern

mystics tend to devalue the ego is that ultimately they consider it unreal. Buddhist and Hindu teachings equate the "real" with the unchanging; since our egos, like our bodies, are in a constant state of flux and alteration, there is no ultimate substance to them. Similarly, God is ultimately not a person, but an impersonal Absolute such as the Hindu Atman or the Buddhist *shunyata* or "void."

Western religions, by contrast, generally teach that God relates to his creation in a radically personal way. From its beginnings, Judaism has had a long tradition of individuals who speak and pray to, and even argue with God (Job is the most famous example), while for Christians the ultimate relationship between self and other is embodied in the Trinity itself, each "person" of which relates to the others through love.

**The possibility of a "way" in daily life.** Many Eastern traditions are fundamentally monastic. Buddhism, for example, started as a discipline for monks, and its earliest rules presuppose the monastic life. (To this day there is no official Buddhist wedding service, though it is possible to have one's wedding blessed by a monk.)

Monasticism exists in the West, certainly, but many Western teachings avoid saying that a life of seclusion is necessary or even preferable to ordinary life for spiritual practice. Some religions, such as Judaism and Paganism, are even devoid of a monastic tradition. On such paths, daily life is not a second-best setting, an indulgence granted to the weak, but the ideal place to put spiritual principles into practice. While it may be more difficult to maintain a discipline in the face of the world's distractions, any gains you do make are more stable and less prone to slippage. The monk who comes down from his mountaintop, on the other hand, may find that the vexations of worldly life disrupt his practice and overturn his accomplishments.

**The role of the teacher.** Nearly all esoteric traditions stress the need for a personal contact with the teaching through a teacher or master. But Eastern and Western traditions see the teacher's role differently. We've already noted that the Eastern conception of the divine is generally much more impersonal than the Western. At the same time, humans seem to need to devote themselves to a higher being or goal. It's hard to feel much devotion for an impersonal Absolute. Hence many Eastern traditions tend to venerate the teacher, or guru, as the representation of the Absolute.

Devotion to the guru is not a confusion of an ordinary human being with the divine but rather a recognition that a certain individual embodies divine consciousness to an unusually high degree. Devotion is directed beyond the teacher, to this divine consciousness; the guru is simply a doorway.

In the West, this veneration of the teacher is rarely practiced. The reason is obvious: worship is for God alone. Even the tradition of Eastern Orthodoxy, which cultivates devotion to the saints and even (in some cases) to living holy men and women, stress that ultimately only God must be worshiped as supreme.

The Western teacher or master provides advice, instruction, and, most important, a connection to the living current of a tradition. As such he or she is worthy of honor and affection, but the relationship is more like that between professor and student or mentor and protégé. And while any true esoteric teaching requires discipline, Western teachers, at least the reputable ones, don't exact unquestioning obedience from their pupils; that kind of power is regarded as too corrupting. In Western paths the discipline may be stringent, but it tends to be a matter of keeping faith with oneself rather than with an outside authority.

There is a final distinction to be made between East and West. In the civilizations of Asia, esoteric teachings have seemed more or less at home. Disciplines such as yoga and meditation are widely known and have been widely practiced. This has not been the case in the West. Esoteric schools have often surfaced for a generation or two, done their work, and vanished; often enough they were deliberately destroyed or suppressed. Historical examples include the Essenes of Qumran; the Gnostics of the early Christian centuries; the schools that built the great Gothic cathedrals; the Rosicrucian Brotherhood of the seventeenth century; and the ancient Jewish sages who used the *merkavah,* the mystical "chariot" mentioned in the Book of Ezekiel, to ascend to higher realms.

We don't know whether these schools survived in any real sense. There is no clear evidence to show they did, although various groups have laid claim to their heritage. In some instances these claims are simply fraudulent; in others, there may be some actual connection, but the tradition has degenerated either into empty forms or into something positively sinister. Still others may indeed offer something genuine.

Thus there's often no clear place to go for the beginner interested in Western esoteric traditions of the past, only a plethora of claims ranging from the credible to the ludicrous. How can one tell what's valid and what isn't? Anyone who has lived through the past twenty years, with their echoes of names like Jonestown, Waco, the Solar Temple, and Heaven's Gate, will know how badly awry the spiritual quest can go.

On a mundane level, it's easy enough to avoid the most egregious offenders. It's wise, for example, to stay away from groups that charge exorbitant fees, encourage members to cut off relations with outside friends and relatives, urge violence, or exact absolute obedience. But these guidelines only apply to extreme cases; they don't tell us how to identify groups and teachers who may be perfectly harmless but ultimately just don't have that much to offer. After all, wasting your time is another hazard to be avoided.

This book will try to refrain from passing judgment on specific organizations, for two reasons. First, there are no objective, universally accepted criteria for validating a "successful" esoteric group. If esoteric work is ultimately internal, then the criteria will have to be internal too. Second, even a good group can go bad, and this can happen in a relatively short time. Therefore any recommendation made today might not hold true tomorrow.

This fact means that the aspirant is responsible for finding his or her own way, and this is as it should be. Indeed, one of the main qualities that the spiritual seeker of any persuasion must develop is discrimination. The British magician William G. Gray writes:

[The] spiritual actuality [of the Western inner way] is indeed surrounded by a vast field of misleading, inaccurate, and diversionary material. We might well suppose that its appointed guardians have camouflaged its paths very cleverly against unworthy entrants and unwelcome intruders. Only those intelligent and determined enough to penetrate the barriers and surmount the formidable obstacles are likely to reach the realities symbolized by the goal. Through this filtering stage, sometimes called the "Outer Court," aspiring souls sort themselves out stage by stage as they respond to various spiritual stimuli.[5]

A Sufi proverb puts it bluntly: "If you *can* be fooled, you *will* be."

Discernment of this kind must be as finely tuned as the gourmet's palate or the perfumer's sense of smell. The Russian esotericist Boris Mouravieff relates an Eastern legend that tells of a certain type of bird known as the "royal swan." If these swans are given milk mixed with water, they can drink the milk and leave the water. The spiritual path demands a similar degree of refined discernment. You need to check out credentials and do all the research in the ordinary way, of course, but you must also bring something much subtler into play.

Nor is this discrimination exclusively intellectual in nature. The ordinary rational mind is too coarse a screen to discern someone with genuine knowledge from someone who merely puts on a good show. This subtler kind of discernment uses what's called "emotional intelligence," and it's closely connected to a quality that's best described by a somewhat old-fashioned word: decency.

Books on spirituality abound with exhortations toward purity of heart and cleanliness of motive, along with examples of those who became ensnared in the web of their own occult ambitions (a main theme of horror films). These warnings should be taken seriously.

Nobody comes to the path totally pure. Along with our hopes of communion with the Infinite, we bring along our ordinary obsessions with money, sex, and power, and our dreams of unearned gain. Much of the spiritual path in fact consists of a subtle purification whereby the dross of these base motives is removed—sometimes gently, sometimes not so gently—so that something purer and finer may emerge.

In any event few seekers entirely manage to avoid playing with power for the sake of gain. A good number get no results whatsoever. Others make a few halting steps in that direction, find that these powers are real enough, and run away in terror, like children frightened by the answers they get from a Ouija board.

Many of the rest will need to make a choice. They have a taste of real power, and they see how they can use it. If they like this power and want more of it, it's a wish that can be granted. But with a proviso: if you're playing the power game (and this is as true in spirituality as it is in daily life), you'll eventually meet someone stronger, smarter, and meaner than you. And then the struggle will be merciless. Sorcerers' battles have long been a staple of magical cultures; some legends tell how whole civilizations have been destroyed by such conflicts.

All this may seem terribly rarefied to someone who's just browsing in the mystical marketplace. But even for a beginner this choice will be an issue. As you encounter various groups and teachers, you'll find some that allow and encourage various forms of abuse—humiliation, dominance, deceit, or other such games. If you are drawn to such groups, you will probably not escape unscathed. But if you feel an instinctive repugnance for harmful machinations, you'll most likely lose interest in these groups, and they'll lose interest in you.

This is probably one inspiration for those tales that tell of innocents whose guiltlessness provides them with an impenetrable defense. But myths are myths, and it is only in such stories that you can rely on your decency alone to protect you. If you put both your decency and discrimination into play, you have a much better chance. On a practical level, your best bet is to find a group that encourages such qualities as humor, open inquiry, and respect for all its members.

There is one final demand that the esoteric path places upon beginners: hard work. Esoteric spirituality does offer the hope of attaining exceptional capacities, but you won't be able to achieve them without making exceptional demands of yourself. Any weight-room trainer knows that unless you push your muscles up to, and even beyond, a certain limit, you won't gain strength.

On the esoteric path much the same is true, except that here it is the totality of your being—your body, mind, emotions, and parts of yourself that you didn't know you had—that you'll have to push beyond their limits. Nearly all traditions speak in terms of "overcoming yourself." You can only accomplish such a thing by enormous work and struggle. G. I. Gurdjieff even went so far as to say that in esoteric work "only super-efforts count."

In the past, aspirants made these "super-efforts" using means that we would consider dangerous or extreme. The Sioux Indians, for example, in their celebrated Sun Dance, pierce the seeker's chest muscles with thongs; the participant dances till the thongs have pulled free, which may take as long as several days. Other traditions have obliged aspirants to fast or subject themselves to other privations or extreme experiences (remember Christ's forty days in the wilderness).

In most of the traditions we'll be exploring, "super-efforts" of this kind are no longer practiced. Demands are still made, but they may appear in subtler forms. For most people today, the challenge will probably lie, for a long time at least, not in enduring pain and privation, but in somehow managing to carry out a spiritual practice during the course of a busy life. Such efforts will probably include study and meditation, as well as certain physical or emotional disciplines. At the outset one should probably plan to devote thirty minutes a day to some kind of practice, as well as an evening a week to a group meeting or similar activity.

Discernment, decency, and hard work are the three basic requirements for the paths we'll be examining; unless you can satisfy these criteria you probably won't get far. Later on you will have to fulfill other requirements, and we will deal with those in due course.

# HIDDEN WISDOM

*One*

# JUNG AND THE DISCOVERY
# OF THE UNCONSCIOUS

Psychology is an infant science. Although reflections on human nature can be found as far back as the written record goes, the scientific investigation of the mind goes back scarcely more than a century; indeed, many date its inception to the publication of Sigmund Freud's *Interpretation of Dreams* in 1900.

Freud's great insight, discussed first in this book and elaborated in his later writings, was actually the discovery of what we *don't* know: the subconscious, that great unfathomed area of the mind that contains fears, hopes, longings, and terrors so deep that we live in complete ignorance of them. Freud regarded the subconscious as the region of primal desires—principally sexual desires—that the conscious mind has deemed unacceptable and chosen to repress. For the rest of his long career, he would attempt to unearth the mysteries of this nether region as they were disclosed in dreams, jokes, and slips of the tongue.

It would be hard to overstate the importance of Freud's discovery; much of twentieth-century thought would have been impossible without it. But Freud's views had been in circulation only a short while when other psychiatrists, including some of his own pupils, began to find fault with them. One of the chief issues had to do with spirituality.

Freud had little patience with religious manifestations of any sort. He regarded mystical experience, with its sense of merging with a greater whole, as an unconscious attempt to recapture the "oceanic" quality of the infantile state, when the individual does not yet see himself as an "I" distinct from the rest of the world. Freud also mistrusted religion, seeing it as the result of a repressed libido or sex drive.

For some of his associates, this view failed to do justice either to the richness of religious experience or to the heights of human spiritual aspiration. Foremost of those who took issue with Freud on this score was Carl Gustav Jung (1875–1961), a Swiss psychiatrist who had long been fascinated by the occult (he wrote his dissertation on psychic phenomena).[1] Jung became interested in Freud's ideas and finally met him in 1907. The two men rapidly became close friends, and at one point Freud even seemed to be grooming Jung to be his successor as leader of the psychoanalytic movement. After several years, however, Freud and Jung began to grow apart. Though personal issues contributed to their estrangement, they had also begun to differ on their views of the psyche, especially the unconscious.

## THE DISCOVERY OF THE ARCHETYPES

Jung spent most of the first decade of the twentieth century as staff psychiatrist of the Burghölzli, a respected Swiss mental hospital. His clinical work there with psychotic and schizophrenic patients led him to make an odd observation. He found that their fantasies and delusions often bore a striking resemblance to ancient myths—even when there was no way they could have read or heard of those myths.

One celebrated case involved a patient diagnosed with paranoid dementia. In Jung's description, "The patient sees in the sun an 'upright tail' similar to an erected penis. When he moves his head back and forth, then, too, the sun's penis sways back and forth in a like manner, and out of that the wind arises."

To most people, this weird delusion might seem meaningless. Not to Jung. He noticed that it resembled a text from the Mithra cult, a mystery religion that flourished in the late Roman Empire. The text reads, "In like manner the so-called tube, the origin of the ministering wind, will become visible. For it will appear to you as a tube hanging down from the sun."[2]

How could this coincidence be explained? The patient was hardly likely to have read the text, since institutionalized psychotics rarely keep abreast of classical scholarship; besides, the man had been admitted to the asylum years before the document was published.[3] To explain this case, and others like it, Jung posited an unconscious layer of the mind that is more than a mere collection of repressed desires. It is common to all humankind and, he felt, serves as a repository not only for the images of our dreams, fantasies, and hallucinations, but also for the universal symbols of myth and religion. Jung would come to call this realm the *collective unconscious*. The symbols themselves were produced by forces he called *archetypes*.

Like Freud, Jung gave central importance to the role of unconscious drives or instincts in the human psyche. Whereas Freud thought these could for the most part be traced to the sex drive, however, Jung considered such a view too simplistic. In addition to the ordinary instincts designed to preserve self and species, Jung came to see another, even more important drive: the drive toward self-realization. He understood the archetypes as forces that urge us, sometimes gently, sometimes harshly, toward this greater wholeness.

Today, books and magazines are full of talk about "self-realization" and "greater wholeness." But the more one looks into these ideas, the more elusive they seem. What is the "self" that I'm supposed to realize? Does it exist already, or do I make it up as I go along? For that matter, how does it differ from the "I" that I am now? Such questions cut to the heart of Jung's psychology. They also show why his ideas have found their way into discussions of esoteric and mystical traditions.

Most forms of psychotherapy have one chief aim: to resolve

various kinds of problems—depression, anxiety, sexual or emotional dysfunction—and help people live more balanced lives. There is nothing wrong with this goal, but it does not address the ultimate meaning of human existence. Jung believed that unless one faces this question, particularly in the second half of life, one cannot, in the deepest sense, be sane or healthy. Why? Because the ordinary street-level self, the "I" that goes to work and pays the bills and watches TV, is not the whole self.

## THE EGO AND THE SELF

Jung distinguished what he called the *ego,* the conscious "I" that we normally identify with, from the *Self,* which is the center of our being, conscious and unconscious, and which of course is much larger than the ego. Jung's pupil Marie-Louise von Franz likened the Self to the center of an enormous dark sphere, with the conscious ego as only a small patch of light on the surface.[4] Most modern people lack any means of extending this patch of light so that it illuminates more of the whole, and this disconnection from our own deepest being accounts for the anomie that troubles our lives.

Jung also tells us, however, that this dissociation is not complete. The archetypes leak through the porous barriers of consciousness in various forms, especially through dreams. Working with dream images can thus help bring the hidden treasures of the unconscious to light.

In Jung's view, dreams have two basic functions. In the first place, they show what's going on in the unconscious. As we grow, change, and adjust to the storms and stresses of daily life, the unconscious must make adjustments of its own. These adjustments are reflected in our dreams, which in their strange, allusive language, with its peculiarly logical illogic, serve as a kind of seismograph, indicating the shifts and movements of the psyche.

Often the unconscious seems entirely capable of regulating our psychic equilibrium without any help from the conscious ego. But this isn't always true, a fact that leads to the second function of dreams: the ego is just as much a part of our nature as anything else, and it too has to be brought into the picture. Sometimes it even has to be told where it's off base. This probably explains those dreams whose meaning is all too clear, even to the rational mind. Jung cites an amusing example:

> There was . . . a lady who was well known for her stupid preju-
> dices and her stubborn resistance to reasoned argument. One
> could have argued with her all night to no effect; she would have
> taken not the slightest notice. Her dreams, however, took a differ-
> ent line of approach. One night, she dreamed she was attending
> an important social occasion. She was greeted by the hostess with
> the words: "How nice that you could come. All your friends are
> here, and they are waiting for you." The hostess then led her to
> the door and opened it, and the dreamer stepped through—into a
> cowshed![5]

Clearly the unconscious has a vested interest in communicating with the street-level ego, which has the choice of accepting or refusing the insights offered. But what about the ego? Is it in its turn interested in listening to and speaking to the unconscious?

Usually it isn't. We are, of course, occasionally disturbed by nightmares or warned away from disaster by some premonitory dream. But in most cases the ego and the unconscious are dissociated from each other, like two completely separate people who rent out different stories of the same building. This is the predicament of modern humanity, which has worked so hard to reinforce the conscious mind at the expense of older, more primitive (but more vital) dimensions. Overcoming this split requires tremendous courage and effort, but only if we do overcome it will we find richness and fulfillment in life. Forging a conscious relationship with the Self is known as *individuation*. It is the goal of Jungian analysis.

## ACTIVE IMAGINATION

How does individuation take place? How does one introduce the ego to the unconscious? As we've seen, the barrier between these two aspects of the psyche is permeable. It is more open in sleep, for example, when mental activity is occupied by dreams, and it tends to be more closed when exposed to the bright light of day-time consciousness.

Yet even when we're awake, the barrier is occasionally let down a bit. This can happen spontaneously during times of emotional crisis or depression; Jung called this state the *abaissement du niveau mental,* or "lowering of the mental level."[6] It is the "dark night of the soul" mentioned by the Spanish mystic St. John of the Cross, the "dark wood" in which Dante finds himself lost at the opening of his *Inferno.* In deeply disturbed cases, like the patient who saw the tube coming out of the sun, this "lowering" is often more or less permanent, allowing unconscious elements to leak through all the time.

Jung evolved his own way of "lowering the mental level" of the psyche during his sessions with patients. He called it *active imagination* and described it as

> a method . . . of introspection for observing the stream of interior images. One concentrates one's attention on some impressive but unintelligible dream-image, or on a spontaneous visual impression, and observes the changes taking place in it. Meanwhile, of course, all criticism must be suspended and the happenings observed and noted with absolute objectivity. Obviously, too, the objection that the whole thing is "arbitrary" and "thought up" must be set aside, since it springs from the anxiety of an ego-consciousness which brooks no master besides itself in its own house.[7]

Active imagination is the chief "meditative practice" of Jungian psychology; indeed Jung was probably thinking of this technique when he urged that Western man "remain true to himself and develop out of his own nature all that the East has brought forth from its inner being."[8]

How does it work? Usually the patient brings in a recent dream, or sometimes a daydream. Then, under the analyst's guidance, he or she is encouraged to take a character or symbol from the dream and work with it in the way described above. Sometimes several dream images or characters are imagined together and allowed to interact in the arena of the patient's imagination. In other cases, say where a dream has ended at a particularly critical or dramatic point, the patient will use active imagination to continue the dream and try to resolve the issues it presents.

Working with an analyst in this fashion over a course of time (usually several years), patients often find that the symbols in their dreams and fantasies change remarkably. Working with many clients over his career, Jung began to find some similarities in the ways their inner lives were changed by exploring the unconscious. Although he always stressed the importance of individual differences, he was eventually able to draw a general portrait of the process of individuation as it happens to most people.

Individuation requires us to face the archetypes that lie hidden below the threshold of conscious thought, as well as the *complexes,* the bundle of emotionally charged individual associations in which the archetypes are wrapped. In his writings, Jung describes a number of common archetypes including the trickster, the hero, and the wise old man. But individuation can be seen primarily as an encounter with three archetypes: the shadow, the anima/ animus, and the Self.

## THE SHADOW KNOWS

A radio show in the 1940s used to ask: "Who knows what evil lurks in the hearts of men? The Shadow knows." This is not far from Jung's view. "The shadow coincides with the 'personal' unconscious (which corresponds to Freud's conception of the unconscious)," he writes. "The shadow personifies everything that the subject refuses to acknowledge about himself and yet is thrusting itself upon him directly or indirectly."[9]

As Jung points out, the realm of the shadow is the area where his psychology most resembles Freud's. Much of Freud's psychology had to do with repressed drives—desires or aversions that the conscious mind cannot accept and must push into the background. But as both Freud and Jung understood, these urges are usually only imperfectly concealed. They "thrust themselves" upon us in various forms, ranging from jokes and slips of the tongue to dreams and phobias. Or, as Jung would say, we may *project* them onto somebody else. *Projection* is Jung's term for that uneasy compromise whereby one sees one's own faults in others but not in oneself.

Because the shadow consists of precisely those things we don't want to admit about ourselves, it's particularly susceptible to projection. Hence Jung's metaphor: the shadow is the dark image that we cast onto others. We all project our shadows as individuals upon other individuals, but Jung also saw this as a collective phenomenon, something to which nations, races, and various social subgroups can succumb. Here the results are disastrous. Of the Third Reich, Jung wrote:

> This spectacle recalls the figure of what Nietzsche so aptly calls the "pale criminal," who in reality shows all the signs of hysteria. He simply will not and cannot admit that he is what he is; he cannot endure his own guilt, just as he could not help incurring it. He will stoop to every kind of self-deception if only he can escape the sight of himself. . . . A feeling of inferiority . . . can easily lead to an hysterical dissociation of the personality, which consists essentially in one hand not knowing what the other is doing, in wanting to jump over one's shadow, and in looking for everything dark, inferior, and culpable *in others.*[10]

This is a good description of shadow projection on the collective level. The remedy, however, is more easily described than carried out: one must recognize these forces in oneself and see them clearly, without yielding to them: "It is everybody's allotted fate to become conscious of and learn to deal with this shadow."[11] Unfortunately, this mandate is still harder to fulfill on a group level, where even comparatively sane people can be overcome by the spirit of the mob. Hence Jung tended to mistrust collective efforts and instead held out more hope for individual transformation. It was no coincidence that he called his method of development "individuation."

Yet the shadow cannot be equated solely with evil. It simply consists of what we can't accept about ourselves; thus its contents, however terrifying they may appear to us personally, are from an objective point of view often quite innocent, and may even include positive qualities that for one reason or another we can't admit we have.

## THE OTHER SEX WITHIN

Having encountered the shadow—and Jungians stress that this encounter will continue throughout our lives—the individual may then find another archetype lurking behind it. "In the unconscious of every man there is hidden a feminine personality, and in that of every woman a masculine personality," Jung wrote.[12] To the female aspect of a man he gave the name *anima;* the male aspect of a woman he called the *animus.*

The anima figure often appears as a man's ideal woman. At one extreme, she may reflect his highest aspirations, as Beatrice did for Dante; or, at the other, she may appear as the embodiment of carnality or debauchery. The anima, like the unconscious in general, tends to compensate for overdeveloped features of the consciousness; the anima of a man who is too rational and controlled may look like a slattern or a whore.

The anima can and does appear in dreams, but she is also projected onto flesh-and-blood women, in a process commonly known as falling in love. Both literature and popular culture furnish examples of disastrous anima projections: the tormented love of the medical student Philip Carey for the vulgar Mildred Rogers in W. Somerset Maugham's *Of Human Bondage*; the tyrannical schoolteacher in Josef von Sternberg's film *The Blue Angel* who succumbs to the charms of a cabaret singer; and more recent examples in films like *Something Wild* and *Desperately Seeking Susan*.

No matter what form the anima takes, she always has the same characteristic: she is not quite human. She remains an abstraction. When a man projects his anima onto a real woman, what he loves is (at least initially) not the woman herself but his own idealized feminine self. Thus he sets the stage for disillusionment. Marcel Proust's character Charles Swann, the unhappy lover of the courtesan Odette, sums it up well when he cries, "To think that I wasted years of my life, that I wanted to die, that I had my greatest love for a woman who didn't appeal to me, who wasn't my type!"

Exactly the same thing happens to women. The animus may appear as a dream lover, the knight in shining armor, or in a darker guise, like Tennessee Williams's Stanley Kowalski. Again there is the same disjunction between ideal and reality, with the same disappointment. The truth, when recognized, casts the relationship into doubt; the lover may be discarded, and a fresher screen for fantasies may be sought in someone else. If not, and if there is enough substance to their bond, the partners face the intricate task of disengaging the real people from the projections of the anima and animus. Jungians generally regard this as the passing of a relationship from infatuation to mature, stable love.

Male and female, conscious and unconscious, darkness and light: such polarities form the dominant theme of the way of individuation. On paper they look innocuous enough, but as experienced in one's own life, they are anything but easy or comfortable. More than most thinkers, Jung understood the radical conflicts that lie in every human being, as well as the suffering they cause. He saw the remedy not in the suppression or conquest of one element by another, but in their reconciliation in a *coniunctio oppositorum,* "the conjunction of opposites"—a type of "mystical marriage."

There is more than one *coniunctio* on the path; indeed, each major stage of the individuation process involves an inner "marriage" of this type. At the stage we're discussing here, once the anima/animus has been confronted, the ego begins to withdraw its projections onto others and unites with its own inner opposite. A woman may absorb some of the strength, courage, and passion she has projected onto men, while a man may find that his hard edges begin to soften. When this process has ripened, the individual is ready to face the archetype that lies behind the anima/animus: the Self.

## MEETING THE SELF

In Marie-Louise von Franz's simile, the ego is like a small illuminated patch on the surface of an enormous dark sphere. The light of consciousness, however brightly it may burn, will probably never encompass the entire sphere; it isn't big enough. But Jung held that through certain kinds of introspection, the conscious mind can enlarge its scope so as to at least catch glimpses of the whole. At this point, the archetype of the Self begins to manifest.

How does the Self make its presence felt? Again, dream imagery is the most familiar way. Here the Self, unlike the anima or animus, is most likely to appear as a being of the *same* sex as the subject: "In the dreams of a woman this center [the Self] is usually personified as a superior female figure—a priestess, sorceress, earth mother, or goddess of nature or love. In the case of a man, it manifests itself as a masculine initiator and guardian (an Indian guru), a wise old man, a spirit of nature, and so forth." While it can often appear as an older figure, it can also take the form of a divine youth, symbolizing "a creative *élan vital,* and a new spiritual orientation." Other guises include helpful animals, hermaphrodites (symbolizing the union of masculine and feminine), and even stones, particularly of the precious and magical variety.[13]

The most famous image of the Self, and one that possessed a special fascination for Jung, is the *mandala. Mandala* means "circle" in Sanskrit, and usually refers to a sacred circle. In recent years these symbolic images have become familiar in the West, partly because of Jung's influence and partly because of the popularity of Tibetan Buddhism, which provides the most familiar examples.

Yet a mandala is more than a circle, however sacred. Jung observes: "There are innumerable variants of the motif . . . but they are all based on the squaring of a circle. Their basic motif is the premonition of a center of personality, a kind of central point within the psyche, to which everything is related, by which everything is arranged, and which is itself a source of energy."[14]

The "squaring of the circle" is a familiar mathematical problem: it refers to the impossibility of constructing a square with exactly the same area as a circle (because a circle's area, unlike that of a square, is determined by *pi,* an irrational number). Jung, however, saw another, more profound meaning in the phrase. For him, as for many mystics, the circle symbolized the divine, the ineffable; he was fond of the medieval aphorism "God is a circle whose circumference is nowhere and whose center is everywhere." The square, on the other hand, is the ultimate symbol of solidity and materiality. The "squaring of the circle" thus refers to the embodiment of the divine nature of man in materiality—the central goal not only of Jungian individuation but, one could argue, of human life as well.

Some descriptions make it seem as if a decisive encounter with the Self, whether as a dream of a mandala or in some other form, is a once-in-a-lifetime event; one is, as it were, "individuated" and can go on to something else. This isn't true. Most Jungians stress that individuation goes on throughout life; the developed individual is constantly exploring the depths of the unconscious and constantly coming up with new riches.

Still, the appearance of the archetype of the Self may well mark a watershed in a person's life. Because individuation is concerned with the meaning of existence, Jung saw it as an issue likely to face a more mature individual; he often noted that most of his patients were in the second half of life.

## THE MEANING OF COINCIDENCE

Dreams are not the only means by which an archetype can manifest itself. Jung encouraged his patients to use art as a means of exploring the unconscious, while today some Jungian child psychologists use "sand play"—involving a sandbox with a large number of various toy figures—to help children express issues they cannot address in words. But of all the ways in which an archetype can make its presence felt, perhaps the most curious involves *synchronicity,* which Jung nebulously defined as "an acausal connecting principle."

Synchronicity is a difficult idea to comprehend, not only because it flies in the face of conventional reason but because our understanding of causality itself is so shadowy. To examine it, we might start with Jung's remark that "it often seems that even inanimate objects co-operate with the unconscious in the arrangement of symbolic patterns." As an example he cites "numerous well-authenticated stories of clocks stopping at the moment of their owner's death," which, happened, for example, to Frederick the Great of Prussia.[15] Synchronicities differ from ordinary coincidences in that they are *meaningful.*

One of the most striking examples can be found in an episode that took place in 1909, when Jung was still close to Freud. Even at this time the two men disagreed about parapsychology. Visiting Freud in Vienna, Jung asked him what he thought about synchronicity. "Because of his materialistic prejudice," Jung recalled, "he rejected this entire complex of questions as nonsensical, and did so in terms of so shallow a positivism that I had difficulty in checking the sharp retort on the end of my tongue."

While Freud was talking, Jung had an odd sensation:

It was as if my diaphragm were made of iron and were becoming red-hot—a glowing vault. And at that moment there was such a loud report in the bookcase, which stood right there next to us, that we both started up in alarm, fearing the thing was going to topple over on us. I said to Freud, "There, that is an example of a so-called catalytic exteriorization phenomenon."

"Oh, come," he exclaimed. "That is sheer bosh."

"It is not," I replied. "You are mistaken, Herr Professor. And to prove my point I now predict that in a moment there will be another such loud report!" Sure enough, no sooner had I said the words than the same detonation went off in the bookcase.[16]

Despite its overwhelming eerieness, this "catalytic exteriorization phenomenon" failed to change Freud's mind. He later brushed it aside in a letter to Jung;[17] after that they never discussed the incident again.

This example, which itself belongs in the literature of the paranormal, is not typical of synchronicities; most of the time they occur entirely in the sphere of ordinary reality. They may take the form of a chance meeting with someone you were just thinking of, the sighting of a bird or animal just as you were asking for a sign, or even "accidentally" opening a book to some passage that tells you exactly what you need to hear at that moment.

## UFOs AND THE UNCONSCIOUS

Synchronicities can occur on a collective level too. The most fascinating example in modern times is the UFO phenomenon. Though UFOs, flying saucers, and their kin have fascinated people at least since the beginning of the century, rumors and sightings of them have become far more common since the end of World War II. Jung, in a 1958 essay entitled "Flying Saucers: A Modern Myth of Things Seen in the Skies," doesn't attempt to explain them as a physical phenomenon. Citing the conclusions of the former head of UFO investigations for the U.S. Air Force, he says simply, "*Something is seen, but one doesn't know what*"[18]—a statement that, forty years later, still seems to sum up our findings about this mystery.

Jung also points out that UFOs often come in circular or

cylindrical shapes, which "have always symbolized the union of opposites." Like the mandala, another circular form, they seem to symbolize the Self, not in an individual, personal sense, but in a collective one. We have, he reminds us, come to an age when "untold millions of so-called Christians have lost their belief in a real and living mediator." Yet at the same time "a political, social, philosophical, and religious conflict of unprecedented proportions has split the consciousness of our age. When such tremendous opposites split asunder, we may expect with certainty that the need for a saviour will make itself felt."[19]

Jung is saying that we as a civilization are projecting our longing for wholeness onto these "things seen in the skies." He is careful to stress that this is a question not of individual but of collective psychology, since UFOs are "mostly seen by people who do not believe in them or who regard the whole problem with indifference."[20] Jung is also careful not to reduce the UFO phenomenon to *merely* a matter of projection, as if it were a collective delusion; UFOs are not only visible but even appear as blips on radar screens. His conclusion:

> It seems to me—speaking with all due reserve—that there is a third possibility: that Ufos [sic] are real material phenomena of an unknown nature, presumably coming from outer space. . . . Just at the moment when the eyes of mankind are turned towards the heavens, partly on account of their fantasies about possible space-ships, and partly in a figurative sense because their earthly existence is threatened, unconscious contents have projected themselves on these inexplicable heavenly phenomena and given them a significance they in no way deserve. Since they seem to have appeared more frequently after the second World War than before, it may be that they are synchronistic phenomena or "meaningful coincidences."[21]

Recent years have seen more sinister UFO rumors, which speak of abductions and abuse and unpleasant little grey aliens with malevolent intentions for humanity. Interestingly, these rumors have especially proliferated since the collapse of the Soviet Union and the end of the Cold War. Now that one major conflict on earth has been removed, are we starting to project our hostile fantasies, not onto other humans, but on races from other planets?

Whatever we may think of such speculations, it's important to remember that Jung would not have seen them reductionistically. Simply because something has taken on a projection does not in and of itself mean it is unreal or "just our imagination." UFOs, close encounters, abductions, and such things may or may not be physical realities apart from our projections. Jung, were he alive today, would most likely have recommended investigations of both the psychological and the material kind.

## A THEORY OF TYPES

One final aspect of Jung's view of the psyche must be briefly addressed: his theory of types. The idea that human beings can be roughly categorized into a small number of recognizable types is not a new one; it goes back at least as far as Aristotle's pupil Theophrastus, who wrote a book about it called *The Characters*.[22] We can find echoes of the same idea in the horoscope section of the newspaper, or in the modern-day theory known as the *enneagram of personality* (which will be discussed in chapter 9).

Jung's version is comparatively simple. To begin with, he distinguished between people he called *extraverts,* those who fundamentally tend to move outward from themselves toward engagement with the world; and *introverts,* those whose basic direction is inward, toward themselves and away from the world.

It's easy enough to see the value of such a theory, if only from the fact that these words have entered the common language. But Jung did not stop there. He also observed that people could be divided into four groups according to their dominant psychological functions. Those who are most inclined toward thought and intellectuality were *thinking* types; *feeling* types are oriented toward the emotions; and *sensing* types tend to focus toward the sensations of the body. To this threefold division of humanity (which boasts considerable antiquity, going as far back as the *Republic* of Plato) Jung added a fourth type: the *intuitive*. "We should speak of . . . intuition if we are dealing with a kind of perception which cannot be traced directly to conscious sensory experience. I have therefore defined sensation as perception through conscious sensory processes, and intuition as perception by way of unconscious contents and connections."[23]

By Jung's theory, every person not only has one dominant function, but is also either extraverted or introverted. Thus one can be either an introverted or an extraverted sensing type, and so on. He further arranged these types in a fourfold scheme (see illustration, below) which, not surprisingly, resembles a mandala. According to this scheme, certain types are clearly opposed to each other: thinking to feeling, sensation to intuition. Jung postulated that if one of these functions is *dominant,* or most developed, the

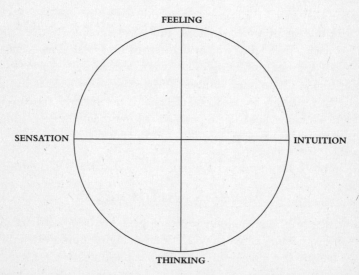

*Figure 1. A schema of Jung's theory of types. The dominant function is the opposite to the inferior function. That is, if your thinking function is the best developed, your feeling function will be the least developed. The inferior function is also the gateway to the unconscious.*

one opposite it will be *inferior,* or least developed. Furthermore, the inferior function is the gateway to the unconscious.

This is an extremely crucial point, and, generally speaking, it applies to all theories of type. For these theories say that we all have certain predispositions in our characters; some are stronger, some weaker. In order to have full access to our potential, we must develop that which is weakest in us.

According to Jung's theory, the philosopher is unlikely to become a good mechanic, while the man who can fix anything in five minutes may never develop superior capacities for abstract thought. The inferior function in any of us will probably never become dominant; our strengths will remain our strengths and our weaknesses our weaknesses. Jung is not saying that the leopard must change its spots, but that unsuspected riches lie buried in the part of the psyche that is most hidden, neglected, and perhaps despised. Cultivating these weaker sides is a vital step in transformation.[24]

You may catch a glimpse of how this works in practice if you chance to visit an esoteric school. You will sometimes notice that things look a little jerrybuilt, or that repairs have been done somewhat clumsily or awkwardly. This is not necessarily a sign of incompetence. Quite often it means that a student has been put to a task that is not his or her forte: the goal is not to have a picture-perfect operation but to help people work on themselves—as Jung would put it, to develop their inferior functions.

## A JUNGIAN RELIGION?

Some questions remain. Jung's psychology, as we have seen, comes out of his therapeutic work with patients ranging from the mildly disturbed to the insane. On the other hand, Jung attached great importance to the mythic and religious symbols that he believed are an intrinsic part of the human psyche. To what extent, then, is Jung's system a form of psychotherapy? To what extent is it a religious system?

Jung took an ambiguous position regarding these issues. He did not want to start a new religion. Indeed, whenever possible he would encourage his patients to return to the religion of their childhood, believing that their greatest hope for inner wholeness lay there. At the same time he saw that the great religion of the West—Christianity—had lost its meaning for many people, and in this he found the cause for much of the turbulence and dislocation of modern life.

Among Jung's followers, however, one encounters people who regard Jungian psychology as their religion and dream analysis as their spiritual practice.[25] Are they right to do this? Did Jung create, intentionally or inadvertently, a new faith that would supplant the waning religions of Western civilization?

In one sense anything that calls itself a religion must attempt to tell us about the unseen powers that rule the universe. It must purport to explain not only the workings of these powers but how we must conduct ourselves toward them—in ritual, worship, or ethical behavior. Most religions (though not all) speak of a God or of gods.

Jung's view of such issues can be gleaned from a famous reply he gave in a BBC interview that was broadcast in 1959. The interviewer asked him if he believed in God. He answered, "I know. I don't have to believe, I know."[26]

This could hardly sound more unequivocal. But in a letter written a few weeks later, Jung explained his statement thus: "[It] does not mean: I do know a certain God (Zeus, Yahweh, Allah, the Trinitarian God, etc.) but rather: I do know that I am obviously confronted with a factor unknown in itself, which I call 'God.' . . . This is the name by which I designate all things which cross my wilful path violently and recklessly, all things which upset my subjective views, plans, and intentions and change the course of my life for better or worse."[27]

This statement points to the crucial difference between Jung's psychology and religion as such. Jung was an empiricist. Metaphysical speculation did not interest him; indeed it is unclear whether he thought anything useful could even be learned by such means. Throughout his career he was concerned not with the abstract truths of the universe, but with leading individuals toward wholeness. One approach he found useful was integrating the various archetypes, including the archetype of the Self. Although the Self may *look like* God to the individual, Jung refused to take the step of saying the Self corresponded to an actual God in the world. For this reason the great Jewish philosopher Martin Buber accused him of equating a transcendent being with psychic processes.[28]

Jung's reluctance to speak about these issues can also be traced to the influence of Immanuel Kant, whom he deeply revered. Kant said we can never perceive the world as it is in its own right; we can only perceive it through certain *categories* of experience, such as time, space, and causality, which are built into the human mind. Jung seemed to include the archetypes among these "categories."[29] They are the filters through which we must look whenever we experience anything, and we must be very cautious in speaking about the world—much less God—as it is apart from them.

## THE PROMISE AND THE COSTS

If Jungianism is not a religion, what is it? What can one expect from Jungian analysis?

The answer is simple: Jungian analysis is a form of psychotherapy. It is generally offered in a therapeutic context, usually in one-hour sessions with an analyst once or twice a week. Because training for Jungian analysts is itself a long and expensive process, the price will be correspondingly high—an estimated $100–$150 per hour. Since the process of Jungian analysis usually spans several years, one can expect treatment to cost thousands, even tens of thousands of dollars. Of all the paths discussed in this book, Jungian analysis is likely to cost the most in sheer financial terms.

On the other hand, Jungian analysis is a respected part of the therapeutic mainstream. This is not to say that every therapist who claims to be a Jungian is reputable and competent—here, as in other realms, one must do one's homework and trust one's best judgment—but Jungian analysis has proved helpful for many. Though any given approach is unlikely to benefit everyone, it's safe to say that if you feel the need for psychotherapy and find yourself in sympathy with the ideas presented in this chapter, you may find Jungian analysis worth exploring.

Today, though, most people who have been touched by these ideas have not gone through formal analysis. The fact is that Jungian concepts have filtered into popular consciousness, not only through Jung's own writings, which are widely available, but also in various other forms. The most obvious of these are books with a strongly Jungian flavor, including Joseph Campbell's *The Hero with a Thousand Faces*, Robert Bly's *Iron John*, Clarissa Pinkola Estés' *Women Who Run with the Wolves*, and the novels of Robertson Davies. But Jung's ideas have also found their way into the collective psyche through other means, including movies (George Lucas's *Stars Wars* films were partly inspired by *The Hero with a Thousand Faces*) and television programs like Bill Moyers' PBS interviews with Joseph Campbell, one of the best-known and best-loved interpreters of myth in our time.

One offspring of Jung's ideas, a system known as *archetypal psychology,* has taken on a direction of its own in recent years, chiefly through the inspiration of James Hillman. Hillman, who was trained as a Jungian analyst, became disaffected with the importance Jung gave to the archetype of the Self. Hillman came to see the psyche "polytheistically": the archetypes, Hillman tells us, live in us in a more egalitarian, free-wheeling, and tumultuous fashion than Jung believed. In this they resemble the lively though troublesome gods of Olympus.

Influenced by writers as diverse as Marsilio Ficino, Keats, and Coleridge, Hillman also emphasizes the notion of *soul,* which he defines as a middle realm between the world of matter and the spirit proper. The neglect of "soul," Hillman believes, is one of the chief sources of our current discontent. Writers influenced by Hillman's works include Robert Sardello and Thomas Moore, author of the best-selling *Care of the Soul*.[30]

It is far from surprising that Jung's intellectual descendants use quasi-religious terms like "soul," for there is an irreducibly religious—or, as he would have said, "numinous"—tone to Jung's ideas. This numinosity reached its crescendo in a curious little document that dates to the winter of 1916–17, at the height of World War I and at a period of great emotional upheaval for Jung himself. In this atmosphere Jung, haunted by strange apparitions, found himself composing what today would be called a piece of "channeled" material—that is, a work that seems to be dictated to the writer by an unseen being or presence.

Jung did not publish the work called *Septem Sermones ad Mortuos*, or *The Seven Sermons to the Dead*,[31] in his lifetime, and only showed it to close friends and associates. Later in his life he even dismissed it as a "youthful indiscretion." But as he also admitted, "These conversations with the dead formed a kind of prelude to what I had to communicate to the world about the unconscious."[32]

The work begins, with a reference to Jerusalem—the holiest of holy cities for both Jews and Christians; the very embodiment of exoteric revealed religion: "The dead came back from Jerusalem, where they found not what they sought." The text that follows, which fills only a few pages, sets out a cryptic esoteric system that speaks of the "Pleroma," which is "the nothingness and the fullness," and of the god Abraxas, who "speaketh that hallowed and accursed word which is life and death at the same time."

As author Stephan Hoeller has observed about Jung, "Some think that he is a spiritual pagan, while others accuse him of being biased in the direction of Christianity. This little book would set both of these opinions in the wrong, for it shows that he is a kind of Gnostic."[33] To understand what this means, we must now turn to Gnosticism itself.

## SUGGESTED READING

Campbell, Joseph. *The Hero with a Thousand Faces*. Princeton: Princeton University Press, 1968.

Joseph Campbell is one of the most celebrated exponents of Jung's ideas. In this, his most famous work, he explicates the archetype of the hero.

Edinger, Edward F. *Ego and Archetype*. Boston: Shambhala, 1992.

An illuminating discussion of the individuation process as expressed in myths and symbols.

Jung, C. G., ed. *Man and His Symbols*. Garden City, N.Y.: Doubleday & Co., 1964.

An accessible and lavishly illustrated introduction to Jung's ideas, written by Jung and some of his closest associates. Perhaps the best starting-point for gaining access to Jung.

Other works by Jung that will be useful at the outset are the following:

*Modern Man in Search of a Soul*. Translated by W. S. Dell and Cary F. Baynes. New York: Harcourt, Brace, & World, 1933.

This collection of essays stresses the connection of Jung's ideas with the dilemmas of modern culture.

*Memories, Dreams, Reflections*. Edited by Aniela Jaffé. Translated by Richard and Clara Winston. New York: Vintage, 1961.

Jung's memoirs; the closest thing to an autobiography that he ever wrote.

*Collected Works*. Princeton: Princeton/Bollingen, 1953–96.

A multivolume edition of Jung's writings translated into English. Many of his more popular writings, such as *Synchronicity* and *Flying Saucers*, are available as paperbacks from the same publisher.

Noll, Richard. *The Jung Cult: The Origins of a Charismatic Movement*. Princeton: Princeton University Press, 1994.

A strong and at times vitriolic critique of Jung and his ideas. Worth reading for its insights into Jung's cultural context, as well as for a dramatically different perspective on Jung than that of Jungians.

Robertson, Robin. *Beginner's Guide to Jungian Psychology*. York Beach, Maine: Nicolas-Hays, 1992.

A lucid account of basic Jungian theory. Probably the best introduction to Jung's ideas apart from those written by Jung himself.

Sharp, Daryl. *C. G. Jung Lexicon: A Primer of Terms and Concepts*. Toronto: Inner City Books, 1991.

A good reference source for Jungian ideas and concepts, citing definitions and explanations from Jung's own works.

## Two

## GNOSTICISM:

## THE SEARCH FOR AN ALIEN GOD

It is probably safe to say that we all have days when it seems that the universe is stacked against us. In fact, for many of us, this is an ongoing sensation. As the T-shirt slogan says: "Life's a bitch/ and then you die." Therapy is one way to cope with our "disease," but even therapy has its limits.

In response to this modern angst, Carl Jung made a point of encouraging his patients to return to the religion of their childhood as part of their growth toward wholeness. It was there, Jung presumed, that they would likely find a sense of connectedness with their earliest memories and roots of meaning. For most people in Jung's Switzerland, as in most of the West, this meant a return to Christianity.

Yet many people have trouble embracing the theological and cultural baggage that comes with calling oneself a Christian. This is hardly surprising. Precisely because Western culture has been so dominated by Christian assumptions and morality—notions brought to a fever pitch in the 1980s and 1990s by politicized fundamentalism—it is hard to step back and see things with a fresh perspective.

What if we were able to put aside the last two millennia of church history and reacquaint ourselves with the powerful spiritual experiences that propelled many of the earliest believers? What we would discover is that among followers of this new religion there were many approaches. One approach—that of the Gnostics—grappled head-on with the same sense of alienation that many feel today.

In exploring Gnosticism we soon discover that it can mean many different things to different people. Is one inclined toward asceticism? One is sure to find early Gnostics from whom to draw inspiration. If, on the other hand, one is inclined toward sexual license or ritual, there too certain Gnostics will pop up as comrades-in-arms. Elitist? Gnosticism fills the bill, with its distinction between those who "know" and those who don't. Populist? How about Gnosticism's struggle with the church hierarchy, its advocacy of female bishops, and validation of individual experience? The very diversity of the Gnostics makes them nearly impossible to typecast, even as it makes them important to understand.

Interest in this area has grown steadily since the 1977 publication of the first complete English translation of a cache of ancient scriptures that were found at Nag Hammadi, Egypt, in 1945. These crumbling codices, dating from the fourth century A.D., were Coptic versions of sacred texts that were older still—apparently from the first and second centuries A.D.[1]

Included among the fifty-two texts were the *Gospel of Thomas*, the *Gospel of Philip*, the *Apocalypse of Peter*, and other early Christian scriptures that never made it into the accepted canon of the New Testament. Scholars have attributed these works to circles of early Christians who were branded as heretics by the early Roman Church. The alternate theologies, symbols, and rituals that they employed have come to be known collectively as Gnosticism.[2]

The resurfacing of Gnostic texts might have remained a matter of mere scholarly interest but for a couple of unusual circumstances. The first involved Jung, whose interest in Gnosticism predated the Nag Hammadi discovery by several decades. Following the 1945 discovery, the translation of the Gnostic codices was tied up for years by interminable wrangling among scholars, the

Egyptian government, and antiquities dealers. Finally the Jung Foundation in Zurich, with the assistance of the Dutch scholar Gilles Quispel, was able to purchase one of the codices through back-channel sources in 1952. Jung's possession of this text, now popularly known as the Jung Codex, combined with his own discussion of Gnostic themes and myths, kindled an interest in Gnosticism in Jungian circles.

The second unexpected event was the ascent onto the best-seller list in 1979 of an eminently readable exploration of the scriptures' implications. This was Elaine Pagels's *The Gnostic Gospels*, which won a National Book Critics Circle Award. Pagels had served on the scholarly team that completed the English translations now known as the *Nag Hammadi Library*. In engaging prose, Pagels championed the Gnostics as upholders of an early Christianity that was more open to the feminine both in mythic-theological terms and in day-to-day leadership and participation. By her account, the early Gnostics represented a brand of Christianity uniquely in tune with late twentieth-century feminism and alternative spiritual interests.

Although scholars have taken issue with some of Pagels's conclusions in the years since the publication of *The Gnostic Gospels*, and even with the usefulness of the word *Gnosticism* as an umbrella term for these early Christian groups, popular interest in the Gnostics has continued to grow. What is it about Gnosticism that has proved so attractive to certain contemporary spiritual seekers?

## IN SEARCH OF GNOSIS

Gnosticism derives its name from *gnosis,* the Greek word denoting experiential knowledge, usually referring to an inner knowledge of God or spiritual matters. In contrast to the agnostic's assertion that God or divine reality is unknowable, the Gnostics affirmed that it is possible to some extent to directly "know" God and the divine. Many claimed that the path to gnosis was the content of Jesus's most secret teachings, imparted to only a few of the Apostles and largely absent from the four canonical Gospels. Elaine Pagels cites a passage from the *Gospel of Thomas* in which Jesus speaks to Thomas and indicates that such transformative knowledge has been passed along:

> Jesus said, "I am not your master. Because you have drunk, you have become drunk from the bubbling stream which I have measured out. . . . He who will drink from my mouth will become as I am: I myself shall become he, and the things that are hidden will be revealed to him."[3]

It is not hard to see how this radical notion—that one who undergoes gnosis ("drinks from Jesus's mouth") in effect "becomes" Christ and sees with his eyes—was deeply threatening to church authorities and orthodox theology. Today, with so many people hungry for some concrete experience of spiritual realities beyond day-to-day material existence, the promise of gnosis is attractive indeed.

What was this knowledge that the Gnostics sought? Is it still accessible to us now, nearly two thousand years later? Unfortunately, because gnosis deals with the nonrational and the ineffable, the Gnostic texts make only oblique references to the experience itself. What's more, because gnosis is an individual inner knowledge, no single description would suffice. By inference, however, and through the Gnostic scriptures, we can get a glimpse of what gnosis encompassed. But first, in order to make sense of it, we need to look at the Gnostic worldview as expressed in its central myths.

## THE DEMIURGE AND SOPHIA

Historically, most Christians down through the centuries have assumed that the God Jesus spoke of in the New Testament, and familiarly referred to as "my Father," was identical to the God portrayed in the Old Testament.[4] The Gnostics weren't so sure.

Many Gnostics had trouble reconciling the jealous and often angry God of the Prophets with the loving God described by Jesus. What's more, they looked at all the pain and suffering in this world and wondered how any God worthy of the name could have created such a seemingly flawed universe.

Their solution to this puzzle was to posit that the true God (sometimes referred to as the Unknown God or Alien God) was wholly good and inhabited a realm of light (usually referred to as the Pleroma) that was distant from material existence. In contrast to the traditional creation account in Genesis, the Unknown God was not directly connected with the creation of this world and its cruelties.

The Gnostic creation myths portrayed the creator of this world as an imperfect lesser god, known as the Demiurge or Yaltabaoth, who was the inadvertent result of an attempt by Sophia (Wisdom)—a feminine facet of the true God—to experience the act of creation on her own. According to some versions of the myth, Yaltabaoth in turn created still lesser planetary rulers called Archons, and the world itself, including Man. The humanity that Yaltabaoth created was a distant echo of the divine, incapable of walking upright. Pitying humanity, Sophia blew fragments or sparks of the divine light into Man, only to have these sparks become trapped in the material world. When Sophia came down into the world to rescue humanity and its sparks, she became trapped herself and it was only through the intervention of Christ, the Son of the Unknown God, that she was rescued.

The ensuing union of Sophia and her consort, the Christ, in the "bridal chamber," serves as a mythic model for the gnosis that will save individual humans from their ignorant state, trapped in matter. By seeing through the charade of the Demiurge and uniting with the true God (perhaps by "becoming" Christ as suggested in the passage from the *Gospel of Thomas* above) our spirits (the sparks of light) can return to their rightful place in the Pleroma.

This is a far more complex version of the creation story than the simple six-day tale told in Genesis. Various Gnostic authors made it more complex still, perhaps inspired by the unique color-ings of their own revelations and imaginations. Depending upon which scripture we read, there are exhaustive descriptions of different Archons (unseen rulers), Aeons (personified aspects of the Pleroma), and Heavens, as well as differences in Sophia's placement in the scheme of things. In one interesting version found in *The Hypostasis of the Archons*, Sophia even enters the Garden of Eden and disguises herself as the Serpent. She directs Adam and Eve to eat of the Tree of Knowledge: in the kind of reverse interpretation that the Gnostics were fond of, this becomes not an act of disobedience to God, but a symbol for outwitting the Demiurge through gnosis.

The spiritual lovers, Sophia and Christ, are portrayed in Gnostic creation myths as cosmic beings or principles that bear little relation to earthly life. It is only when the cosmic becomes grounded in the human that we find ourselves on more familiar terrain. Yet the portrayal of Jesus found in Gnostic scriptures such as the *Gospel of Philip* plays havoc with the traditional image depicted in the canonical Gospels. In perhaps the most famous passage in the *Gospel of Philip*, we find Christ and Sophia symbolized by Jesus and Mary Magdalene:

> . . . the companion of the [Savior is] Mary Magdalene. [But Christ loved] her more than [all] the disciples and used to kiss her [often] on her [mouth]. The rest of [the disciples were offended by it . . .]. They said to him, "Why do you love her more than all of us?" The Savior answered and said to them, "Why do I not love you as [I love] her?"[5]

To contemporary ears, this passage makes the official portrayal of Jesus seem hopelessly bowdlerized. To accept it even as a provisionally accurate picture of infighting among the disciples calls into question the notion of the male disciples as Jesus's closest intimates and undercuts the foundations of Catholic Christianity with its roots in Peter's leadership. By embodying Christ (as Logos)[6] and Sophia (as Wisdom) in a human relationship, the Gnostics encouraged their followers to build a bridge between their own material lives and the divine.

Clearly we are on dangerous ground here, and it is small wonder that the Gnostics were declared heretical as the Church began to coalesce and homogenize. To read the Nag Hammadi scriptures is to travel back to a time when Christianity was still free-form and numerous sects proliferated, each with its own interpretation of the meaning of Christ's life and teaching. In this respect, the Gnostics stand as our contemporaries, and their subversions and reverse readings of accepted texts and myths parallel the preoccupations of our own era.

## FINDING MEANING IN MYTH

Making sense of the Gnostic myths is far from easy. If many modern-day Westerners are disinclined to accept the usual Genesis account of Creation as literally true, the Gnostic version with its Demiurge and Archons and Aeons is, in many ways, even harder to swallow. But myths, as Joseph Campbell has underscored, are not meant to be taken literally. They speak of eternal truths and recurring archetypes that exist outside linear time.

Jung saw the Gnostic myths as significant descriptions of psychological reality and viewed the early Gnostics as the first psychologists. For Jung, the Demiurge of the Creation myth symbolizes the inflated ego, which assumes it is the one true God. Sophia, trapped in matter, represents the archetypal Self hidden in the unconscious. The path of individuation is the embrace of inner androgyny, the union of our "masculine" and "feminine" aspects in the bridal chamber. The return to the Pleroma is symbolic of the emergence of the Self from unconsciousness, leading to the wholeness that is our ultimate destiny and to psychological salvation.

Jung took great pains to maintain that his psychological theories were "scientific" and thus only applied to the psyche. His escape clause was that the archetype of the Self, while residing in the collective unconscious of humanity, transcends the psyche of any single individual. We might say that in his effort to make religious issues relevant to modern man, Jung recast them in psychological terms.

Two contemporary Jungians, Stephan Hoeller and June Singer, have taken Jung's analysis of Gnosticism and redirected it back into the spiritual realm. For instance, note the following passage from the *Gospel of Thomas* and June Singer's commentary.

[Christ says:] . . . When you come to know yourselves, you will become known and you will realize that it is you who are the sons of the living Father.[7]

Singer comments:

The "living Jesus" who speaks his wisdom is not the one who died on the cross but the one who descended to this plane from the level of reality that we call the invisible world and whose essence returned to the invisible world when he departed from his earthly form. His words reveal to us that the Kingdom of Eternity is within us, as it is within him, and it is within all human beings. As seekers, we may be astonished when we find that the Kingdom to which we aspire is so close at hand! In the intimacy of our quiet meditations, we come to know our own darkness, and when we have penetrated it, we may find there the hidden fragment of the boundless Light that is the treasure of the Kingdom within.[8]

Hoeller, for his part, closely follows Jung's concepts and terminology in his writings on Gnosticism, noting, for instance, that

to Jung, God is never a theological or philosophical postulate, but a psychological reality; not an essence, but an experience. Thus it is only natural that this God may be experienced as remote and at the same time be also intimately involved both as subject and object in human transformation. Once again, we are dealing with the principle of the opposites which converge in the experience of the psyche.[9]

Yet Hoeller has gone far beyond Jung. Ordained and consecrated as a bishop in independent Catholic lines, he subsequently founded a Gnostic church based in Los Angeles, the Ecclesia Gnostica, which celebrates a Gnostic Mass and promulgates its own line of priesthood. He has become an influential exponent of a contemporary Gnosticism that melds Jung's ideas with religious ritual and concerns.

## IS WISDOM FEMININE?

The Jungian and neo-Jungian approaches described above are significant ways of finding meaning in the Gnostic worldview, but there are others as well. In fact, because it is both oddly familiar and yet so strange, Gnosticism serves as a kind of spiritual Rorschach test into which spiritual seekers can read their own preoccupations and preferences.

Proponents of feminist spirituality have taken Elaine Pagels's lead and celebrate Sophia as a theological balance to the masculine emphasis of Father and Son in the Christian Trinity. In this reading, Sophia becomes either a feminine rendering of the usual neutral Holy Spirit or a goddess in her own right—a manifestation of the Divine Feminine.[10] Indeed, much of the present enthusiasm for Gnosticism comes from those who perceive the God of the Bible (both Jewish and Christian) as unsalvageably patriarchal and who feel much kinship with His demotion in the Gnostic myths to the status of a self-serving Demiurge. For women (and men) who still identify with Christian values but reject the institutional establishment, the welcoming of Sophia back into Christian theology represents a way to transform Christianity from within.

How did Sophia ascend to prominence among the Gnostics, and why was she later eclipsed? Was she an external symbol for an inner facet of the human psyche, as Jung alleged? Or was she a designation for an important aspect of divine reality that was banished from view when the Gnostics were suppressed?

As it turns out, Sophia did exist as a goddess in her own right in pre-Christian Hellenic culture.[11] (Philosophy, after all, is "the love of wisdom" in Greek.) Similarly, the notion of Logos (assigned to Christ as the "Word" of God) is also of Hellenic origin and predates Christianity. As Margaret Starbird has pointed out, the pattern of paired male and female deities who unite in a *hieros gamos* (divine marriage) recurs in numerous pre-Christian religions, and the parallels with the Gnostic models of Sophia as bride and Christ as bridegroom suggest the continuation of an archetypal myth in Gnostic garb.[12]

Thus, to a certain degree, Gnosticism can be read as a meeting of the feminine and masculine. In the creation myths, a one-sided feminine power (Sophia) spawns a one-sided masculine power (Yaltabaoth) that masks humanity from the Pleroma (Wholeness). The path of return is through the union of the feminine with a higher masculine (Christ).

Less charitable interpretations also exist. The religious scholar Pheme Perkins points out that in Gnostic myth, Sophia's "fall into the lower world becomes a fault or disobedience for which she is blamed. She must await the gracious coming of the Spirit and the redeemer in order to be restored. . . . Identifying the female Wisdom with the dyad of material creation makes her ontologically inferior to beings who belong to the world of light."[13]

Whether we focus on the fall or its resolution, it is difficult to cast Sophia as a completely positive and autonomous goddess, though this has not stopped some modern interpreters from trying. A controversial conference held in Minneapolis in 1993, called "Re-Imagining Christianity," included prayers and rituals directed to Sophia as a quasi-Christian goddess more or less replacing God the Father. This is an intriguing development within mainstream Christianity (the conference was partially funded by the United Methodist and the Presbyterian churches), but it sidesteps Sophia's ambiguous role in Gnosticism by removing her from the context of the Gnostic myths that give her prominence in the first place.

Some verses, such as these in the *Gospel of Thomas*, are, at best, ambivalent about the feminine and about women as women:

> Simon Peter said to them, "Let Mary leave us, for women are not worthy of life."
>
> Jesus said, "I myself shall lead her in order to make her male, so that she too may become a living spirit resembling you males. For every woman who will make herself male will enter the kingdom of heaven."[14]

Is this the Gnostic Jesus defending his women followers against the chauvinism of male apostles like Simon Peter? It would certainly seem so. But it remains uncertain whether he is doing so at the expense of their femininity. If maleness, in Jesus's time, represented thinking for oneself and the autonomy necessary to strike free of one's family and upbringing in order to follow Jesus, then a "woman who will make herself male" could be seen as coming into her own (becoming "a living spirit"), not abnegating herself. On the other hand, perhaps this is an exercise in anachronistic projection.

Such questions bring us face to face with the challenge of interpreting esoteric teachings. Because mystical sects were so often suppressed, forced underground, or eradicated altogether, there are many puzzling gaps in our understanding of their teachings. Thus the student of these paths is forced to cultivate his or her spiritual intuition by trying to understand them, and spiritual intuition plays a large part in the acquisition of gnosis.

Nevertheless, it is all too tempting to stitch together fragments of past teachings into a satisfying patchwork quilt that is primarily composed of hunches and wishful thinking. In a way, this is no better than blindly following a dogmatic belief system. Rosamonde Miller, a contemporary gnostic bishop, has pointed out that it takes an agnostic to make a gnostic. In other words, in order to open up the interior space in which to "know," one must first be ruthlessly honest with oneself about what one doesn't know. As far as Gnosticism is concerned, there is much that we simply do not know.

## COSMIC ALIENATION

Some readings of the Gnostics focus on their world-rejecting side, which at its most extreme resembles the dark vision of nihilism. This is an aspect of Gnosticism that many contemporary enthusiasts tend to skip over or minimize. However, if we seriously delve into the Gnostic scriptures and teachings, sooner or later we will confront the deep alienation that lurks within the Gnostic worldview. Sophia and the sparks of light within us are all very well, but the Gnostic myths emphasize that this world is ruled by the Demiurge and his Archons.

A modern-day Gnostic organization in Australia, the Institute for Gnostic Studies, asserts that this is indeed still the case:

> In contradiction to modern holistic philosophy, the Gnostic has always known there is a conflict between matter and spirit. Whether we consider the biblical view of flesh battling Spirit or the cosmic dualism of many Zoroastrians (where Ahura Mazda and Ahriman battle across the universe), the essential truth is that matter and spirit do not work well together. . . . While man's physical existence accelerates and his technology reaches greater and greater heights, the cost has been great; far greater than may be first appreciated. Most of us tend to believe that evolution has dragged man from the primeval waters of earth and slowly transformed him into the half-divine animal he presently is. What of his spirit, his "Light Self," at what point did he "lose his Soul"? . . . Mankind has lost its vision, the "Particles of Light" have been suppressed and the mindless force of matter has taken ascendancy. If you doubt our evaluation of the situation, watch the "News at Seven" and weep.[15]

Another Australian Gnostic group, the Life Science Fellowship, takes this view to its logical extreme:

> Behind all the mundane conspiracies and cover-ups in the world there is a vast cosmic conspiracy. Ultimately the conspiracy view of history aims to unveil the source of human suffering and pain. Conspiratologists search for the unity behind the mask of apparent complexity. They struggle to pinpoint and clarify those elements that poison the lifestream of history. The Gnostics have already unmasked the grand charade and exposed the ignorant "god of this world," along with his Earthly dupes. They urge us to escape from the trap of the world order and open our eyes to the higher level of transcendence.[16]

This comes uncomfortably close to the Christian fundamentalist worldview whereby Satan is seen lurking behind every action or cultural manifestation that doesn't match the believers' values. It is but a short step from identifying "Earthly dupes" to scapegoating those so designated. Here is the shadow side of a Gnosticism that succumbs to the temptation to engage in the power struggles of politics and history. Given the tendency of all institutions to stray from their original inspiration over time, it may be just as well that the Gnostics didn't win the battle with the embryonic Catholic Church and ascend to power.

## IS GNOSIS GNOSTIC?

At first glance, there seems to be a choice between two interpretations of gnosis. It has been described as knowledge of divine reality—but knowledge of what sort? Usually knowledge is conceived as some *thing* that is known, some kind of *information*. In dealing with paradoxical notions like the Unknown God, however, what exactly is there to know? The Gnostics seemed to define the remote God of the Pleroma as ineffable, which means indescribable, indicating that God is beyond the realm of mere things.

One possible answer is that gnosis is knowledge of how we stand *in relation to* the Unknown God and the material universe. For the Gnostics, without knowledge of the Demiurge, the Archons, the bridal chamber, and most importantly, the route back to the Pleroma, we cannot be "saved" but are doomed to wander in illusion both in this life and beyond. As in the Tibetan Buddhist doctrine of the *bardos,* one must maintain consciousness at one's death and, armed with the right passwords, pass through a maze of astral worlds (referred to as "the middle" in the *Gospel of Philip*) until one reaches the Realm of Light. Such an approach to gnosis links it to specific crucial information (perhaps acquired experientially) that is necessary for salvation.

The *Gospel of Philip* appears to be speaking of this when it encourages "resurrection" prior to one's death:

> In this world there is good and evil. Its good things are not good, and its evil things are not evil. But there is evil after this world which is truly evil—what is called "the middle." It is death. While we are in this world it is fitting for us to acquire the resurrection, so that when we strip off the flesh we may be found in rest and not walk in the middle. For many go astray on the way. For it is good to come forth from the world before one has sinned.[17]

The same Gospel later speaks of gnosis as receiving the light from the bridal chamber. Such a person will not be able to be seen (by the Archons) or detained (in the "middle") after death:

> If anyone becomes a son of the bridal chamber, he will receive the light. If anyone does not receive it while he is here, he will not be able to receive it in the other place. He who will receive that light will not be seen, nor can he be detained. And none shall be able to torment a person like this even while he dwells in the world. And again when he leaves the world he has already received the truth in the images. The world has become the eternal realm (aeon), for the eternal realm is fullness for him.[18]

Another interpretation sees gnosis as the mystical experience of union with God itself. From this perspective, gnosis is the experience of the infinite: a consciousness beyond time, space, and the individual ego, which numerous mystical paths all speak of. Gnosis, from this viewpoint, is synonymous with the states of enlightenment and illumination found in religions and esoteric paths the world over.

In a sense, early Gnosticism embodied both of these aspects: gnosis as secret esoteric knowledge and gnosis as a unitive experience in which God and human are one. In this fashion, Gnosticism set in motion two approaches to the inner life, which have sometimes merged and more often diverged as they have evolved in the Western tradition.

Building on the first approach, it is possible to say that "gnosis was Gnostic" in that the elaborate details specified in the Gnostic scriptures were imaginative attempts to describe, through metaphor and koan-like puzzles, what the Gnostics experienced in meditation and inner exploration.

For example, the fall of consciousness into matter parallels the trauma we all undergo at birth, as we are expelled from the unity of the womb. In a visceral sense, we are all exiled in this world. The complicated effort the Gnostics described, of rising through spiritual levels and eluding the Archons, might be seen as a metaphor for the journey our consciousness takes during meditation or prayer in trying to ascend again to the state of gnosis with our consciousness intact. Yet once achieved, union proves temporary; the ineffable God or Absolute, from which existence emanates "downward," can be seen as symbolizing the Gnostic's attempt to express the inner experience of returning from a meditative state of unity (gnosis) back into differentiation, limitation, and ego-identification.

According to the second approach to gnosis, gnosis isn't only Gnostic, but is the universal experience of cosmic consciousness that is potentially accessible to all seekers, no matter what the model used or the symbols employed to describe it. It is as relevant today as it was two thousand years ago—the ultimate gift of mystical attainment.

When Gnostic ideas are considered in this way, the scholarly game of trying to identify the roots of Gnosticism in earlier religions and cosmologies becomes almost irrelevant. Earlier myths and symbols that seem to parallel those of the Gnostics may have had some influence on how Gnostics framed or interpreted their experiences of gnosis, but it is just as likely that similarities between Gnostic cosmologies and earlier systems stem from similarities in the experience of gnosis itself, which has never been the possession of any one ideology.

## THE METAPHYSICAL TRAGEDY

Gnosticism is often called tragic, and this is true in more ways than one. Tragedy is implicit in the myths that tell of Sophia's error, the entrapment of divine light in matter, and the struggle against the Archons and material temptations that is needed for the Gnostic to return to the Pleroma. But if these myths are primarily an imaginative rendering of the Gnostic's consciousness ascending to and descending from the unity of gnosis, the effort they describe is an instrumental or practical challenge. It is the struggle that every meditator undergoes in trying to quiet the mind and enter a contemplative state, and in facing the challenge of coming to terms with daily life outside of the bliss of union.

Perhaps the greater tragedy of Gnosticism is that this "practical" struggle was seemingly interpreted as a *moral* one, lending itself to a deprecation of Creation itself. In this "detour," asceticism commonly became a *moral requirement* for reaching gnosis—not merely one approach among many to assist the seeker in relinquishing the attachments that preoccupy the mind. Confronted with a world of both suffering and joy, the chronic water-glass dilemma was decided in favor of the pessimistic "half empty" instead of the optimistic "half full" or the paradoxical "both."

The Gnostic scriptures tried to elucidate the ineffable and paradoxical, but when interpreted from a literalist perspective outside of gnosis, the myths they portrayed were also capable of masking gnosis and pulling the hapless seeker into a cul-de-sac where behavior and belief, not gnosis, became the central focus. The experience of gnosis itself is a vital and dynamic process. When that vitality succumbs to systematization, metaphors become mistaken for facts, and spiritual truths become static.

The biggest stumbling block of ancient Gnosticism (or at least of any dogmatic reading of it, whether ancient or modern) was the self-fulfilling alienation built into its very structure. Rather than seeing the universe at root as fundamentally benign—the common perception of the mystic suffused with divine love—the Gnostic perceived it as an enormous illusion that one has to see through.

Rather than attaining gnosis through a "letting go" (of ego, of attachments, of fear), the Gnostic on the journey to the Pleroma must exert tremendous will and perseverance and obtain special knowledge. The ignorant ones, those who weren't even aware of the need for gnosis in order to be saved, are doomed to oblivion.

## THE GNOSTIC LEGACY

Gnostic ideas lived on as a recurring form of spiritual protest perhaps precisely because the Gnostics were banished by the Church hierarchy. Not only did Gnostic motifs reappear in later heresies such as the Bogomils and the Cathars of the Middle Ages, but Gnostic premises have formed the underpinnings of the Western esoteric paths as found in Rosicrucianism and Hermeticism. The promise of secret knowledge and of hidden techniques for overcoming material limitations are a feature of most of the traditions examined in this book.

Similarly, the union of the bridal chamber—the embrace of both feminine and masculine qualities and aspects—recurs as a motif within Western esotericism. While exoteric Western religion has been accused of emphasizing the masculine over the feminine, the Western esoteric tradition has served as a counter-weight, assuring that the feminine is in balance with the masculine.

The Gnostic scriptures of the Nag Hammadi library reveal a cluster of myths that elude our full understanding. These myths spoke to the ancient Gnostics in the context of their own time and place. Accordingly, any attempt to revive an "authentic" Gnosticism is doomed to failure. Too much has changed in the intervening centuries. At the same time, one need not disregard the potential that the myths still have to inspire a contemporary quest for gnosis.

Our souls hunger for a union with the divine and for a sense of wholeness where both feminine and masculine qualities can be embraced. Sophia is still alive in our efforts to find the divine spark amidst the darkness of daily life. The Archons confront us in the form of social strictures and pressures that do not always have our best interests in mind. And the Demiurge lives on when we succumb to rigid concepts of God and religion that haven't been confirmed by our own living experience.

For those wishing to pursue an interest in the Gnostic myths, an increasing number of groups and churches of a Gnostic persuasion can be found by doing a keyword search on the Web for "gnostic," "gnosticism," or "gnosis." Other such groups advertise in local New Age guides or even the Yellow Pages. Commonly, these are small, one-of-a-kind churches, founded by bishops who have been consecrated in one of the lines of independent Catholic or Orthodox apostolic succession.[19]

A word of caution is in order here. Not every group that describes itself as "gnostic" necessarily works with the ancient Gnostic myths. The Gnostic Association of Cultural and Anthropological Studies, founded by the late Samael Aun Weor, has a Tantric orientation and is strongest in Hispanic communities and Latin America. The Ecclesia Gnostica Catholica, despite its name, promulgates the philosophy of Thelema, derived from Aleister Crowley (whose work is discussed in chapter 5); other gnostic denominations are intertwined with magical orders as well. Some gnostic churches consider themselves Christian, while others, such as the Ecclesia Gnostica Mysteriorum of Bishop Rosamonde Miller in Palo Alto, California, transcend any single label. In this way, contemporary gnostics bear an uncanny resemblance to the ancient Gnostic sects, with their often conflicting myths, loyalty to different leaders, and varying degrees of heresy and orthodoxy.

Of course, the Gnostic current is not the only approach to a rediscovery of Christianity's mystical heritage. The next chapter looks at esoteric aspects of Christianity that have stayed alive despite the eclipse of the original Gnostic sects.

## SUGGESTED READING

Hoeller, Stephan A. *The Gnostic Jung and the Seven Sermons to the Dead*. Wheaton, Ill.: Quest Books, 1982; and *Jung and the Lost Gospels*. Wheaton: Quest Books, 1989.

With these two volumes, Hoeller has become the most prominent interpreter of Jung as Gnostic and of Gnosticism as a mythic path to psychological individuation.

Jonas, Hans. *The Gnostic Religion*. Boston: Beacon, 1963.

Jonas was the first to draw parallels between the ancient Gnostics and modern existentialism and nihilism. This scholarly examination of Gnosticism largely relies on sources other than the Nag Hammadi library and particularly emphasizes the dualistic aspects among the ancient Gnostics.

Layton, Bentley. *The Gnostic Scriptures*. Garden City, N.Y.: Doubleday, 1987.

In this book, Layton, one of the team of scholars translating the Nag Hammadi scriptures, renders many of the texts into his own more literary translation, thereby making them far more accessible than the official academic translations. Supplemented by very helpful commentaries.

Pagels, Elaine. *The Gnostic Gospels*. New York: Random House, 1978.

By far the most readable introduction to the Gnostics and the Nag Hammadi Library. Recent scholarship has challenged some of Pagels's conclusions, but this remains the single most influential book among people first discovering Gnosticism.

Robinson, James M., ed. *The Nag Hammadi Library in English*. San Francisco: Harper & Row, 1988. (First edition, 1977.)

The complete translated texts of all the scriptures found at Nag Hammadi. The abundance of interpolations and ellipses make for a sometimes choppy read. This is probably the most widespread reference book for exploring what the Gnostics had to say themselves.

Singer, June. *A Gnostic Book of Hours: Keys to Inner Wisdom*. San Francisco: HarperSanFrancisco, 1992.

A lovely book of meditations on Gnostic scriptures, modeled on the format of late medieval prayer books. Singer combines insights from depth psychology with her own spiritual reading of the Gnostic myths.

*Three*

# FINDING THE INNER CHRIST:
## ESOTERIC CHRISTIANITY

Today many people like to think of themselves as irreverent and iconoclastic. While most civilizations have shown an instinctive reverence for the heritage of the past, ours often shows an equally automatic contempt for it. Orthodoxies and received wisdom receive harsh treatment today.

Nowhere is this mistrust of the past so evident as in current attitudes toward Christianity. The Christian faith, the central one of Western civilization, obviously retains its fascination for us, as evidenced by the tidal wave of new Bible translations and the endless debates about the historical Jesus in recent decades. But in addition to this allure, there is also widespread criticism and even disgust. In fact much of today's restless spiritual searching seems to be inspired by the conviction that Christianity has nothing to offer the inner life, that it has become simply a collection of dogmas and hierarchies and politicking.

It would be a gross mistake to think that Christianity has no inner dimension. Examples to the contrary include the Quakers, with their relentless search for the Inner Light; great visionaries like St. Teresa of Avila; Emanuel Swedenborg; and Jacob Boehme, a seventeenth-century German cobbler who received illumination while entranced by a glimmer of light on a pewter dish. There are great medieval contemplatives like Meister Eckhart, Thomas à Kempis, and the anonymous fourteenth-century English mystic who urges the seeker to "strike that thick cloud of unknowing" that separates Creator from created.[1]

The twentieth century offers its own examples: Boris Mouravieff, an enigmatic Russian émigré who claimed to be expounding the esoteric "Doctrine" of Orthodox Christianity; Valentin Tomberg, another Russian émigré, who wrote one of the most compelling expositions of modern Catholic mysticism in the form of commentaries on the Tarot; and Stylianos Atteshlis, or "Daskalos," the Cypriot magus portrayed in the works of Kyriakos Markides.[2]

Esotericism can be considered as a more or less systematic way of exploring the unseen, whereby the practices of meditation and contemplation are combined with a structured and sometimes rigorous theoretical framework (usually rooted in a particular spiritual tradition). By contrast, mysticism may be seen as more preoccupied with the naked experience of the divine; theories and ideas may be merely rudimentary or may even be ignored altogether. By this view the Quakers, who have always stressed the pure experience of the Inner Light, would be mystics but not esotericists. Jacob Boehme, who outlined a great baroque system that purported to show the very structure and dynamics of the Godhead, would be more of an esotericist.[3]

The categories overlap, but it would be true to say that both mystical and esoteric Christianity are preoccupied with that famous verse from the Gospels "The kingdom of God is within you" (Luke 17:21).[4] Rather than accepting this text merely as a bland reassurance, these inner forms of Christianity ask very specifically *what* the kingdom of God is and *where* within us it can be found.

## BEING BORN AGAIN

It has often been stated that being "born again" is essential for the Christian life, yet few seem sure about what rebirth exactly entails.

It seems to have something to do with "accepting Jesus in your heart," but is that all? Does it mean anything more than going to the front of the hall after a moving evangelical performance?

Esoteric Christianity also stresses the need to be "born again," but it sees this process as both subtler and more demanding than is generally believed. According to Boris Mouravieff, the "second birth" requires an enormous amount of work, "much greater than that required for example from the student from the time when he starts his elementary education until he obtains his doctorate."[5]

To understand why the "second birth" takes so much effort, we might begin by going back to Christ's famous words: "Except a man be born of water and of the Spirit, he cannot enter into the kingdom of God" (John 3:5). Christ does not say exactly what he means by "water and the Spirit," but other references in the New Testament help to clarify his statement. St. Paul tells the Thessalonians, "I pray God your whole spirit and soul and body be preserved blameless unto the coming of our Lord Jesus Christ" (1 Thess. 5:23).

This verse suggests how the early Christians understood the makeup of the human being. They saw it as consisting of three parts: the physical body, the soul, and the spirit.[6] They believed that human development can be gauged by knowing which of these elements is dominant.[7] The lowest level is that of the *fleshly,* or, as the King James Version puts it, "carnal" man, the one who is governed by the desires and aversions centered on the body: "For whereas there is among you envying, and strife, and divisions, are ye not carnal?" (1 Cor. 3:3).

The second level is that of the soul—the *psychic,* or, as we might say today, the "psychological." The King James Version translates the Greek word *psychikos* as "natural" (see, e.g., 1 Cor. 15:44). While this word may seem a trifle misleading, it is less so if we regard this level as being occupied with what is naturally human—the emotions and the intellect. As Jung often stressed, one of the most common symbols for the psyche is water, an image that accurately reflects the flowing, liquid, turbulent quality of the mind.

The third level is the *spiritual* (Greek, *pneumatikos*). The spirit is, to use a contemporary catchword, "transpersonal": it has to do with the eternal and unchanging, with what is far beyond mere desires, thoughts, and emotions. It is the part of us that reaches toward God.

In Christian doctrine, humanity was originally created to be governed by the spirit, which in turn answered to God. But the Fall of Adam (often seen as a mythic truth rather than a factual event) reversed the orientation of human nature: human beings became subject to the desires of the body, which usually dictate our thoughts and feelings. In the language of Christ's parable, this is the predicament of the man who built his house on sand (Matt. 7:26): our loves and hatreds constantly shift and change, offering no solid foundation for our lives.

The Christian tradition refers to this state as *passion;* passions (in the plural) are the urges that we experience as a result. As the sixth-century mystic St. Isaac of Syria said, "Passions are like dogs, accustomed to lick the blood in a butcher's shop; when they are not given their usual meal they stand and bark."[8] To be ruled by passions is the human condition, according to Christianity, and anyone who looks at his or her own motivations honestly will see that this is true.

The way to overcome the passions is *repentance.* Like so many familiar Christian terms, this one has acquired an unwholesome savor; it is often associated with guilt, noisy breast-beating, or complacent hypocrisy. But for esoteric Christians, repentance is something far different. The Greek word (Greek was the language in which Christianity was first spread throughout the ancient world) is *metanoia,* whose roots literally mean "change of mind."[9] Repentance in this sense may well entail regret for past sins and a firm resolve to abandon them, but it also means a change in orientation.

In the ordinary human condition, one's orientation is external, toward the world of sensation and appearances; the emotions and mind more or less follow along. Christian "repentance" or "change of mind" is a reversal of this orientation, a movement from the exterior to the interior. One turns from the "carnal" to the psycho-logical or "natural," then from the "natural" to the spiritual. And at the center of the spirit is Christ: "for ye are Christ's, and Christ is God's" (1 Cor. 3:23).

This is what it means to be "born again of water and of the Spirit." To "enter the kingdom of God"—that is, to reach the point where God, and not the body or the ego, is really at the core of one's being—one must be "reborn" on two levels: that of the psyche and that of the spirit. As St. Paul says, "It is sown a natural body; it is raised a spiritual body" (1 Cor. 15:44). Some esotericists even see this idea as meaning that the Christian develops subtle bodies that the ordinary human does not possess.

If this is so, one can easily see how, as Mouravieff says, the ef-forts required would far exceed the amount of schoolwork as-signed between kindergarten and a Ph.D. But what does it mean in practice? The notion of developing psychological and spiritual "bodies" may sound arcane or even ridiculous. It makes more sense, however, if one thinks of a body as an organized structure.

In a healthy person, the physical or "carnal" body is an intricate and well-designed mechanism. Everything is oriented toward a single, coherent purpose: staying alive. Christianity says we are not so well organized on a psychological or spiritual level. Our minds and spirits have nothing toward which they can turn; they have no purpose, no center. As a default, they orient themselves around the body, becoming enslaved to its interests. This is passion, also known as *sin,* or the condition of the Fall. To be redeemed from this state, the seeker accepts Christ as the center of his being, or, as it is often put, he "accepts Jesus into his heart."

Esoteric Christians, like Christians of all types, differ enor-mously about the nature and person of Christ. To judge from the long lists of heresies and polemics that the religion has spawned since its birth, there has never been a unanimous answer to Christ's searching question to the disciples: "Whom say ye that I am?" (Mark 8:29). Yet however one understands Jesus Christ, Christ must remain central to the Christian's spiritual aspiration, for the simple reason that this is what Christianity *is.*

## MYSTERY AND SACRAMENT

Esoteric Christianity, like more familiar forms of the faith, sees the death and resurrection of Christ as its central mystery, indeed as the central mystery of human existence. But mainstream Christianity stresses the passion of Christ as a one-time event, something that happened in a unique historical moment. For esoteric Christians the passion of Christ also serves as a prototype for the rebirth that each seeker must undergo.

Not every Christian of an esoteric bent denies that Christ literally died and rose again as an act of redemption. Swedenborg did not. Nor did Rudolf Steiner, the founder of the twentieth-century esoteric school known as Anthroposophy. Nor did most of the writers we will cite. Some esoteric Christians, however, do see the passion of Christ as a myth—meaning that, although it has deep significance for the psyche, it may not have happened in fact. Those who see the story in this way tend more toward the Gnostic end of the doctrinal spectrum, whereas esoteric Christians with a more orthodox perspective see Christ's sacrifice both as an objective act of redemption and as a symbolic key to the journey of the seeker.

To understand how Christ's passion refers to the individual journey, we might begin by citing a basic esoteric idea, made famous by the Greek philosopher Protagoras: "Man is the measure of all things." Each of us is a microcosm of the universe; nothing exists in the universe that does not also exist in us.

If this is so, then it stands to reason that there would be something in us that has the same role God has in the universe. It has many names; Jung called it the Self. Under ordinary conditions, this "God within" is not only transcendent, but cut off and distant; the ordinary ego, with its passions and distractions, has little contact with it.

Esoteric Christianity, by certain practices and methods (as well as by the intervention of divine grace), helps open up these channels so that the ego makes contact with the God within—the divine indwelling that lies at the core of our being. Thus the seeker who turns toward God finds that God also turns toward him. At this point the Christ within looks down upon our sins and our suffering and, through a subtle inner mystery, takes part in them. Out of love and compassion this inner self "dies" to its former isolation; yet, being immortal, it cannot truly die. Indeed, because it contains all life and potency, it resurrects the ego from its own deadness. (Again, most esoteric Christians would say that this inner Self has some connection with the historical Jesus Christ, the incarnate Son of God.)

Over the past two centuries, chiefly through the influence of John Wesley's Methodism, many Protestants have come to view this transformation as a completely individual process—"making a personal commitment to Christ." But Catholicism, Orthodoxy, and much of the Anglican communion see this process as being enacted through rites and symbols as well, especially through the rituals of worship Christians know as the sacraments.

The Catholic and Orthodox churches celebrate seven sacraments: baptism, confirmation, Eucharist, penance, matrimony, ordination, and extreme unction. The esoteric significance of the first sacrament, baptism, should now be obvious: it marks the Christian's rebirth "of water and of the spirit." Alan Watts sums up the meaning of this ritual immersion:

> Clearly, it involves the most extraordinarily complex of symbols, since the water is all in one the Womb of the Virgin, the stuff of the world, the emblem of Purity or Voidness in which the past leaves no stain, and the depths into which the neophyte descends with Christ in his death, and from which he rises with Christ in his Resurrection.[10]

Not surprisingly, the early Christians usually performed baptism only on adults. Infant baptism came later, chiefly as a means of enveloping the child under a "canopy of grace" and protecting it from evil spirits until maturity, when the individual could accept its effects consciously.[11] Infant mortality was also undoubtedly a factor, as parents wanted to ensure that their children would go to heaven even if they died young.

The central ritual of the Christian religion is the Eucharist, which Catholics call the mass and the Eastern Orthodox know as the liturgy. On the simplest level this offering of bread and wine is commemorative—a fulfillment of Christ's instruction to "do this in remembrance of me." What else does it accomplish?

The Eucharist is a *mystery,* and the word *mystery* has a specific esoteric sense. It does not mean a puzzle or a conundrum to be figured out. On the contrary: though a mystery may give rise to many interpretations, it can't be exhausted by any of them. Rather it serves as a window to a higher reality; it speaks of, and elicits, a deeper truth within the mind.

Hence whatever can be said about the Eucharist will of necessity be only partial. But that doesn't mean one can't speak of it at all. To explicate a mystery is like drawing a pailful of water from an inexhaustible well—as long as one remembers that the pailful is not the well.

Primarily, of course, this ritual symbolizes the work of Christ himself. "The order of the mass," said Pope Innocent II, "is arranged upon a plan so well conceived that everything done by Jesus Christ or concerning Him, from His Incarnation to His Ascension, is there largely contained either in words or in actions, wonderfully presented."[12] Most centrally, the offering of bread and wine represents Christ's sacrifice of his own body and blood to atone for sin.

At the same time, the Eucharist symbolizes the Christian's own inner journey. For example, the materials used in the ritual—bread and wine—are not really natural materials. Although they make use of natural substances—grain and grapes—a great deal has to happen before these substances become bread and wine. The crops must be planted, cultivated, and harvested, then crushed and mixed with other things before they can yield the final results.

In esoteric Christianity, each of these materials, and each stage of their production, relates to inner development. It is no coincidence that so many of Christ's parables speak of "wheat," "vines," "harvest," "leaven," and so on.[13] For example, the "seed" must be sown into "good ground" (Matt. 13:23): that is, the "word," the impulse toward a higher consciousness, must find its home in a receptive individual. It must be given time to mature; when it is harvested, it must be threshed, and so on.

In simple terms, this all means that Christians must start with good material *in* themselves: one must be sincere to begin with. Then one must work on one's own mind and emotions, as well as allowing the teachings of Christ to work on them, before one can be an acceptable sacrifice on the altar of God. At that point one dies as "bread"—as an ordinary personality—but is reborn as part of what Catholics call the Mystical Body of Christ. Then, as St. Paul says, "I live; yet not I, but Christ liveth in me" (Gal. 2:20).

There are, of course, many other aspects to the Eucharist and the other sacraments. Early in this century C. W. Leadbeater, an early Theosophist who claimed to be clairvoyant (and who was also a bishop in a splinter sect of Catholicism), wrote a thick book describing his visions of "thought-forms," the unseen forces that the sacraments brought down from heaven.[14]

The sacraments are, from Leadbeater's perspective, a rite of *theurgy.* Theurgy is ritual magic—but magic that enacts the will of God, not of the magician. It brings divine energies down to earth, elevating and spiritualizing the world of matter, including the very being and substance of the participants. Each time the believer takes part with attention and devotion, he or she becomes more attuned to God.

## DIVINE READING

Another means of mystical exploration in Christianity is scriptural study. Over the centuries the Bible has been put to many uses: some preachers treat it like a sacred amulet, which they brandish before their congregations to command awe; modern critical scholars portray it as a well-intentioned but rather haphazard collection of earlier texts, cobbled together at various times and for various purposes.

In general, esoteric Christians steer between these two extremes, both of which, despite their different conclusions, are concerned with the literal meaning of the Bible. Although it holds Scripture in the highest regard, esoteric Christianity has never held that the Bible is literally true at all points. As the third-century Church Father Origen wrote:

> Very many mistakes have been made because the right method of examining the holy texts has not been discovered by the greater number of readers . . . because it is their habit to follow the bare letter. . . .
>
> Scripture interweaves the imaginary with the historical, sometimes introducing what is utterly impossible, sometimes what is possible but never occurred. . . . [The Word] has done the same with the Gospels and the writings of the Apostles; for not even they are purely historical, incidents which never occurred being interwoven in the "corporeal" sense. . . .
>
> And who is so silly as to imagine that God, like a husbandman, planted a garden in Eden eastward, and put in it a tree of life, which could be seen and felt. . . . And if God is also said to walk in the garden in the evening, and Adam to hide himself under a tree, I do not suppose that any one will doubt that these passages, by means of seeming history, though the incidents never occurred, figuratively reveal certain mysteries.[15]

Evidently fundamentalism was a problem even in Origen's time.

Esoteric Christians have traditionally taught that Scripture has four levels of meaning: the *literal,* which is the lowest, being directed only at the level of the senses; the *moral* or psychological meaning, which impels one to act according to the teachings of Scripture; the *allegorical,* in which the symbolic meaning of the text begins to penetrate into one's unconscious; and finally the *mystical* or unitive level, where the message of Scripture has become integrated into the deepest fiber of one's being.[16]

Some, for example, say the story of the Flood is an allegory of meditation: Noah (whose name in Hebrew means "rest") builds an "ark" of meditation in order to float upon the waters of the psyche. The story of the Exodus from Egypt is said to be a symbolic account of the soul's journey from enslavement under the "Pharaoh" of the body to the "Promised Land" of spiritual freedom.[17] Much of Christian (and Jewish) literature interprets Scripture this way.

Just as important, though, is the correspondence of these four levels to states of being. The noted Benedictine monk David Steindl-Rast describes the contemplative practice of *lectio divina,* or "divine reading":

> It consists of . . . reading not as much as you can but as little as you can. So you read only one word, maybe, of a passage. . . . And then this reading sends you into—I would not say reflecting on what you have read, because that is too active—but into basking in it, savoring it, and that usually lasts for a little while, depending on your psychological state. Sooner or later you begin to daydream, and then you can come back to the next word or the next sentence or the next page, so that the reading is really like a landing strip from which to take off, and whenever you can't stay in the air anymore, you come back down to it, taxi, and take off again.[18]

In the Benedictine tradition there are four states to which one can attain by means of this "divine reading" and, not surprisingly, they correspond to the four levels of meaning. In the first place there is *lectio* or "reading," which has to do with comprehension on the most literal level. The second level is *meditatio* or visualization, the use of mental imagery, which may lead to *oratio*—spontaneous affective prayer—and finally to *contemplatio,* where one simply rests silently in the presence of God.[19]

Another contemplative use of Scripture involves the best-loved of all the books of the Bible: the Psalms. This collection of 150 songs and prayers, many of them attributed to the biblical King David, has long formed a central part of the Christian path. St.

Benedict of Nursia, the founder of monasticism in the West, ordered his monks to recite the entire Psalter at least once a week, saying, "We read that our holy Fathers strenuously performed that task in a single day. May we, lukewarm that we are, perform it at least in a whole week!"[20]

When we approach the Psalms today, our reactions may be mixed. There are the old favorites: the Twenty-third Psalm, "The Lord is my shepherd," which many know by heart; Psalm 91, with its promise of divine protection, whose written text has often been given as a talisman to soldiers going off to war; and Psalm 51, with its heartrending plea of contrition, written, it is said, by King David after he had stolen Bathsheba from her husband.

Yet other Psalms may be confusing and even dismaying: Psalm 119, the longest chapter in the Bible, written in the original as a series of acrostics on the twenty-two Hebrew letters and containing, according to some, a hidden esoteric doctrine in digest form;[21] or Psalm 137, which begins hauntingly with "By the waters of Babylon there we sat down, yea, we wept, when we remembered Zion" but ends grimly with "Happy shall he be, that taketh and dasheth thy little ones against the stones"; and many others that call for retribution against the Psalmist's "enemies."

We may be tempted to dismiss these texts as expressions of the hopes and fears of half-savage people long since dead. On an inner level, though, contact with the Psalms may have a completely different import.

Going through these dense, elusive poems arouses a perplexing array of emotions in one. The reader is catapulted from ecstasies of bliss and thanksgiving to anger, despair, and emptiness and back again. Reading them gives the impression not of a sagelike serenity but of struggling human beings with lives every bit as turbulent as our own. And this may be the very point. The Psalms are not an emotional sedative. Quite the contrary: they seek to touch every layer of feeling that we are capable of—and to turn them all toward God.

In the fifth century, John Cassian traveled to monasteries in the Middle East and brought back some of their practices to the

West. During his travels he met a monk named the Abbot Isaac, who recommended reciting a version of Psalm 70:1—"O God, make speed to save me; O Lord, make haste to help me"—as a sure means of attaining a state of perpetual prayer. Cassian wrote:

> It is not without good reason that this verse has been chosen from the whole of scripture as a device. It carries within it all the feelings of which human nature is capable. . . . It carries within it a cry to God in the face of every danger. It expresses the humility of a pious confession. It conveys the watchfulness born of unending worry and fear. It conveys a sense of our frailty, the assurance of being heard, the confidence in help that is always and everywhere present. . . . This is the voice filled with the ardor of love and charity. This is the terrified cry of someone who sees the snares of the enemy, the cry of someone besieged day and night and exclaiming that he cannot escape unless his protector comes to his rescue.[22]

Much the same could be said about reciting the other Psalms. "Divine reading" is not simply a means of concentrating the mind; it also requires the attention of the heart. The reader who can open up both the mind and the emotions to the divine spirit may glimpse some of the higher meanings of Scripture, and the corresponding states of being, of which the tradition speaks.

Recent years have seen a new fascination with Gregorian chant.[23] The use of chant and music in Christian services has had a long and respected history from the religion's earliest times, producing such masterpieces as the grave medieval hymn *Dies Irae* and Bach's *B Minor Mass*. Some scholars even say that the magisterial opening of the Gospel of St. John is an adaptation of an early Christian hymn. Yet the whole history of Western sacred music could be seen as an elaboration of this one fundamental urge: to use every means, including sound, with its inexplicably touching rhythms and harmonies, to turn the attention of both head and heart toward God.

## REPENTANCE, OR TURNING WITHIN

Perhaps the most powerful attempt at Christian inner exploration was made by an odd assortment of men who withdrew to the wildernesses of Egypt and Syria in the first three or four centuries after Christ. They have since become known as the Desert Fathers.

Few clues have been left regarding their motives. Some were perhaps disgusted with the urban noise and squalor of the late Roman Empire; some no doubt wanted to draw closer to the God whose presence they had tasted in Christian worship; some may not have even known why they went but felt themselves obscurely drawn to the solitude of the desert, which has given birth to so many of the great world faiths.

In the silence and peace that they had sought out, the Desert Fathers pursued devotions including prayers, hymns, fasting, and ascetic practices, punctuated by stretches of physical labor as well as the chanting of Psalms.

What was their goal? The word they used was *theosis,* or "deification." Particularly in Eastern Christianity, *theosis* has been seen as the final goal of human effort and as the ultimate purpose of Christ's mission on earth. In the words of the fourth-century Church Father St. Athanasius the Great, "God became man so that man might become God."

For most Christians, this ultimate union with God is expected to come in the afterlife, either in heaven (assuming one makes it there) or after the Last Judgment. (Reincarnation has not played a large role in Christian doctrine, though this belief is fairly common among esoteric Christians today.) But for those who want to go the extra mile, "deification" can take place in this lifetime. This is what transforms a human being into a saint, and this is the goal that the Desert Fathers were aiming for. Through the practice of repentance, or *metanoia,* these ascetics attempted to "put aside the old man" and centered their being upon the living Christ within.

Repentance cannot be a merely intellectual process. Indeed in classic Christian mysticism it takes place not in the head but in the

heart, and is felt there. One of the most important Christian devotional practices is known as the Prayer of the Heart. This method
goes back at least to the Desert Fathers and possibly to the earliest
days of the faith, inspired by Paul's command to "pray without
ceasing" (1 Thess. 5:17). How is this possible? Even if one spends
long hours reciting formal prayers, how can prayer be taken into
daily life, where even monks must occupy themselves with eating,
sleeping, and mundane chores?

The answer is that somehow the prayer must take root and
perpetuate itself automatically, like the beating of the heart. As the
process continues, the prayer comes to lodge itself in the deepest,
most unconscious aspects of one's being, drawing the practitioner
ever closer to God.

To pray in this way requires some short formula. Its exact form
varies; one of the earliest is the verse cited by John Cassian: "O
God, make speed to save me; O Lord, make haste to help me."
Sometimes it can be as brief as a word or two. The fourteenth-
century English mystical classic *The Cloud of Unknowing* recommends using a single word, such as "God" or "love."[24] The most
common form, however, the Jesus Prayer, usually consists of some
version of the sentence "Lord Jesus Christ, Son of God, have
mercy on me, a sinner." This too can be abbreviated. David
Steindl-Rast, for example, says he uses the phrase "Lord Jesus,
mercy" in his devotions.

The basic method of the Jesus Prayer is simple: one repeats the
words, as few as a dozen times a day for lay people, or, in certain
monasteries, as many as ten thousand times a day. At the beginning, one repeats the phrase aloud or at least mouths it with the
lips and tongue. Later the prayer becomes more internal and automatic; the mind begins to repeat it without a conscious act of will.
Still later the prayer comes to penetrate one's whole being and
even merges with the rhythm of the heartbeat.

Use of the Jesus Prayer (or a similar contemplative method) can
produce a subtle internal sensation of burning. This is the "re-
finer's fire" of which the Bible speaks (Mal. 3:2), a certain inner
process by which that which is base and coarse in oneself is trans-

muted into the fine.[25] To work consciously with this process is to cultivate *apatheia,* which is not "apathy" but passionlessness, freedom from passion: as St. Isaac the Syrian writes, "Passionlessness does not mean not feeling passions, but not accepting them within."[26]

After this stage one reaches a state of inner stillness known in the Orthodox tradition as *hesychia,* in which one does not have any specific experiences or see any images but rests quietly in the presence of God. Finally one may encounter what Orthodox mystics call the Uncreated Light, the overwhelming radiance that emanates from the Divine Being itself.

Such a technique can be powerful. One of the great obstacles humans face is inner conflict: part of one's being wants something that the other parts do not want. Few escape this conflict entirely. The Jesus Prayer is intended to unify one's being to the point where even the heartbeat obeys the presence of the living God, so that "it is not I that liveth, but Christ in me."

This process is not, as in certain forms of Eastern mysticism like yoga, the same as making contact with an impersonal Absolute. Though some mystical Christians, like Meister Eckhart, speak of the Godhead this way, as "God beyond God, utterly without numeration or distinctive marks,"[27] most see the confrontation with the radically *personal* God as the essence of Christianity. "The Jesus Prayer is not a method," observes one monk on Mount Athos, a Greek peninsula that has for centuries been the center of Orthodox spirituality. "Properly, it is a relationship, something personal, emotional. If one treats it as a method, intellectually, then you are missing the point . . . which is a personal relationship with Jesus."[28]

This practice has its dangers too, which have been rigorously detailed by Orthodox mystics. Foremost of them is what the Russians call *prelest* or "glamour," a state of delusion in which one takes superficial or transitory supernatural experiences for the true presence of God or Christ. Not every light is the Uncreated Light. (This danger is recognized by all great traditions; it is one reason they warn against cultivating psychic powers for their own sake.)

A more mundane problem has to do with physical health. Directed attention is a powerful force—more powerful than we may think. For most of us, the heart works quite well without any conscious attention; to interfere with it, even by using a prayer, may throw the system out of kilter. This is partly why people are encouraged to practice the Jesus Prayer only under the guidance of a competent spiritual director. This too corresponds to the advice of most traditions, which urge meditators to talk with a teacher from time to time as a means of checking any possible dangers or digressions, or simply to make sure they're still doing the practice right.

## CENTERING PRAYER

The Jesus Prayer casts a merciless light on inner foibles and applies the same remedy to all of them: the call to Jesus Christ to "have mercy on me, a sinner." It is intended to set up a powerful inner dynamic between the perfection of God and the weaknesses of ordinary human beings. It is strong medicine—stronger, perhaps, than many might feel they can take.

It's no surprise, then, that some contemporary Christian mystics have shifted the emphasis of inner prayer somewhat. One of the most influential of these is Thomas Keating, a Trappist Benedictine monk who has updated Christian contemplative prayer in a version known as Centering Prayer. Based on *The Cloud of Unknowing*, it shows the tremendous resiliency of traditional mysticism and its application to the modern experience. Though Centering Prayer does resemble the Prayer of the Heart in some ways, it speaks more of healing the "woundedness" of the seeker than atoning for "sin."

According to Keating, Centering Prayer also differs from most forms of meditation in that it doesn't begin with attention but with *intention*. In this practice the practitioner simply tries to rest in the presence of God beyond all thought and emotion. A sacred word or phrase, such as "God" or "love," may be used, but rather than being repeated incessantly, it is simply used as a reminder to return to the heart of the practice—resting in the presence of God.

The benefits of meditation have been widely advertised: it's supposed to promote relaxation, reduce blood pressure, lower cholesterol. Oddly enough, people who have tried Centering Prayer sometimes report the opposite: resting in the presence of God in this way can summon forth hidden emotions, fears, and desires. And this is part of the point—to unearth the unconscious motivations that constitute "passion" as it is understood by Christianity. Only in this way can the darker part of one's nature be purified, freeing the seeker to rest in the clear presence of God.

As new as Centering Prayer is, it harks back to much in the Christian heritage. Remember the turmoil experienced by the Desert Fathers, most famously expressed in the Temptation of St. Anthony, which has formed a compelling artistic motif for centuries. Here too it is a matter of confronting inner demons, and this is no mere metaphor. The further within the seeker penetrates, the more he or she will tend to experience the desires of the body or the ego as *external:* what formerly seemed to be one's own thoughts or feelings start to seem more like the arguments of noisy neighbors—or evil spirits.

This suggests why repentance in the deepest sense is a delicate process; if not undertaken under competent guidance, it can lead to dissociation and breakdown. In his book *The Presence of Other Worlds*, the psychologist Wilson Van Dusen describes the strong resemblance between the "voices" heard by schizophrenics and evil spirits as described by Emanuel Swedenborg.[29] And those afflicted by what today's psychology calls complexes, neuroses, or emotional trauma may find that their experience parallels the old mystics' struggle with demons or even the Devil himself.

## WHO IS THE DEVIL?

The notion of a real, personal (or superpersonal) embodiment of evil is not fashionable today. But the Gospels portray the Devil and his minions as real enough. Christ goes into the wilderness "to be tempted of the devil," and much of his healing work consists of exorcising demons from the Galilean populace. Is this a quaint superstition, or is it central to the teaching of Christianity?

To grapple with these questions, it may be easiest to begin by remembering that Christianity is a *way*. Jesus's earliest followers, in fact, were simply known as "the way" even before the name "Christian" was coined (Acts 9:2; 11:26). A way implies direction, here the direction of the seeker as he or she moves toward God. Human beings who are not on "the way" are knocked about by the forces of nature. This is the state of ordinary life, of people as they are carried in various directions by the upheavals of accident. But they can't be said to have lost their direction, because they didn't have one to start with.

Everything changes when one embarks upon "the way." Having decided to move toward God, one finds that certain forces help while other forces stand in opposition. The seeker who notices these forces of opposition may begin to glimpse in them a certain personal quality.

Of all the great religions, Christianity is the one that most strongly emphasizes the radically *personal* nature both of human beings (as contrasted to Buddhism, which denies the ultimate reality of a Self) and of the Absolute. God himself is a person (or three persons) and chooses to relate to his creation in a personal way.

Hence Christianity tends to view the opposition in much the same fashion; the Hebrew word *satan,* from which the Devil's proper name is derived, means "opponent." The Devil is simply the sum total of the cosmic forces that oppose the journey toward God—viewed as a conscious person.[30] Individual thoughts and desires that oppose our way are known as "demons" or "evil spirits"; esoterically these are the "enemies" mentioned by the Psalmists. While Christianity is not the first of the world religions to view evil in this light (that honor probably goes to Zoroastrianism), it is the one that has emphasized it the most.

The struggle with the Devil can be viewed, then, as wrestling with everything that moves us away from God. The ancient monks and hermits experienced this force of opposition as a deliberate, conscious source of evil, even as a vast infernal hierarchy that imitates, in inverse form, the angelic ranks of heaven.

It's possible, of course, to become obsessed with the Devil and to see his pernicious influence in the smallest misfortune that may befall us. But then here, as in most areas of life, we have the choice of focusing on the goal or on the obstacles.

## A COURSE IN MIRACLES

To believe in God, must we believe in the Devil? The more orthodox versions of Christianity say we must. Even the Lord's Prayer implores the Almighty to "deliver us from evil"—which the original Greek states more clearly as "the evil one." Nevertheless, some versions of Christianity see the dark powers of the world from a different perspective. Among the most popular of these today is one expounded in a strange blue-bound book entitled *A Course in Miracles*.

The *Course*, as its admirers call it, is an anomaly in Christian history. Most Christian mystical writings are considered to have been written by humans on earth—inspired by the Holy Spirit, perhaps, or informed by a deep inner experience, but still composed more or less in the ordinary manner. Not so the *Course*. Dictated to a skeptical New York psychologist named Helen Schucman in the 1960s and 1970s by an inner voice claiming to be that of Jesus Christ himself, it thus falls into the burgeoning category of "channeled" materials, meaning that those who wrote them down believed they were transmitting them from a source outside their own minds.[31]

The *Course*, which has attracted a large following since its publication in 1975, inspiring a number of best-selling books by Marianne Williamson and Jerry Jampolsky, is not a religion or a church. To enter its world, one simply needs to get hold of the book (originally bound in three volumes consisting of a "Text," a

"Workbook," and "A Manual for Teachers," today they are available in a single volume) and do the assignments—for the term "course" applies very literally. The heart of the *Course* is its Workbook containing 365 daily lessons, whose goal it is to undo "false perception" and help the student acquire "true perception."[32]

"False perception," according to the *Course*, is the world we see—a world of bodies, of distinctions, of separation. The "real world," on the other hand, can only be seen through the eyes of forgiveness, which acknowledges that all evil is merely delusion and that God's love is the only reality.

The *Course* also focuses on a personal relationship with Jesus, less as God and savior than as an "elder brother" who would show us the way. This idea, combined with its view that the physical world is the result of error and delusion (the *Course* recognizes no conscious figure of evil like the Devil), sets it apart from conventional Christianity. That may explain why the *Course* has been most welcomed in New Age circles that emphasize positive thinking.

The *Course* teaches that in the beginning "God extended Himself to His creations and imbued them with the same loving will to create."[33] This collective creation is known in the *Course* as the "Son" or the "Sonship" and includes not only Jesus Christ but each of us. Regarding the historical Jesus, the *Course* says, "Is he the Christ? O yes, along with you."[34]

At some point, however, the Son chose to exercise his free will and believed he could be separate from God. Hence the Fall or "separation," which engenders the illusion that we exist as beings independent from each other and from God. Indeed the closest thing the *Course* has to the Devil is what it calls "the ego." The Fall encompasses the world we ordinarily see—time, space, the physical realm, even our own bodies.

The remedy God has given in response is known as the Atonement, also known as the Holy Spirit. According to the *Course*, "Jesus is the manifestation of the Holy Spirit," who "has established Jesus as the leader in carrying out his plan since he was the first to complete his own part perfectly. All power in Heaven and earth is therefore given him and he will share it with you when you have completed yours."[35]

In contrast to conventional Christianity, this representation of the Atonement ultimately consists of recognizing that the Fall never really occurred. God's will cannot be gainsaid. For this reason miracles are not only possible but "natural. When they do not occur something has gone wrong. . . . Miracles transcend the body. They are sudden shifts into invisibility, away from the bodily level. That is why they heal."[36]

What can one make of the *Course*? It's impossible to say whether it was telepathically dictated by Jesus Christ—how could anyone tell? Even comparing it with Christ's words in the Gospels is useless, since the *Course* insists that the Apostles got parts of his message wrong. (Many modern scholars agree.)

In a sense, the *Course*'s popularizers have done it a disservice in weakening its insights, making it sound much like another update of the gospel of positive thinking. In its hard-headed rigor it resembles the teaching of the Desert Fathers, urging students to scrutinize their minds for "attack thoughts" or "grievances," which, the *Course* says, "hide the light of the world in me."[37] However, it differs from the teaching of the Desert Fathers, and from much of Christianity, in seeing the consequences of the Fall not as sin, but as a *belief* in sin.

Some have said the *Course* is ultimately not Christian at all. The *Course*'s notion of Atonement, for example, is not the conventional Christian one: the book claims that "the crucifixion did not establish the Atonement; the resurrection did."[38] It even speaks of the journey to the cross as "the last useless journey."[39] Yet esoteric Christianity embraces a vast landscape of theologies, and in its inner "turning" toward God through the mediation of Jesus Christ, the *Course* is indeed Christian. How one will reconcile it with other versions of Christianity will in the end depend upon one's own beliefs and experience.

## ORTHODOXY AND HERESY

The *Course* aside, most of the Christian teachings and practices discussed in this chapter are consistent with an orthodox view of the faith. This is not a coincidence. Popular misconceptions to the contrary, Christianity has not generally persecuted or suppressed its mystics or forced them to turn to heresy. Most Christian mystics of most periods have had no quarrel with the creeds or the dogmas of the Church. The Benedictines have always been loyal Catholics, just as the monks and ascetics who taught the Prayer of the Heart remained true to Orthodoxy.

Yet certain streams of esoteric and mystical Christianity have been at odds with ecclesiastical authority. The Gnostics were one such group. Jacob Boehme was hounded by the doctrinaire ministers of his home town for his apparent divergences from Protestant teaching; and the Quakers were persecuted by the seventeenth-century Church of England. In more recent centuries, as official Christianity has mellowed or weakened, many Christians with a mystical bent have tended to exclude themselves from the churches instead of being excluded by them.

One of the greatest concerns in recent years has had to do with Christianity's perceived masculine bias. If the Christian Church has insisted on a personal God, it has also fostered a masculine image of this God: the Trinity, after all, is described as "Father, Son, and Holy Ghost." Today more and more people recognize that these male images, though initially intended as metaphors, have come to be taken too literally over the centuries. Some people have broken away and attempted to revive (or create) a religion of the Goddess; others have searched the Christian tradition for more feminine images of God.

The most obvious one is of course the Blessed Virgin. Over the years she has repeatedly appeared to people in various places around the world, including Fatima, Medjugorje, and Bayside, Queens. These apparitions have inspired popular cults that have sometimes dismayed the ecclesiastics. Though there is little evidence that the Virgin was venerated in the earliest centuries of

Christianity, today it would be hard to imagine Catholicism or Orthodoxy without her. Many would probably find it easier to live without God the Father than without the Virgin.

A less familiar candidate for the feminine face of God goes back further in the Christian tradition, even to the Bible itself. This is Sophia, known to the Gnostics as the personification of Wisdom, who says in Proverbs, "I was set up from everlasting, from the beginning or ever the earth was" (Prov. 8:23). Though Holy Wisdom has not received much honor in recent centuries, at one time she was central to Christianity: the greatest of all Byzantine churches, Hagia Sophia in today's Istanbul, was dedicated to her.

Sophia has never been regarded by orthodox forms of Christianity as part of the Godhead, but some esoteric Christians regard her as the active power of God in the world, "the living soul of nature and of the universe."[40] As such she is the closest feminine figure in Christianity to the actual person of God, and so she has attracted some interest from Christians of various stripes who are seeking to give God a more feminine face. At times she has been identified with the Blessed Virgin.[41]

One interesting idea about the feminine aspect of God has been propounded by the Russian mystic Daniel Andreev (1906–59), who wrote a visionary book called *The Rose of the World* while incarcerated in the gulag. In this powerful work, which has only recently appeared in English, Andreev contends that Sophia, manifesting as the Blessed Virgin, is in fact the Third Person of the Trinity, so that the Trinity really consists of "the Father—the Virgin Mother—the Son."[42] While this doctrine would no doubt be condemned by orthodox theologians, it could go far toward remedying the perceived masculine bias of the conventional Trinity.

## FINDING ESOTERIC CHRISTIANITY

Despite the richness of its heritage, esoteric Christianity is not always easy to encounter. Most clergymen of any denomination may never have heard of the ideas and practices mentioned here. And, to return to a distinction made at the beginning of this chapter, Christianity has always had a bias toward the mystical rather than the esoteric. This is to say that Christians who seek the "divine indwelling" within themselves have tended to resist theorizing, preferring to leave such matters to theologians. Many monks and other Christian seekers, their own deep experience notwithstanding, would deny that they knew anything about "esoteric Christianity."

Christians with a mystical bent can find avenues for their aspirations in Protestant or Catholic contexts—a small contemplative group meeting in an Episcopal church, a Benedictine monastery that offers retreats, or a workshop in Centering Prayer. These are often likely to be open, at least to some extent, to people who may not feel tied to a denomination or to Christian doctrine as it is narrowly understood. Eastern Orthodoxy, on the other hand, is more rigorous; for the Orthodox, dogma, ritual, and mysticism are an indissoluble whole, so experimentation is less likely to be encouraged except perhaps as a prelude to conversion.

For approaches to esoteric Christianity as such, one may turn to the writings of Maurice Nicoll, a British psychiatrist who studied with both Jung and Gurdjieff. Valentin Tomberg (1900–73), a Russian esotericist who converted to Catholicism in middle age, wrote a profound book entitled *Meditations on the Tarot*, in which he related the arcana of these curious cards to the mysteries of Christian faith and practice.[43]

Esoteric Christianity takes on other forms as well. The Liberal Catholic Church, for example, was started early in the twentieth century as a means of understanding the Catholic sacraments in the light of esotericism (Leadbeater was one of its founders); it has always had a close bond to H. P. Blavatsky's Theosophy and shares most of its doctrines, including reincarnation.[44] The Liberal Catholic Church has had a powerful impact in helping define the theory and practice of such well-known twentieth-century magicians as Dion Fortune, W. E. Butler, and Gareth Knight.

There are many other small splinter churches with elaborate

names (usually with "Orthodox," "Catholic," or "Apostolic" in the title). These often consist of a more or less independent bishop and a flock that numbers no more than a handful.[45] Often ornate in liturgy and mystical in doctrine, these churches are very much a mixed bag. On the one hand, at their best they can offer a sense of the ineffable that is frequently lacking in middle-of-the-road denominations; on the other hand, the eccentricities of both members and leaders are often real enough and need to be taken with a good deal of caution.

## THE SILENT CENTER

One idea that is central to all versions of Christianity remains to be addressed. It forms the focus, not only for the teachings we've talked about here, but all of the manifold dimensions of the Christian religion, from the Catholic veneration of the Virgin to the stillness of the Quaker seeking the Inner Light. It is the reason God became man, the means by which the divine Lord communes with the redeemed Christian, the force that brings Atonement to a shattered universe.

This force is love. *Love* is a dangerous word; it can be applied to anything from violent passion to a bland sentimentality. Yet without love Christianity is incomprehensible. We've seen that the Christian worldview is ultimately a *personal* one—God is not an abstract Absolute or a cosmic energy but a person (or three indissoluble persons) who relates to his creation directly and intimately. The medium of this relationship is love.

Christian mystics have sometimes been chided for insisting on the "otherness" of God, especially compared to Eastern mystics, who emphasize the essential unity of the Self with the Absolute. Christian mystics do, of course, speak of mystical union with the Divine, but they also stress that an unbridgeable gulf separates Creator from created.

Perhaps Christianity insists upon this gulf so powerfully because it views love—which, in Dante's famous words, "moves the sun and the other stars"[46]—as the central force of the universe. And love in its truest sense can ultimately exist only between two distinct entities; even self-love requires us to see ourselves (or part of ourselves) as in some way "other."

Yet isn't it also true that we experience anyone we genuinely love as part of our own being? Perhaps the ultimate mystery of love is that it constantly shifts focus between one and two, between otherness and unity. We cannot dissect the secrets of love with the knives of logic. To analyze it is to destroy it, and there is a point at which indeed it passes our understanding. Yet in its strange silent way it conveys us to the living heart of the universe.

## SUGGESTED READING

Amis, Robin. *A Different Christianity: Early Christian Esotericism and Modern Thought*. Albany: State University of New York Press, 1995.
    Perhaps the best introduction to Orthodox mysticism and its relation to the modern experience.

*The Cloud of Unknowing and Other Works*. Translated by Clifton Wolters. Harmondsworth, Middlesex, U.K.: Penguin, 1961.
    This anonymous fourteenth-century text is one of the greatest Christian mystical works of all time.

*A Course in Miracles*. Three vols.: Text, Workbook, A Manual for Teachers. Tiburon, Calif.: Foundation for Inner Peace, 1975.
    Many of the *Course*'s admirers regard it virtually as a sacred text. The Text, the first volume, is the most difficult; it's easier to start with the Workbook or the Teacher's Manual. Recent editions include all three parts in a single volume.

Kadloubovsky, E., and G. E. H. Palmer, trans. *Writings from the Philokalia on Prayer of the Heart*. London: Faber & Faber, 1951.
    A selection from the primary texts of the Eastern monastic tradition.

Keating, Thomas. *Open Mind, Open Heart: The Contemplative Dimension of the Gospel*. Rockport, Mass.: Element Books, 1986.
    A good introduction to the ideas of the founder of Centering Prayer, including instructions on how to carry it out.

Mouravieff, Boris. *Gnosis: Study and Commentaries on the Esoteric Tradition of Eastern Orthodoxy*. Three vols. Translated by Maneck d'Oncieu et al. Newburyport, Mass.: Praxis Institute Publishing, 1989–93.

Mouravieff claimed to be giving the first complete exposition of the hidden "Doctrine" of esoteric Christianity. A compelling, challenging work.

Needleman, Jacob. *Lost Christianity*. San Francisco: Harper & Row, 1980.

A distinguished philosopher tells about his search for the inner meaning of Christianity.

Swedenborg, Emanuel. *Heaven and Hell*. Translated by George F. Dole. New York: Swedenborg Foundation, 1976.

The best introduction to the ideas of the great eighteenth-century visionary, this book describes his experiences of the realms of the spirit and the afterlife.

Watts. Alan W. *Myth and Ritual in Christianity*. Boston: Beacon Press, 1968.

An eloquent examination of the Christian mystery using the cycle of the sacred year.

*The Way of a Pilgrim and The Pilgrim Continues His Way*. Translated by Helen Bacovcin. Garden City, N.Y.: Image Books, 1978.

This consists of a pair of works written by an anonymous Russian pilgrim of the nineteenth century. It is probably the most engaging and accessible introduction to the Prayer of the Heart.

# Four

# A LADDER BETWEEN HEAVEN AND EARTH: THE KABBALAH

On the face of it Judaism offers a great paradox. One of the great world religions, it is also the religion of a people. How can a faith of a single people have universal significance?

Judaism itself has tried to answer this question in many ways. There is the famous claim that the Jews are God's chosen people, uniquely entrusted with the divine Law, but there is also the wry legend that God offered his covenant to the Jews only after every other nation had refused it.[1]

The idea of God forming a covenant with a people is not unusual. It harks back to an older phase of religious history, when a nation or a tribe often came to an agreement with the gods or spirits of a land; in exchange for rights of possession, they were entrusted with certain sacred duties. The identity of the Cheyenne tribe of the Great Plains, for example, was crystallized around a sacred ceremony called the Massaum, which commemorated the Cheyenne's relationship with, and obligations toward, the spirits and animals of the territory.[2] Such covenants sometimes entailed more cosmic functions as well: in his travels Jung met Pueblo Indian holy men who believed it was their tribe's task to assist the sun in its course across the sky.[3]

Such a covenant often prescribes rules that determine how the people should live. Many such law codes have been handed down in traditional contexts: the Romans had their Twelve Tables; the Chinese have the Five Classics; the Hindus have the Laws of Manu. But the most famous legal revelation belongs to the Jewish tradition: it takes the form of the commandments given to Moses on Sinai.

Today the word *law* has two meanings that are somewhat at odds with each other. On the one hand, we apply it to patterns of nature, like the law of gravity or the first law of thermodynamics. On the other hand, we also use it to refer to human legislation, such as criminal law or tax law.

What is immediately obvious is that the laws of nature are immutable, while human laws change. Moreover human laws, though they are (at least ideally) grounded in universal ethical principles, are often matters of convention: in the United States, the law tells people to drive on the right side of the road, while in Britain it tells people to drive on the left. Such laws, though convenient and necessary, are neither holy nor immutable; nobody imagines that they have been sanctioned by God.

This distinction between natural and human law is a comparatively recent one. It can be traced back no further than to the ancient Greeks, who were the first in recorded history to distinguish between "nature" and "convention" in this manner.

Judaism, embodying a more ancient understanding, draws no clear line between the rules governing the universe and the laws by which human beings must live: both are fixed, unchanging, and ordained by divine intelligence. Indeed Jewish lore says that the Law, written in letters of black fire on white fire, existed before the foundation of the world and that God himself consulted it before beginning creation.

The Law is thus an act of revelation; it cannot be altered by parliaments or legislatures. In this sense it is universal. But its application to the life of a specific nation is particular. Jews have never believed that the Law of Moses is meant to apply to other peoples. Some Jewish authorities believe that only the laws given to Noah after the Flood (Gen. 9:1–9) apply to all humanity. In recent years, in fact, this has given rise to the fledgling Noachide Movement, whose non-Jewish adherents worship the God of Israel but adhere only to the Noachian commandments, which include prohibitions against killing, stealing, sexual misconduct, and, curiously, eating flesh cut from a live animal.[4]

The written Law that has been given to the Jews as a people is known as Torah, a term that strictly applies only to the Pentateuch, the five books of Moses, though it is often extended to the rest of the Hebrew Bible as well. But Judaism has always held that there is more to the Law than the Bible as we know it. The Talmud, which takes the form of extensive multivolume commentaries on the Torah, proceeds further into the deeper recesses of the Law. Talmud consists of *halakhah,* the rabbinic law as such, and *aggadah,* a genre of exposition that includes legends, homilies, proverbs, and allegories.[5] Beyond the Talmud there is an esoteric core of Jewish teaching, not written but transmitted orally. This teaching is known as the Kabbalah.[6]

Sometimes people mistakenly refer to the Kabbalah as if it were a book or a text like the Bible itself. Although there are many Kabbalistic writings, there is no single text that embodies the Kabbalah in the way that the Hebrew Bible embodies the written Law. The Kabbalah is primarily an oral teaching; though many of its doctrines have been written down (often in the time-honored form of commentaries on the Torah), others have not been and may never be.

The word *Kabbalah* is clearly derived from the Hebrew verb *qaval,* "to receive."[7] But what this "receiving" exactly refers to is not so clear. At times it is understood to mean something passed down over the course of generations; hence it is often translated as "tradition."[8] At other times Kabbalah is taken to mean the receiving of influences from higher spiritual levels.

In a sense, both views are right, for sacred traditions are handed down in both ways. Theories, techniques, and texts are all passed from generation to generation with modifications over the course of time. Every form of human knowledge, from surgery to woodworking, is transmitted this way. But what distinguishes Kabbalah and other esoteric teachings in general is that the knowledge must also be transmitted "from above": that is, the aspirant must make contact with higher levels through gnosis. This contact not only transforms his inner nature but gives him the authority and the knowledge to pass the tradition on to others in turn.

If the Kabbalah is regarded as another Torah that has been transmitted orally alongside the Bible, does this mean that, like the written Law, it contains its own set of precepts and codes that the Kabbalist must follow? Ultimately, no. The Law of the Kabbalah—though it does involve certain techniques and practices—does not add to the commandments of written Torah but rather explicates the principles behind them.

Judaism is a religion that values learning. Indeed, though the word *Torah* is usually translated as "Law," it is more accurately translated as "Teaching." Innumerable Jewish proverbs expound the value of study for its own sake, and it is said that Eastern European Jews used to smear the blackboards with honey on the first day of school; new pupils were told to lick the honey so that they would know that learning is sweet.

Hence Jews have always taken a lively interest in knowing the reasons behind the rules. On the other hand, not all Jews, not even all of the devout, have a deep understanding of the reasons behind their traditions. They may well not know the cosmic principles that underlie the divine instructions, the dietary prescriptions, ethical rules, and ritual observances. It is the task of the sage to penetrate the mysteries of the divine commandments and to understand why they must be followed. Throughout the history of Israel, these sages have taken on many guises, sometimes as priests and prophets, as the rabbinic masters of the Talmud, and often as mystics and Kabbalists.

The oral Law of the Kabbalah, then, is not so much a matter of codes of conduct as an investigation into the hidden structure of the universe—of the "natural law" that undergirds the rules and practices of Torah. Astonishingly enough, this inquiry into the nature of things dares to penetrate into the essence of God himself.

The Kabbalah provides a *theosophy,* a systematic exploration of the structure and nature of the divine.[9] Its answers not only help explain various Jewish customs and practices, but help the Kabbalist to know God.

But isn't the divine nature so far beyond human comprehension that our minds can't grasp it? It is, Kabbalists agree; no matter how closely we may approach God or how intimately we may come to know him, there will always be more for us to know. They even have a name for this unknown and unknowable dimension of the divine: they call it the *Ain Sof,* which is Hebrew for the "limitless" or "infinite." Because of its very nature, we can say nothing about it; we can only describe it in negative ways, by saying what it is *not.* It has no form or shape or quality; the nearest the human mind can come to understanding it is by imagining endless, empty space.

This space is not dead or lifeless, however; in fact it is the source of all life. As such it wishes to create, to manifest itself. For millennia theologians have been asking why the inconceivable void of the Godhead should have chosen to disclose itself in appearance. One answer that Kabbalists give is that God wished to behold God. By this view the entire universe, is nothing more than an immeasurable mirror in which the Holy One can view his own glory. The essence of God as he has chosen to make himself known is portrayed in a diagram called the Tree of Life (figure 2).

The Kabbalistic Tree entered into the public domain sometime in the fifteenth century. Since then it has become part of the common tradition of nearly all corners of Western esotericism; most of the people and teachings discussed in this book have been influenced by it to one degree or another. Most crucially, it has become a mainstay of magicians and occultists, and indeed one would hardly be able to understand the Western magical tradition without some acquaintance with Kabbalah. Hence its teachings are worth exploring in some detail. Its structure and dynamics, Kabbalists say, can be used to analyze any process from the creation of the universe to the writing of a book.

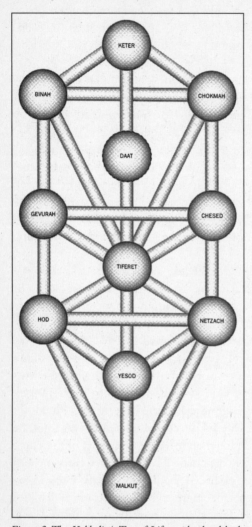

*Figure 2. The Kabbalistic Tree of Life can be dated back to thirteenth-century Spain, though it may well be much older. The structure of the ten sefirot indicates a map of the processes of manifestation, beginning with Keter, "Crown," and ending in Malkut, "Kingdom," or material reality. But the sefirot also delineate human qualities and faculties.*

## THE TREE AND THE *SEFIROT*

The Kabbalistic Tree exists partly to deal with the question of how the many arose from the One. If we can at times glimpse an underlying unity that gives birth to all we perceive, we also see that the world displays a lavish and bewildering multiplicity. How did one generate the other? Kabbalah's answer lies in the *sefirot*.

This is a difficult term to translate (*sefirot* is the plural form; *sefirah* is the singular). In the earliest of all Kabbalistic texts, the brief and enigmatic *Sefer Yetzirah*, or "Book of Formation," *sefirah* means little more than "number." In the medieval period, when Kabbalah took the form in which it is known today, the word came to refer to the divine emanations, the various aspects in which God makes himself known.[10] For our purposes perhaps the most straightforward translation is "principle."

The individual *sefirot* are represented visually in three vertical columns known as "pillars." On the right is the Pillar of Mercy, associated with all that is expansive and energizing. The left pillar is the Pillar of Severity, which is concerned with all that limits and gives form. (Those familiar with the popular Taoist terms *yang* and *yin* would not be far off in associating them with these two pillars respectively.) In the center is the Pillar of Mildness, which mediates between the two extremes. Here there is room for choice between mercy and rigor. Because this choice requires some kind of conscious decision, this pillar also has to do with consciousness at its many levels.

At the top is *Keter,* or "Crown." Notice that it is on the middle pillar, so it is concerned with consciousness, in this case a conscious decision to manifest. At this point everything begins, yet still exists only in potentiality.

The best way of coming to terms with Keter is as a point as defined in geometry: having no dimension itself, it nonetheless is the basis of all lines and shapes. Contemporary science provides another metaphor when it tells us that at one time all the matter of the universe was compressed into a space the size of an electron before exploding into manifestation with the Big Bang. (A Kabbalist would add, however, that this process did not merely happen once fifteen billion years ago, but is forever occurring moment to moment as God continuously wills to sustain the universe. If this process stopped even for an instant, everything would cease to exist.)

To continue the physicist's metaphor, if Keter is the point that contained everything before the Big Bang, then *Hokhmah* is the explosion itself. It is pure activity and dynamism, the relentless will to create and expand. The Hebrew word *hokhmah* means "wisdom," and if at first it seems odd to associate the state of wisdom with this pure explosive energy, we might recall that even ordinarily we regard wisdom as the capacity to see the innumerable possibilities in any situation.

As the diagram of the Tree indicates, the process of manifestation follows a definite order. From its zigzag pattern it is known as the lightning flash; as the *Sefer Yetzirah* says, "The ten *sefirot* appear out of Nothingness like a lightning-flash."[11]

With Keter there is the will to create; Hokhmah provides the energy. Now we need form to give it shape. Here is where *Binah,* "Understanding," comes in. Wisdom can, as it were, exist in a pure state, but to understand always means to understand *something:* Or, to view it another way, we may wish to create, but *what* shall we create? The answer to this question lies in Binah.

Binah consists of all the qualities inherent in something and all the possibilities it admits—and excludes. Hokhmah, pure energy, contains all possibilities, but for something to manifest in definite form it must admit some possibilities and exclude others. To be a human being means that you can't also be a fish. Binah is the realm in which "yes" and "no" first appear. Hence it is known both as "the Bright Fertile Mother" and the "Dark Sterile Mother";[12] the primordial *yin* or feminine, Binah, decides what to bring to life and what to abort.

Next comes one of the most curious aspects of the Tree: *Da'at,* "Knowledge," which is not, strictly speaking, one of the *sefirot;* some, like the contemporary British Kabbalist Z'ev ben Shimon Halevi (Warren Kenton), refer to it as an "unmanifest *sefirah*" or even a "non-*sefirah*." Da'at is sometimes known as the Abyss; it is the point at which the lightning flash pauses between manifestation in the abstract (as pure energy and form) and material appearance.

The next *sefirah* is *Hesed,* "Mercy." On the Tree it is right below Hokhmah; hence it also has to do with the energy of expansion. But because the lightning flash has already passed through Binah, the mother of form, Hesed entails a more orderly expansion; it is what makes growth possible within the limits of form. Because it is the principle connected with "room to grow," it is associated with mercy and charity.

Opposite Hesed is *Gevurah,* "Strength," also known as *Din,*

"Judgment," or *Pachad*, "Fear." Gevurah is concerned with limits and boundaries. While the connection between limitation and strength may not be immediately apparent, it is not all that mysterious. The karate expert cracks bricks with a blow of his hand because he can concentrate his force at a very specific point. Without limitation, strength would not be possible; the expansive energy would continue till it was dissipated.

Gevurah sets limits; if Hesed says yes, Gevurah says no. As the sixteenth-century Kabbalist Moses Cordovero says, "Among the actions of Gevurah are harsh judgment, as indicated by its name. It is a lash to discipline humanity."[13]

This aspect of the divine is among the most problematic for the modern mind. We read stories of heavenly wrath in the Old Testament or come across verses like "The Lord is a man of war" (Exod. 15:3) and wonder how we can reconcile them with the idea of an omnipotent yet benevolent God.

The Kabbalah is not quite so preoccupied with the exclusive goodness of the Deity. As God says, in the Bible, "I form the light, and create darkness: I make peace, and create evil: I the Lord do all these things" (Isa. 45:7). The central tenet of Judaism is "Hear, O Israel: The Lord is God, the Lord is One." God is the unique source of all that exists—light and darkness, peace and evil.

Does this mean that God is as responsible for evil as for good? At times that *is* what it seems to mean. Like Christianity, Jewish Kabbalah certainly regards Satan as an adversary to human beings, but unlike Christianity, it generally doesn't consider him an adversary to God. Rather he is a kind of celestial quality-control officer: it is Satan's job to test people to see how good they really are—and this is exactly his function as set out in the prologue to the Book of Job. This is why Cordovero also says that from Gevurah "stem all the aliens that seduce and denounce."[14]

The Kabbalah also occasionally speaks of evil as being outside the pale of the divine intent. By this view the Fall of Adam was not merely a tragedy for humankind but a cosmic event. At this point the lower *sefirot* were sundered from the higher ones, producing a bizarre, inverted mirror of the *sefirot* known as the *kelipot*. These cast-off fragments of the higher worlds have managed to survive by a kind of psychic parasitism: they incite people to evil deeds, from which they take their sustenance.[15] The word *kelipot* means "husks" or "shells," but if the idea had been phrased in modern terms, perhaps the image of a virus might have been chosen instead.

Hesed is growth and Gevurah limitation; Hesed love and Gevurah hate. From the dynamic interaction of these two forces comes the essence of a thing, for what we love and what we hate make up the deepest core of our essence. This is no mere sentimental utterance; it speaks of what a being's nature can and cannot endure. It is the nature of a cactus that it loves heat and hates damp; an air-fern is exactly the opposite. To put either one in the wrong environment is to push it past its limits; it cannot grow and will die.

This essential nature of a thing is symbolized by the *sefirah* called *Tiferet*, "Beauty," by which the Kabbalah seems to hint at the beauty that lies at the core of all things. Tiferet reconciles Hesed and Gevurah, but as the diagram shows, Tiferet is also at the very center of the Tree. No other *sefirah* is connected to so many of the rest. In terms of the human psyche—of which the Tree also serves as a prototype—Tiferet is what Jung called the Self.[16] Through the Abyss of Da'at (roughly equivalent to the collective unconscious), it is directly linked to the infinite at Keter.

Once anything exists as itself, it naturally has the urge to perpetuate itself. This is the province of *Netzach,* sometimes mistranslated as "victory," but which really means "endurance" or "perpetuation."[17] Netzach is the third and lowest *sefirah* on the Pillar of Force. Here the natural expansion and dynamism of the right-hand pillar is now firmly under the control of form. At this point it is channeled back into itself. As such Netzach is the sphere that governs all repetition, including the cycles of nature and the self-sustaining mechanisms of the body.

Next we come to *Hod*. Though this is usually translated as "Glory" or "Majesty," the root of the word actually means "crashing" or "reverberation."[18] Hod is what enables things to "reverberate"—to recognize and respond to the outside world. Hence Hod has to do with perception. But even inanimate things are not devoid of this principle. We all know, for example, that when a sodium atom encounters a chlorine atom, a reaction occurs and they form salt. Hod is the underlying principle that enables even something as basic as an atom to "recognize" and respond to something outside of it.

*Yesod,* the ninth *sefirah,* means "Foundation." Sometimes it is called *Tzaddik,* "the Righteous," because, as the Bible says, "The righteous one is the foundation of the world" (Prov. 10:12). This verse, so far from being merely a pious string of words, highlights a fundamental point.

The Kabbalah envisions manifestation in a way completely opposite to that of modern materialism. The materialist claims that matter arose first; all things, including consciousness, are mere by-products of matter. The Kabbalah, on the other hand, like most esoteric philosophies, insists that the visible is undergirded by the invisible; matter came not first but last. And what underlies matter is Yesod, the subtle form of a thing, which constitutes its "foundation."

Yesod is the realm of subtle matter, of what is known to esotericists as "the astral plane," and has to do with dreams, oracles, visions, and the like—in short, everything that has manifested in this subtle realm before making its descent into visible appearance. Whatever has already taken shape in Yesod can be perceived in certain circumstances. Some say this is the mechanism that explains precognition, clairvoyance, and other psychic phenomena. Shaping and manipulating this subtle matter is the essence of magic.

The tenth and final aspect, *Malkut,* "Kingdom," also known as *Shekinah* or "Presence," deals with manifestation in the physical world. It is the realm of solidity and stability. Viewed from the perspective of the higher *sefirot,* it is ultimate passivity (since only Malkut receives from above without giving to anything below it) as well as rest. Therefore Malkut is connected with the Sabbath, the day of rest that commemorates God's repose after creation.

## THE *SEFIROT* AND THE LAW

The Sabbath provides one of the most accessible examples of how the cosmic order of the *sefirot* underpins the laws of Jewish observance. For a pious Jew, the Sabbath is quintessentially the day when the Shekinah, the "Sabbath Queen," descends to earth. A Jew greets the arrival of this feminine aspect of God not only by imitating the divine rest, but with an elevation of spirit that helps unite the world above with the world below:

> The Kabbalists in Safed took this personification of the Sabbath as bride and queen literally. They would go, late Friday afternoon, in a procession outside the town to greet the queen and bride Sabbath; they sang certain Psalms and they would end with, "Come, bride; come, bride!"[19]

A pious Jew need not know about these ideas to experience the joy and blessings of the Sabbath. But understanding the esoteric dimension—which is really only possible through the Kabbalah—makes it possible to know why the Sabbath is kept. And knowledge is central to the Jewish tradition.

To take another example: the Kabbalah teaches that the movement represented on the celebrated image of Jacob's ladder, with "the angels of God ascending and descending on it" (Gen. 28:12), also takes place in the human heart. The heart contains the *yetzer ha-tov,* the "good impulse," which draws one upward toward God. But there is also the *yetzer ha-ra,* "the evil impulse," which pulls one away from God and toward the physical world.

This teaching casts light on the abstinence from leavened bread that is commanded for Passover. The eighteenth-century Kabbalist Moses Luzzatto explains:

> Bread is designated as man's primary food, and it is therefore precisely what is required by the state that God desired for man in this world. Leaven is a natural element of bread, making it more digestible and flavorous. This also is a result of man's appropriate

nature, since he must have an Evil Urge (*Yetzer HaRa*) and an inclination toward the physical.

At a particular determined time, however, Israel was required to abstain from leaven, and be nourished by Matzah, which is unleavened bread. This reduced the strength of each individual's Evil Urge and inclination toward the physical, thus enhancing his closeness to the spiritual.[20]

To take a final, and somewhat more obscure, example, the Book of Exodus describes making the priests' garments of specific colors: "And they made upon the hems of the robe pomegranates of blue, and purple, and scarlet, and twined linen" (Exod. 39:24). This small detail is a reference to Kabbalistic teaching. The "pomegranates" are a common image of the *sefirot*. But the colors refer to something different: they represent four Kabbalistic "worlds" that make up the universe in both its visible and invisible guises.[21]

## THE FOUR WORLDS

The Kabbalah teaches that Jacob's ladder comprises four worlds, or dimensions of existence, that stretch from heaven to earth. Each contains a Tree of Life in its own right.

The first world is known as *Atzilut,* from a Hebrew root meaning "standing near," for this is the world that "stands nearest" to God himself. Atzilut is the realm of the divine emanations proper, the energies of God that extend into manifestation. One could see it as the world of principles that constitute the universe. It is a realm that few people reach, except perhaps in a rare glimpse of illumination; even mystics do not often attain to an experience of Atzilut. Because of its dazzling purity and luminosity, it is connected with the color white—presumably the color of the "twined linen" in the priests' garments.

The second world is called *Briah,* or "Creation." If Atzilut is the dimension of principle, Briah has to do with the possibilities

that arise out of these principles. It is equated with heaven in all
the manifold meanings of that word, and so the color blue is associated with Briah. It is the world of the spirit. From the perspective of humans on earth, it is a step closer to ordinary world, but is
still extremely rarefied, abstract, and impersonal. Although it can
be attained through certain meditative and contemplative practices, it has comparatively little form.

In the next world, *Yetzirah,* "Formation," the possibilities that
arise out of Briah begin to take form, and so Yetzirah is the world
of forms and images, whether they are communications from a
higher world (as certain dreams and visions may be) or merely the
by-products of the customary churning of the mind.

At its highest reaches, Yetzirah contains the forces of Jung's collective unconscious, the great archetypes that are the building
blocks of our individual psyches. At lower levels it is the realm of
psychological drives and impulses, both conscious and unconscious, that motivate us on a daily basis. Much of our ordinary experience takes place at these lower levels of Yetzirah. Because it is
the meeting place between the "heaven" of Briah and earth (the
former symbolized by the color blue, the latter by red), Yetzirah's
color is purple.

The final world is *Assiyah,* "Action"; Assiyah is the kingdom of
doing. It is in this realm that all our daily actions are carried out,
as well as the sphere of the operations of nature. Assiyah is concerned with the earthly, and Hebrew thought has traditionally associated the earth with the color red.

Hence the four colors of the threads of the priests' garments
disclose a teaching about the four worlds, which subtly interact
with and interpenetrate each other. Some Kabbalists see them as
stacked one atop the other; the Keter of one is the Malkut of the
next.[22] Others see a more intricate connection between the two,
where the Tiferet of one world is the Keter of the next.[23]

## THE KABBALISTIC FILES

What we have said so far about the *sefirot* and the four worlds is more or less standard among most Kabbalists. Beyond this point matters become more nebulous. The Kabbalistic Tree can serve as an intricate symbolic filing system: each *sefirah* corresponds to names of God in the Bible, planets, angels, archangels, colors, minerals, types of incense, even drugs and pagan deities.[24] Unfortunately, these various systems often disagree with one another.

Some Kabbalists say, for example, that Binah's color is green, where others say it is black or red. One system connects blue with Hokhmah, where another links it to Hesed.[25] One system regards the Hebrew God-name connected with Gevurah as Elohim; another says it is Yah.[26]

To avoid reaching an impasse over these matters, the most sensible approach is probably to learn one Kabbalistic system well; later on one can add on to one's knowledge with less chance of confusion. If one finds a good teacher, of course, he or she is most likely to teach a particular system. Choosing a teacher may be simpler for the beginner than trying to choose from among various systems.

Nonetheless one wonders why there are so many inconsistencies among the works of even the greatest authorities. Is there one pure, "correct" system? Or is each a misinterpretation in its own right, suggesting that the "real" truth has been lost?

One might come to grips with this issue by remembering that Judaism, though far from a cold religion, is ultimately a rather cerebral one; no other faith gives such centrality to the study of texts. The most revered figure in the Jewish tradition is not the meditating monk or the saint in prayer but the scholar musing over the books of the Law.

Understanding this fact helps us understand why such forests of different associations have arisen. The Kabbalistic approach seems to work in the opposite way of the now-familiar Zen *koan*. The latter makes use of riddles and paradoxes ("What is the sound of one hand clapping?" "What did your face look like before your mother was born?") to stymie the rational mind and lead it to an impasse; the resulting confusion will presumably give way to enlightenment.

Kabbalistic study, on the other hand, does not attempt to arrest the mind in its course, but rather looks to lead it along many trains of associations. Anyone who picks up a book containing rabbinic disputations on the Torah can see this: the disputing parties cite various verses of the Bible to back them up, and each of these references adds its own dimension to the debate.[27] As the sage continues to ponder and debate about the texts, eventually, perhaps, the strings of associations become so intricate that each verse of the Torah will be linked to all others. The Kabbalist may do something similar with the associations triggered by the *sefirot*. And it may be that it is this web of interlinked and interpenetrating ideas that brings about illumination.

## KABBALISTIC PRACTICE

Bible study is clearly one main area of Kabbalistic practice. In a manner that resembles esoteric Christian perspectives, Jewish mystics envisage four different levels of meaning in the Bible, symbolized by the Hebrew word *pardes,* "garden" or "paradise." The four letters of this word (vowels are for the most part not written in Hebrew) are often taken as an acronym for these levels: "the literal (*peshat*), the allegorical (*remez*), the hermeneutical or homiletical (*derash*), and the mystical (*sod*)."[28] These four levels correlate with the four worlds.

A number of Kabbalistic techniques are used to grasp these levels. Some resemble the allegorical methods already seen in esoteric Christianity; others are more distinctively Jewish. One of the most important of the latter is *gematria.*

This word, derived from the Greek *geometria* ("geometry"), consists principally of "explaining a word or group of words according to the numerical value of the letters."[29] The most popular example of this method—which is in fact a descendant of ancient *gematria*—is numerology. By adding up the numerical values of the letters in your name (the values are usually given in a chart), you come up with a number that is supposed to give a key to your inner essence.

This may seem a bit artificial in English. It is less so in Hebrew, which, unlike our language, does not have separate characters for numerals but uses the letters of the alphabet to denote numbers as well. Kabbalists use *gematria* as a means of unlocking the *sod,* the mystical essence, of sacred texts.

The *Sefer Yetzirah*, for example, says of the *sefirot* that "their end is imbedded in their beginning . . . like a flame in a burning coal." Abraham Abulafia, a medieval Kabbalist particularly fond of *gematria,* noted that the numerical value of letters of the word *gachelet,* "coal," is 441. The word *emet, "*truth," has exactly the same value. This points to an essential equivalence: it is truth that binds all things together, just as the coal binds the flame to it.[30]

Why such emphasis on the minutiae of letters? What significance do these mere marks on a page have for mystical knowledge?

It is clear that Judaism views the Torah not as a mere collection of rules and covenants, but as a blueprint for the construction of the universe. These mysteries are concealed, not only in the meanings of the words, but in the very shapes and forms of the letters.

Hebrew, like another great sacred language, Sanskrit, does not have an alphabet of its own but has made use of a number of scripts. Before the Babylonian Exile in the sixth century B.C., it was written in Phoenician letters; after the Exile, Hebrew came to use the Ashurite or Assyrian script. The Midrash Rabbah says, "Hebrew is a spoken tongue but has no script of its own. The Hebrews chose for themselves the Assyrian script and the Hebrew tongue."[31] (It is the "Assyrian script"—presumably learned in Babylonia—that we now call the Hebrew alphabet.) This and other statements in Jewish lore suggest that the Hebrew tradition underwent a major reformulation during the Exile.

At any rate, contemplating the shapes and sounds of letters, as well as combining them according to various schemes, lies at the center of Kabbalistic practice. Even apart from the reasons mentioned above, it is not hard to see why. The second commandment forbids making any "graven image" of anything "that is in the heaven above, or that is in the earth beneath, or that is in the water under the earth" (Exod. 20:4). Under this ban, there can be no likenesses of God, leading Jewish mystics to use letters (which are not, strictly speaking, images *of* anything) as a means of contemplating the divine.

The central example is the most important of the many names of God—YHWH, also known as the Tetragrammaton. The exact pronunciation of this name in antiquity is unknown; the most common guess is "Yahweh."[32] This name, presumably used by everyone in biblical times, was later regarded as so holy that it could only be uttered once a year, by the high priest in the Holy of Holies of the Temple on Yom Kippur.

Implicit in this is the idea, deeply rooted in Judaism, that the name of something is identical with its essence. A Kabbalistic proverb says, "God and his name are one." Not only are the *sefirot* associated with various names of God, but, as Moses Cordovero puts it:

> These names are the *sefirot*. It is not that these names are ascribed to the *sefirot*, God forbid. On the contrary, the [divine] names [themselves] are the *sefirot*, and the names are appellations of *Eyn Sof* according to His actions.[33]

Here too the connections of names with various *sefirot* vary: YHWH, יהוה, is associated either with Hokhmah or Tiferet.[34] More significantly, though, this name epitomizes the whole Tree. Keter, the junction point between the Absolute and manifestation, is signified only by the topmost point of the first letter. The entire letter *yod*, י, signifies the primordial power of Hokhmah; the first ה, H or *heh*, which at the end of a word marks the feminine gender in Hebrew, is associated with Binah, the primordial feminine. The letter ו, W or *waw*—which in Hebrew is used as a connective, signifying "and" when placed at the front of a word—signifies the next six *sefirot,* which connect the supernal *sefirot* to the lower. The final ה or H denotes Malkut, which is again feminine in its ultimate receptivity.

Thus the Tetragrammaton in itself contains a capsule summary of the Tree. To delve even deeper into these mysteries, Kabbalists contemplate this quintessential name of God in various forms. Some visualize the Hebrew letters before them, taking their inspiration from Psalm 16:8: "I have set יהוה before me always."[35] Others, reluctant to create images even in the mind's eye, prefer to meditate upon the sounds of the name, often permutated with the various vowels. Each permutation can be associated with a particular *sefirah.*[36]

These practices obviously resemble the Eastern technique of mantra recitation, and indeed the earliest Jewish mystics about whom we know anything—the *merkavah* mystics, the "riders of the chariot"—chanted holy names in preparation for their ecstatic journeys.[37]

*Ma'aseh Merkavah,* or "The Work of the Chariot," owes its inspiration to the beginning of the Book of Ezekiel, which describes an intricate and terrifying revelation of the divine presence in the form of "the likeness of a throne" resting upon a chariot consisting of "four living creatures" each accompanied by "wheels" (Ezek. 1:5, 1:15ff.).

The *merkavah* mystics did not merely seek to understand Ezekiel's vision of the celestial chariot; they wanted to attain it for themselves. After rigorous austerities, hymns, prayers, and recitations of divine names, they sought to ascend in their meditations through the seven *hekhalot* or "palaces" of heaven. Here they hoped to encounter "the likeness of the glory of the Lord" (Ezek. 1:28) seated on his throne.[38]

The practices of the *merkavah* were always seen as dangerous, as shown by a famous Talmudic account of four rabbis who ascended to the "Garden" of Paradise:

Four men entered the "Garden," namely Ben Azzai, Ben Zoma, Aher, and R. Akiva. Ben Azzai cast a look and died. . . . Ben

Zoma looked and became demented. . . . Aher mutilated the
shoots [became a heretic]. R. Akiva departed unhurt.[39]

Mystical ascent, in its many forms, makes up one half of Kabbalistic practice. The other half is descent, typified by *Ma'aseh
Bereshit* or "the work of Genesis." As the *merkavah* practices are derived from Ezekiel's vision, this latter work is inspired by the creation story in *Bereshit* (the Hebrew name for the book of Genesis).

*Ma'aseh Bereshit* attempts nothing less than to duplicate the efforts of God, who created the universe using letters and numbers.
The letters of the alphabet were considered to have such power
that under certain circumstances they could even be used to create
life. One amusing story tells of two rabbis who created a calf by
this means, upon which they then dined very satisfactorily.

With such methods, it is taught, one can even create a *golem,*
The *golem,* which has been the subject of innumerable legends and
stories, is a kind of Frankenstein's monster formed from earth by
means of certain rituals, recitations, and letter permutations.[40] The
most famous *golem* was supposedly created by Rabbi Yehuda Loew
in the late sixteenth century to acquit the Jews of Prague of the
charge of murdering Christian babies. According to legend, the
*golem* uncovered the true criminal, saving the Jews from a pogrom.[41]

It is hard to tell how literally a Kabbalistic adept would take such
stories; some say constructing a *golem* is meant to be a kind of meditative visualization.[42] Even so, one may wonder about the point of
these elaborate practices. Is it merely a kind of metaphysical hobby-
ism—building *golems* in one's workshop instead of, say, a bookcase?

The answer lies in Jacob's ladder, with its image of ascent and
descent. Kabbalah strives to elevate the consciousness of the practitioner so as to bring it closer to God; this is the "work of the
chariot." Then this heightened awareness must be incorporated
into the world of doing; this is "the work of Genesis." The two
processes constitute an ascent and a descent—"returning" to God
and "running forth" into manifestation.[43]

For the ordinary pious Jew, this "running and returning" is accomplished chiefly by fulfilling the commandments of the Torah.

For the Kabbalistic adept, it involves meditations upon the names of God, and, when the need arises, possibly even acts of ritual magic.

These awesome functions point to the centrality of the human role in creation. As envisaged by the Kabbalah, humanity is not an accidental by-product of a mechanistic universe. On the contrary: we have a central role in this universe. We are the only beings who function in all four worlds; even the angels cannot do this, but exist in their own narrow spheres, without free will. As unique, conscious beings, we are vitally needed for the *yechidut,* the "unification," of above and below. As the contemporary scholar Daniel C. Matt says:

> According to Kabbalah, every human action here on earth affects the divine realm, either promoting or hindering the union of Shekhinah and her partner—the Holy One, blessed be he. God is not static being, but dynamic becoming. Without human participation, God remains incomplete, unrealized. It is up to us to actualize the divine potential in the world. God needs us.[44]

## TODAY'S POSSIBILITIES

In the earliest centuries of the Common Era, only small, secret circles had access to mystical teachings. The Talmud warns that the mystical aspects of the creation story "should not be expounded before two persons, nor the chapter on the Chariot before one person, unless he is a sage and already has an independent understanding."[45]

And for many centuries the sage was almost always a "he." "There have been no women Kabbalists," states Gershom Scholem, the most eminent academic scholar of Kabbalah. He blames "this rather exclusive masculinity" on a tendency to stress "the demonic nature of woman and the feminine element of the cosmos."[46] Woman has been associated with the Pillar of Form, which gives rise to all limitation and evil.[47]

The Kabbalah was not even accessible to all males. Traditionally the aspirant had to be learned in Torah and Talmud, married, and forty years old (regarded as the age at which one attains Binah or "Understanding"). These requirements were meant to ensure that the aspirant was mature and well-grounded in practical life.

On the other hand, the stipulations have not always been strictly enforced. Some Kabbalists assert that women have always taken part in the tradition, though discreetly. Moreover a number of the greatest Kabbalists did not obey the age limit: Cordovero said one could start at age twenty,[48] and he himself completed his great book, *Pardes Rimmonim* ("A Garden of Pomegranates"), when he was twenty-seven. The medieval rabbi Joseph Gikatilla was publishing books on Kabbalah by the time he was twenty-six. Isaac Luria died at thirty-eight.[49] We would not have much Kabbalah today if everyone had obeyed the rules.

In fact over the centuries Kabbalah has undergone a slow but continuous process of democratization. The Middle Ages saw the appearance of works like the *Sefer ha-Bahir* (usually dated to the eleventh century) and the *Zohar* ("The Book of Splendor"), the greatest of all Kabbalistic texts, attributed to a second-century rabbi but almost certainly written by the thirteenth-century Spanish Kabbalist Moses de Leon. With the publication of these works, Kabbalistic ideas became available to anyone who could read Hebrew and Aramaic. During the Renaissance, the Kabbalah was expounded by Christian esotericists like Pico della Mirandola and Johannes Reuchlin, giving rise to a line of Kabbalah that has thrived for five hundred years outside a Jewish context. And later still, in the eighteenth century, the Jewish communities of Eastern Europe gave rise to Hasidism, a popular movement that stressed joy and devotion in worship and offered the treasures of Kabbalistic wisdom to every pious Jew.

A Jew who approaches this teaching today faces two major issues. In the first place, Kabbalah has been chiefly preserved in ultraconservative corners of the faith; the more liberal and rationalistic forms of Judaism have tended to shun it as a superstitious relic of the ghettos of medieval Europe. As a result, traditional teachers of Kabbalah may expect the aspirant to fulfill the traditional requirements. Even for most Jews, these requirements are likely to be prohibitive; studying the Talmud alone is a task of many years.

The second issue comes from the fact that much of Kabbalistic practice and teaching has been lost over the past few generations. This is partly because of the disgrace into which Kabbalah fell among educated Jews during the Enlightenment, partly because of the destruction wrought by the Third Reich on traditional Jewish life. Hence even rabbis with longstanding interests in the subject will sometimes admit that they have had to learn practices from books rather than from living teachers.

The Dalai Lama, meeting with leaders of the Jewish community in 1991, urged them to make the esoteric side of their own teaching more accessible to ordinary Jews.[50] Indeed, there has been some movement in this direction over the last generation, with particular inspiration from the Hasidic community, which continues to thrive. Its most prominent exponent in recent years has been Menachem Mendel Schneerson, who inherited leadership of the Lubavitcher line of Hasidism from his father-in-law. (Leadership in Hasidic traditions is partly charismatic, that is, based on sheer personal authority, and partly handed down by inheritance.) By the time of his death in 1994, Schneerson had become the single most influential figure in Judaism worldwide, and his house in Brooklyn became a center of pilgrimage. Many of his followers regard him as the Messiah.[51]

Though Hasidism remains by and large a closed community, some well-known contemporary teachers, such as Zalman Schachter-Shalomi and Shlomo Carlebach, have tried to bring Hasidic and Kabbalistic ideas into the mainstream. The Kabbalah Society in London, headed by Warren Kenton, offers access to the tradition from a nonsectarian perspective. Others are rediscovering such disciplines as *devekut* (a type of meditation that involves "cleaving to God") and *hitbodedut* (the Hasidic practice of pouring out one's heart to God aloud in prayer).[52] Today Kabbalah is more accessible to all, including women, than it has ever been. Ironically, some of its most able popularizers have been in the Western magical tradition, whose practitioners are for the most part not Jews; many are not even Christians or monotheists in the strict sense of the term.

## SUGGESTED READING

*The Book of Legends: Sefer Ha-Aggadah.* Edited by Hayim Nahman Bialik and Yehoshua Hana Ravnitzky. Translated by William G. Braude. New York: Schocken, 1992.

*Aggadah* is the term applied to the legends and lore of the Talmud. This classic edition offers a tremendous amount of material in a single volume.

Buber, Martin. *The Legend of the Baal-Shem.* Translated by Maurice Friedman. Princeton: Princeton University Press, 1995 (1955).

The Baal-Shem Tov, the "master of the good name," was the semi-legendary founder of Hasidism in the eighteenth century. This is an engaging collection of tales about him, edited by one of this century's foremost Jewish philosophers.

Fortune, Dion. *The Mystical Qabalah.* London: Ernest Benn Ltd., 1935.

Probably the best introduction to the Kabbalah from the perspective of the Western magical tradition.

Halevi, Z'ev ben Shimon (Warren Kenton). *Introduction to the Cabala.* York Beach, Maine: Samuel Weiser, 1972.

Formerly entitled *Tree of Life*, this lucid guide by one of the most prolific contemporary writers on Kabbalah gives a detailed discussion of the Tree of Life, with practical applications.

Other valuable works by Halevi include *Kabbalah: Tradition of Hidden Knowledge* (London: Thames & Hudson, 1979); *The Work of the Kabbalist; School of the Soul* (formerly entitled *School of Kabbalah*); *Adam and the Kabbalistic Tree*; and *A Kabbalistic Universe* (all published by Samuel Weiser). *School of the Soul* is especially useful as a discussion of group work.

Matt, Daniel C. *The Essential Kabbalah.* San Francisco: HarperSanFrancisco, 1994.

An excellent short anthology of excerpts from traditional Kabbalistic texts.

Scholem, Gershom G. *Major Trends in Jewish Mysticism*. New York: Schocken, 1961.

Scholem remains the single greatest academic scholar of Kabbalah. This collection of lectures, originally delivered in 1938, offers a superb historical overview.

————. *Kabbalah*. New York: Dorset Press, 1974.

A collection of Scholem's articles on Kabbalah for the *Jewish Encyclopedia*. First-rate, but more for reference than for reading.

*Sefer Yetzirah: The Book of Creation*. Translated by Aryeh Kaplan. York Beach, Maine: Samuel Weiser, 1990.

Many translations have been made of this mysterious text. Kaplan's is one of the most recent and comprehensive.

Steinsaltz, Adin. *The Thirteen-Petalled Rose*. Translated by Yehuda Hanegbi. New York: Basic Books, 1980.

Perhaps the best single introduction to mystical Judaism.

Weiner, Herbert. *Nine and One-Half Mystics: The Kabbala Today*. New York: Macmillan, 1969.

An engaging account of the author's search for living Kabbalists in the U.S. and Israel.

*The Zohar: The Book of Splendor*.

The *Zohar* is the central Kabbalistic text. No complete or entirely satisfactory translation of this multivolume work exists in English. The most complete is *The Zohar*, translated by Harry Sperling and Maurice Simon (London: Soncino Press, 1934). Daniel C. Matt, *Zohar: The Book of Enlightenment* (Mahwah, N.J.: Paulist Press, 1983) offers small sections of the *Zohar* translated into verse form.

S. L. MacGregor Mathers, *The Kabbalah Unveiled*, 1887. Reprint. New York: Samuel Weiser, 1974. Mathers presents sections of the more mystical aspects of the *Zohar*, translated from a Latin version rather than from the original Aramaic.

*The Zohar: Bereshith* (*Genesis*), translated by Nurho de Manhar (San Diego, Calif.: Wizards Bookshelf, 1995), is an intriguing presentation of the part of the *Zohar* that deals with Genesis. The text is interspersed with comments by the translator, however, and this is not always noted.

*Five*

# MAGICIANS:
# SCULPTORS OF THE ASTRAL LIGHT

In 1628, Pope Urban VIII, fearing that a coming eclipse por-
tended his death, called upon an erstwhile Dominican friar named
Tommasso Campanella for help. Campanella, who was known for
his occult knowledge, sealed off a room from the outside air; there
he and the pope conducted a magical ritual that replicated the solar system in miniature, using two lamps to represent the sun and
the moon and five torches to represent the other planets known at
the time. In this secluded setting, in which beneficent plants and
gems had been collected, they drank liquors that had been distilled
under the wholesome influences of Jupiter and Venus and played
therapeutic music. The performance was apparently successful, for
the pope lived another sixteen years.[1]

Today it may seem strange that a pope should have turned to
occult means for help, but in fact many in the Renaissance agreed
with the magus Cornelius Agrippa (1486–1535), who asserted
that "a magician doth not among learned men signify a sorcerer,
or one that is superstitious, or devilish; but a wise man, a priest, a
prophet" and that magic "was accounted by all ancient philosophers the chiefest science."[2]

For many centuries this appraisal was accurate. The sorcerers of
Egypt and Babylonia frequented monarchs' courts, ready to pre-

dict the future or repel evil. The Greco-Roman world produced magicians like Apollonius of Tyana and the Neoplatonist philosopher Iamblichus, who expounded a technique of theurgy, a means of bringing the gods down to earth. Medieval savants like Albertus Magnus and Roger Bacon were as renowned for their occult powers as for their theological and philosophical acumen. In the Renaissance, magicians such as Agrippa himself or John Dee, a favorite of Queen Elizabeth I, gained entrance into royal palaces.

There have been few eras, however, in which some amount of hostility has not fallen upon the magus, and many have tasted the full gamut of fortune's possibilities. Roger Bacon was imprisoned for sorcery, Agrippa and Campanella for heresy, and Dee's house (together with its library, one of the best of its age) was ransacked by a wizard-hunting mob.

As the Renaissance waned, the emerging scientific worldview—which owes more to magic than most scientists realize—accorded its older cousin neither the fear nor the respect that it had enjoyed in earlier eras. In the West, magic as a systematic spiritual practice was certainly not dead in the eighteenth and early nineteenth centuries: many Masonic groups in France and Germany were practicing ritual magic, and Francis Barrett was operating a magical school in London's Marylebone district at the turn of the nineteenth century. Still, the tradition was in something of an eclipse during this period, and it was only with the work of the French occultist Éliphas Lévi (1810–75) that the magical arts came to widespread attention.[3]

Lévi, a former seminarian who passed through a phase of political radicalism before being drawn into the occult currents swirling around in the Paris of his age, created a grand synthesis of esoteric knowledge. Nearly all that falls under the category of Western magic today owes a great debt to Lévi's work, particularly to his masterpiece, *Dogme et rituel de la haute magie* ("Dogma and Ritual of High Magic," 1854–56).[4] Many of the terms used in this chapter can be traced back to him, even though they are themselves reformulations of much older ideas.

Lévi's influence passed into the English-speaking world chiefly through a British society known as the Hermetic Order of the Golden Dawn. Founded in 1888, the Golden Dawn lasted a mere twelve years before it was shattered by personal conflicts. At its height it probably never had more than a hundred members. Yet its influence on magic and esoteric thought in the English-speaking world would be hard to overestimate.

The Golden Dawn's membership comprised a fascinating cast of characters, including the poet William Butler Yeats; S. L. MacGregor Mathers, author and translator of many occult texts; A. E. Waite, whose design for the Tarot deck remains the most popular in English-speaking countries today; and Aleister Crowley, the *enfant terrible* of modern magic, whose fascination with drugs and sexual magic would inspire British tabloids to dub him "The Wickedest Man on Earth." (Crowley's presence in the order, in fact, did much to hasten its dissolution in 1900.)

Today the authority of the Golden Dawn is perpetuated by in-numerable little groups and lodges that lay claim to its heritage with varying degrees of legitimacy. Its chief legacy, however, lies in the books and teachings that it has inspired. Though the Golden Dawn's rituals and doctrines were not for public consumption, nearly all of them have managed to find their way into print.[5]

The most influential perpetuator of the Golden Dawn tradi-tion is probably Violet Firth (1890–1946). She is best known un-der her pen name, Dion Fortune, derived from a Latin phrase she had taken as a magical motto, *Deo Non Fortuna*—"By God, not by luck."[6] She was only ten years old when the Golden Dawn itself collapsed, but she studied with several of its principal initiates, in-cluding Moina Mathers, wife of MacGregor Mathers and sister of the philosopher Henri Bergson.[7] Her struggles with Moina Math-ers, which, Fortune believed, included battles on the psychic level, provoked her to compose a book entitled *Psychic Self-Defence*.[8]

Despite these adversities, Fortune came away from her training with enough knowledge to write several of the most influential works on magic in this century. Her masterpiece, *The Mystical Qa-balah*, remains the best primer on the Kabbalah from a Western magical perspective. She also founded an occult lodge called the Society of the Inner Light, which still operates in London.

What exactly did the Golden Dawn accomplish? Certainly not the revival of magic per se. Magic is always with us. We attempt to perform it whenever we cross our fingers or say "God bless you!" when someone sneezes, for all superstition is magical in inspiration. But this magic, like most of the folk magic that has been performed over the centuries by the old wives and "cunning men" of the countryside, is far from systematic or well thought-out. "The primitive magician knows magic only on its practical side," wrote J. G. Frazer in his classic work *The Golden Bough.* "He never analyzes the mental processes on which his practice is based, never reflects on the abstract principles involved in his actions."[9]

This step was precisely what Lévi and the members of the Golden Dawn contributed. They were not the first in history to construct a coherent worldview out of magic—that had been done in ancient Egypt and Mesopotamia. But they were the first to make it intelligible and appealing to the contemporary man—and woman, for the modern occult magic of the West does not relegate women to second-class status.

## THE ART OF WILL

Although in recent years—thanks partly to Hollywood and partly to fundamentalist Christian opponents—the term *occult* has taken on a sinister connotation, a few generations ago it was used in a neutral or even positive sense. In the way the term will be used here, the *magician* or *occultist* is concerned with practical operations in the unseen realms.

The mystic, as described earlier, is principally concerned with reaching the Divine using the most direct path; everything else is a mere distraction. The esotericist, on the other hand, while also seeking ultimate union with the Divine, wants to learn about the landscape that appears along the way. The occultist or magician wants not only to view the landscape but to interact with it as well.

Since magic has to do with operations and their effects (even though they may be unseen to the ordinary eye), it is very much concerned with the practical. Aleister Crowley, who for all his quirks was a serious and intelligent practitioner of the art, defined magic as "the Science and Art of causing Change to occur in conformity with Will." Crowley then somewhat whimsically went on to describe the creation of a book as a magical process: "I write 'incantations'—these sentences—in the 'magical language' i.e., that which is understood by the people I wish to instruct; I call forth 'spirits,' such as printers, publishers, booksellers, and so forth, and constrain them to convey my message to those people."[10]

However amusing Crowley's example may be, few of us regard the publication of a book as a magical act. Something genuinely magical seems to require means that are hidden or unknown. Éliphas Lévi defines the word more precisely:

> Magic is the traditional science of the secrets of Nature which has been transmitted to us from the Magi. By means of this science the adept is invested with a species of relative omnipotence and can operate superhumanly—that is, after a manner which transcends the normal possibility of men.[11]

Why does Lévi call it a *science?* Science deals with the empirical—with experience, with the repeatable, and with the systematic. Yet remarkably enough, much the same could be said of magic. The difference lies in the levels of reality in which the two disciplines operate.

The previous chapter touched upon the four worlds of the Kabbalah. (Nearly every esoteric teaching has some analogous system, but the Kabbalistic system is the most common one in magic today—again, largely thanks to Lévi and the Golden Dawn.) Each of these worlds encompasses a unique level of existence. Of the higher worlds we have little conscious experience; our deepest insights and profoundest visions only touch upon their outskirts.

A little more can be said, however, about the two lower worlds. The lowest, known as Assiyah or "doing," makes up reality as we usually understand it. This is the realm of conventional science: the operation of matter and molecules, or in short the physical world.

We encounter the next lowest world, Yetzirah or "forms," chiefly through subjective experience, through thoughts, dreams, images, emotions, and the like. In some systems, it is also known as the "astral" realm. Yetzirah is the world in which magic takes place.

Each of the four worlds emanates from the one above it; nothing can come into physical existence unless it first takes shape in the higher worlds. Though this idea runs against modern scientific understanding, it is essential to magic.

Magic is indeed, as Crowley said, "causing Change to occur in conformity with Will." Magical workings are intended to create a "form" in this subtle, "astral" world of thoughts and images that will then give birth to an event in the physical world.

Thus magic is in its way quite "scientific"—specific causes produce specific effects. Like science, it is regular, systematic, and rational. Furthermore, like science, magic is essentially amoral; it can be turned to both good and bad ends.

## THE ASTRAL LIGHT

To begin to consider magical operations in their manifold forms, one needs to understand a concept that has fallen into disuse in recent years but still occupies a central place in Western magic: the *astral light,* or, as Éliphas Lévi resonantly called it in his native tongue, *la lumière astrale.* Some esoteric texts, such as Agrippa's, refer to it as the *anima mundi,* or "the Soul of the World."

"God is light," the Bible tells us (1 John 1:5). Esotericism regards this image as a specific and accurate picture of reality. This light pervades the universe; there is nowhere and nothing it is not, but it is modified, its purity and intensity are filtered and diluted, as it proceeds through various levels of manifestation. Esoteric theory holds that this light reaches us on earth only after passing through the zones of the stars and planets, whose influences it absorbs; hence its name.[12]

Astral light must not be confused with physical starlight. It is a subtle matter, imperceptible to the five senses and to the implements of science. "It is the common mirror of all thoughts and forms," says Lévi, "the images of all that has been are preserved therein and sketches of things to come, for which reason it is the instrument of thaumaturgy and divination."[13]

To form a more or less accurate picture of this light, one need only ask, what is the substance of a thought? Neurochemical responses, a scientist may say. While that may be true enough, we don't experience these images and forms as neurochemical events; we experience them subjectively as images and forms. In Kabbalistic terms, they exist both in the physical world of Assiyah and the psychic world of Yetzirah. They are made up not only of electrochemical interactions, but of astral light.

A more topical analogy comes from the world of computers. Hardware, software, and networks together form cyberspace, a dimension that, while in no way separate from the workings of computers, seems to obey its own laws and possess its own reality. This resemblance between the apparently outmoded world of the occult and the sophisticated ideas of cutting-edge science has not eluded computer scientists: Silicon Valley is a hotbed of interest in the esoteric, and hackers sometimes speak of cyberspace as a kind of *bardo*—a term used in *The Tibetan Book of the Dead* to designate the astral plane.

The fine matter of the *lumière astrale* is also believed to form the subtle or "astral body" of humans, giving literal force to the words of Shakespeare's Prospero: we are indeed "such stuff as dreams are made on." Shakespeare, of course, meant these words metaphorically; he was saying that we are frail, transitory, ephemeral. But then so are dreams and mental images.

This is not to say that the astral light is itself a frail substance;

occultists even consider it indestructible. But this subtle matter does not hold shapes well. Dream figures constantly shift form, and even before our waking eyes mental images rise and fall like waves. For this reason some esoteric teachings refer to this substance figuratively as "water." At its core, occult magic is concerned with navigating the watery world of the astral light, usually by astral travel, divination, or ritual.

*Astral travel* involves detaching the astral body—that is, the part of one's own being that is composed of the astral light—and making it journey to other places, in this world and in others. Magicians may, in the mind's eye, journey to Mars or Neptune or even beyond the solar system; they may encounter gods, devils, or fairies, or experience heavens and hells. Usually this ends up as little more than a voyage in the imagination; at times, though, it may step over the threshold into verifiable reality. Magicians may be able to see remote objects or places as if they were there personally. Some occultists claim that their presences have been felt, or even seen, at the sites they were visiting in the astral plane (a phenomenon known as *bilocation*).

*Divination* uses various means to tell the future or take a reading of some present situation.[14] Here the tools of divination reflect patterns in the astral light that are about to manifest in the physical world; the similarity to Jung's notion of synchronicity is obvious.

Each of the two most popular forms of divination today—the ancient Chinese oracle known as the *I Ching* and Tarot cards—encompasses an esoteric system in its own right. Confucius said if he had fifty years added to his life, he would spend them studying the *I Ching*.[15] The Tarot embodies teachings that some of its devotees trace back to ancient Egypt. The *I Ching* is beyond our scope of discussion here; we will take up the Tarot in more detail in chapter 8.

Other forms of divination rely more directly on the practitioner's own intuition.[16] Here one does not toss coins or lay out cards, but gazes into some object—usually a reflective one, like a glass or a crystal ball—and falls into a light trance. The images that then arise in the mind give insight into the question or problem at hand.

This type of divination is sometimes known as *skrying*. It has produced remarkable results, but it only works if the skryer can set aside the "editor"—the critical, analytical function of the mind. (Children, whose critical minds are not yet fully developed, have often been used as skryers for this very reason.) Hence skrying requires a certain mental deftness: the magician must be able to set aside the "editor" without disabling it, for the critical faculty is essential for evaluating one's experiences in the astral world (not to mention everyday life).

The third, and perhaps most important, aspect of magical attainment has to do with forming, holding, and energizing a shape composed of astral light. If enough power and skill are used in its creation, the image will sooner or later manifest in the physical world.

In theory the process sounds simple enough, and in a way it is; but it is not so easy to accomplish. To begin with, in order to manifest in the physical world, an image must have a steady, consistent form in the mind's eye. In practice, however, few things are more difficult to achieve, since it is notoriously hard to hold an image in one's mind for all but the briefest time. This may be partly due to a lack of mental discipline, but it also reflects the nature of the astral light itself. It is fluid and slippery; trying to hold it is like trying to grab water with one's bare hands. Thus much of magical practice is intended, in one way or another, to devise various means of containing and molding this elusive substance. Hence magical training emphasizes, above all else, mental concentration and will.

## WILL AND SACRIFICE

Look at some object near you. Now close your eyes and try to visualize it. Then open your eyes again, and compare your mental picture of the object with the object itself.

If you're like most people, you'll find some discrepancy between the object and your picture of it. You may find that you were able to imagine some parts of it better than others, or that you could imagine it as seen from one angle but not from another. You'll probably find not only that it's hard to keep your mind on the same picture, but that it's difficult to create an entirely accurate image even of an everyday object right in front of you.

One part of magical training is intended to hone the skill of visualization. The magician may begin by taking extremely simple objects or forms—geometric shapes, for example, like triangles and circles—and attempting to visualize them. Later on, the aspirant may be able to proceed to more complicated things like three-dimensional objects. A piece of fruit like an orange is a good thing to use, since one can imagine not only its appearance, but also its taste, smell, and texture.

However, visualization and imagination form only one aspect of the discipline. The second and more important part is the conditioning of the will. The mind is not likely to enjoy concentrated imagination at first; it will probably rebel and drift on to its ordinary worries and fantasies. The only way to train it is to constantly bring it back to the object.

Such work is often tedious, and the beginner may be able to practice for only a few minutes a day before concentration gives out. Gradually, however, these practices will achieve their end. The act of constantly bringing the mind back to the object, despite boredom or frustration, begins to form a small core around which the will can constellate. And the will is the magician's principal tool.

So far this procedure resembles the "creative visualization" that has been the subject of numerous books. Creative visualization as it's generally described, however, doesn't go past this point. Nothing more may be needed: sometimes the greatest hurdle lies in simply formulating a clear goal. But often the enterprise requires some sacrifice: an additional investment of vital energy to literally give life to the desired image.

The life force, as esoterically conceived, is another subtle substance, similar to but not identical with the astral light. There is no precise word for this force in English, so writers have used terms from other languages, especially *prana,* a Sanskrit word, or *chi,* a Chinese term. This life force is a slightly denser substance than the *lumière astrale,* though it is still too rarefied to be measured scientifically. Under certain conditions—say, in an acupuncture session—one can feel it as a subtle, almost electrical current coursing through the body.

If a magical image can be infused with *prana,* it will have much more power to manifest itself. The magician can accomplish this most easily by using his or her own vital force—for example, by generating emotional excitement, even to the point of frenzy, until it is felt as a palpable physical energy inside the body. Incantations are made and sacred names invoked, such as *El Hai Shaddai, Adonai Tzvaot,* or other Kabbalistic names of God; the magician may even intone portentous but meaningless syllables.

Though most magicians ascribe tremendous power to sacred words and names, this power does not lie so much in the word's meaning as in its emotional effect on the participants and, some say, in the very vibrations of the sounds. YHWH, the Tetragrammaton, is believed to have such power that if pronounced correctly it will shatter the universe (one reason, perhaps, why this pronunciation has been lost).[17]

Once emotional energy has been generated, at a climactic moment of the ritual the magician releases it toward the image desired. Crowley alludes to this process when he says, "The whole secret may be summarised in these four words: *Enflame thyself in praying.*"[18]

Magicians who use such an approach may sometimes feel drained or ill after the ceremony. But there are other, possibly less demanding means of applying energy. According to esoteric theory, *prana* is connected to various bodily fluids, such as the blood.[19] One way of adding energy to the "sacrifice" is to use a small amount of venous blood—but also semen or menstrual blood—in the ritual, smearing it, say, on a magical emblem. However bizarre this practice may seem, it explains the importance these substances have had in magical ceremonies worldwide.[20]

The magician may, however, want to use the energy of another. In this case an animal may be ritually slaughtered; its *prana,* released in death, will then give life to the image of the thing desired. Throughout history nearly every type of animal has been used for this purpose. Human beings have been sacrificed as well, but of course this is not part of Western magical tradition today, despite recent scares over "ritual abuse" or "ritual murder." A study conducted for the National Center on Child Abuse and Neglect in 1994 surveyed more than 12,000 accusations of group cult abuse, but found none that could be substantiated.[21] Even animal sacrifice is rare in the Western magical tradition today, though it is common in Voudoun and Santería, the Caribbean strains of magic that have become increasingly popular in urban America. (These are discussed in chapter 6.)

## THE WORLD OF SPIRITS

Sacrifice in spiritual traditions is usually made *to* someone or something—usually a god or spirit believed to be capable of granting one's wish. In primitive magic, the spirit is "fed" with the life force of the victim and grants the favor in return. In more sophisticated systems, the spirit or god is fed with the emotional energy of the aspirant, that is, with devotion. Indeed much of what passes for prayer in any faith is really "sacrifice" of this kind.

The world of spirits—those to whom the sacrifice is offered— is sometimes described as a sea or an ocean, for one of the prime metaphors used to describe the astral light is water. The analogy can be carried further, for, like the sea, the watery world of forms seems to contain a whole ecosystem in its own right, harboring entities from the rudimentary to the superhuman.

The magician who works in the world of forms will inevitably come across such entities, just as someone who goes diving will inevitably see fish. Encountering them is even part of the process, for they not only provide valuable help in accomplishing one's ends, but can teach us a great deal about ourselves. Hence a great part of ritual consists of *invocation*—"calling up spirits from the vasty deep," as Shakespeare put it. The magician can invoke angels, archangels, and gods, or summon demons and devils.

Over the past century we have come to view such things in highly psychologized terms, and magicians today vigorously debate whether these entities exist at all outside our own minds. Many occultists view them in the light of Jung's ideas, equating the gods with the archetypes of the collective unconscious, while demons, unclean spirits, and other unwholesome entities are likened to what Jung called complexes.[22]

Crowley (who had no connection with Jung) echoes such a view in discussing how to deal with a troublesome spirit:

> The spirit is merely a recalcitrant part of one's own organism. To evoke him is therefore to become conscious of some part of one's own character; to command and constrain him is to bring that part into subjection.[23]

The reader may find something comforting—or disappointing—in the notion that "it's all in your imagination." But many who encounter spirits find the experience real enough. In the early part of this century, Alexandra David-Neel, an indomitable explorer of Tibetan occultism, saw an aspirant in the mountains being driven mad by demons he had invoked. She complained to the man's teacher:

> "Rimpoche," I said. "I warn you seriously. I have some medical knowledge; your disciple may gravely injure his health and be driven to madness by the terror he experiences. He really appeared to feel himself being eaten alive."
>
> "No doubt he is," answered the lama, with the same calm, "but he does not understand that he is himself the eater. May be that he will learn it later on . . ."[24]

The aspirant who explores the astral plane finds that it truly is a different world from the physical realm. At the astral level it can be difficult to determine what is "inside" or "outside" oneself. Horror movies create a false picture: spirits, both good and evil, rarely appear in visible form. Instead the magician experiences them as unseen presences, inner voices, or simply as thoughts or emotions.

In such cases one can easily become confused about what is alien and what is really one's own. Past thoughts, grudges, hatreds, and other forms of unfinished business can easily resemble psychic intruders, whereas extraneous impulses may look like "my" thoughts and feelings. (These experiences parallel the "inner combat" of mystical Christianity.) This is why madness and obsession constitute potential hazards for any magician. They need not deter the serious aspirant, just as the risk of being killed on the freeway need not keep one from learning how to drive; but they do drive home the need for caution.

## RITUAL AND IMPLEMENTS

If magical work takes place in the realm of the astral light, then the magician's safeguards will have to lie in that realm as well. Thus adequate protection will have to involve some clearly imagined visual image. And for some practitioners this is enough—they are quite capable of guarding their psychic spaces by means of purely mental images, such as donning an imaginary robe of protection or envisaging themselves surrounded by a globe of light. Most magicians do not stop there, however, but prefer to strengthen their protection by means of operations in the physical realm.

The fact that magic is principally concerned with a world normally unseen to us doesn't mean it is totally cut off from manifest reality. Indeed, ritual operations—actions that take place in the physical world but are intended to have an effect in the astral— have always been an integral part of magical practice.

Why does the physical world need to be involved at all? In the first place, a large segment of the human mind is slavishly literal and refuses to acknowledge what it cannot see and touch. Hence a ritual operation strengthens the mental form in the magician's own mind. In the second place, magic, like many of the approaches we'll examine in this book, relies upon the doctrine of correspondences. The most famous expression of this idea comes from an ancient document called *The Emerald Tablet*, attributed to the legendary Egyptian magus Hermes Trismegistus: *Quod est superius est sicut quod est inferius; et quod est inferius est sicut quod est superius, ad perpetranda miracula rei unius.* "What is above is like what is below; and what is below is like what is above, to accomplish the wonders of one thing."

In magical terms, this means that one can affect the astral world by performing a corresponding operation in the physical. When magicians draw a sacred circle with a consecrated sword, they are not only making a physical circle but are creating a form in the astral light as well. (Crowley goes so far as to say, "The first task of every Magician is . . . to render his Circle absolutely impregnable.")[25] Such an operation is perhaps the simplest example of creating a holy space in which to work. Probably all sacred spaces, from Megalithic stone circles to Gothic cathedrals, are elaborations of this basic idea.

The magical function of the sword is to cut or sever, that is, to draw distinctions, in this case between sacred and profane space. (Sometimes the sword is supplemented by a ritual knife known as an *athame*.) The other basic magical implements are a wand, a cup, and a pentacle or a disk. They are associated with the four traditional elements: the wand with fire, the sword with air, the cup with water, and the disk with earth. More importantly, they point to the four basic skills a magician must command: to raise power (symbolized by the wand); contain it (symbolized by the cup); cut away extraneous forces (the sword); and ground the energy on earth (the disk).

The implements themselves can be elaborate or simple or even rude in design; their workmanship is not as important as the power and significance attached to them. Generally speaking, they must be procured in ways that accord with their ultimate function. The instructions can be quite intricate. Here is Éliphas Lévi on how to make a wand:

> The true and absolute magical wand must be one perfectly straight branch of almond or hazel, cut at a single blow with the magical pruning-knife or golden sickle, before the rising of the sun, at that moment when the tree is ready to blossom. It must be pierced through its whole length without splitting or breaking it, and a long needle of magnetised iron must occupy its whole length.[26]

The directions become even more elaborate, requiring gilded prisms and fillets inscribed with Hebrew characters. "The more trouble and difficulty your weapon costs, the more useful you will find it," says Aleister Crowley.[27] Lévi himself explains why:

> If a peasant rose up every morning at two or three o'clock and went a long distance from home to gather a sprig of the same herb before the rising of the sun, he would be able to perform a great number of prodigies by merely carrying this herb upon his person, for it would be the sign of his will, and in virtue thereof would be all that he required it to become in the interest of his desires.[28]

Few magicians use such intricately fashioned implements. In fact a good number buy them in occult shops. In these cases, though, magicians generally at least make the effort to consecrate the tools—to charge them with the energy of intention. Once this is done, the implements are reserved for this purpose alone: they are unlikely to do double duty in the kitchen or workshop.

## CHAOS AND CORRESPONDENCES

If the power in any magical tool only comes from the practitioner's mind, it follows that you can use anything in magic so long as you believe in it. That is the fundamental premise of a new movement called Chaos Magic, whose central tenet is the idea "Nothing is true; everything is permitted." A mélange of the influences of Crowley, the British visionary artist Austin Osman Spare, the horror writer H. P. Lovecraft, and a host of other sources including scientific chaos theory, it is regarded by some of its adherents as "postmodern shamanism." The writer Siobhán Houston observes:

> Chaos magicians are perfectly willing to use traditional beliefs and rituals. They avoid attaching any ultimate truth or meaning to these devices, however, and are willing to discard them as soon as they are ineffectual.[29]

Chaos magicians stress the vacuity of all beliefs and practices. The British occultist Peter J. Carroll, one of the movement's guiding geniuses, urges aspirants to use any means available, including "heresy," "sacrilege," and even "anathemism" or self-destruction to dislocate the consciousness from its customary moorings: "Eat all loathsome things till they no longer revolt. Seek union with all that you normally reject. Scheme against your most sacred principles in thought, word, and deed."[30]

Despite its riotous iconoclasm, in the end Chaos Magic is not so different from more conventional forms of ritual magic. Here *Chaos* is simply the name given for the force that animates the universe—a force that others call God. And though Carroll uses exotic terms like *Kia* and *Aether,* these turn out to be remarkably similar in meaning to "life force" and "astral light." Even the apparently repugnant practices are simply means of weakening the ego so that one can come to know the Higher Self—a common goal of spiritual practice.

Chaos Magic is clearly a path for those who like strong, dark, and pungent flavors; not many are so disposed. Nor is every magician prepared to accept the complete arbitrariness of his or her own belief and practice. Most, in one way or another, use the doctrine of correspondences, a system of associations linked to the Kabbalistic Tree as well as to the planets.

The view of astral light as emanating from God through the stars and planets can be found in such great Western thinkers as Plato, Plotinus, and Dante. In ancient and medieval times this was understood quite literally. The earth was seen as the center of the universe, but also as the part furthest removed from God, encircled by the zones of the planets, and, above them, the fixed stars. Beyond lies God's heaven. As the divine light passes through each of these spheres, it loses some of its purity and intensity until it reaches the earth. Each of the planets was thought to beam a certain type of influence toward earth: some, like the sun, Jupiter, and Venus, are beneficial; others, like Saturn and Mars, mostly baleful. (This is the traditional understanding of why the planets are supposed to influence us; astrology in all its forms is an attempt to gauge these influences and work with them.)

The reader will at once recognize this as the discredited Ptolemaic or geocentric paradigm. Today we know that the earth isn't the center of the universe. So why does anybody still base a worldview on it?

Whatever we may know about the solar system and the vastnesses beyond it, the earth is still the center of *our* universe. If modern magicians no longer accept the cosmology that went with this view, they regard it as psychologically true. And as we have seen, magic is centrally concerned with the psyche.

In the magical worldview, every aspect of human character and activity is assigned to one or another of the planets. (Many magicians are well versed in astrology.) This includes virtues, vices, professions (quick, clever Mercury rules writers and journalists, graceful Venus, artists and musicians) as well as colors and metals. After the Kabbalah entered the public domain in the late Middle Ages, these spheres were also equated with the Kabbalistic *sefirot*. The following table gives some of the basic correspondences:

| Sefirah | Planet | Color | Metal |
|---------|--------|-------|-------|
| Keter | [Neptune] | white | - |
| Hokhmah | [Uranus] | pearl grey | - |
| Binah | Saturn | black | lead |
| Daat | [Pluto] | - | - |
| Hesed | Jupiter | blue | tin |
| Gevurah | Mars | red | iron |
| Tiferet | Sun | yellow | gold |
| Netzach | Venus | green | copper |
| Hod | Mercury | orange | quicksilver |
| Yesod | Moon | purple | silver |
| Malkut | Earth | multicolored | lead[31] |

To this list could be added a range of associations from perfumes and drugs to classes of angels and demons.[32] This helps explain why the Kabbalistic Tree of Life has played such a central role in Western occultism.

This systematization could be viewed as the "scientific" aspect of magic. To conduct an operation in Hesed—that is, to arouse mercy, charity, or loving-kindness—one would use objects and clothing that are blue, invoke *El* (the Hebrew name of God associated with this *sefirah*), and visualize a king sitting on his throne, the magical symbol of Hesed.[33] Working with specific associations in this way produces specific results.

At least in theory. But in practice magical correspondences are not like scientific formulae, however much some magicians may insist they are. They are too fluid, too contradictory, to have the hard-and-fast connections that we see in material causality. Richard Cavendish, in his book *The Black Arts*, is probably closer to the truth when he describes these connections as poetic.[34] They are fluid, tenuous, and elusive, like the astral light itself. Moreover, of course, different systems do not always jibe.

All the same there is a certain logic to the associations. Jupiter, for example, is known astrologically as the "great benefic"; its presence in a sign of the zodiac generally marks good fortune. This relates well to the mercy and loving-kindness of Hesed. Blue is also a natural choice, as Jupiter is the sky god. As for tin, it is among the softest and therefore the most "merciful" of all the metals. Red, by contrast, is naturally associated with Mars, which has a ruddy aspect in the sky; red is also the color of blood, correlating with Mars's warlike quality (it is the root of the word *martial*). Iron, used to forge weapons, is its logical metal counterpart.

## FOR LOVE OR MONEY

By now it should be obvious that magic cannot be verified in the strict scientific sense.[35] Science is concerned purely with externals; the experimenter's mental attitude has little if any effect on the result, so long as she correctly carries out the procedures. In magic nothing could be further from the truth. Here the actual operations performed are secondary; some occultists, like Chaos Magicians, even regard them as more or less arbitrary. Will and intention are all.

The issue is more complicated than that, however, for at a fairly early stage the magician is forced to ask what she wants. Usually the answer boils down to some combination of love, money, and fame. Most magicians, no matter how pure, have probably made some attempt at one point or another to use their occult powers for these ends, and the majority, if they speak honestly, will probably admit that they have had mixed results.

The reason can be best understood by recalling a corny old joke. A man somehow gets hold of a lamp with a genie in it. He rubs the lamp. The genie appears and tells him he has three wishes. The man, a bit at a loss, thinks for a moment, and finally commands, "Make me a hamburger." Whereupon the genie dutifully turns him into a hamburger.

This silly story has some truth to it. You can of course concoct rituals to attract love or generate money; magical texts old and new are full of them. But it is no small thing to specify exactly what you want and then get it in a way you will be happy with.

Here is another story, this one true. A woman's boyfriend was starting a business and needed money, so she performed a magical ritual that would produce $10,000 for him. She got her wish, though perhaps not in the way she intended: A short time later, she was moving out of town and had loaded all her belongings into her car. She was robbed at gunpoint. The insurance settlement for her losses came to $10,000.

One need not draw moralistic conclusions from such incidents. The astral light resembles photographic film; it reproduces what is presented to it more or less literally. It is very hard to specify what one wants clearly enough to generate flawless results.

This is what distinguishes magic from prayer. The magician knows, or thinks she knows, what she wants, and conducts a ritual to get it. One who prays approaches the matter more diffidently. She also knows what she wants—but cannot be completely sure that it will be good for her. So she directs her request to a beneficent higher power, with the understanding that the higher power may well deny the request if it is unsuitable. (This also provides a reassuring explanation for unanswered prayers, whereas an unsuccessful magician can only blame her own lack of skill.)

Not all magicians, of course, share this view of their art. A great number refuse to perform magic for personal gain, and most of those who do add "if it harm none" or some other proviso to the request as a means of disarming any unwanted side effects.

This leads to the issue of *black magic* versus *white magic*. The simplest means of differentiating the two is by means of their motivation. White magic is intended to promote some beneficial end, whether it is healing or simply greater cosmic harmony. Black magic involves some harm to someone else—if not directly, then obliquely, say, by disarming his free will. *Grey magic* (a less common term) generally applies to magic that is performed with mixed motives. Whatever the practitioners may think they're doing, grey magic probably constitutes the majority of magic performed.

We can see the distinction more clearly by taking a common example: the magician may want a lover. Most white magicians would regard this as an acceptable motivation, provided it is open-ended—that is, provided it does not specify *who* the lover should be. In this case the magic is simply intended to draw a suitable partner (who presumably wants the same thing) to the practitioner. A rite intended to win the love of a specific person, on the other hand, involves interference with another's will, something at which most responsible magicians will balk.[36]

It's not always possible to distinguish a black from a white magician by mere externals: a scowling Satanist with shaved head and goatee may turn out to be a sincere and ethical individual, whereas someone with an ethereal glow who prattles on about "white light" may be the lowest form of manipulator. With some experience, one can tell the good from the bad, but it is chiefly a matter of gut feeling and common sense—ultimately not all that different from deciding whom to trust in everyday life.

## THE HOLY GUARDIAN ANGEL

Working to attain personal goals plays too great a role in magic to be completely ignored, but the best occultists regard it as low magic. Some even advise against looking for any palpable results from a ritual at all. What, then, is the end of high magic? Objectives vary, but Crowley's view has gained wide acceptance:

> It is the uniting of the Microcosm with the Macrocosm. The Supreme and Complete Ritual is therefore the Invocation of the Holy Guardian Angel; or, in the language of Mysticism, Union with God.[37]

The mysterious entity known as the Holy Guardian Angel has analogues in various traditions. The Romans called it the *genius;* the kahunas, the wizards of Hawaii, refer to it as the *aumakua,* the "Great Father Spirit." It is, of course, similar to Jung's notion of the Self, and like Jung's version, this higher Self is not experienced immediately as part of one's own being, but as another.[38] It is both united with and detached from the personal ego.

One of the most famous magical procedures for contacting

one's Holy Guardian Angel appears in a curious work entitled *The Book of the Sacred Magic of Abramelin the Mage*. It was unearthed from the Bibliothèque de l'Arsenal in Paris in the late nineteenth century by MacGregor Mathers, who published its first and only English translation.[39] Purporting to be the work of a fifteenth-century Jewish magus, it exercised a great influence on many of the Golden Dawn magicians, especially Crowley.

In Abramelin's method, the aspirant goes into seclusion for some six months while performing rites and purifications that gradually grow more intense. In the end, if the operation is successful, he is rewarded with the vision of this Guardian Angel, who gives him powers over spirits both evil and good.

Abramelin's general plan accords well with what we have already seen of high magic. Its rites and rigors enable the magus to climb the ladder of the astral world. By dint of this work he not only gains power over good and evil spirits, or, as some magicians would say, the diverse facets of his own psyche, but is granted a vision of his own higher Self—which is itself only a particular manifestation of the omnipresent light and power that is God. Here the magician's and the mystic's paths converge: as Dion Fortune once observed, "Every magician worth his salt ends up a mystic."

The work of any legitimate magician does not merely satisfy personal ends, however, for by linking the higher with the lower worlds, the magician helps unite all the diverse aspects of creation. That this is reminiscent of the work of the Kabbalist should come as no surprise: Western magic is indebted to Kabbalah for far more than diagrams and Hebrew words.

## PATHS TO MAGIC TODAY

Where can someone begin to investigate magic? The answer is usually the same as it is for nearly all other esoteric traditions: through reading. Most magicians would probably say their first encounter with magic was through a book that they came upon whose ideas rang true to them. The metaphysical bookstore—

whether the cluttered, old-fashioned type or the bright, crystal-festooned New Age variety—has played a tremendous and generally underrated role in promoting alternative spirituality of all types.

Other people may come to magic not through reading but through experience. Some paranormal event, some glimpse into higher realities may propel one into investigating the occult. Someone else, a college student say, may perform an improvised rite as an experiment or even as a joke and find the results to be more impressive than expected.

However one may approach the field, the issue rapidly becomes how to study and how to advance. Magic requires a number of basic skills, and mastering them is a long and not always enjoyable process. But the aspirant who does learn some measure of discipline and concentration will in the end find they are useful skills in any area of life.

Many magicians practice on their own, and some even say that one can traverse the whole of the magical path alone. But at a certain point many aspirants discover they can really only progress with the help of others. Although the institution of the occult lodge is not as common in the United States as in Britain—where it has a heritage of centuries, if not millennia—lodges do exist in this country. They can be encountered through word of mouth (the metaphysical bookstore is again a useful resource) or through seminars and workshops or even correspondence courses. Unfortunately, here as elsewhere in esotericism, there seems to be an inverse correlation between celebrity and depth of knowledge. It must also be added that there are a number of lodges are both fraudulent and corrupt.

The lodge is often arranged on a strictly hierarchical basis. The Golden Dawn—which serves as the prototype of many twentieth-century lodges—included ten grades corresponding to the ten *sefirot* of the Kabbalah, from Zelator or "aspirant," through Neophyte, Theoreticus, and Practicus, to Adeptus Minor, the grade corresponding to the *sefirah* Tiferet. The nature of the higher grades is a bit more nebulous. The further one ascends in the hierarchy, the more improper it becomes to claim any such status in public. The great credo of magical aspiration is in fact "To know, to will, to dare, to keep silent."

The Golden Dawn grades required mastery of occult theory as well as the acquisition of paranormal powers like clairvoyance and telepathy. (These faculties, though partly a matter of aptitude, can be enhanced by training and practice.) Indeed grades of initiation in any system of magic are meant more to reflect attainment than to confer it. Though it may provide contact with certain levels of reality, the initiation itself is not nearly as important as the work the initiate has put in. Some, though by no means all, magicians say it is possible to initiate oneself.

Some of the Golden Dawn's heirs, notably Dion Fortune, have also stressed the importance of an "inner-plane contact"—access to some intelligence that is not in embodied human form. "Knowledge of the Holy Guardian Angel" is one form this encounter can take, but there are many others. Kabbalists sometimes speak of "the Academy on High," which the mystic may visit in dreams or meditation. Here disincarnate masters provide instruction that the student may not be able to find on the physical level.

Such inner-plane contacts pose their share of risks, notably obsession and delusion. Here as in so many other areas, the magician treads a narrow ledge: credulity may lead to foolish mistakes, while doubt can close the doors to higher realities. But those drawn to magical work generally relish such challenges. At any rate they should be ready to face them.

A good number of magicians practice in less formal groups than an organized hierarchical lodge. Today many practicing magicians are connected with Witchcraft or Neopaganism—movements that have many affinities with high magic.

## SUGGESTED READING

Agrippa, Henry Cornelius of Nettesheim. *Three Books of Occult Philosophy*. Translated by James Freake. Edited by Donald Tyson. St. Paul, Minn.: Llewellyn, 1993.

The great classic of Renaissance magic. Dense reading (the translation dates from the seventeenth century), but it contains a seminal discussion of the doctrine of correspondences.

Butler, W. E. *Apprenticed to Magic and Magic and the Qabalah*. Wellingborough, Northamptonshire, England: Aquarian Press, 1990.

Butler (1898–1978) studied with Dion Fortune. This pair of short works is the best introduction to his solid, genial, and pragmatic approach to magic. Other works of his include *The Magician: His Training and Work* (Hollywood, Calif.: Wilshire Books, 1979); *Lords of Light: The Path of Initiation in the Western Mysteries* (Rochester, Vt.: Destiny Books, 1990) and *Practical Magic and the Western Mystery Tradition*, edited by Dolores Ashcroft-Nowicki (Aquarian, 1986).

Carroll, Peter J. *Liber Null and Psychonaut*. York Beach, Maine: Samuel Weiser, 1987.

The single most important text of Chaos Magic.

Cavendish, Richard. *The Black Arts*. New York: G. P. Putnam's Sons, 1967.

Despite its title, this engaging, literate guide to the teachings and personalities of magic covers both black and white varieties. The British edition is entitled *The Magical Arts*.

Crowley, Aleister. *Magick in Theory and Practice*. New York: Castle Books, 1929.

Crowley has his admirers and detractors, but he remains one of the most important figures in the magical tradition of this century. This is probably his best book; *777 and Other Qabalistic Writings of Aleister Crowley* (New York: Samuel Weiser, 1977) contains his exhaustive tables of correspondences to the *sefirot*.

Fortune, Dion. *Psychic Self-Defence*. Wellingborough: Aquarian, 1957.

Dion Fortune had the curious fate of encountering numerous episodes of psychic attack and vampirism. This work contains her discussions of her experiences, as well as practical advice about these issues. Her masterpiece *The Mystical Qabalah* remains *de rigueur* for anyone interested in Kabbalistic magic.

Knight, Gareth. *Experience of the Inner Worlds*. York Beach, Maine: Samuel Weiser, 1993.

A step-by-step introduction to experiencing the astral plane; strongly Christian in tenor.

Lévi, Éliphas. *Transcendental Magic: Its Doctrine and Ritual*. Translated by A. E. Waite. London: Bracken Books, 1995.

Though many scoff at Lévi today for his penchant for hyperbole, it remains astonishing how much the magical tradition owes to him. One of the most important works of Western occultism.

Regardie, Israel. *The Complete Golden Dawn System of Magic*. Phoenix, Ariz.: New Falcon, 1994.

Regardie, a pupil of Crowley's, took it upon himself to publish all the Golden Dawn rituals, teachings, and other material he could get his hands on. This is the most recent and compendious version; an earlier one is *The Golden Dawn* (St. Paul., Minn.: Llewellyn, 1982).

Tyson, Donald. *The New Magus: Ritual Magic as a Personal Process*. St. Paul: Llewellyn, 1988.

An intelligent and comprehensive discussion of most of the major issues that face the magician.

## Six

# THE RETURN OF THE PAGANS:
# WITCHCRAFT AND NEOPAGANISM

*Let my worship be within the heart that rejoiceth*
*for behold, all acts of love and pleasure are my rituals.*
—THE CHARGE OF THE GODDESS

Most people think witches are like ghosts or fairies—entities that once haunted superstitious imaginations but which more enlightened times have found to be illusory. Modernity has relegated the image of the witch to cartoons and Halloween cutouts or, in the strange metamorphosis worked by American popular culture, to sanitized figures like Sabrina, the Teenage Witch.

Yet witches do exist. In fact many of them have stepped forward and identified themselves.

Few of them resemble either the stereotypical snag-toothed crones or the carefully-coifed witches of television, but they are certainly real. Indeed, modern Witchcraft and its near relative, Neopaganism, are among the fastest-growing religions in America today. Nor are they limited to simple folk hidden up in the hills; adherents include academics, artists, and professionals as well as many otherwise ordinary men and women. (Contrary to popular belief, men as well as women can be witches.)

Witchcraft is both ancient and universal. In literature, witches can be found as far back as the Circe of Homer's *Odyssey*. The Bible tells of the Witch of Endor, who conjured the shade of the judge Samuel for King Saul (1 Sam. 28:7–25). The Roman poet Sextus Propertius besought "those who know the trick of calling down the moon" to help him win the favors of his coy mistress. And in *The Golden Ass*, a novel of the third century A.D., Lucius Apuleius (himself believed to be an initiate of the mysteries) tells the story of a man changed into a donkey by a witch's ointment.

These, of course, are literary allusions, and we grant a great deal of license to the literary imagination, whether it belongs to Apuleius or to Stephen King. But how was witchcraft, along with its close kin paganism, brought back to life in the glaring light of modernity? Appropriately enough, the story begins with the last witchcraft trial in Britain, which took place during the Second World War.

It seems that a Spiritualist medium had made contact with the spirit of a drowned British sailor. The dead sailor revealed that his ship had been sunk, which the medium disclosed several days before it was officially acknowledged. The discomfited authorities tried the medium under the Witchcraft Act of 1735, which was still on the books. (This law replaced an earlier statute that had punished witchcraft by hanging.) She was convicted and served nine months' imprisonment.

The Spiritualists, a movement chiefly dedicated to contacting the spirits of the dead, were understandably displeased by this ruling and after the war agitated to have the Witchcraft Act repealed. In 1951 they succeeded and soon afterward people who claimed to be witches emerged into the public light and began publishing books and offering teachings. They have been doing so ever since.[2]

Like many of the terms encountered here, the word *witchcraft* carries a number of meanings. In its broadest sense, it simply means any kind of exercise of occult power. (Many magicians have faced charges of witchcraft at one point or another.) Often it means causing damage by occult means: witches of old were frequently charged with harming crops, livestock, or their neighbors.

For most contemporary Witches, however, the term has a different sense. It refers to the "Old Religion," the form of Paganism that prevailed in Europe before the coming of Christianity. Though it does involve the exercise of occult power—including the power to curse as well as bless—its modern adherents see it not so much as a collection of occult techniques but rather as a distinct faith that worships the divine immanence in the dual form of the Horned God and the Great Goddess. Contrary to most assumptions, they insist that this Old Religion has survived underground for centuries despite the relentless efforts of Christian authorities to wipe it out. It is also called "Wicca," whose adherents style themselves "Wiccans,"[3] and is part of a larger movement called Neopaganism, which encompasses all who venerate gods of revived Pagan pantheons.

One of the first people to emerge in public with a claim of access to the Old Religion was Gerald Gardner (1884–1964), a retired English customs official. Gardner said he had encountered a coven of practicing witches in the New Forest of Hampshire, and had been initiated into the coven himself in 1939. Although he discussed the subject in a fictional context in a 1949 novel entitled *High Magic's Aid*, it was only after the Witchcraft Act was repealed two years later that he felt free to enter fully into the public light. He published his first nonfiction book, *Witchcraft Today*, in 1954.[4] He is the central figure of the Witchcraft revival.

Gardner insisted that his coven could trace its lineage back to pre-Christian days. However, the Neopagan writer Aidan Kelly, after extensive research into Gardner's manuscripts, concluded that Gardner invented nearly everything that has come to be known as modern Witchcraft[5]—a suggestion that has aroused considerable indignation among many Witches. Taking a middle course, the Neopagan Isaac Bonewits has suggested that the modern Craft (as Witchcraft is often known to its practitioners) was founded in the 1920s, when some folklorists combined forces with some Fam-Trads (short for "familial traditions," this is a nickname for Witches who have had the Craft handed down through their families) and magicians from the Golden Dawn.[6]

Whether true or not in fact, Bonewits's idea has the merit of acknowledging the three chief influences on modern Witchcraft. The first is the remnant of European Paganism that survived centuries of Christian dominance. It is hard to say exactly how much of this religion endured, but it is probably safe to say that at least a small part of it did. Driven underground by persecution, many Pagan traditions were handed down along family lines—some handed down in the male line, others only in the female, still others across gender lines. Some families practice formal initiation, but with others it seems to be a matter of upbringing, much as in any religion. One member of a family tradition from Yorkshire describes it thus:

> Fundamentally, the belief that was handed down to me was this: that the world and everything in it was driven by an awesome power which could be seen everywhere—but only in its effects and results. This power was generally considered to be female, mother nature if you like, although that expression is now so overused that it seems it's become a cliché. We didn't need to make representations of her like statues and the like because she was all around, everywhere, and it was simply a matter of looking and learning how to find her.

He goes on to describe his earliest instruction, conducted by his grandmother, which took the form of nature walks. "Did we worship?" he says. "No, not really. To us being alive and part of the body of the mother was worship . . . staying true to the tradition and marking the special time, being open to the natural powers was enough."[7]

If this is typical of the Paganism of family traditions, Aidan Kelly might be right: modern Witchcraft may not owe many of its rituals and practices to the heritage of the past. Where, then, did they come from?

Gardnerian Witchcraft, as we've seen, surfaced in the 1950s. At this time the works of the magicians of the Golden Dawn and their spiritual progeny were in wide circulation in Britain. Dion Fortune's novel *The Sea Priestess*, published in 1938, had already hinted that magical ritual could open the way for the return of the Goddess, the feminine aspect of deity that reflects the immanent, embodied aspect of the Absolute. In 1948 a far more influential book was published: Robert Graves's *White Goddess*, which argued that all of prehistoric Europe had worshiped the ancient goddess of the moon.

Graves was fundamentally a poet; indeed he said he wrote *The White Goddess* in a kind of Muse-inspired frenzy,[8] and his theory has never gained much acceptance among scholars. But Witchcraft had received a boost from more systematic researchers as well. The American folklorist Charles Godfrey Leland (1824–1903), whose book *Aradia: The Gospel of the Witches*, published in 1899, described the lore of "la Vecchia Religione" as received from an old witch he had come to know in Tuscany. Many of Gardner's rites were adapted from this book.

An even more important figure was Margaret Murray (1863–1963), a British scholar who started as an Egyptologist but became fascinated with pagan survivals into the Christian period. In her book *The Witch-Cult in Western Europe*, Murray offered a bold new thesis. Using firsthand accounts of the witch trials, she contended that witchcraft was an actual religion that competed with Christianity throughout the Middle Ages.

In this and later works, especially *The God of the Witches* (1931), Murray set out a lengthy description of this faith. It was dedicated to the worship of the Goddess, known as Diana, and the Horned God (Janus or Dianus) who appeared at witches' gatherings, known as *esbats*.[9] From the witches' many descriptions of the hard, leathery surface of his skin, Murray concluded that this Horned God was in fact a priest of the religion wearing a costume.

Taking her cue from the New England Puritan Cotton Mather, who wrote, "The witches do say that they form themselves much after the manner of Congregational Churches, and that they have a Baptism, a Supper, and Officers among them, abominably resembling those of our Lord." Murray also contended that witches were organized into more or less independent *covens,* each composed of thirteen members.[10]

Murray further claimed that this Old Religion, or Dianic Cult, was the legacy of the "fairies" or "little people." These were not supernatural entities but a diminutive race who inhabited Europe before the coming of its present population and who to some extent coexisted with them. To support her argument, Murray used records describing encounters with fairies and even interracial marriages in which humans took fairy husbands and wives.

Citing descriptions of "fairy cattle," Murray said this elusive race had lived not by farming but by raising livestock—a fact she connected with the four main festivals, or "Sabbaths," of the Old Religion: Candlemas (February 2), the Eve of May (May 1), Lammas (August 1), and All Hallow E'en, which today we know as Halloween.[11] These were not agricultural but pastoral festivals, she contended, Candlemas marking the beginning and Halloween the end of the breeding season.

Murray's theory grew more extravagant: The Old Religion counted among its adherents a good number of the English royal family up to the time of the Stuarts. Indeed William Rufus, the English king who was killed in 1100 by the arrow of a man in his hunting party, was a "sacred king" offered as a sacrifice on behalf of his people, and who moreover knew that his death was coming. The "dying god" was not always a sovereign, however; other embodiments of this divine victim included Thomas à Becket, Joan of Arc, and her associate Gilles de Rais.[12]

Most crucially, Murray said, the witch hunts that swept Europe from roughly 1450 to 1750 were not the result of a delusion concocted by the Inquisition (as most scholars had believed) but a struggle between two great religions—the venerable religion of the Horned God and the interloper known as Christianity.

Murray's work, like Graves's, is not taken seriously by current historians, who fault her selective use of evidence and her reliance on inferior sources.[13] Today the standard academic view has reverted to the idea that witchcraft was a delusion chiefly generated by anxieties rampant in the early modern era and fueled by social and economic crisis. The Oxford historian Robin Briggs observes, "Virtually everywhere it was the half-century between 1580 and 1630 which included the great majority of all [witch] trials; however dubious one may be about mere chronological links, it is hard to avoid the *prima facie* inference that a simultaneous sharp decline in living standards and individual security played a large part in this."[14]

By this view, witch persecutions were a matter more of neighbor pitted against neighbor than of the schemings of the Inquisition. Certainly the Catholic Church fueled the witch-hunt craze at its outset in the fifteenth century, with a 1484 bull by Pope Innocent VIII declaring witchcraft a heresy (the Church had previously taught that it did not exist) and with the publication of the notorious *Malleus maleficarum* ("The Hammer of Witches") in 1486. Written by a pair of Dominican monks, this lurid book described such things as "the way whereby a formal pact with evil is made" and "the way whereby witches copulate with those devils known as Incubi."[15] It was to gain a wide readership and must be accounted the key text of the witch mania.

Yet over the next two centuries the officials of the Inquisition became increasingly skeptical of witchcraft claims and, strange as it may sound, often exercised a moderating influence on rabid witch-hunters in local courts. The countries where the Inquisition was the strongest—Spain and Italy—had very few witch trials.[16]

Contemporary scholars are skeptical of many other features of Murray's account: another Oxford historian, Keith Thomas, writes: "In England there can be little doubt that there was never a 'witch-cult' of the type envisaged by contemporary demonologists or their modern disciples. Malevolent magic was practiced, though usually by individuals rather than groups. But witches' 'sabbaths' were almost certainly non-existent."[17] If Thomas is right, the "Old Religion" probably resembled the simple nature worship described by the Yorkshireman above rather than the carefully networked covens of Margaret Murray.

Modern scholars also believe that witch hunts were not princi-

pally the persecution of another way of worship. Though witchcraft was regarded as a heresy, most witchcraft accusations in
England "did not relate to any alleged heretical activities on the
part of the witch, but to her *maleficium* (or 'sorcery')."[18] In those
days people believed that witchcraft could do harm; it was thus
understandable that they might prosecute for it, though the extreme difficulty of proving such charges made the judiciary in-
creasingly skeptical of witchcraft claims.

These issues would be merely academic if not for the fact that
much of modern Wicca owes its inspiration to Murray's ideas. Today's covens are organized in the "congregational" manner she describes; modern Witches venerate the Horned God and Great
Goddess as she characterizes them; and contemporary festivals are
often constellated around the four "Sabbaths" of the year as described by Murray.

Murray herself hinted that she had had some contact with in-
formants who kept up the Old Religion, but she does not mention them; rather she presents her work entirely as a study of
documentary material. Unless some new evidence comes to light,
it is simplest to take the modern Witchcraft revival not as the
reemergence of old traditions, but as having been inspired by
Murray's books—especially since the revival took its current form
in the 1950s and 1960s, when her views were more widely accepted than they are today.

The debt that the revived Witchcraft owes to anthropology can
be seen in another of its central tenets: the idea that before the
coming of "patriarchy"—the social structure that favors males and
causes us to see the divine in masculine form—there was another
civilization that worshiped divinity in the form of woman. This is
the Great Goddess that is represented in so many Neolithic figurines. Reviving this heritage, many feminist Neopagans argue,
can counteract the devaluation not only of women but of feminine qualities such as nurturing and intuition in our hyperrational,
technologized, male-run society.

The idea of a prehistoric civilization in which women were
equal or superior to men is not new. It first appeared in *Das*

*Muterrecht* ("Mother Right"), a book published in 1861 by the Swiss jurist J. J. Bachofen. Analyzing details in Greek myths and historical texts, Bachofen argued that "(1) mother right belongs to a cultural period preceding that of the patriarchal system; (2) it began to decline only with the victorious development of the paternal system."[19] Whereas Bachofen believed that the prior civilization was matriarchal, however, the Lithuanian anthropologist Marija Gimbutas contended that "Old Europe and Anatolia, as well as Minoan Crete, were a gylany." (*Gylany,* a term Gimbutas borrowed from the feminist historian Riane Eisler, refers to a "social structure where both sexes are equal."[20])

According to Gimbutas, this peaceful, egalitarian society covered much of Europe and Asia Minor from at least the beginning of the Neolithic period some eight or nine thousand years ago until it was ended by the incursions of a warlike, patriarchal nation that she identified with the Indo-Europeans. "We are still living under the sway of that aggressive male invasion and only beginning to discover our long alienation from our authentic European Heritage—gylanic, nonviolent, earth-centered culture."[21] Gimbutas, who died in 1993, is a much more contemporary figure than either Bachofen or Murray. But here again many scholars are reluctant to support her sweeping conclusions about a shadowy epoch that left no written records, only the famous figurines depicting naked women, often with extremely large breasts, bellies, and buttocks.

In his study of Greek religion, Walter Burkert argues that the famous site of Çatal Hüyük in Asia Minor points unambiguously to the worship of a Mother Goddess of the sort Gimbutas describes; the cult, moreover, continued from Neolithic into classical times, revering the Great Mother of Greek religion, often known as Cybele. On a broader scale, however, Burkert says the evidence is far more ambiguous; "consequently the Mother Goddess interpretation has come to be regarded with increasing skepticism."[22]

In the case of both the Neolithic Goddess and the witch trials, scholars can only make tentative conclusions—in one case, because of the lack of written evidence; in the other, because of the strangeness of the written evidence. What is one to make of a court case where a man confesses that he has turned himself into a toad in order to torment his neighbor?[23] The man was mad, we might conclude—but then how do we evaluate a court that takes him at his word? Were they all under the grip of some form of collective insanity? Or are scholars simply not capable of dealing with occult phenomena?

These issues are likely to offer material for academic disputes for decades to come. Nevertheless both the existence of the Old Religion (in Murray's sense of the term) and the Neolithic worship of the Mother Goddess are taken as fact by many contemporary Witches and Neopagans while scholars see these issues as moot. One also detects a certain tendency to exaggerate: Neopagan writers often insist that some nine million accused witches were put to death during the witch hunts, whereas more sober estimates suggest that these persecutions in fact claimed between forty and fifty thousand victims over three centuries.[24]

Perhaps the most clear-headed conclusion we can reach is this: humans seem to have a natural inclination to glorify the past; they also have an urge to seek roots and find predecessors in antiquity as a way of legitimizing their own aspirations. As the history of religions shows, most faiths incorporate some mythologizing of this sort. Nevertheless, there is no reason to state something as proven fact when it has not been proven. The basic drives behind Witchcraft and Neopaganism—to honor the divine as manifested in the feminine and in the forces of nature, and to live in accord with the rhythms of the earth and the seasons—are entirely honorable; they do not need an imagined past to legitimize them.

## THE GODDESS AND GOD

Many of the doctrines of today's Witchcraft resemble those of its parent, ceremonial magic. Books on Witchcraft often include discussions of the astral light and the life force, and many witches find the conceptual scheme of the Kabbalistic Tree to be quite congenial. Still there are some major differences.

In the first place, modern Witchcraft is a religion, not a technique. The principal motivation for a rite is not occult "working" for one purpose or another—though "workings" do take place—but veneration of the Goddess and the Horned God.

The Goddess, according to both Leland and Murray, is identified with Diana, the Roman goddess of the moon (or Artemis, as she was known to the Greeks). The moon is central to Witchcraft, for it is the quintessential symbol not only of the vital force embodied in woman (since women's monthly cycles often accord with those of the moon) but of the astral light, the primordial "mind-stuff" that generates all material things. Leland's Tuscan witches were enjoined to meet "once in the month, and when the moon is full."[25]

At first it is hard to see how Diana, the chaste virgin goddess, has anything to do with the raw powers of fecundity and sexuality. But the virgin is only one aspect of the Goddess, who in classical antiquity was linked both to Eileithyia, the goddess of childbirth, and to Hecate, who ruled over night and the underworld. These three figures represent the three phases of the moon—waxing, full, waning—and to the three phases of woman: Virgin, Mother, Crone. Taken together, they embody the cycle of gestation, a cycle that is the central mystery not only of Witchcraft but of life itself.[26] And they help us understand why in most countries Witchcraft is envisaged as a women's mystery.

The Great Goddess in her triple aspect represents the sum of all the forces that give life, that lead to physical embodiment. The Horned God, her male consort, is of course the inseminating male principle, but he is also often equated with death, the force that *goes against* embodiment, that moves toward the formless. Here the theme of ascent and descent, the double movement of Jacob's ladder, is set out in a completely different context.

It should be noted that the Horned God has nothing to do with the Christian Devil. As Witches are fond of pointing out, believing in the Devil implies believing in the Christian God, which they do not. Witches do not accept the notion of a personal embodiment of absolute evil; they usually see the dark side of the universe either as a necessary complement to the light or as an imbalance in the workings of a fundamentally harmonious cosmos. Thus, although there are people who call themselves Satanists, Witches in general cannot be classed among them.

The horns of the male God—sometimes known as Cernunnos or Karnayna, "the horned one"—have several meanings. First, they represent male sexual vigor (compare the contemporary slang term *horny*). An animal's horns are also weapons of war, representing the destructive aspect of nature.[27] Finally, horns are sometimes regarded as symbols not of evil, but of mystical attainment: some oral traditions say that those who are exercising powers of extrasensory perception may feel as if they have immaterial "horns" extending from the head or forehead.

Modern Witchcraft differs from Murray's version in one notable respect: whereas the Old Religion as she characterized it was centered around the Horned God, today the Goddess is usually the more important figure. (Certain "Dianic" feminist covens eschew the God altogether.) Some modern Witches say this is because the old witch-hunters, always on the lookout for the Devil, were much more preoccupied with the Horned God than with his female counterpart. But it may also be a question of modern proclivities: indeed its emphasis on the Divine Feminine is one of the chief reasons for the appeal of revived Witchcraft.[28]

These considerations all lead to an interesting question: are today's Witchcraft and Neopagan movements monotheistic, polytheistic, or, for that matter, duotheistic? Most contemporary Witches and Neopagans regard the source of all things as being an unnamable, unmanifest Oneness, akin to the *Ain Sof* of the Kabbalists. Though this Oneness transcends sex as we know it, Witches generally portray it as female: the Great Goddess. All things, male and female, visible and invisible, deities, planets, nature, and human beings—even the Horned God—are her manifestations.

Not all Pagans regard the Great Goddess as the source of all being. Nonetheless, unlike orthodox versions of Christianity, which stress the radical otherness of God, most forms of Paganism say that divinity permeates us and constitutes the truest core of our being; they stress the *immanence* rather than the *transcendence* of divinity. Thus a fundamental notion of unity underlies Paganism (and indeed nearly all forms of polytheism, understood at their deepest level), although this unity does not necessarily resemble the conventional view of God.

## THE CONE OF POWER

In practice as in doctrine, Witchcraft owes a great debt to high ceremonial magic. Many of the tools are the same: the wand, the cup, the sword, the disk, the athame or sacred knife. So is the setting, which is the magical circle. But there are differences.

In the first place, modern Witchcraft is generally less solitary than ritual magic. Although many Witches do practice on their own, this is often a matter of logistics: there may be no covens near them, or they may not know of any. Witchcraft as a whole encourages group work: "You shall not be a witch alone" is a common maxim in the Craft.[29] One reason for this is the tremendous emphasis laid on male-female polarity, particularly in the Gardnerian line: to be truly effective, a rite must include both a priest and a priestess. The priest invokes the energy of the Goddess into the priestess; this is what is called, at least in modern Wicca, the "drawing down of the moon." Similarly the consecrations, whether of ritual objects or food like the traditional cakes and wine, must as a rule be done both by a man and a woman. (All-women covens exist, but they are in a minority; all-male covens are still rarer.)

Another difference has to do with the type of energy used. Witches do, like magicians, attempt to generate "forms" in the astral light. As the influential contemporary Witch Starhawk puts it, "Witches conceive of the subtle energies as being, to a trained awareness, tangible, visible, and malleable.... We can learn to sense them and mold them into form."[30]

Witchcraft, however, is more concerned with the use of the life force than is high ceremonial magic. Witches regard this as a tellurian force as well as a biological one: they say it can be found in the currents of earth energy. James Lovelock's Gaia hypothesis, which holds that the Earth is itself an enormous living being, has found enormous favor among Witches. (*Gaia* is the name of the Greek Earth goddess, the first-born of all the gods after Chaos.)[31]

The connection between Gaia and the Great Goddess helps explain the Neopagan sympathy for Green causes. It also means that for ceremonies they tend to favor "power spots," areas where the earth energy is believed to be particularly strong or auspicious. In Britain, old stone circles are favored sites for working; in America, spots sacred to the Indians may be chosen.

Leland's Tuscan witches, who seemed to have a touch of the anarchist about them, were enjoined by the Goddess, "As a sign that ye are truly free, / Ye shall be naked in your rites."[32] Indeed many Witches, especially those of the Gardnerian lineage, do work their rituals naked, or "sky-clad." The purpose is not to titillate (although sexuality is not out of place in a coven) but rather to allow the body's energies to circulate freely; nakedness is also a mark of equality. A recent survey conducted of Pagans worldwide by the Wiccans Janet and Stewart Farrar and Gavin Bone revealed that 63 percent of respondents worked sky-clad at least sometimes.[33] "Fam-Trads," by contrast, favor working in black robes.[34]

Whether robed or sky-clad, the ritual of a coven generally involves raising "the Cone of Power," a vortex of vital energy seen as ascending in a cone or spiral from the circle (which may explain the popular view of witches as wearing conical hats). This is usually done by dancing around the circle, either *deosil* (clockwise) or *widdershins* (counterclockwise). Deosil is the direction for raising energy for positive or harmonious ends; widdershins is danced for negative ends such as banishing. Many Gardnerian Witches also use ritual flagellation, a light whipping that is intended not to

cause pain, but, again, to raise energy. Here is a description of the
procedure in Gardner's coven:

> The Cone of Power. This was the old way. The circle was marked
> out and people stationed to whip up the dancers. A fire or candle
> was within it, in the direction where the object of the rite was
> supposed to be. Then all danced round until they felt they had
> raised enough power. If the rite was to banish, they started deosil
> and finished widdershins, so many rounds of each. Then they
> formed a line with linked hands and rushed towards the fire
> shouting the thing they wanted. They kept it up till they were ex-
> hausted or until someone fell in a faint, when they were said to
> have taken the spell to its destination.[35]

The energy is then directed toward the intended goal, although, as Isaac Bonewits dryly remarks, "There is some confusion
among various groups as to what exactly should be *done* with the
energies at the moment of firing."[36]

According to Gardner, his coven cast spells during the Battle of
Britain to keep Hitler from invading their homeland. After raising
the Power, the members shouted in a rhythmic chant: "Can't cross
the sea! Can't cross the sea! Not able to come! Not able to come!"
To ensure the spell worked, they used another ancient expedient:
human sacrifice. A frail, elderly member of the coven agreed to
serve as the victim. The sky-clad ceremony took place over a
whole night in May (still a cold month in England); shortly thereafter the aged member fell ill and died.[37]

Whatever one may think of the ethics of this procedure—an
unusual if not unique one in modern Witchcraft—it clearly recalls
the tradition of the "Dying God," a figure who goes willingly to
death so "that one man should die for the people, and the whole
nation perish not," to use the words of the Gospel (John 11:50).
Although Christianity and the "Old Religion" approach this theme
very differently, the resemblance is more than coincidental; indeed
this motif forms the central theme of J. G. Frazer's *Golden Bough*.

Did Gardner's spell work? Who can say? But historians often wonder why Hitler, instead of attacking comparatively defenseless Britain, chose to turn on his erstwhile ally the Soviet Union— which proved to be his undoing. A similar legend, which persists to this day in British occult circles, claims that the magus John Dee conjured up the storm that destroyed the Spanish Armada.

## INITIATION

How does one become a Witch? In a few cases it is a matter of inheritance. But for most people it is a matter of individual commitment and often involves *initiation*. This procedure is by no means limited to witches; it can take the form of ritual inductions in fraternal lodges; the Christian sacraments of baptism and confirmation; the Jewish puberty rite known as the *bar mitzvah;* and, in a debased form, the hazing rituals of college fraternities.

Esoteric initiation has several purposes:

1. To confirm the candidate's sense of purpose and dedication.
2. To admit an individual to a group. This is often enacted through rites that carry out a ritual "death" of the candidate's old self and "rebirth" to a new, higher identity. This new identity is often marked by the bestowal of a new name, sometimes kept secret, sometimes made public.
3. As a kind of graduation ceremony, confirming that the initiate has attained knowledge and power of a certain degree.
4. As a means of transmitting a subtle force that transforms the individual into a being of greater power and wisdom.

Note also that the very word "initiation" conveys a sense of *beginning;* it is not the end but the start of the work.

Traditionally-minded Wiccans occasionally insist that "only a Witch can make a Witch"—that is, one must be initiated by a Witch in order to become a Witch in the true sense of the word— but this sentiment is a minority position in Witchcraft today.

Doreen Valiente, one of Gardner's associates, has even published a rite of self-initiation.[38] The Farrars' survey of world Pagans disclosed that only a quarter of their respondents had been initiated by somebody else.[39] Yet it's easy to see that self-initiation really only satisfies the first of the basic purposes of esoteric initiation—which would seem to make it highly problematic.

In Wicca as well as in most traditions, it's a good idea to seek out initiation from a competent and respected practitioner. (The process of finding such a person can be instructive in its own right.) Failing this, most authorities agree that nothing prevents one from carrying out the rituals and practices on one's own, and these are available in any number of books. If you work on your own with sincerity and dedication, you may eventually meet someone who can then confer initiation in the formal sense. As the saying goes, "When the pupil is ready, the master appears."

There is also the question of initiation on the "inner planes." In such cases a person has a mystical experience in which he or she encounters invisible entities who confer power, knowledge, or authority. For the occultist, the astral realm has a reality that is nearly as palpable as that of the physical, and such experiences can be not only convincing but overwhelming. Still, one inevitably faces the question of whether it "really" happened or was merely imagined.

Probably the best answer is that such an experience will have its own authority for the person who undergoes it, but one would be foolish to flaunt it as a credential. Credentials and certifications are not the fundamental purpose of initiation, and supposed adepts who boast of degrees and titles usually end up as objects of ridicule.

## THE GREAT RITE

Gardnerian initiation consists of three degrees.[40] The first confers the identity of a Witch pure and simple. The second degree makes the Witch a High Priest or Priestess, although it does not necessarily qualify one to operate independently. The third and highest degree makes the initiate a fully independent practitioner who may then "hive off" to form an independent coven.[41]

The ceremony for the third-degree initiation as described by Gardner involves the *Great Rite,* an act of ritual intercourse between the candidate and the conferring Priest or Priestess (whichever is of the opposite sex). Janet and Stewart Farrar explain it thus:

> Why *does* the Craft use a sex-ritual, or a gender-ritual, to mark its highest degree of initiation? Because it expresses three fundamental principles of the Craft. First, that the basis of all magical or creative working is polarity, the interaction of complementary aspects. Second, "as above, so below"; we are of the nature of the Gods, and a fully realized man or woman is a channel for that divinity, a manifestation of the God or the Goddess (and each in fact manifesting elements of both). And third, that all the levels from physical to spiritual are equally holy.[42]

The Farrars stress that the practice is consensual and private; other members of the coven leave the room when the Great Rite is performed. It is also up to the participants whether they will perform the Great Rite actually or symbolically; the initiation has equal legitimacy either way. One Witch puts it thus: "Being unwilling to share one's sexuality is not a bar to Third Degree. Unwillingness to perform a physical Great Rite with anyone but a lover is a personal feeling, and a personal decision. No one, not even the Gods, have the right to make decisions regarding personal sexual activity."[43]

Certainly the centrality of the Great Rite points to Wicca's affirmation of physicality in all its aspects, including sex. Other ceremonies often involve a ritual dipping of the athame into the cup to depict the union of the primal forces of nature. These forces operate not only outside of us but within us; to invoke them symbolically can wield great power. The sexual act itself, conducted under the right circumstances, can wield much more.

Wiccans place so much emphasis on male-female polarity that

many covens require a more or less equal balance between men and women; gays and lesbians are sometimes (though rarely) excluded for similar reasons. On the other hand, there are all-women, or, less often, all-male covens that may have predominantly homosexual membership; in any event few Witches condemn homosexuality. The Wiccan Rede, the ethical touchstone of the religion, is "An it harm none, do what thou wilt."

## VARIETIES OF NEOPAGANISM

Most Neopagans identify themselves with Wiccan ideas and practices, and since Neopaganism in the English-speaking world was given its greatest impetus by Gardner, to this day "Wicca remains the 'spearhead' of the Pagan revival."[44] But there are other varieties of Paganism, including the following:

**Alexandrians.** This line, which has much in common with Gardnerians in ritual and doctrine, traces its beginning to the British Witches Alex and Maxine Sanders, who led covens in the 1960s and 1970s. There is probably more of a pronounced element of ceremonial magic in this tradition than in most varieties of Neopaganism.[45]

**Hereditary.** Witches who claim to have learned the Craft from a continuing family tradition; the nickname "Fam-Trad" is often applied to them.

**Eclectic.** Those who practice using gods and practices from a mixture of different traditions, including Celtic, Germanic, Greco-Roman, and Egyptian.

**Dianic.** Women's groups who concentrate on the feminine aspect of divinity; they often have a strongly feminist aspect and include such well-known Witches as Starhawk and Z Budapest. The term is obviously taken from Margaret Murray's references to the "Dianic cult." Some Dianic groups have a separatist tendency.

**Fairy/Faerie.** In Europe, a term used for those working with nature spirits. In the United States it is applied to a tradition formulated by Victor Anderson and Gwyddion Pendderwen and incorporating much European material. These should not be confused with Radical Faeries, gay male Wiccans devoted to the Goddess.

**Ethnic Paganism.** People who are attempting to revive the pre-Christian religions of various national groups. The Wiccans (who use much Celtic material) may be classed under this category, but other Pagans have explored the religious roots of Scandinavian, Slavic, Baltic, and other European nations. Probably the most numerous and visible are those worshiping the gods of the old Germanic pantheon; branches of this tradition are Asatru and Odinism.

There are of course many possible subcategories, such as Druidism, which attempts to revive the Druidic heritage of the Celtic nations and encompasses groups ranging from some quasi-Masonic British fraternal lodges to contemporary Neopagans (Isaac Bonewits is the most prominent of the latter). Other trends in Neopaganism overlap with those of ritual magic, including Chaos Magick and Thelema (the name applied as a general rubric to groups inspired by Aleister Crowley). Despite its name, the Western Mystery Tradition focuses chiefly on British archetypes, including the Arthurian legends and the Grail cycle, as well as on Christian motifs.[46]

The most visible Neopagan organization in America is probably the Church of All Worlds, which pursues themes as diverse as Gaia, science fiction, and polyfidelity; it publishes *Green Egg*, probably the best-known Neopagan magazine. The Covenant of the Goddess is a Neopagan religious denomination organized along congregational lines. The Circle Sanctuary, through its quarterly newspaper, *Circle Network News*, assists Neopagans with networking and with legal defense issues.[47]

## GODS OF THE AFRICAN DIASPORA

One living Pagan tradition in America cannot be classified under the Neopagan rubric. It is not a recent revival; it owes no debt to

Gardner, the Golden Dawn, or to contemporary scholarship; nor is it primarily a white, middle-class phenomenon.

Some call it the tradition of the African diaspora. In Haiti it is known as Voudoun; in Cuba, as Santería or Lucumí; in Brazil, as Macumba and Candomblé.[48] New Orleans has long had its own version, which gives us our most familiar name for this tradition: Voodoo. These religions differ in rites, practices, terminology, and the gods they worship, but they are similar enough to permit some generalizations.

Between the discovery of the New World and the end of slavery in the nineteenth century, an estimated six hundred thousand Africans were imported to the Western Hemisphere as slaves. Most came from West Africa. Though their white masters made attempts—often perfunctory—to Christianize them, many of the blacks, especially in South America and the Caribbean, remained faithful to the religion of their homeland, sometimes disguising it under a thin veneer of Christianity.

This syncretization between African religion and the faith of the whites was particularly easy in Catholic countries, where the Africans found a natural resemblance between their own gods (called *orishas* in Santería, *loa* in Voudoun) and the Catholic saints. Like the saints, the *orishas* are not omnipotent but have certain spheres of influence; one can heal, another can help out in matters of love, and so on. Thus their devotees came to equate the two: Ogun, the war god, was connected with St. George the knight; Oshun, the goddess of love, with Our Lady of Charity; Elegguá, god of the crossroads, with St. Peter. Sometimes the correlations cross gender lines: the dynamic storm god Changó was identified with St. Barbara, the patron saint of thunder and lightning.[49] And just as the Catholic saints are subordinate to God Almighty, the *orishas* are all emanations of the supreme Creator, Oludumare.

Textbooks often draw a sharp contrast between monotheism, the worship of one God, and polytheism, the worship of many gods. Yet even the most lavishly polytheistic religions usually have some concept of a supreme unity that gives rise to the many gods; similarly, monotheistic faiths often worship God under different aspects and names. Jews and Muslims have accused Christianity of polytheism on the grounds that the Trinity is really three gods; but the Jewish Kabbalah portrays different aspects of the One in the *sefirot,* and Muslims have a similar concept in the 99 Names of Allah, which represent his different manifestations. A Kabbalistic legend even says that mankind was originally monotheistic, but became polytheistic when people began to worship the *sefirot* as different gods.

This resemblance between two apparently contradictory worldviews need not surprise us. The relation of the One to the Many is a problem that has preoccupied the human race for millennia. People have always perceived an underlying unity behind things, which they have then tried to reconcile with the multiplicity of manifest reality. For the Yorubas, the West African tribe whose religion is the ancestor of Santería, this underlying unity is the god Olodumare:

> Be there 1400 divinities of the home
> Be there 1200 divinities of the marketplace
> Yet there is no one divinity to compare with Olodumare
> Olodumare is the king unique.[50]

Like the God of Western religions, Olodumare is revered and praised, but his relationship with the individual worshiper is a bit distant. Olodumare "made the whole world and the sun and the stars," as one initiate put it. "Then he made the *orishas,* to take care of things here on earth while he carried on with his business elsewhere in the universe."[51] And it is to the *orishas* that the individual must go for help.

The relation between god and devotee is not an arbitrary one. The intricate forms of divination found in the religions of West Africa and their New World offspring are needed partly to discern which *orisha* a given person belongs to: to be initiated into the ceremony of the wrong one will bring disaster.

Moreover this connection is intimately tied to the deepest structure of the individual's psyche. A Creole proverb says, "*Tem-*

*perament mun, ce temperament loa-li*"—a person's character is the character of his *loa*. The *loa* proper to one's nature is known in Voudoun as the *maît-tête,* the "master of the head."[52]

Although everyone belongs to one *orisha* or another, religion exists to strengthen this connection. Initiation in Santería, known as *hacer el santo* (literally, "making the saint"),[53] is an intricate and expensive process, requiring large quantities of food and animals for the ceremonial sacrifice. Poorer aspirants may have to save for years before they can afford the rite. The preparations impose other austerities, including wearing fresh clothes every day, avoiding mirrors for three months, and abstaining from sex for at least several days before the ceremony.

Each devotee may also need to be initiated into the mysteries of more than one god. In Santería this decision can only be made by the *babalawo,* the high priest, who uses a complicated form of cowrie-shell divination known as Ifa for this purpose.[54] (Higher initiations confer various authorities such as the priesthood itself.)

Once a devotee has "made the saint," he or she may experience possession. In the faiths of the African diaspora, possession is both a common and (by and large) a positive experience that takes place in the context of a religious ceremony. When it is over, the one possessed returns to a normal state. Usually it takes place during a ceremony where the god is "danced"—that is, the participants perform specific types of music and dance that invite the god to descend. Once he or she arrives and takes over the body of one of the participants, the one possessed begins to behave like the god. This is not always pleasant or even welcome: Ghédé or Baron Samedi, the Voudoun god of death, often shows up at the ceremonies of other *loa* and sometimes must be gotten rid of tactfully, usually at the cost of much food, for he has an enormous appetite.

The phenomenon of possession relates to how these traditions view the human makeup. In addition to the body, a human being has what is known in Voudoun as the *ti-bon-ange* (the "little good angel"), more or less equivalent to the Higher Self or conscience, and the *gros-bon-ange* (the "big good angel")—roughly equivalent to what in Western magic is known as the astral body. In possession the *gros-bon-ange* is displaced for a time so the body can serve as a vehicle for the god.[55]

The skeptic may be tempted to dismiss this as a subjective delusion, but the participants find it real enough; they even regard anything done under possession as an act of the god rather than of the human. Migene González-Wippler, a Puerto Rican author who has considerable experience with Santería, describes a rite whereby *santeros* (initiates) possessed by three different *orishas* drink the spurting blood of two sacrificed doves. González-Wippler, remembering taboos against human consumption of blood, asks her teacher why the *santeros* should have drunk it.

"But the *santeros* don't drink it," the teacher replies. "The *orishas* do. You'll never see a *santero* drink blood when he's not possessed by an *orisha*. . . . The *orishas* are manifestations of God. And as such, blood also belongs to them."[56]

The typical American may find such rites repugnant and may question not only their morality but their legality; devotees of these religions have encountered opposition from animal-protection groups and municipal authorities. In a 1993 case, the Supreme Court vindicated the right of a Florida Santería church to conduct such sacrifices in the face of a local ordinance opposing them.[57] Devotees claim that they perform their offerings with respect, which makes them superior to the commercial slaughter of millions of animals each year by the meat industry. Whether one agrees or not, one must acknowledge that, unlike most contemporary Neopagan groups, the traditions of the African diaspora do sacrifice animals as an integral part of their practice. If you object in principle to such a thing, you are unlikely to find a congenial home in these religions.

## SATANISM

Nearly all followers of the religions of the African diaspora, like Witches and Neopagans, would no doubt insist that their religion is a positive and wholesome influence on their lives. But sinister associations have often been attached to such things as Voodoo and witchcraft. Is there such a thing as Satanism? Does anyone actually serve the Devil?

Nearly all Witches and Pagans today would, if asked, insist that they do *not* serve the Christian Devil. They regard the divine in a different way from mainstream religion—God is feminine as well as masculine, plural as well as singular, immanent as well as transcendent—but they would deny that the Goddess or even the Horned God has anything to do with the Satan of theology, that is, the conscious, transpersonal embodiment of cosmic evil. Believing in the Christian Devil implies believing in the Christian God, and Witches do not. Consequently, from their perspective, Witches are not Satanists.

Yet there are people who do claim to serve Satan. By all accounts they form an almost insignificant part of the general population, but because charges of Satanism and "ritual abuse" have created such public unease in the 1980s and 1990s, the matter is worth some attention.

It is true that certain crimes are connected with some element of Satanism or the occult. Most of these, however, are acts of adolescent rebellion: scrawling graffiti saying "Satan Lives," desecrating churches, disemboweling animals, and other sinister acts are motivated, in the words of Arthur Lyons, a modern historian of Satanism, "more by the use of narcotics or the deviant attraction of the acts themselves than by any real commitment to or knowledge of Satanism."[58]

At its crudest level, Satanism is a self-conscious inversion of the forms of Christianity.[59] The Lord's Prayer is said backwards, the mass is performed using the body of a naked woman as an altar, and so on. The most famous description of this "Black Mass" occurs in the novel *Là-Bas* ("Over There"), by the nineteenth-century French novelist J.-K. Huysmans. Another such rite is the hideous Mass of St. Secaire, which, according to Gascon folklore, can only be said in a deconsecrated church, using a black, triangular Host. The mass is performed in order to lay a curse on a designated victim, who wastes away slowly with no hope of recovery. It

is considered so evil that only the pope himself can grant absolu-
tion to those who perform it.[60]

But these strange inversions of Christian ritual occur far more
often in horror films than in real life. In modern America it would
be hard to find a Black Mass even if one tried. To the extent that
they exist at all, they are chiefly motivated by the desire to shock,
as is obvious from the use of quasi-Satanic paraphernalia by certain heavy-metal bands.

Ultimately, the Satanic impulse is centered in rebellion. Many
Satanists take their cue from the old Gnostics, who, we have seen,
saw the God of the Old Testament as the flawed creator of a defective cosmos. It would naturally follow that the opponent of
such a God must be good, producing the odd and often con-
founding inversion of "good" and "evil" that is the hallmark of
Satanism. Indeed the best account of the Satanist's psychology
appears in Bernard Shaw's 1897 play *The Devil's Disciple*, set in the
gloomy New England of the Puritans. The hero, Richard Dud-
geon, disgusted by the oppressive and Pharisaical religion around
him, decides that if these people are serving God, he will stand up
for "the other party." He is, of course, the most appealing character
in the play.

Similarly, contemporary Satanism constitutes a revolt, not so
much against God—who is often regarded as a product of the human imagination—as against the hypocrisy and sexual repression
that Satanists blame on Christianity. Rather than embodying cosmic evil, the Devil is simply seen as the personification of liberation and self-gratification. The late Anton Szandor LaVey, founder
of San Francisco's Church of Satan and the best-known exponent
of Satanism, proclaimed:

Satan represents indulgence, instead of abstinence! . . .
Satan represents vital existence, instead of spiritual pipe
    dreams! . . .
Satan represents undefiled wisdom, instead of hypocritical
    self-defeat! . . .

Satan represents kindness to those who deserve it, instead
of love wasted on ingrates! . . .
Satan represents vengeance, instead of turning the other
cheek![61]

LaVey advocated a form of conscious egotism. His writings are
sprinkled with references to Aleister Crowley and to Enochian
magic, a cryptic system originating with John Dee; yet Massimo
Introvigne, an Italian scholar of religions, observed that the greatest influence on LaVey was Ayn Rand, whose radically individual-
istic philosophy of "Objectivism" propounds an ideal of rational
self-interest rather than Christian self-sacrifice.[62]

The Church of Satan went through a schism in 1975, when
LaVey began selling initiations to anyone who would pay the
price. Michael Aquino, a U.S. Army officer who belonged to the
church in San Francisco, broke away, dissatisfied not only with
LaVey's commercial motives but also with his reluctance to commit to belief in the actual existence of Satan as a metaphysical
entity.[63]

On his own, Aquino founded the Temple of Set, dedicated to
the Egyptian god who slew the divine Osiris. According to
Aquino, Set is the embodiment of enlightened, self-conscious
awareness in opposition to a blind and mechanical universe.[64] His
name, says Aquino, was later corrupted into the Hebrew "Satan."

Despite their differences, both LaVey and Aquino espouse not
evil as such, but rather a kind of enlightened self-interest or
worldly wisdom. If there is anything horrifying in their teachings, it is chiefly that they expound principles by which most
people live most of the time—usually without admitting it even to
themselves.

Contrary to rumors of an enormous Satanic conspiracy, the
movement is extremely small, numbering most likely in the hundreds rather than the thousands; and it has never been connected
with the kind of cult abuse that remains a perennial obsession
among the tabloids; indeed it has gone out of its way to condemn

such activity.[65] In any real sense the social danger posed by organized Satanists is infinitesimal. While psychopaths and other disturbed people may sometimes use Satanic signs and slogans, far more crimes are committed in the name of God or of some political ideology, or for no reason at all, than in the name of the Devil.

## PAGAN POSSIBILITIES

No one really knows how many Witches and Pagans there are in the U.S. today. One educated estimate suggests a range from 200,000 to 500,000,[66] but many who are attracted to Neopaganism are averse to denominations, organizations, or record-keeping of any kind. And given that Paganism is, if not actively persecuted, at least regarded with suspicion throughout many parts of the nation, a number of people who practice it may feel the need to keep their preferences quiet. Anecdotal evidence suggests that Paganism is a religion that is growing very fast; sales of one basic text, *Buckland's Complete Book of Witchcraft*, have risen from 12,000 copies a year to 48,000 in the course of the 1990s.

The reasons for this interest are clear. Like many other alternative spiritual paths, Paganism offers the promise of direct experience instead of received ideas and dogma. The possibility of a closer contact with nature is another attraction, since urbanization has led many to feel the loss of a deeper connection with the natural world. Paganism and Witchcraft, which base their observances on the seasonal cycles and work rituals using the energies of the body and the earth, seem able to heal the alarming rift between human beings and nature. Finally, in revering the feminine aspect of the divine at least as much as the masculine, Witchcraft and Paganism teach that both sexes have equal dignity and status—an idea that has been obscured in the West for centuries.

There are other reasons as well. People drawn to exploring their ethnic roots sometimes approach the Pagan traditions of their heritage as means of gaining access to what Jung regarded as the racial stratum of the collective unconscious. Others seem to take comfort in the ambiance of many Pagan gatherings, which often have a strong flavor of the 1960s Counterculture. Still others, who wish to explore unseen dimensions with a minimum of doctrinal baggage, find these paths supportive but not confining structures in which to conduct a search.

Pagans and Witches pride themselves on their individualism and iconoclasm, but Americans will probably find these paths most congenial if they feel a strong affinity for Green causes, feminism, or various elements of the old Counterculture. Not all Pagans and Witches fall under these rubrics, but many do, particularly those the beginner is likely to meet. This is less true in Britain and other countries where people have a stronger connection with the "old ways."

## SUGGESTED READING

Adler, Margot. *Drawing Down the Moon: Witches, Druids, Goddess-Worshippers, and Other Pagans in America Today*. Rev. ed. New York: Arkana, 1997.

This remains the most intelligent and sympathetic account of Witchcraft and Paganism as a modern social phenomenon.

Clifton, Chas S., ed. *Witchcraft Today*. St. Paul, Minn.: Llewellyn, 1992–95.

A multivolume series containing essays exploring the modern Craft movement, rites of passage in Witchcraft, and Witchcraft and shamanism.

Deren, Maya. *Divine Horsemen: The Living Gods of Haiti*. 1953. Reprint. New Paltz, N.Y.: DocumenText, 1970.

Deren went to Haiti to record Voudoun ceremonies for her film *Divine Horsemen*. This book is an eloquent account of her experiences.

Farrar, Stewart. *What Witches Do*. New York: Coward, McCann, & Geoghegan, 1971.

A readable account of the author's initial experiences with the coven of the well-known British Witch Alex Sanders. Farrar's *A Witches' Bible*, (Custer, Wash.: Phoenix Publishing, 1996), coauthored with his wife, Janet, contains a compendium of practical information, including rituals, spells, and a discussion of initiation.

González-Wippler, Migene. *Santería: The Religion*. New York: Harmony Books, 1989.

A lively account of the author's firsthand experience with Santería in Puerto Rico and the U.S. mainland. This volume contains parts of two earlier books of hers, *Santería: African Religion in Latin America* (New York: Doubleday Anchor, 1975) and *The Santería Experience* (Englewood Cliffs, N.J.: Prentice-Hall, 1982).

Hopman, Ellen Evert, and Lawrence Bond. *People of the Earth: The New Pagans Speak Out*. Rochester, Vt.: Destiny Books, 1996.

Contains interviews with most leading Neopagans in America, including Starhawk and Margot Adler. Useful in giving a sense of the factions and controversies in Neopaganism today.

LaVey, Anton Szandor. *The Satanic Bible*. New York: Avon Books, 1969.

Perhaps not quite as shocking as it was when first published. Blunt, cynical, and often witty, but not entirely accurate in its discussions of magic.

Murray, Margaret A. *The God of the Witches*. Oxford: Oxford University Press, 1931.

Not to be taken face value as a work of scholarship, Murray's book remains useful for the light it throws on how modern Witches view themselves. Her earlier book, *The Witch Cult in Western Europe* (Oxford: Oxford University Press, 1921), is more cautious and more heavily documented.

Starhawk. *The Spiral Dance: A Rebirth of the Ancient Religion of the Great Goddess*. Rev. ed. San Francisco: Harper & Row, 1989.

The first edition of *The Spiral Dance*, published in 1979, was so influential that some Wiccans divide the current movement into pre- and post-Starhawk eras. Often tendentious, strident, and historically inaccurate, this book has nevertheless galvanized modern Neopaganism in a way that no other single work has.

Thomas, Keith. *Religion and the Decline of Magic*. New York: Charles Scribner's Sons, 1971.

An eminent historian examines why people stopped believing in witches and magic in the early modern period. An excellent overview of the social milieu of the witch hunts.

Valiente, Doreen. *Witchcraft for Tomorrow*. Custer, Wash.: Phoenix Publishing, 1978.

A discussion of practical contemporary Witchcraft by one of Gerald Gardner's closest associates. Another book by Valiente, *The Rebirth of Witchcraft* (Phoenix, 1989), gives a history of the modern movement.

*Seven*

# SHAMANS:
# TECHNICIANS OF ECSTASY

Today the word *shaman* turns up in a wide array of contexts. We come across urban shamans, psychedelic shamans, shamanologists, even technoshamans. Some of them claim to have been initiated into the world of indigenous wisdom, but many others have no more connection to that world than one can attain from the comfortable removes of Marin County or Beverly Hills.

Shamanic techniques of ecstasy have been widely practiced around the world. And anthropological literature has given us a more accurate understanding of these methods today than any society has probably ever had. Moreover, the unslakable thirst for a deeper contact with the forces of earth and nature—a thirst that, as we've seen, has given a new birth to Paganism—ensures that many seekers will undertake the shaman's quest. It may come as a surprise, then, to learn that according to some authorities, nobody in our society today can be a shaman.

Why not? Because in the strict sense a shaman is not merely a practitioner of certain mystical techniques; to be a shaman is to fulfill a social role. This role properly exists only in simple societies, where tasks and functions are far less differentiated than in our own specialized culture. Indeed, one scholar has found that true shamans can be found only in hunter-gatherer cultures,

156

where the shaman operates as a combined priest, doctor, medium, poet, and scientist. He or she may conduct religious rites, prescribe medicine for the sick, counsel the chiefs on matters of state, and serve as keeper of the tribe's history.[1] No one in the developed world can be a shaman in this sense, any more than a modern man can be a galley slave or feudal baron.

The word *shaman* itself comes from the language of a Siberian tribe known as the Tungus. Mircea Eliade, the great Romanian scholar of comparative religions, says, "Shamanism in the strict sense is preeminently a religious phenomenon of Siberia and Central Asia." Yet he adds that shamanism is a universal phenomenon found in North America, Indonesia, Oceania, and elsewhere. The use of a Siberian term seems to stem mostly from the fact that the phenomenon was first described among the tribes of Central Asia.[2]

Everything that will be said here about shamanism must be understood in light of the fact that this concept is the creation of scholars and anthropologists. Jews regards themselves as a Jews, Christians as Christians, even Witches as Witches; but most native shamans do not call themselves that, nor do they think of their religion as "shamanism." The term has been created by academics to describe a certain facet of religious experience. This is not to say that it is a false picture—it goes far toward explaining religious practices that are remarkably consistent around the world—but it *is* a scholarly construct, and the three most important figures in the modern shamanic revival are not shamans but academicians. Besides Mircea Eliade, whose book *Shamanism: Archaic Techniques of Ecstasy* remains the central text on the subject, a second figure is Michael Harner, an anthropologist who spent years with Amazon tribes in the 1950s and 1960s. His experiences there, as well as his studies of other cultures, led him to formulate what he called "core shamanism"—a set of visionary techniques that he and his organization, the Foundation for Shamanic Studies, now teach in an extremely successful series of weekend workshops.

The third and best known, as well as the most controversial, is Carlos Castaneda, whose doctoral dissertation about his encounters with a Yaqui Indian "sorcerer" named don Juan eventually became the best-selling book *Teachings of Don Juan: A Yaqui Way of Knowledge*. Since this book appeared, a number of authorities have criticized it along with Castaneda's later books, citing inaccuracies in detail about Yaqui practice and claiming that these works are little more than fiction. Whether or not this is true, they have shaped the popular understanding of shamanism more than anything else in modern times.

Eliade worked chiefly from published writings, but both Harner and Castaneda have (at least by their own accounts) encountered shamans and sorcerers in their native contexts through fieldwork. Having approached these cultures from the outside, at some point each one felt the need for more immediate experience. Harner writes:

> My anthropological research on the culture of the Conibo had been going well, but my attempts to elicit information on their religion met with little success. The people were friendly, but reluctant to talk about the supernatural. Finally they told me that if I really wished to learn, I must take the shamans' sacred drink made from *ayahuasca,* the "soul vine."[3]

Such statements abound in today's shamanic literature. The writer often begins as an anthropologist, approaching a native culture from the outside. At some point he or she feels the need to experience the shamanic states of reality directly. (Harner's initiation took place by means of the psychedelic beverage *ayahuasca,* but drugs are not always used.) Having been initiated and trained, the writer then returns to the Western world to serve as a bridge between indigenous wisdom and the modern sensibility.

Although over the last generation academic anthropology has come to recognize the value of "partipicatory observation," this impulse presents difficulties of its own. Castaneda remarks that his method of apprenticeship to don Juan, which had to conform to his academic schedule, "retarded the advent of the full commitment I needed to become a sorcerer. Yet the method was beneficial from my personal standpoint in that it allowed me a modicum of detachment, and that in turn fostered a sense of critical examination."[4]

In a traditional context, the shaman is often seen as one who walks between worlds: between the ordinary reality that we know and the hidden realms that are accessible only to those with the right power and knowledge. The modern shaman-anthropologist walks between worlds in another sense, for he or she must hold true to two visions, the indigenous and the modern: the one who has experienced altered states of consciousness and the one who maintains a critical detachment.

## DISMEMBERMENT AND REASSEMBLY

Eliade defined shamanism as a set of "archaic techniques of ecstasy. . . . The shaman specializes in a trance during which his soul is believed to leave his body and ascend to the sky or descend to the underworld."[5] For Timothy White, editor of *Shaman's Drum*, a "journal of experiential shamanism," a shaman is "somebody who moves into alternate states of consciousness and brings back information or healing from the other side."[6]

Even within indigenous cultures, which usually have a much more vivid sense of alternate realities than our own, not everybody can master these feats; they require some combination of training and innate ability. There are many ways of embarking upon such a path. In certain tribes it is hereditary. Some choose the shaman's way as a kind of career move: A Mayan *h'men* or "man of knowledge" named Don Eligio Panti says that he became a shaman at the age of fifteen, when he lost his job as a gatherer of chicle. Encountering an elderly initiate, he begged him to take him on as an apprentice.[7]

Others are called by the spirits—a process that is not always agreeable. The message can come in a dream or a vision, but it can also take the form of restlessness, illness, or mental dysfunction. Some shamans take up their work after years of sickness; after the local practitioners have failed to cure them, they must learn to "shamanize" for themselves. The mental states that lead up to the shaman's call have often been compared to epilepsy, schizophrenia, and other disorders.

The actual initiation can be equally excruciating. Most initiations in most cultures involve a symbolic death and rebirth: the candidate "dies" to his old identity and is reborn to a new one. Shamanic initiates often experience this resurrection in gruesome ways. When the *rai* (spirits) make a shaman in western Australia, they take him to their home.

> There they cut him up and hang up his insides. . . . His body is dead, but his soul remains there, and on the order of the *rai* to look steadily at the part hanging up, he recognizes [his organs]. His body is put over a hot earth-oven, with magic cooking stones in it, and covered with paper-bark. The perspiration streams down. The *rai* then replace his insides and close up the flesh. He is told that he can henceforth travel in the air like a bird or under the ground like a goanna.[8]

However odd this description may seem as objective fact, it no doubt gives an accurate picture of the initiate's subjective experience. Such states can be brought about by drugs, fasting, seclusion, or other austerities. No matter what the means, the initiation is no formality, but requires a willingness to sacrifice the very fiber of one's being. Hence candidates must be exceptional: they must have some freedom from identification with the body;[9] they must also be endowed with psychological courage, for these encounters with the spirits are bound to be terrifying even for those of the strongest character.

This occult dismemberment also has a deeper import. The shaman stands on the threshold between the potent but invisible realm of the spirits and solid day-to-day reality. As such he or she serves as a conduit for bringing extraordinary energies to earth, and for this purpose the ordinary physical form will not suffice. The shaman's body itself must undergo a transformation; only then can one accomplish the work the spirits have in mind. Stories of disembowelment, dismemberment, and reassembly (usually with magic stones or crystals installed into the shaman's frame) are probably best understood in this light. (One might even wonder whether today's science-fiction tales of androids and bionic creatures are an unconscious recollection of this motif.)

Such initiatory experiences are not a shaman's only encounter with the spirits; they are a first step, a means of opening the portals of communication. The shaman goes on to receive instruction in such things as magical songs and the healing powers of specific herbs from the spirits, whom the shaman will also consult to diagnose individual cases. (Most shamans, of course, learn techniques from human instructors as well.)

## ANIMALS AND THE WORLD BELOW

Shamans understand the cosmos as being composed of many levels and dimensions. The specific views of these dimensions vary, but basically we can portray the shamanic universe as consisting of three levels: ordinary, street-level reality; the world of heaven, of celestial powers and influences; and the world beneath the earth, the abode of the natural powers. Depending on the task, the shaman may visit one or the other, or both, of these alternate realities.

This picture differs in one striking respect from that of Judaism and Christianity. These major traditions tend to view the cosmos in terms of Jacob's ladder, where heaven is the highest and earth the lowest point of the divine order. Anything "beneath the earth" is usually seen as evil or diabolical, like Dante's hell, which is a series of concentric circles below the surface of the earth. But many shamanic traditions do not regard the "world beneath" as morally any better or worse than heaven.

Here it's important to stress a point that may already be obvious. There is often an overwhelming temptation, when presented with different systems, to try to show that they're really all saying the same thing. Although there are strong similarities among traditions, it's dangerous to try to reduce them all to a lowest common denominator. At the very least one may end up obscuring crucial differences; at worst, one may even demonize another vision of the world.

"My God is dark," wrote the poet Rilke, "like a knot with a hundred roots that drink in silence." Shamans might well agree. For them, the underworld is not necessarily a place where devils take refuge or sinners are punished, but where the powers of earth and nature reside.

This nether realm even has its own family of gods and spirits— a fact that helps explain an odd detail in the ancient Greek pantheon, which had two sets of gods: the familiar Olympians and their darker counterparts, the chthonic deities (from the Greek *chthon,* "earth"). Even Zeus, the sky god *par excellence,* has his chthonic double. These gods of the underworld are powers to be reckoned with, for they rule the mysteries of death and regeneration. "The other Zeus, the Zeus of the dead, may simply be another name for Hades; but nevertheless it is from him that the growth of the crops is expected," says the scholar Walter Burkert.[10] Similarly Haitian Voudoun has its brighter Rada clan of deities and the darker and more sinister Petro clan.[11]

Why would the shaman want to encounter these baleful powers? In the first place, to gain power and knowledge. Such a descent may coincide with initiation, when the candidate may have the experience of making a descent to the underworld, even to the land of the dead. This journey symbolizes the initiate's own figurative death and renewal, but it also suggests an encounter with forces that lie outside the human realm—for, symbolically speaking, to go past the gates of death is to go beyond the limits of human existence as we know it. Here the shaman may meet and ally with one or more spirits, often in the form of animals.

Even today many people feel a peculiar affinity for a certain type of animal, wild or domestic. It may be expressed in an unusual rapport with a particular species, or sometimes simply as a passion for collecting frog or bear figurines. In a shamanic context, such an animal may represent a tutelary spirit. This is not so much a specific individual animal (which makes it different from the common notion of the witch's "familiar") as it is a kind of collective spirit of the species. Some tribal traditions say that every person has such a guardian spirit, that it is in fact almost impossible to reach adulthood without one. Others say it can only be acquired by initiation. This "totem," "animal ally," or "power animal," as it is sometimes called, is essential to shamanic practice.[12] An ally may also represent a set of specific skills that the shaman needs to acquire: a dragonfly ally, for example, often represents the ability to find water.

Michael Harner advises aspiring shamans who have acquired such an ally to "dance the animal"—to move around in the manner of the animal, experiencing what it's like to be that creature. This practice is recommended not only to maintain access to the spirit's power, but to give it what it wants: an experience of human embodiment. Harner distinguishes this practice from possession in the classic sense, which is more or less involuntary. "You possess the guardian spirit," he stresses, "it never possesses you."[13]

In native cultures the shaman may spend months studying the animal, learning its habits, and imitating its behavior as a means of becoming one with its spirit. In some cases the shaman is literally thought to be transformed into the power animal. Don Eligio Panti says he saw his teacher change into a jaguar. And a friend of the late Tuscarora medicine man Mad Bear said, "You know, sometimes I think he's really a bear. I'm not saying I'm convinced, but again and again, I've had hints from things he's said, or little glimpses I've had, that he takes on a bear or a bearlike form. Or maybe he uses an existing bear."[14] Similarly, under don Juan's guidance Castaneda felt he was transformed into a crow.[15]

In most shamanic traditions, the descent to the lower world is mirrored in the ascent: instead of going down into the earth, the shaman makes an inner journey up to heaven. Rather than animal spirits, he or she may encounter gods, spirits, or teachers in human form. Whether ascending or descending, the shaman typically makes this journey for some purpose; one of the most common purposes is healing.

## EXTRACTIONS AND RETRIEVALS

For shamans, both mental and physical illnesses are caused by occult means, so occult remedies are required. Many disorders are seen as the result of intrusions of spirits or other invisible entities—that is, possession on what Western occultists would call the astral level. Such ailments may be caused by the deliberate work of black magicians, by the more or less accidental intrusion of alien entities, or by negative energy sent by human, for in the shamanic worldview, we are constantly emitting and receiving energy, both positive and negative. Though this may be done unconsciously, it may also be performed on purpose through sorcery.

The Jivaro tribe of South America believe illness is caused by *tsentsak,* or magical darts. " 'Bad' or bewitching shamans send these spirits helpers into victims' bodies to make them ill or to kill them," writes Harner. " 'Good' shamans, or healers, use their own *tsentsak* to help them suck out spirits from the bodies of ill tribesmen."

The *tsentsak* take the form of small objects like plants, stones, or even living insects or worms. To heal a patient, a Jivaro shaman will use his paranormal powers, often heightened by *ayahuasca,* to diagnose where in the body the intruding entity can be found. He will then literally suck it out, keeping his own *tsentsak* in his mouth. The intruding spirit will be caught in the shaman's *tsentsak,* and the healer will show this object to the patient as proof of the cure.

This practice obviously raises the issue of fraud. "The non-shamans may think that the material object itself is what has been sucked out, and the shaman does not disillusion them," Harner adds. "At the same time he is not lying, because he knows that the only important aspect of a *tsentsak* is its nonmaterial or nonordinary aspect."[16]

Healing by extraction is also performed by the faith healers of the Philippines. They use some combination of genuine paranormal power and sleight-of-hand to perform "bloody extractions," whereby they magically seem to reach into a patient's body with their fingers, without surgery or implements, and extract harmful objects ranging from worms to safety pins. Though these healers have been shown to use some measure of trickery, many patients go away from the procedure much improved or even completely healed. If this is a matter of healing by suggestion, it seems to work often enough. Far more than Western doctors, shamans regard the mental and emotional condition of the patient as paramount in the healing process.[17]

Another form of healing has to do with the opposite problem: a loss of power or life force. Again this idea has a parallel in Western medicine: the concept of resistance, whereby a person weakened by malnutrition, overexertion, or emotional stress is more vulnerable to disease. But shamans differ from Western doctors not only in placing the cause and cure in occult dimensions, but in saying the weakness arises from a literal loss of soul.

Many esoteric systems posit various unseen dimensions, including subtle bodies of which we are generally unaware. Shamans would agree with this view, but they would add that these different aspects of the human makeup are not so well-integrated as we might think. In fact trauma can split off one or more of these "souls," leaving its possessor weakened and vulnerable. This severed shard of the soul—which may be a power animal but which may also be part of one's human nature—wanders in the nether world, longing for its former home but not knowing how to return.

Entering into a trance, the shaman makes the journey to retrieve the lost soul. Among the Chukchee of Central Asia, the shaman will return with the soul in the form of a fly or a bee, which he then "blows" into an opening he is believed to make in the patient's head.[18] As far-fetched as this practice may sound, it recalls an idea found in many traditions, in which the soul leaves the dying body through the crown of the head. (Practitioners of the Tibetan Buddhist technique known as *phowa,* for example, learn how to "blow" the soul out of the crown at death into the visualized heart of a Buddha, ensuring enlightenment or an auspicious rebirth.)

Shamanic healing is not limited to extractions and retrievals. It also employs herbal remedies, and many shamans serve as living repositories of their tribes' herbal lore. If the case is a simple one, the shaman may already know which herb to use; otherwise he or she may have to make a journey to the unseen worlds to find out. Sometimes it happens that the patient has offended one of the gods or spirits and must make recompense through sacrifice.

## DRUMS AND PSYCHEDELICS

The shaman's initial encounter with the spirits by way of some kind of physical and psychological ordeal is obviously a once-in-a-lifetime experience; he or she cannot undergo a dissolution of the self every time a patient needs help. Routine visits to the worlds above and below are most often made through the drum. "For an experienced shaman," Harner writes, even a few minutes of drumming "is usually sufficient to achieve the light trance in which most shamanic work is done."[19] (The shaman may start the drumming, though usually at some point an assistant will take over.)

Steady, low-percussion rhythms have long been used to alter consciousness. Drummers once accompanied men into battle to sustain the martial spirit, while today's discos and rock concerts use a pounding bass to shift moods in a different direction. For shamans, the association of drumming with trance is heightened because by and large they do not use it for other purposes.

The drum is more than a mere utensil; shamans sometimes speak of it poetically as the "horse" they ride into higher realms. Moreover, as Eliade notes, the symbolism of the drum itself recapitulates the shamanic worldview. In the initiatory journey, the shaman may make a visit to the spiritual center of the world, "to the seat of the Cosmic Tree and the Universal Lord. It is from a branch of this Tree, which the Lord causes to fall for the purpose, that the shaman makes the shell of his drum. . . . *By the fact that the shell of his drum is derived from the actual wood of the Cosmic Tree, the shaman, through his drumming, is magically projected into the vicinity of the Tree;* he is projected to the 'Center of the World,' and thus can ascend to the sky."[20]

Other methods also involve music. The rattle is a common instrument, typically producing a rhythm of a higher frequency than the drum. The shaman may also chant power songs, sometimes handed down through a tribal tradition, though the most powerful ones are those learned directly from the spirits. According to Harner, the shaman must have at least one power song before attempting to perform "soul retrieval."[21]

A far more controversial means of attaining ecstasy involves psychedelic plants. Besides *ayahuasca,* plants used for this purpose include peyote; psilocybin mushrooms; mandrake root; ibogaine, a West African root; datura or jimsonweed; and *Amanita muscaria,* a psychedelic mushroom.

The role of psychedelic plants, both in shamanism proper and in the genesis of the great world religions, is much debated, but these materials have probably been far more influential than is generally believed. There is some evidence that initiates of the Eleusinian Mysteries in ancient Greece used a potion containing the hallucinogenic fungus ergot (a chemical precursor of LSD) to know "the end of life and its god-sent beginning," as the poet Pindar put it. The Vedic hymns of India, among the oldest religious texts known to mankind, sing the praises of *soma,* a mysterious intoxicant "all-pervading, swift as thought."[22] Medieval witches may have used datura, which can precipitate out-of-body experiences, as an ingredient of their "flying ointments."[23]

Because much of shamanism is clearly psychedelic in nature, it has especially intrigued people who came of age in the 1960s and experimented with psychedelics in those years. Plant psychedelics tend to differ from synthetic products like LSD, mescaline, and MDMA (Ecstasy) in several respects. In the first place, synthetic chemicals are much simpler; by contrast, a plant like peyote has a complex of different psychoactive compounds that may influence the experience.

The most striking contrast between synthetic and natural psychedelics lies in their effects on the body. For most users, synthetic psychedelics produce comparatively few immediate physical side effects such as vomiting or nausea. But many plant psychedelics have side effects that are intensely disagreeable. During his first experience with *ayahuasca* Harner thought he was dying and had to be revived with an antidote. Most neophytes who take peyote or *ayahuasca* vomit it up soon after; the trick is often to be able to keep it down long enough to allow the psychedelic properties to engage.

From a shamanic point of view, even these unpleasant aspects have a certain value: they are seen as purgations of impurities, initiatory thresholds to be crossed, or triggers of the death-and-rebirth process. (They also ensure that few of these drugs are candidates for widespread recreational abuse.) Experienced users tend to suffer fewer and milder side effects.

Plant psychedelics have another curious property that distinguishes them from their synthetic cousins: users frequently feel they are meeting the personified spirits of the plants. Potent entities, capable of conferring power and knowledge, these spirits are often regarded as teachers in their own right. Coming to know them is a chief reason for taking these drugs.

In Carlos Castaneda's books, the entity or intelligence behind peyote is Mescalito. Castaneda reports: "Don Juan spoke with deep fervor about Mescalito's being the teacher of the proper way to live."[24] The Huichol Indians equate this personification of the peyote spirit with the spirit of the deer and the corn, while in other contexts it is known as "Grandfather Peyote."

Similarly, users of ibogaine may encounter "Mr. Ibogaine," an entity capable of relentlessly forcing the user to face the issues in his or her life. This may help explain why some research suggests that ibogaine can cure heroin addiction.

Today there are two main camps of people interested in using psychedelics for inner exploration. The first can be traced back to the 1950s and 1960s, when synthetic psychedelics first became widely known among writers like the British novelist Aldous Huxley, who began to take—and write about—materials such as LSD and mescaline;[25] psychologists and psychiatrists also began to conduct research on them. (LSD and mescaline were legal in the United States until the late 1960s.) From these explorations, psychedelic enthusiasts, most famously Timothy Leary, contended that these materials can be profitably used for inner work, provided they are used in the right "set and setting"—that is, with a positive attitude in serene and supportive circumstances, often with an experienced guide present.

Employed in such a way, psychedelics can give even the first-time user genuine access to the numinous as well as to repressed unconscious material. It is then up to the individual to sort through his or her experiences and integrate them into everyday consciousness. Sometimes a psychotherapist may help with this process. Though it's not widely known, a sizable number of therapists work with patients in this way, administering psychedelics as a means of increasing insight and then using counseling to help them sort out the contents. Certain relationship counselors administer MDMA, which usually produces overwhelming feelings of empathy, to create a loving mood in which couples can sort out their difficulties. Of course this work is done *sub rosa*, since current laws do not permit the use of these materials even therapeutically.[26]

The second category of psychedelic voyagers are those who are curious about the shamanic uses of psychotropic plants; of these seekers, many have tried natural as well as synthetic materials. But as Timothy White puts it, "The successful shamanic use of any psychotropic involves a lot more than just taking a prescribed dosage in a safe set and setting—it requires mastery of an entire complex of shamanic disciplines." White quotes California psychedelic explorers Gracie and Zarkov, who contend, "In traditional shamanic societies, there exist specific traditions, histories, rituals, and practices which provide a stable, long-term set and setting by which the drug experiences [are] interpreted and controlled."[27]

These rituals and practices even extend to the way the plant is approached, for some psychedelic plants are considered to be dangerous. Folklore says the only safe way to harvest mandrake root is to tie a dog to the plant and make it pull it up; the dog will die soon after.[28] Among the Huichol Indians of Mexico, peyote is not so malevolent but almost as exacting. Since the plant does not grow in the tribe's mountainous home, annual pilgrimages two hundred miles west to the Huichols' sacred land, which they call Wirikuta, must be undertaken to gather the plant. During this pilgrimage, the wayfarers must live like gods themselves, abstaining from sex and taking only minimal amounts of food.[29] One visitor to Christianized members of another Mexican tribe, the Tarahumara, was told to make the sign of the cross in the peyote's presence.[30]

Peyote is the central sacrament of a comparatively recent religious movement among American Indians known as the Native American Church. The plant has long been sacred in Mexico, its native habitat, but it was only in the nineteenth century that a number of North American tribes, resettled in Oklahoma by the U.S. government, came into contact with it. It rapidly became the focus of a new religion with Christian overtones: the ceremony is likened to the Eucharist, the peyote itself to the body of Christ. "God made peyote," an Indian told one anthropologist. "It is His power. Jesus came afterwards on this earth, after peyote. . . . God (through peyote) told the Delawares the same things that Jesus told the whites."[31]

When the federal government tried to ban peyote, the Indians responded by forming the Native American Church in 1918 to protect their rights under the First Amendment. Since then the church and its supporters have managed to overcome various legislative attempts to interfere with their use of the plant.[32]

For the shaman, encounters with the spirits of psychedelic plants is not a matter of recreation or even self-knowledge, but of practical results. These may include weather control, ensuring favorable results in a hunt, and of course healing. The Peruvian *ayahuascero* Don Agustín Rivas-Vasquez reports, "During the healing ceremonies, the spirits would show me a plant, and I would try to remember the shape and color of its leaves and bark. Then I would find that same plant the next day, and I would give it to the patient, and he would be healed."

Rivas-Vasquez even claims to perform psychic surgery: "During the *ayahuasca* ceremony, I can operate on a person's body and cut out the illness with my mind. A young man with tumors in his head came to see me. The doctors wanted to open him up, and I told him I could help him. He had prepared himself with a lot of faith. During the first night of *ayahuasca,* I took the tumors out of his head. . . . After that, he didn't feel the problem."

The shaman cannot become a healer of any repute after only a few sessions with psychedelic plants. As with most forms of shamanism, he or she faces a long and arduous apprenticeship. Rivas-Vasquez says he spent a year in isolation, eating nothing but rice and plantains, and adds that it took "six years of sacrifice" before he could even undergo the "test" to determine whether he could become a shaman.[33]

## AMERICAN INDIAN RELIGION

Shamanic practices the world over pay a great deal of attention to the spirit of place. Though they almost always have some sense of a larger cosmology and theology, shamans also attach great importance to the purely local realm—the flora and fauna, visible and invisible, that are attached to the vicinity in which they find themselves. For Americans, this brings the traditions of American Indian religion to the foreground.[34]

C. G. Jung viewed the psyche as composed of several strata: At the surface is the purely personal, at the bottom the universal forces of the collective unconscious. Between these extremes he saw a racial stratum, as well as a layer connected to the spirit of place. In an obscure 1930 essay entitled "The Complications of American Psychology," he discussed the tension between the ancestral heritage of white Americans and the spirit they have inherited from the land itself.

> The foreign country somehow gets under the skin of those born in it. Certain very primitive tribes are convinced that it is not possible to usurp foreign territory, because children born there would inherit the wrong ancestor-spirits who dwell in the trees, the rocks, and the water of that country. There seems to be some subtle truth in this primitive intuition.
>
> That would mean the spirit of the Indian gets at the American from within and without.[35]

Jung's theory may help explain why the American Indian remains such a source of fascination—even apart from the perpetual allure of the "noble savage" imagined by the French philosopher Jean-Jacques Rousseau.

Indians don't always appreciate this interest. "What's at issue here is the same old question that Europeans have always posed with regard to American Indians," says the well-known Indian activist Russell Means, "whether what's ours isn't somehow theirs. When they wanted our land, they just announced they had a right to it and therefore owned it. Now, being spiritually bankrupt themselves, they want our spirituality as well."[36]

This raises an important issue concerning Native American spirituality. With the possible exception of some ultra-Orthodox Jewish Kabbalists, the seeker can assume that practically every exponent of the traditions we are discussing will be sympathetic to his or her interest. Certain teachers may at the outset seem a bit standoffish, but this is often only a means of winnowing out the idly curious.

With American Indians, this may not be the case. In Means's

words, "Our religions are *ours*. Period. We have very strong reasons for keeping things private, whether you understand them or not. And we have every human right to deny them to you, whether you like it or not."[37]

Indian activists like Means have harsh words for whites who imitate traditional Native rituals like the sweat lodge or the Sun Dance. But they are often even harsher on Indians whom they believe have sold out to the dominant culture. The late Sun Bear, one of the more visible exponents of Native spirituality, often saw his workshops picketed by Indian activists.[38]

Most responsible Native teachers, however, are chiefly interested in the depth of the seeker's interest regardless of ethnicity. Such teachers try to avoid both commercialism and exclusivism. Indian tradition generally forbids selling teachings for a profit (though most medicine men and women will accept an offering in the form of money, food, or tobacco). They also distinguish between teachings that can be widely disseminated and those that cannot. Steve Coyote, a part-Cheyenne writer and counselor, remarks, "Most of the stuff I do I've been given permission to do. There are things I know about I would not do publicly. I don't have permission, or I've been requested not to."[39] And the Western Shoshone spiritual leader Corbin Harney says of the sweat lodge ritual, "We've been bringing white people into the sweat to teach them the true understanding. . . . The rocks, the water, the prayers, and all the herbs that are used are totally secret. . . . I'm just giving the surface of the whole thing—that we use the sweat for sacred things."[40]

Moreover, Native religion has itself been radically affected by its contact with Western civilization, as in the case of the Native American Church, with its use of Christian symbolism in its peyote ritual. Johnny Moses, a well-known teacher among Pacific Northwest Indians, belongs to the Indian Shaker Church, a denomination that represents "a mixture of Christianity and the old Native beliefs."[41]

Most striking of all is the case of Black Elk (1863–1950), the Oglala Sioux medicine man whose memoirs, as recorded by John

G. Neihardt in *Black Elk Speaks*, has become one of the central texts of today's American Indian theological canon.[42] Neihardt fails to mention, however, that Black Elk spent the last forty-six years of his life (including the time he knew Neihardt) as a devout and proselytizing Roman Catholic. One scholar has even linked many motifs in Black Elk's celebrated visions to a missionary teaching device, the "Two Roads Map," that depicts Christian salvation history in graphic form.[43]

Another reason why it may be difficult for non-Natives to entirely understand the religious ways of the Indians is that these teachings do not always lend themselves well to systematic exposition. Their logic is the logic of dreams and myths rather than of the text (except for certain Mesoamerican traditions like that of the Maya, Indians have no sacred written texts that predate the coming of the whites). Anthropologist Gladys A. Reichard notes with some frustration that among the Navajo, several mythic figures, including Coyote, Frog, and Rainboy, are all said to have control over rain. "By this time we may well ask, 'Who *is* in charge of rain?,' for Changing Woman too has charge of female rain and vegetation of all kinds. . . . No particular being is in charge of rain, because one is dependent upon another."[44]

Despite such ambiguities, and despite the fact that each tribe has its own myths and cosmology, we can make some generalizations. "The great mystery is God or the creator," says Johnny Moses. "The love of God moves all things. When we begin to use the love of God, we see the love of God everywhere, in trees, animals, rocks—the same sacred breath." This creator spirit has different names in various traditions: the Cheyenne call him Maheo; the Sioux, Wakan Tanka; the Blackfoot refer to him as "the Old Man."

The creator is not always worshiped. Like Olodumare in Santería, he is sometimes regarded as a *deus otiosus,* or "idle god." A Lakota Sioux speaking around the turn of the century said, "*Wakan Tanka* was the Great Spirit. He was above all spirits. He did nothing. . . . Indians did not know much about him. They invoked only the spirits that were under him."[45] Anthropologist Clark Wissler observed of the Blackfoot, "Whenever the writer asked if the Old Man was ever prayed to, the absurdity of the question provoked merriment. The usual reply was that no one had enough confidence in him to make such an appeal."[46] (Old Man is usually a disagreeable, lecherous character, the subject of off-color stories.)

But for most Indian traditions, the universe is pervaded by a numinous force that is either identical with the Great Spirit or has been created by him. American Indian religion is animistic; that is to say, it sees this numinous force as present not only in all humans, but in all things animate and inanimate. "Our God isn't somewhere up in the clouds," says the well-known medicine man Rolling Thunder. "He's in the trees and the rocks and the four-leggeds [animals]."[47] As Corbin Harney puts it:

> This is the Native way: all of us are related to everything else, to the elements, to all the animal life. We're all connected to the tree life, too—you name it. We're all the same. . . .
>
> We're part of everything here on Earth, and we're part of the moon, sun, and stars. . . . Indian people always pray to all those things so that they keep moving in the right direction, so that they'll keep us nice and clean, and so that we can have a healthier life. . . .
>
> The Native way is to pray for everything.[48]

Unlike most of the world's religions, which consider humanity to be the pinnacle or centerpiece of the divine creation, Indians do not see humans, or for that matter the gods, as having a privileged position in the cosmos. "In Navaho religion no one thing has more absolute significance than another," writes Gladys Reichard. "We may speak of 'high gods' as members of an elaborate pantheon, but Changing Woman or Sun is no more important at a particular moment than the humble roadrunner or a grain of corn."[49]

If all things are indeed pervaded by an omnipresent sacred force, it naturally follows that humans must honor all things, even plants and minerals. Respect is to Native American spirituality what love is to Christianity. A medicine man who decides to harvest sage for use in rites of purification may begin by asking permission of the largest (and hence senior) of the plants he is about to cut. Medicine men even speak to stones they are using in sweat ceremonies, explaining to them why they have been taken and to what use they will be put.

The earth too deserves respect, a consideration that has inspired some Native holy men to publicize their traditions in a way that was formerly deemed unacceptable. "All the living things on this planet of ours, everything has a vision," says Corbin Harney. "Even the planet itself has a vision, and now it's beginning to warn us that something's going to become different pretty quick, if we don't do something about it."[50] Harney attributes his own vocation to spread Indian teachings more widely to this need on the part of the earth, which he, like many in his tradition, blames on environmental depredation.

To some extent ecological issues have enabled—or forced—Indian teachers to move into a more public arena. Like many indigenous people, they view themselves as caretakers of the earth, so the current ecological crisis is of great concern to them. Many indigenous tribes have also directly felt the effects of environmental degradation. Corbin Harney has led protests against underground nuclear testing on Western Shoshone land, while the Cree Indians have fought to keep a hydroelectric dam from being built on their territory in Quebec.[51] Similar issues have affected indigenous peoples around the world; the magazine *Shaman's Drum* runs a regular column, "Earth Circles," specifically devoted to these matters.

Issues like the environment and relations between Indians and white culture will come up for any seeker who makes direct contact with American Indian traditions. Nearly all the teachings we cover in this book are fundamentally apolitical. Though a spiritual path may change one's political attitudes, it usually doesn't determine what these attitudes will be. This is not entirely true for Native American religion: any interest in it on the part of a non-Native will often lead to a political challenge to become involved with Native or environmental causes. Given the grim history of the conflict between whites and Indians over the past five hundred years, this is not surprising, and many who are drawn to these traditions will have no difficulty with becoming involved in this fashion.

## THE SACRED COSMOS

American Indian spirituality must not be mistaken for certain forms of liberal Protestantism in which social activism has more or less displaced religious sentiment. The Indian sense of the sacred is alive and powerful; it is expressed not only in a cosmology but in practices that are intended to help the individual make contact with the divine. There are again many differences among tribal traditions, but the features described below are common to most.

To begin with, there is the image of the circle. "The circle is the emblem of our religion," says Rolling Thunder. "It's in all things that have life. There's no such thing as a straight line. If you shoot a beam of light into space, eventually it will come back." The circle includes "Mother earth and the universe—which also travels in a circle. Everything in life is composed of those circles. That's why we dance in a circle. Our drum is a circle."[52]

The circle, which symbolizes totality, is often divided into four quadrants known as the four directions. Black Elk likens the four ribbons hanging from his pipe to these four sacred quarters: "The black one is for the west where the thunder beings live to send us rain; the white one for the north, whence comes the great white cleansing wind; the red one for the east, whence springs the light and where the morning star lives to give men wisdom; the yellow for the south, whence come the summer and the power to grow."[53]

Because Black Elk's vision has become so influential among both Indians and non-Natives, one will often see these colors attributed to these directions. But there is nothing particularly consistent about them from tribe to tribe; even the number of directions vary.

No matter how it is divided or what colors are assigned to it, this image of the circle with four quadrants evokes associations with the mandalas that held such great significance for Jung as a mystical symbol evoking unity, wholeness, and transcendence. Among the Wichita, this quaternity extends to time as well: the Wichita cosmology speaks of four ages of the universe, which are repeated cyclically.[54]

Another important symbol is the pipe: the Lakota have an elaborate myth of how Wohpe, the Beautiful Woman, gave the pipe to them so that "when the smoke came from the pipe she would be present and hear their prayers and take them to the *Wakan Tanka*" or Great Spirit. The pipe may seem an odd thing to invest with sacred power, but upon reflection it is not so surprising. In nearly all cultures, burning is a way of turning something corporeal, whether incense or a sacrificial offering, into something incorporeal. The offering ascends through the smoke into heaven, where the gods, who are of subtler form than we are, can enjoy it. Tobacco, which Indians revere as the sacred plant *par excellence,* has an added dimension, for the pipe allows humans to partake of the smoke as well. Hence Indians see it as the great symbol of concord; men smoke because "the spirit in the pipe will make their spirits all agree."[55]

Among the most common sacred rituals is the sweat lodge, which, according to Lakota holy man George Sword, "strengthens the ghost" of a human being and "drives away all evil spirits." It is, of course, a rite of purification, but, far more than that, it is a reentry into the primordial womb, symbolizing rebirth. Tom Flanders, an Eastern Cherokee, explains:

> The sweat lodge represents the womb of our true Mother, the Earth. It is a traditional American Indian belief that the Earth is, in fact, the first Mother and we are, therefore, direct descendants of Her. There are many things in the sweat lodge which help to reinforce this relationship. All the elements are present: Water (which is poured on the hot rocks), Fire (which is represented by

the heat in the rocks), Air (which is made visible by the steam), and, most important, Earth (the Lodge itself and the rocks themselves).[56]

The sweat lodge is undertaken among the Lakota before any major endeavor, including a vision quest—itself a preliminary to any great undertaking. According to George Sword, the usual way to pursue a vision is to purify the body in a sweat lodge. Then the seeker proceeds naked, wearing only a robe, to the top of a hill. There he waits without eating, drinking, or speaking to anyone and thinking only of his vision. He will stay there either until a vision comes or until he is sure he will not receive one. If he does have a vision, he will tell of it to the elders. If its meaning is clear, they will advise him what to do; otherwise they will repair to the sweat lodge and contemplate it further until they understand it.[57]

The vision quest, like the pipe and the sweat lodge, appear in the traditions of many tribes. It embodies much of what is most characteristic of American Indian spirituality: the exposure of the individual to the forces of nature and the supernatural; an often severe asceticism; and the underlying assumption that the individual must seek out his or her own inner truth. While medicine men and women can provide help and guidance, ultimately the seeker must confront the spirit powers alone.

From all this it should be clear that while Native spirituality has many features in common with shamanism, it cannot be reduced to shamanism alone. In the end shamanism (as defined by Eliade and his school) is a "technique of ecstasy," whereas the American Indian tradition is a religion.

## WHO CAN BE A SHAMAN?

More than many other traditions, shamanism offers acute difficulties for the modern seeker. In its indigenous context, shamanic initiation is clearly often a long and excruciating process; not everyone will be able to commit to five or ten years in the jungle, studying an enormous pharmacopoeia of herbs and ingesting nauseating hallucinogenic brews. And yet the numbers of self-styled shamans seem to be growing exponentially. Often such teachers offer workshops that sound suspiciously like package tours: join us on a five-day trip to Central America, see the Mayan ruins, and be initiated into an ancient way of knowledge.

Is there a sensible middle course? Some weekend workshops, particularly those that emphasize a straightforward approach to learning the technique of shamanic journeying, can be useful, provided one doesn't believe that this can be equivalent to twenty or thirty years' work in a traditional context. Workshops are merely entrance points; taken with a serious and respectful intent, they can be stepping-stones to greater knowledge, but it would be foolish to pretend that they are more.

What of those who want to go further? Native teachers are difficult to approach, not always because of hostility or suspicion toward outsiders, but sometimes simply because they live in remote areas; they may also, with genuine humility, deny that they know anything.

When dealing with Native American traditions, it is well to remember that indigenous peoples often put much more emphasis on gestures of deference (such as avoiding direct eye contact) than our brash American culture does. However, there is no need to be excessively fawning or obsequious toward Native teachers. In this area it is best to take on the ideals of the Indians themselves: to behave at all times with dignity and respect.

If you should be so lucky as to gain access to a genuine Native teacher—someone who enjoys the respect of his or her own tribe or community—it would be a mistake to expect rapid-fire instruction or instant initiation. The ways of indigenous cultures are, by the hectic standards of our era, extremely slow-moving and far more in accordance with the rhythms of the seasons. You should expect to take a long time—a matter of years rather than weeks or months—to get to know the teacher and the people around him or her. Not only will this give you ample opportunity to gain a clear sense of what they are about, but you will also over the course of time be imparted with a certain indefinable quality that comes with immersion in a tradition. This flavors one's being with a subtle "seasoning" that is far closer to the essence of true initiation than the amassing of facts or credentials.

Books and other forms of written text, while useful in providing preliminary information, are perhaps less to the point with shamanism and indigenous traditions than they are with most of the teachings we have covered. Most of these cultures were not literate; their knowledge was handed down not in written texts or scriptures, but orally, through practice. The heart of shamanism is to penetrate into the mysteries of nature, and by and large the most successful seekers on this path will be those who feel an unmistakable affinity for the ways of the earth.

## SUGGESTED READING

Castaneda, Carlos. *The Teachings of Don Juan: A Yaqui Way of Knowledge.* Berkeley: University of California Press, 1968.

As controversial as it is, Castaneda's has shaped the popular perception of shamanism. This is his first book; he has written a number of others, which are widely available. *The Art of Dreaming* (New York: Harper-Collins, 1993) is a good summary of his ideas on the dream state.

Eliade, Mircea. *Shamanism: Archaic Techniques of Ecstasy.* Princeton: Princeton/Bollingen, 1972.

Extremely dry, Eliade's book also suffers from a certain tendency to overgeneralize. Nonetheless it remains the most authoritative work on shamanism overall.

Elkin, A. P. *Aboriginal Men of High Degree.* Rochester, Vt.: Inner Traditions, 1994.

A readable and intelligent account of shamanic traditions among the Australian aborigines, first published in 1945.

Harner, Michael. *The Way of the Shaman.* New York: Bantam, 1982.

The most accessible and popular how-to text. Contains directions on attaining the shamanic journey similar to those given in Harner's popular workshops.

Lévi-Strauss, Claude. *Tristes Tropiques.* Translated by John and Doreen Weightman. New York: Atheneum, 1974.

This memoir by the great anthropologist contains little on shamanism, but as a meditation on the impact of European cultures on indigenous peoples, it is unsurpassed.

Long, Max Freedom. *The Secret Science behind Miracles.* Los Angeles, Kosmon Press, 1948.

An odd but wonderful work recounting Long's attempt at investigating Huna, the Hawaiian form of shamanism. Other books of his are *The Secret Science at Work* (Marina del Ray, Calif.: DeVorss & Co., 1953) and *Mana* (Cape Girardeau, Mo.: Huna Research, 1981).

Neihardt, John G. *Black Elk Speaks.* 1932. Reprint. Lincoln: University of Nebraska Press, 1988.

The central text of the current revival of American Indian spirituality. It also contains Black Elk's reminiscences of the wars between the Sioux and the U.S. cavalry.

*Shaman's Drum: A Journal of Experiental Shamanism.*

This quarterly journal, published since 1984, provides scholarly but readable accounts of shamanic rites and traditions worldwide.

Walsh, Roger N. *The Spirit of Shamanism.* Los Angeles: Jeremy Tarcher, 1990.

A discussion of shamanism from a cognitive point of view. Particularly useful for its comparison of shamanic ecstasy with other mystical states of consciousness.

## Eight

# THE GOLD OF THE PHILOSOPHERS:
# ALCHEMY AND HERMETICISM

One day the seventeenth-century Flemish scientist Jean-Baptiste van Helmont received a curious visitor to his laboratory. The stranger, who did not identify himself, led Van Helmont into a discussion of alchemy, the mysterious art whose practitioners were said to transmute base metals into gold by means of a substance called the Philosophers' Stone.

Van Helmont said he did not believe in any such thing. The stranger then offered to give his host a piece of the Stone itself. Van Helmont accepted on the condition that he be allowed to conduct his own experiments on it in the stranger's absence. His guest readily agreed, asking nothing in return for the substance; the scientist's conversion, he said, would be reward enough. The stranger left, never to be seen again.

"I saw and handled the Philosophers' Stone," Van Helmont wrote. "It was a saffron-colored powder, very heavy, and it glittered like splinters of glass."

Van Helmont had his assistants melt eight ounces of mercury in a crucible. He then added the powder and sealed the vessel. Fifteen minutes later he opened it and was astounded to find a lump of gold.

In 1666, the Dutch scientist Helvetius had a similar experience.

183

Given the Stone by a stranger, he was able to transmute a piece of lead pipe into gold that an assayer called the finest he had ever seen. Later, when the gold was melted down, mixed with silver, and separated out again, there was more gold than there had been at the beginning. Evidently some of the silver had been transformed by contact with this alchemical gold.[1]

Such stories abound in the literature of that time. We read not only of visits by elusive strangers visiting early scientists, but of such figures as the fifteenth-century French alchemist Nicolas Flamel, who, having learned the secret of the Great Art (as alchemists call their practice), not only amassed a tremendous personal fortune but endowed many churches and hospitals. Another Frenchman, Jacques Coeur, allegedly used his alchemically created wealth to bail out his bankrupt nation after the Hundred Years' War.[2] Alchemists were particularly welcome at the Hapsburg court of Austria in the seventeenth century, where they would commemorate their feats by striking their transmuted gold into elaborate medallions, at least one of which still exists.[3]

Today the word *alchemist* conjures up images of an old man wearing a conical hat emblazoned with astrological symbols, laboring in a darkened room crowded with vessels and retorts to find the nonexistent secret of turning the base into the precious. If we accord any honor to alchemy now, it is as a clumsy precursor of scientific chemistry. Yet others have seen more of an inner side to alchemy. Jung in particular gave much attention to alchemical texts; his difficult late work *Mysterium Coniunctionis*, which many consider his magnum opus, is almost completely devoted to relating alchemical images to the process of individuation.

Jung, however, was principally concerned with the symbolism of alchemy, with its intricate descriptions of green dragons, red lions, and the "union of the sun and the moon." He saw in these old texts a naïve projection of unconscious processes onto matter. Analyzing alchemical texts like dreams, he insisted that "the alchemists did not know what they were writing about."[4]

Whether we side with Jung or with today's chemists, we seem to reach the same conclusion: alchemy is the relic of a simpler age when people believed there were only four elements and barely guessed at the existence of atoms and molecules. Alchemists today are relegated to the same ranks as creationists or flat-earthers—amusing, irritating if they expect to be taken seriously, and doomed to extinction in the Darwinian march of scientific progress.

Even so, we may find ourselves wondering what Van Helmont and Helvetius stumbled onto. It is a matter of experimental fact that gold can be produced in small amounts by the nuclear bombardment of mercury (the two substances stand next to each other in the periodic table, gold with an atomic weight of 79, mercury with a weight of 80).[5] But it seems unlikely that the primitive laboratories of the seventeenth century could have accomplished anything of the kind—and even if they did, what does it matter? Gold may be good for wedding rings, dental crowns, and diversifying portfolios, but it has lost much of its allure; we don't even use it as money anymore. To produce it as the centerpiece of a spiritual search seems both laughable and sacrilegious.

Yet we may be doing the old alchemists an injustice. Their fanciful descriptions of the processes of chemical change may have amounted to more than crude approximations of later science or the spontaneous outpourings of the unconscious. Although, as we have seen, there are hints of the actual transmutation of base metals into gold, there are also indications of a subtler, more profound, and more universal transformation. As the alchemists themselves insisted, "Our gold is not the gold of the vulgar."

Alchemy forms part of a larger current within the Western esoteric traditions known as Hermeticism.[6] At the head of this line stands a remote figure called Hermes Trismegistus, "Hermes Thrice-Greatest." No one knows if he ever walked the face of the earth. Sometimes he is identified with Thoth, the ibis-headed Egyptian god of wisdom, sometimes with Hermes, the Greek messenger of the gods. The cathedral of Siena in Italy has an inlaid floor dating from 1488 that portrays this semidivine being; its legend reads *"Hermes Trismegistus, contemporaneus Moysi"*—"Hermes Trismegistus, contemporary of Moses."

Hermes Trismegistus is a founder-figure not unlike Moses himself. Practically no scholar believes that Moses wrote the books of the Bible attributed to him; they are generally understood to have been composed centuries after he lived. Many writers of earlier times, particularly writers of sacred literature, attributed works to men long dead, partly as an act of humility, partly to confer greater authority upon their writings, partly because they believed they were continuing the founder's heritage.

Such is the case with the body of Greek writings called the *Corpus Hermeticum*, or "Hermetic corpus." When these works first came to Western Europe after the collapse of the Byzantine Empire in 1453, they were believed to be literally as old, and as important, as the books of Moses. The great Florentine patron Cosimo de' Medici even asked the scholar Marsilio Ficino to interrupt his translations of Plato into Latin and translate the Hermetic texts first.

Ficino complied, and for the next two centuries the Hermetic writings enjoyed enormous prestige among the intellectuals of Europe. These years marked the golden age of alchemy, when many of the great alchemical texts were produced and alchemists had easy access to the courts of princes. It was only after 1614, when a scholar named Isaac Casaubon proved that the Hermetic writings dated to the first few centuries after Christ, that these documents fell in esteem.[7]

Though modern scholars still agree with Casaubon's dating, they are of mixed opinions about the sources of the texts. Some say they represent a peculiar admixture of Greco-Roman paganism and philosophy with Jewish and Christian ideas. Others argue that the Hermetic texts reflect ancient Egyptian esoteric ideas that were merely written down in Greek at that time.[8]

This is not as fanciful as it might seem. As early as the third century A.D., the Roman Emperor Diocletian denounced "the old writings of the Egyptians, which treat of the transmutation of gold and silver." The word he used for "transmutation" was *chemia,* a Greek word that is derived from the Egyptian *khem. Khem* (literally, "black")[9] was the Egyptian word for Egypt itself—the "black land" surrounded by the desert—but it has another, more important meaning that takes us to the heart of the alchemical search.

## OSIRIS SLAIN AND REBORN

Lovers of Egyptian mythology will remember the story of Osiris, the divine king who ruled over Egypt in the legendary past until he was slain by his jealous brother Set or Typhon (whose modern-day worshipers we have already encountered with the Temple of Set). Set dismembered his dead brother and cast the parts of his body over the land. After defeating Set in battle, Osiris' son Horus gathered up the pieces of his father's body and, with assistance from his mother, Isis, the goddess of life, brought Osiris back to life.

The meaning of this story has been much disputed. The most common explanation is that Osiris symbolizes the death and rebirth of vegetative life in the cycles of the seasons: Frazer's *Golden Bough*, which examined such myths from all over the world, is the greatest exposition of this point of view. But it is not a new idea. Even in the first century A.D., the historian Plutarch expressed his impatience with the "dull crowd" who said "Osiris is buried when the sown corn is hidden by the earth, and comes to life and shows himself again when it begins to sprout."[10]

A small detail in the myth, however, may open a window onto another perspective. Plutarch wrote further that according to the Egyptians, "Typhon was red-skinned, Horus white, and Osiris black."[11] The description is particularly intriguing if one realizes that the three main stages of alchemical transformation are *nigredo* or "blackening," *albedo* or "whitening," and *rubedo* or "reddening." Even more crucially, the process that the divine Osiris undergoes is the same one that is summed up in the central precept of alchemy: *solve et coagula,* "dissolve" and "coagulate." Is the myth of Osiris attempting to reveal something about alchemical transformation? And if so, what does it say about human transformation?

Alchemical terms are symbolic: they point to a deeper meaning than appears on the surface. Usually this is explained by saying that the secrets of the art must be kept hidden from the vulgar. But this is only part of the reason. The alchemists speak in these allusive terms principally because ordinary language cannot express what they are trying to say. The alchemists carve up reality differently from the customary way, and unless one tries to see things from their perspective, their writings will seem impenetrable or even ridiculous.

## SOL AND LUNA

The Hermetic arts speak of two fundamental principles called *sol* and *luna*. The epithets applied to them are numerous and confusing: *sol* is Sun, gold, heaven, light; *luna* is Moon, silver, water, stone, ocean, night, and much more. Baron Julius Evola (1898–1974), an Italian esotericist who discusses alchemy in his book *The Hermetic Tradition*, says such strings of words "are symbols in the hermetic cipher language that refer, often in the same passage, to one continuous object and thereby create an enormous difficulty for the inexperienced reader."[12]

Evola goes on to quote Cornelius Agrippa: "No one can excel in the alchemical art without knowing these principles *in himself;* and the greater knowledge of self, the greater will be the magnetic power attained thereby and the greater the wonders to be realized."[13] Evola himself explained these principles "in ourselves" as follows:

> We can say that in general the Sun is "form" and the power of individuation, while the Moon—which preserves the archaic Mother and Woman symbols—expresses the "material" and universal; to the undifferentiated vitality, to the cosmic spirit or the ether-light, corresponds the feminine.[14]

To simplify, one could say that *sol,* the Sun, gold, represents the principle of consciousness, that which experiences—the "I." The

Theosophist Annie Besant calls this the Self, the Knower, "that conscious, feeling, ever-existing One that in each of us knows himself as existing."[15]

*Luna,* on the other hand, is a name for that which *is experienced.* The Greeks called it *hyle.* This word is usually translated as "matter," but it seems more to resemble Éliphas Lévi's astral light—an ethereal substance that has no form of its own but can take on the shapes of specific things.

Experience has no qualities in a pure state. We never just experience; rather, we experience *something,* and we experience it *as* something,—a specific object. In alchemical terms this is matter in its fixed state, or "lead." It is associated with the color black, which connotes ultimate darkness, passivity, receptiveness. Similarly, when we experience the world in an ordinary state of consciousness, it is radically external to us. Objects are dead, lifeless, without any inner vitality or consciousness of their own.

If so, then Hermeticism could have to do with transmuting the "lead" of ordinary experience into the "gold" of consciousness. Alchemists say you have to have gold in order to make gold. This would mean that you have to use what consciousness you already have to create more consciousness.

To have an experiential glimpse of these ideas, look around the room you are in and take in the things you see. Probably your first impulse will be to see them as familiar, obvious, or drab: a table, a book, a chair, and so on. This is matter in its fixed state— "lead."

Now look around you again, and as much as possible try to forget that you know what these things are or have seen them before. In fact you haven't: even if you know the room well, you have never seen them as they are *now.* Try to experience them as they are in the moment, without any labels or associations.

If you make an effort to see things this way, you may find that the quality of your experience, even the atmosphere of the room, changes slightly. You may start to see things, not so much as distinct objects, but as patches of light and color. Reality may start to have a more fluid quality, reflecting your own shift in consciousness. This may be like what the alchemists meant when they spoke of *luna*.

Persisting long enough in this exercise, you may notice that these ordinary objects begin to manifest a certain vividness and dynamism. You may even find yourself with the odd impression that *they are watching you*. That is to say, there seems to be some innate—but usually hidden—"knowing" quality even in inanimate objects that is evoked by your own shift in consciousness.[16] This may correspond to the alchemists' *sol* or "gold."

## STAGES OF ASCENT

The alchemical process, then, can be seen as an elaborate allegory of the descent of consciousness into matter and its return to its pristine state. Another version of this idea, in the Western magical tradition, sees the world as being surrounded by the concentric spheres of the seven planets. The light of God descends through each of these until it reaches earth. If we also remember that each of these planets is associated with a metal (see p. 114–115), we will have an exact representation of the Hermetic worldview. (In fact Hermeticism is the source of the theory of correspondences.) The metals represent various aspects of consciousness as it both descends from and ascends to God.

A Zoroastrian myth elucidates this idea. Ahriman, the principle of evil, succeeds in slaying the primordial man, Gayomart. As he falls into the state of conditioned reality, seven metals issue from his body, like white light passing through a prism and then differentiated into the seven colors of the spectrum.[17]

Each metal represents some aspect of life or consciousness. Mercury symbolizes the means by which the mind mediates between the knower and the known. Mercury, or quicksilver, is what we have in our thermometers: changing shape, it tells us the temperature. Similarly our sense-perceptions "change their shape" to reflect the world around us. Copper, the metal of Venus, the goddess of love and sex, is known for its ability to conduct the vital force of electricity; instead of rusting, it turns green with verdigris, recalling the vegetative world. And every cook knows that copper bowls are particularly good for mixing eggs. But gold is preeminent among the metals: impervious to rust and tarnish, it "outshines the splendors of mortal wealth," in the words of the poet Pindar.

The alchemical texts depict the ascent of consciousness as a series of changes in color of the material the alchemist works on. In keeping with the axiom *solve et coagula,* "dissolve and coagulate," the process entails a series of dissolutions followed by reconstitutions—a constant purification.

The first stage, *nigredo,* or blackness, is thus a descent. Consciousness plunges into matter, embracing a bondage to form and materiality. At this stage the "I" experiences desire, which distracts it and pulls it in many directions. Hence alchemists regard the *nigredo* as a corruption or dissolution not unlike the death and dismemberment of Osiris. The process is summed up in the word *vitriol,* which alchemists read acrostically as *Visita interiora terrae; rectificando invenies occultum lapidem:* "Visit the depths of the earth; by purifying you will find the hidden stone."[18] Vitriol, of course, is known for its corrosive properties.

To realize the truth of this death and dismemberment brings about the second stage in the alchemical process: whiteness, or *albedo*—the triumph of purity, the freedom from desire. Julius Evola suggests that this transformation can be accomplished in two opposite ways. There is the familiar means of asceticism (also associated with Mars and iron, suggesting struggle and discipline), which is the conquest of desire. But there is also the method of embracing passion, especially sexual passion, and transmuting it into a higher energy. A number of teachings the world over, including Tantrism and Taoism in Asia, promote this idea, but few people seem to know what it really involves. Evola bluntly warns, "This is an extremely dangerous path!"[19]

The stage of *albedo* imparts immortality. Alchemy, like certain other esoteric teachings, does not seem to regard immortality as a human birthright; rather it is something that can be attained only

by dint of almost unimaginable strivings. At the white stage the alchemist achieves this condition: "The 'white stone' having been
obtained," says Evola, "the preservation of consciousness stops depending on the ordinary body state and its continuity can maintain itself in states and modes of existence that no longer
participate in the material world."[20]

Finally there is *rubedo,* or reddening. If white is associated with
purity, the red stage adds or discloses another characteristic of the
transformed consciousness: warmth, ardor, life. Evola characterizes
it as the "return to earth"—if consciousness must first be corrupted and purified, it must in the end return to make contact
with the earth.

This is a rough schematic view of the process of alchemical
transformation. Other stages are mentioned, sometimes as many as
seven.[21] The most common of these, *xanthosis* or yellowing, which
occurs after (or sometimes before) the *rubedo,* emphasizes illumination or gnosis. But many alchemical texts do not mention the
*xanthosis.* There are many enigmas and ambiguities in the texts,
and without instruction by one who already knows, the aspirant is likely to go astray (the theme of many warnings in the
literature).

In essence, alchemy has to do with the liberation and transformation of consciousness. But it is a transformation of a very specific kind. One might say that *the gold of the alchemists is the body of
resurrection.*[22]

The achievement of the "resurrection body" of alchemy resembles divinization or *theosis* as understood in esoteric Christianity. (This is not surprising, for the Christian tradition owes more to
ancient Egypt than it admits.) This "resurrection body," achieved
only after superhuman discipline, seems to consist of a heightened
consciousness, an "I" that includes the whole of one's being, physical, mental, and emotional. It is also possessed of certain properties
that human beings typically do not possess—notably immortality.

If this is so, it helps explain why the alchemists say "our gold is
not the gold of the vulgar." It also suggests why one cannot

achieve the Hermetic Great Work (as this great transformation is called) without being free from greed. Only an idiot, given the choice between enlightenment and immortality on the one hand and material wealth on the other, would choose the latter.

What techniques make such inner transformation possible? Practices such as meditation and breathing exercises have probably played a part; there are also suggestions that, as in Chinese alchemy, the sublimation of sexual energies is employed.[23] But another thread occasionally surfaces in the literature, involving a practice that very likely goes back to the ancient Egyptians, though it has acquired a new name in the modern world: *proprioception,* or the sensation of one's own body.

Egyptian sacred texts contain allusions to such practices. The *Papyrus of Nu* suggests that one meditation might have had to do with connecting the individual parts of the body with different gods:

> *My hair is the hair of Nu.*
> *My face is the face of the Disk.*
> *My ears are the ear of Ap-uat.*
> *My nose is the nose of Khentikas. . . .*
> *My backbone is the backbone of Suti.*
> *My phallus is the phallus of Osiris. . . .*[24]

The *Egyptian Book of the Dead* includes the following passage:

> He counts his bones. He assembles his members. He turns his face toward Amentet, the beautiful West. He comes renewed, reborn every day, for this is his image, a body of gold carrying the light of Light.[25]

Specific techniques of proprioception, of conscious sensing of the body, are still taught today in various esoteric schools, some of which trace their teachings back to Egypt itself.[26]

## LAB WORK

Nothing of what we have said up to this point accounts for the literal claims made by alchemy. The stories of Helvetius and Van Helmont suggest that alchemists believed they could actually turn base metals into gold. So it would be a mistake to think that the Great Work is entirely a metaphor for the construction of an indestructible body of light. Rather the alchemist seems to undergo a dual process: what he or she must undergo symbolically within must also be carried out literally in the laboratory.[27]

Again, this process cannot be reduced to scientific chemistry, however crude, for it is not merely a matter of technique and replicable results: the internal state of the experimenter, far from being irrelevant to the undertaking, is its most vital aspect. François Trojani, one of the foremost practitioners of the art in France today, observes, "The history of alchemy has shown that innocence and simplicity may succeed where the most sophisticated abilities fail."[28]

Some information is available about the transformation that takes place in the laboratory, although it is often very difficult to understand what the alchemists are saying. Even the material one starts with, called the *materia prima,* is spoken of in cryptic terms. "It is indeed veritably a stone," says the early twentieth-century alchemist Fulcanelli, "because it presents, when out of the mine, the same outward characteristics that are common to all ores."[29]

From this hint one might suspect that the material is an ore. This is confirmed by a work called the *Collectanea Chemica*, which says: "We can no longer be silent concerning the seed of metals, but declare that it is contained in the ores of metals, as wheat is in the grain." The author chides those who start with refined metals, "herein acting as foolishly as if a man should sow bread and expect corn from it, or *from an egg which is boiled hope to produce a chicken.*"[30]

From this ore—the ore of lead is said to be the easiest to work with—the alchemist seeks to obtain "mercury." This is not ordinary quicksilver but the "seed of metal," which "contains in it a seminal quality whose perfect ripeness is only in gold; in the other metals it is crude, like fruits which are yet green."[31] One might say that it is to metals what the life force or *prana* is to living creatures, for the Hermeticists have never drawn a sharp line between the animate and inanimate.

This "mercury" is one member of the primordial alchemical trinity; the other two are "sulfur" and "salt." None of these are the familiar versions of these substances; rather they are more like forces or principles. *Sulfur* has to do with all that is quintessentially active; *salt,* with what is inert or passive; and *mercury,* the "volatile force," is that which mediates between them.[32]

Having found the *materia prima,* the alchemist then must prepare the "secret fire" or "natural fire," paradoxically described as "a dry water that does not wet the hands, and as "a fire burning without flames."[33] This "secret fire" is then mixed with the *materia prima,* moistened with spring dew, and placed in a hermetically sealed vessel called the "Philosophical Egg." The "Egg" is then heated very slowly in the alchemist's furnace, or *athanor,* designed to provide a constant amount of heat for a long period of time.

The stages of transformation are those we have already encountered. The combined materials first disintegrate and turn "blacker than black," and this phase, the *nigredo,* is the first sign the alchemist is on the right track. One Hermetic aphorism says, "No generation without corruption."

Eventually the end of the *nigredo* is signaled by the appearance of a starry pattern on the surface of the material, which is likened to the Star of Bethlehem that heralded the birth of Christ. Then there appears "the metallic, volatile humidity which is known as the Mercury of the Wise."

This volatile mercury rushes through the egg like a wind until it begins to settle on the solid residue, the "New Earth." At this point the alchemist turns up the heat in the athanor, and a pattern of beautiful colors appears, in a phase known as the *cauda pavonis,* or Peacock's Tail.

After this comes the *albedo,* or whitening. Just as the alchemist himself at this stage is thought to have overcome death, the substance now has enough strength to resist the fire—presumably meaning it can no longer be ruined by overheating—and a white substance, the Sulfur of the Wise, appears.

The third stage begins with the "chemical marriage" of the alchemical king and queen, the sulfur and the mercury; from their union arises either the Philosopher's Stone or gold itself. This is the *rubedo* or "reddening." Remember from Van Helmont's testimony that the Philosopher's Stone was the color of saffron. Saffron, of course, is a reddish substance that, when used in cooking or as a dye, turns things the color of gold. Moreover, good-quality gold often has a ruddy tinge.

There are many obscurities in these details, and the identity of the various substances remains a mystery. Are they anything like materials we might recognize? Or do they exist only in the sealed vessel of the Hermeticist, like those curious elements at the end of the periodic table that are artificially created in physics labs and last for only a few microseconds? We cannot say. But however fanciful or paradoxical the images produced by the alchemists may seem, we cannot write them off as mere symbols. They have always been understood as corresponding to something real that takes place in a laboratory.

## THE PURPOSE OF ALCHEMY

The work of the alchemist is never easy. One twentieth-century practitioner, Eugène Canseliet, admitted that after fifty years he had only been able to try the third stage of transformation (presumably the *rubedo*) four times, and had failed each time. "One must wait and deserve the great miracle," he said, "to hold oneself ready, each spring, to utilize the unforeseeable week of weeks—*hebdomas hebdomadum*—when, exceptionally, the work of man and that of Nature shall meet."[34]

Canseliet here alludes to yet another demand the alchemist must face. For the intricate correspondences that prevail between the higher and lower worlds requires that the work be begun only in the spring, under the signs of Aries, Taurus, or Gemini (Aries is reckoned most auspicious). Indeed the alchemist should cast a horoscope to determine the most favorable time.[35]

Similar strictures govern the gathering of the *materia prima,* even the spring dew used in the mixture. The process is so rigorous that anyone reading about it is likely to ask, "Why go through all this trouble?" If it were merely a matter of making money, one could do it more easily and reliably on the stock market or by real-estate speculation. But money is not the object. As we have seen, greed is a disqualification for the Great Work. So what is its purpose?

One of the central doctrines of Hermeticism is that of living nature. Certainly everyone agrees that plants and animals possess some vital principle like the one that operates in us. Hermeticism goes further, for it teaches that the inanimate world too is endowed with life.[36] It is the alchemist's task to nourish and propagate this life, even in metal. His purpose is "to unite his soul so intimately with that of the metals that he could remind them that they are in God, that is, that they are gold"—the most perfect of metals, which possesses the most spiritual light.[37]

This work resembles the transformation that Christians believe takes place in the Eucharist. Just as the ordinary materials of bread and wine are changed into the body and blood of Christ, so base metals become precious and incorruptible through alchemy. "Copper, because of its nature, can become silver, and silver, by its nature, can become gold: so neither one nor the other stops nor pauses until this identity is realized," writes the Christian mystic Meister Eckhart.[38]

The Hermetic path thus has a slightly different view of the familiar teaching of the Fall. Hermeticists do not so much see man as the creature in need of redemption, but rather as the redeemer of the light of consciousness that has become trapped in the darkness of matter.

Such an act would, of course, require great purity on the redeemer's part. And few can live up to such a heroic task, which helps explain why alchemy is such a mysterious and rarefied path.

Even among those who seriously undertake it, those who actually accomplish the Great Work seem to be few. This may be a matter of the impurities that may remain in the practitioner, or it may be dictated by the logic of the times: "The alchemist could transmute every 'imperfect metal'," writes one contemporary authority, "but he did it only rarely, for as a saint, he knew that the time for cosmic transfiguration had not yet come." And if he were not a saint, he would not be able to transform gold at all.[39]

Nonetheless alchemical techniques have been applied to an enormous number of ends and enterprises, ranging from the distillation of brandy to the making of fertilizer. What they have in common with the most familiar types of alchemy are analogous processes and similar symbols. The central idea that gives rise to all these manifold forms of activity is the notion that nature is alive, that it has an inner intelligence that can be cultivated by the wise.

## ALCHEMY TODAY

Alchemy is a tradition to which it is often difficult to gain access. There are certainly more practitioners of the art than are generally recognized, but they are notoriously secretive. They are probably more numerous in Europe, where a continuous Hermetic tradition has persisted since the Renaissance, than in the United States.

One of the few public schools of the Hermetic arts was maintained for a number of years in Salt Lake City, Utah, by Albert Riedel (who styled himself Frater Albertus). Students at his Paracelsus Research Society would learn such arts as the making of a "plant stone," a stonelike matter derived from a plant or herb and believed to have curative powers.[40] Experience with the vegetable world, he asserted, would make it easier to undertake the more laborious work with metals later on.

Frater Albertus died in 1984, and his organization did not survive him, but various students of his continue to work independently in the U.S. and abroad. There are also other groups, more or less public, that teach a version of alchemy, including an organization headquartered in France, Les Philosophes de Nature, which offers a seven-year training course in laboratory alchemy.

For the most part, however, alchemy tends to be a solitary path. François Trojani advises:

> Learning about alchemy is very much a path of reading and studying. It not only includes study of the alchemical corpus, but of other types of Hermetic subjects, as well as comparative studies of philosophy and religion. It is not a discipline for those who don't love research, at least not in our era. . . .
>
> When the time is right, you will begin laboratory work in your own way, perhaps with an appropriate guide. At a certain point, I would recommend some courses in beginning chemistry, with emphasis on simple, practical lab techniques such as mixing, melting, and distilling.

Trojani also recommends that serious students learn Latin, as many alchemical texts have never been translated into modern languages.[41]

## THE ELUSIVE TAROT

There remains one corner of the Hermetic tradition that needs to be discussed—if indeed it is Hermetic. This is the Tarot, a deck of seventy-eight cards that is believed to embody all the wisdom of ancient Egypt in its cryptic figures. This idea comes from the eighteenth-century savant Antoine Court de Gébelin, who claimed that Egyptian priests had created the deck to preserve their knowledge. By disguising it in the form of an innocuous card game, they hoped to spare it from the destruction visited upon their libraries.[42]

There is no direct evidence to support this claim. Though it has become a cliché that "the origins of the Tarot are shrouded in mystery," it is nevertheless true.

The first surviving Tarot decks come not from Egypt but from

Italy, where in the mid-fifteenth century it was the fashion among noble families to have elaborate hand-painted decks of cards for playing *tarocchi* (*Tarot* is a French form of this word). *Tarocchi,* which is still played on the European continent, is basically a trick-taking game not unlike bridge. Unlike bridge, however, it is not played with an ordinary deck. Instead the Tarot deck has, in addition to four regular suits, a permanent set of twenty-two trumps. It is these trumps that have attracted the particular attention of occultists, who refer to them as the Major Arcana (the Minor Arcana are the four suits that resemble those of ordinary playing cards).

As scholars have shown, there is little evidence that the *tarocchi* or Tarot cards were used for esoteric purposes before Court de Gébelin published his theory in 1781.[43] There is even little to suggest that they—or any other playing cards—were used for fortune-telling before then: one of the earliest written references to cartomancy appears, oddly enough, in the memoirs of Casanova, who offhandedly remarks that a Russian serf girl he had bought in 1765 was much given to this practice.[44]

Since there is no evidence for the existence of the cards themselves before around 1450, an Egyptian source would seem unlikely. Yet we can't say there was no esoteric intent in their creation; given the intense interest in esotericism in fifteenth-century Italy, there probably was. There is also the indirect testimony of the Tarocchi di Mantegna, a similar type of deck that has fifty trumps, going from the lowest (called *Misero,* "The Beggar," and identical to the Fool) to the highest (*Prima Causa* or "First Cause") and taking in the nine Muses, the liberal arts, the planets, and various mythological figures in between.[45] This type of deck seems to embody a much more obviously esoteric system. If so, it may be an expanded version of the familiar Tarot, since it appears to have arisen slightly later.

One solution that would explain both the known facts about the Tarot and the legend of an Egyptian source is simply this: As we shall see in more detail in chapter 11, esoteric schools do sometimes trace their origins to remote antiquity; for example, a twentieth-century Italian esotericist named Arturo Reghini belonged to a school that claimed to go back to the philosopher Pythagoras in the sixth century B.C.[46] We can almost never say whether these claims have any truth to them, since we are usually dealing with societies that have kept themselves secret for centuries, but it is not implausible to suppose that the Tarot was created by esotericists in the Italian Renaissance who traced their spiritual lineage back to Egypt.[47]

Whether the Tarot was created by a school of adepts or by a gamesmaster trying to amuse bored aristocrats, its power cannot be denied. Figures like the Fool, the Magician, the Hanged Man, and the World seem to address depths in the mind like characters in a dream. The Tarot's unwearying allure is apparent from the thousands of different types of decks created, ranging from the splendid gilt versions done for the Visconti-Sforzas to the most whimsical recent creations. Today one can find Hawaiian, Japanese, and Mayan Tarots; the Daughters of the Moon Tarot (a women's deck with round cards); the Tarot of the Cat People; a Tobacco Tarot; and even a scratch-'n'-sniff deck (the Devil, symbolizing temptation, has the scent of chocolate).[48]

In the two centuries since Court de Gébelin, occultists have devoted much attention to understanding the Tarot's haunting images. At the end of his *Dogme et rituel de la haute magie*, Éliphas Lévi reveals the "universal key" of "the book of Hermes":

> Among the ancients the use of this key was permitted to none but the high priests, and even so its secret was confided only to the flower of initiates, Now, this was the key in question: (1) a hieroglyphic and numeral alphabet, expressing by characters and numbers a series of universal and absolute ideas; (2) a scale of ten numbers, multiplied by four symbols and connected with twelve figures representing the twelve signs of the zodiac; (3) plus the four *genii* of the cardinal points.[49]

Anyone familiar with the Tarot will recognize its structure here: the twenty-two Major Arcana are the "hieroglyphic alpha-

bet," and the "scale of ten numbers multiplied by four" is the
Minor Arcana, with its four suits of ten cards each. (Each suit
also has four court cards each: the King, Queen, Knight, and
Page.) "The four *genii* of the cardinal points" evidently refers to
the four elements associated with each suit: fire, symbolized by
wands; air, symbolized by coins; water, by cups, and earth, by
swords.[50]

Lévi also connected the twenty-two Tarot trumps with the
twenty-two letters of the Hebrew alphabet. The Hebrew letters,
like Egyptian hieroglyphs, were originally derived from represen-
tations of familiar things. *Gimel,* the third letter, is said by some
Kabbalists to mean "harvest": Lévi connects it with the Empress,
the third Tarot trump, which symbolizes "plenitude, fecundity, Nature." *Zayin,* the seventh letter, means "sword" and is linked to the
Chariot, the seventh card, "weapon, sword, . . . triumph, royalty,
priesthood." Lévi places the unnumbered Fool card, seemingly ar-
bitrarily, between the twentieth and the twenty-first trumps; associated with the letter *shin,* it means "the sensitive principle, flesh,
eternal life." *Shin* means "tooth," and the card shows the Fool being bitten by a dog.[51]

Since there are also twenty-two paths connecting the *sefirot* of
the Kabbalistic Tree, on which the Hebrew letters are placed, it's
natural to associate the Tarot cards with the paths of the Tree as
well. (Lévi was the first explicitly to connect the Tarot with the
Kabbalah, though again it is quite possible that these links existed
long before his time.) Unfortunately there is no universally accepted system of attributing Tarot cards to the paths of the Tree.
The Golden Dawn's version is the most widespread, but not necessarily the most authoritative. Occult writers tend to extricate
themselves from this problem by saying, "The *sefirot* are objective,
the paths subjective."

In Western occultism, the arcana of the Tarot form part of a
great system of symbols that, if mastered, is intended to to unlock
certain dimensions of the mind and lead the student toward illumination. Valentin Tomberg, author of the profound and subtle
*Meditations on the Tarot,* explains:

The Major Arcana of the Tarot are authentic symbols. They conceal and reveal their sense at one and the same time according to the depth of meditation. That which they reveal are not *secrets,* i.e. things hidden by human will, but are *arcana,* which is something quite different. An arcanum is that which it is necessary to "know" in order to be fruitful in a given domain of spiritual life. . . . An arcanum is a "ferment" or an "enzyme" whose presence stimulates the spiritual and the psychic life of man.[52]

To view them from another perspective, one could say that the Major Arcana form a concise index of the Jungian archetypes of the collective unconscious. And there are few, if any, major archetypes that do not appear in some form in the Tarot: the shadow can be seen in the Devil; the anima in the Empress or the High Priestess; the Self in the Wheel of Fortune or the World. One use for these images is, as suggested above, to contemplate them, integrating them more completely into the psyche.

By far the most familiar use for the Tarot is for divination. Magicians and occultists often consider this purpose to be somewhat inferior to contemplation, but most people who take up the Tarot probably first employ it for this purpose.

The basic method of reading Tarot is simply to shuffle the cards while concentrating on a question and then to lay them out in a given pattern. The most popular spread is known as the Celtic Cross, where six cards are laid out in a cross around a "significator" (a court card chosen to represent the querent); four others, which comment further on the situation, are then set out to the right. But there are other spreads as well, including one based on the Kabbalistic Tree.

To be an adroit Tarot reader, one should ideally have memorized the meanings of the cards—no small feat considering that each card has two meanings depending on whether it is upright or reversed (unlike conventional playing cards, Tarot cards are not horizontally symmetrical). This fact helps explain the great popularity of what is known as the Rider-Waite deck in the English-speaking world.

The Rider-Waite deck was designed by the occultist A.E. Waite and executed by the visionary artist Pamela Colman Smith—both members of the Golden Dawn—in 1909. (The name "Rider" comes from its first publisher, the London firm of Rider & Co.) It differs from most other decks in depicting an image on each of the Minor Arcana that indicates its meaning, making divinatory readings far easier than with most decks. The Three of Wands, for example, shows a wealthy merchant looking out over his ships; in a divination this indicates prosperity. The Four of Swords shows a knight entombed in a crypt, indicating a deathlike standstill; the Ten of Cups displays a family rejoicing in good fortune.

This helpful feature did not originate with the Rider-Waite deck; in fact several of its images are taken directly from a late fifteenth-century Italian deck called the Sola-Busca Tarot.[53] But the Sola-Busca deck has not survived in complete form, and most Tarots since then have been content simply to depict, say, four swords or ten cups in some kind of symmetrical pattern.

Among French occultists, the Tarot of Marseilles has the highest authority, chiefly because the deck has predominated in France, and indeed on the rest of the Continent apart from Italy, since the eighteenth century.[54] Unlike the Rider-Waite deck, with its Pre-Raphaelite flavor, the Tarot of Marseilles is crude in execution, its style falling somewhere between medieval woodblocks and the stylized forms of modern playing-cards. Many writers, however, including the author of *Meditations on the Tarot*, regard this deck as the most authentic.

Divination and contemplation do not exclude each other; in some ways they are complementary. In the past, divination tended to be seen as more or less deterministic: the prediction foretold what would happen. Whether from increasing psychological sophistication or reluctance to commit themselves, modern occultists have turned away from such fatalism. A Tarot layout is not necessarily seen as a forecast but rather as suggesting what principles are at play and how the querent might understand the situation and proceed. Since these principles are regarded as operating in oneself foremost, a proper understanding of divinatory messages becomes a means of self-knowledge. As two contemporary authorities put it, "For when we know ourselves, and why we do the things we do, we can begin the process of deliberate change, using the Tarot images to help us move into new ways of being."[55]

## SUGGESTED READING

Burckhardt, Titus. *Alchemy.* Baltimore, Md.: Penguin, 1971.

A concise if somewhat abstract discussion of the basic cosmological teachings of Hermeticism.

Copenhaver, Brian P. *Hermetica: The Greek Hermetica and the Latin Asclepius in a New English Translation with Notes and Introduction.* Cambridge: Cambridge University Press, 1992.

No completely satisfactory edition of the *Corpus Hermeticum* is available; Copenhaver's is probably the best. Walter Scott's old edition, *Hermetica: The Ancient Greek and Latin Writings Which Contain Religious or Philosophical Teachings Ascribed to Hermes Trismegistus* (1924; reprint, Boston: Shambhala, 1985) takes considerable liberties with the texts, but does provide the original Greek and Latin.

Evola, Julius. *The Hermetic Tradition: Symbols and Teachings of the Royal Art.* Translated by E. E. Rehmus. Rochester, Vt.: Inner Traditions, 1995.

Probably the best discussion of alchemy as a mystical path.

Frater Albertus. *The Alchemist's Handbook.* New York: Samuel Weiser, 1960.

By far the most lucid guide to practical alchemy. Includes instructions on making "plant stones."

Klossowski de Rola, Stanislas. *Alchemy: The Secret Art* London: Thames & Hudson, 1973.

This engaging volume is chiefly composed of alchemical illustrations, but the author's introduction is useful as well.

Mead, G. R. S. *Thrice-Greatest Hermes: Studies in Hellenistic Theosophy and Gnosis.* 1906. Reprint. York Beach, Maine: Samuel Weiser, 1992.

Mead's work, though nearly a century old, still contains much valuable material, including ancient sources. Mead, himself a Theosophist, had more innate respect for the material he discusses than many mainstream scholars display.

Papus [Gérard Encausse]. *The Tarot of the Bohemians*. Translated by A. P. Morton. London: Chapman & Hall, 1892.

The most influential of all explications of the Tarot as a mystical system, it begins where Éliphas Lévi's works leave off. It has been reprinted often.

*Paracelsus: Selected Writings*. Edited by Jolande Jacobi. Princeton: Princeton/Bollingen, 1951.

A readable anthology of the writings of the most famous of the Renaissance alchemists.

[Tomberg, Valentin.] *Meditations on the Tarot: A Journey into Christian Hermeticism*. Translated by Robert A. Powell. Warwick, N.Y.: Amity House, 1985.

At the author's request, this dense but profound exploration into the mystical Tarot was published posthumously and anonymously. Unquestionably the greatest book on the Tarot.

*Nine*

# THE WAY OF THE SLY MAN:
# THE TEACHINGS OF
# G. I. GURDJIEFF

It has happened to everyone. You go into a room only to find you have no recollection of why you went there; someone reminds you of a promise you made but have completely forgotten; or you realize you've set down your keys but can't remember where. Nor are such cases always matters of failure: sometimes you discover that you have done a perfectly good job of making coffee or writing a check even though you have no memory of it.

We usually take these harmless instances of forgetting for granted; certainly it's hard to believe that they can tell us anything important about the human condition. But according to George Ivanovich Gurdjieff, they point to the heart of our predicament.

Long before the twentieth century's discovery of the unconscious, people have always known there are unseen parts to themselves. "I cannot totally grasp all that I am," wrote St. Augustine in the fifth century A.D. "For that darkness is lamentable in which the possibilities in me are hidden from myself: so that my mind, questioning itself upon its own powers, feels that it cannot rightly trust its own report."[1]

Gurdjieff would have agreed. Indeed he insisted that we are not awake even in the so-called waking state, but go about our lives in a hypnotic stupor. "It may surprise you," he said, "if I say that the chief feature of a modern man's being which *explains everything else that is lacking in him* is *sleep*. A modern man lives in sleep, in sleep he is born and in sleep he dies."[2]

## SLEEP AND KUNDALINI

Of all the figures discussed in this book, Gurdjieff is the most thoroughly misunderstood. Many writers dismiss him as a fraud or a trickster, yet few have bothered to acquaint themselves with his ideas in any but the most superficial way.

It is true that Gurdjieff made himself more than a bit mysterious. Even his birth year is questionable. One of his numerous passports listed the date as 1877; his most recent biographer, James Moore, offers an intelligent argument for 1866, but even this is not decisive.[3] Gurdjieff's birthplace can be fairly well established as Alexandropol, a small town on the Russo-Turkish border. His father was Greek, his mother Armenian.

This much can be said. But for the rest of the first forty-seven years (more or less) of Gurdjieff's life, we have no other authority than his own writings, particularly the autobiographical *Meetings with Remarkable Men*. As entertaining and profound as it is, this book is intended not as a comprehensive record but as a means of acquainting the reader "with the material required for a new creation and to prove the soundness and good quality of it."[4] As such it leaves many questions unanswered about Gurdjieff's early life. Even serious scholars have used speculation, rumor, and sheer fiction to fill the gap.

The most intriguing—and most believable—part of Gurdjieff's legend is one he fostered himself: that he began at an early age to search for some deeper truth about humanity and the universe. Along with a small band of fellow seekers, he eventually made his way to an esoteric school in Central Asia called the Sarmoung Brotherhood and there learned the secrets that he would later impart to his students.[5]

Where this brotherhood was, or even if it really existed, has never been verified. Nor do we have any clear picture of Gurdjieff's companions in his search. Gurdjieff did his best to cover his tracks, and to a large extent he succeeded. The first conclusive evidence we have of his whereabouts is in Moscow around 1914, where he began to teach the system for which he is now renowned. (Gurdjieff's disciples refer to his teaching as "the Work"; those attempting to follow it are said to be "in the Work.")

In 1915 in St. Petersburg, Gurdjieff met his most famous student, the man who, more than Gurdjieff himself, would become the most widely read exponent of his teaching: Piotr Demianovich Ouspensky (1878–1947). Ouspensky, a journalist preoccupied with the nature of the universe, had already published a book entitled *Tertium Organum* offering "a key to the enigmas of the world." (An exploration of the fourth dimension, it bears some resemblance to those ideas in Edwin Abbott's classic *Flatland*.) Nonetheless Ouspensky knew he had more to learn, having just returned from an unsuccessful journey to India to find hidden teachings, and he suspected Gurdjieff had what he'd been searching for.

Ouspensky's account of his experiences appears in what is perhaps the best and most famous book about Gurdjieff's teaching: *In Search of the Miraculous: Fragments of an Unknown Teaching*, which Gurdjieff himself endorsed as an accurate picture of his views. It presents an intricate and fantastic esoteric system that included many novel ideas. One theme is the "sleep" of ordinary life. Another is the disunity of the human being. Gurdjieff says:

> Man such as we know him . . . cannot have a permanent and single I. His I changes as quickly as his thoughts, feelings, and moods, and he makes a profound mistake in considering himself always one and the same person; in reality he is *always a different person,* not the one he was a moment ago. . . .
>
> Each minute, each moment, man is saying or thinking "I." And each time his I is different. Just now it was a thought, now it is a desire, now a sensation, now another thought, and so on, endlessly. *Man is a plurality.* Man's name is legion.[6]

Gurdjieff is here alluding to an ancient view of the human mind, which regards human beings as essentially tripartite, consisting of the intellect, the emotions, and the instinctive and motor functions of the body.[7]

These three "centers," as Gurdjieff called them, "instead of fusing inwardly in the normal way to produce common outer manifestations, have become, especially of late, quite independent outward functions. . . . [Man] cannot be master of himself, for not only does he not control these centres, which ought to function in complete subordination to his consciousness, but he does not even know which of his centres governs them all."[8]

This disjunction would be bad enough on its own, but it is compounded by "sleep," the hypnotic trance in which we habitually live. Gurdjieff links this "sleep" to the concept of *kundalini*.

The spread of Eastern teachings over the past generation has made *kundalini* a comparatively familiar term. Most esotericists use this Sanskrit word to refer to the "serpent fire" at the base of the spine. This subtle energy is said to lie dormant in most people, but can be awakened through meditation or yogic practices. Traveling up the spine, it brings about illumination when it reaches the head.

Gurdjieff thought this view of kundalini was completely wrong. "In reality Kundalini is the power of imagination, the power of fantasy, *which takes the place of a real function*. When a man dreams instead of acting, when his dreams take the place of reality, . . . it is the force of Kundalini acting in him. Kundalini can act in all centers and with its help all the centers can be satisfied with the imaginary instead of the real."[9]

In his immense and difficult magnum opus, *Beelzebub's Tales to His Grandson*, Gurdjieff speaks of "the crystallized consequences of the properties of the organ kundabuffer."[10] *Kundabuffer*, a coinage of Gurdjieff's, is a portmanteau word formed from "kundalini" and "buffer"; "buffers" were what he called those psychic mechanisms that keep the different "I" 's from confronting each other.[11] (The idea resembles the modern psychological concept of dissociation.)

But what Gurdjieff calls "the terror of the situation" is still worse than this. For it might not matter if we lived our lives in sleep; perhaps we would not achieve all we could, but that almost inevitably happens anyway. According to conventional religion, if we are good, we will still go to heaven (or obtain a favorable rebirth) when we die.

But Gurdjieff does not subscribe to the conventional views of immortality, which generally come down to one of two: either we have immortal souls or we don't. For Gurdjieff, we possess the *possibility* of having immortal souls, or what he calls "higher being-bodies," but we almost never attain them because we live in sleep. And for undeveloped human beings, there is no immortality. "The 'man-machine' . . . who is now one, the next moment another, the next moment a third, has no future of any kind; he is buried and that is all."[12]

## FOOD FOR THE MOON

This incontestably bleak view of human fate is reminiscent of the gloomier Gnostic cosmologies, and to many who have read *In Search of the Miraculous*, Gurdjieff sounds like a Gnostic. "Kundalini is a force put into men in order to keep them in their present state," he asserts. "One would think that there are forces for whom it is useful and profitable to keep man in a hypnotic state."[13]

There is some truth to the idea that Gurdjieff is a kind of Gnostic, but only some. To understand it fully, we need to grasp something of his intricate cosmology. It can be best seen in a diagram known as the Ray of Creation (Figure 3). Gurdjieff did not claim to have originated it but said it "belongs to ancient knowledge." Many other esoteric systems, including those that set forth a naïve geocentric view, are, he adds, distorted or incomplete versions of this system.[14]

As one can see from the diagram, the Ray of Creation rather resembles the way children sometimes address envelopes: after listing the street, city, and state, they will add "North America, Planet

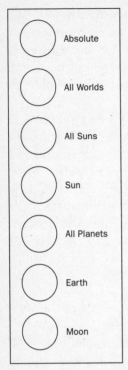

Figure 3. *Gurdjieff's Ray of Creation*

Earth, the Solar System, the Milky Way, the Universe." It also resembles the levels of manifestation seen in other systems, like the Kabbalistic Tree of Life. But Gurdjieff depicts the cosmic levels in terms of *scale*. The Absolute, or God, is all-encompassing. The next level is that of "All Worlds," that is, all galaxies (and perhaps all universes) taken as one. The next stage is that of "all suns" in our own galaxy, and so on. Each level, as it descends, is subject to a new set of cosmic laws of its own in addition to those of all the levels above it.

As one can see, in contrast to the higher realms, where there is comparative freedom, we on earth are subject to many cosmic laws. In fact we are very nearly at the bottom rung of the ladder—but not at the absolute bottom, for that rung is occupied by the moon. For Gurdjieff, contrary to the prevailing scientific views both of his time and of our own, the moon is not cold and dead but is rather "an unborn planet, one that is, so to speak, being born. It is becoming warm gradually and in time (given a favorable development of the Ray of Creation) it will become like the earth and have a satellite of its own."[15]

In order for the moon to grow, however, it needs to be fed by certain cosmic energies. What Gurdjieff calls "a huge accumulator" exists on earth to accomplish this end. This "accumulator" is organic life in all its forms: "Everything living sets free at its death a certain amount of the energy that has 'animated' it: this energy, or the 'souls' of everything living—plants, animals, people—is attracted to the moon as though by a huge electromagnet." Human beings, like the rest of life on earth, are thus merely "food for the moon."[16]

Such is the view set out in *In Search of the Miraculous*. Because this book is much more readable than Gurdjieff's own *Beelzebub's Tales to His Grandson*, many take it as the final word. But *Beelzebub* amends this picture in an important way. For while Gurdjieff here reiterates that humanity was indeed designed as "food for the moon," he adds that we have a choice of how to serve this end.

Buried toward the end of *Beelzebub*, in a convoluted passage on war, Gurdjieff makes an important and often overlooked disclosure: that the energy needed to "feed the moon" is precisely the same as that given off by people "forming and perfecting . . . their higher bodies by means of conscious labors and intentional sufferings."[17] If people do not serve the purposes of "Great Nature" by inner work, this energy will be extracted from them on a massive scale by means of wars and epidemics.

Gurdjieff's picture of the universe, stated so baldly, seems improbable. What are we to make of "higher being-bodies," "kundabuffer," and the idea that we are "food for the moon"? Does he mean these things literally? There was always a touch of the rogue about Gurdjieff, and the reader is sometimes struck by his writing in the same way that some people were struck by him in life: he seems to be staring at you with a penetrating gaze and asking you to decide whether or not he is kidding.

Yet there is nothing in Gurdjieff's life and work to indicate that he did not mean what he said. He despised conventional wisdom, and indeed one of the main themes interwoven throughout *Beelzebub*'s 1,200 pages is that modern people are so stuffed with absurdities that they have lost sight of cosmic truths. So Gurdjieff would hardly be concerned that today's scientists and psychologists might differ with certain points of his teaching.

At the same time there is an elegance and sublimity to Gurdjieff's vision. He is telling us not only that we are here for a purpose, but that the universe is benign and intricately constructed: if we fulfill its designs, we will be rewarded with immortality.

Even "the organ kundabuffer" itself is something of a mistake (Gurdjieff portrays the cosmic hierarchy as benevolent but not infallible). Installed in humans in prehistoric times "at the base of their spinal column, at the root of their tail—which they also, at that time, still had," it was intended by certain "Sacred Individuals" (also known as archangels) as a means of keeping people from prematurely comprehending "the real cause of their arising" (that is, to "feed the moon").[18] Later this organ was removed by the same higher beings, but its effects persist in us mostly through inertia.

To rescue us from this plight, Gurdjieff brought what he called "the Fourth Way." He contrasts his approach with three more familiar ways: (1) the way of the fakir, who masters his body to the point where he can stand "motionless in the same position for hours, days, months, or years";[19] (2) the way of the monk, who, by prayer and devotion to God, masters the emotions; (3) the way of the yogi, the one who gains control over the mind.

Unlike these paths, the Fourth Way, "the way of the sly man," does not require withdrawal from the world, but can and should be pursued in the course of everyday life; and instead of working with the mind, the body, or the emotions alone, it works with all three. It is, Gurdjieff claimed, faster and more efficient than the other three ways. "The 'sly man' knows the secret," said Gurdjieff, "and with its help outstrips the fakir, the monk, and the yogi."[20]

What is the sly man's "secret"? It is a higher force, an energy that is able to penetrate the being of man and create unity in his centers where there was none before. This energy must come from above, but it will not come by itself; Gurdjieff does not preach quietism but advocates "conscious labors and intentional suffering." For a long time these "labors" and "sufferings" will consist, not in some sophisticated form of masochism, but in striving to overcome the slumber of daily life and see oneself as one really is.

## REMEMBER YOURSELF

A central practice of the Fourth Way is *self-remembering.* "*You do not remember yourselves,*" Gurdjieff chides Ouspensky's Petersburg group. "You do not feel *yourselves;* you are not conscious of your-selves. With you, 'it observes' just as 'it speaks,' 'it thinks,' 'it laughs.' You do not feel: *I* observe, *I* notice, *I* see."[21]

Anyone who has read even a little in the literature of contem-porary spirituality will find familiar resonances here, for many books emphasize the need for awareness and mindfulness. Gurd-jieff's teaching goes still further, for it puts this effort at the center of the spiritual search. It also gives many more specific practices for "self-remembering": people in the Work often receive instruc-tions about being consciously present at certain moments of the day or during particular tasks. Psychologist Charles Tart, a veteran of a Gurdjieff group, remarks, "I still find the Gurdjieffian tech-niques of self-remembering to be a better way of being present in everyday life than the Buddhist admonition that you ought to be present in everyday life without any specific technique for doing anything about it."[22]

Many who have read about—or even practiced Gurdjieff's teaching seem to fall into the trap of seeing "self-remembering" as a completely cerebral practice; trying to carry it out, one ends up simply being self-conscious in the ordinary sense. They miss an es-sential part of the practice: that self-remembering entails a con-scious effort at sensing the body.

Self-remembering begins with the body because, as the French Gurdjieffian Jean Vaysse puts it, the body "is solid and concrete, with an apparently stable form which can . . . be relied on to some degree. It is the instrument through which we perceive and our means of action. It can stay still voluntarily and thus is easier than the other parts for us to observe. It is relatively obedient, and we have a certain amount of control over it (in any case more than over our other parts). In addition, it is the one solid material base in us."[23]

How does one work with the body in this way? A Gurdjieffian reading this book might attempt to read while giving some atten-tion to the sensation of some part of the body, the foot or hand, say, or even the body as a whole. This may sound simple, but if you try it, you'll find it isn't: if you're lucky, you may be able to keep this "divided attention" for a few seconds before you lose it again. For a long time the Work in fact involves returning to this sensation of the body over and over again no matter what you're doing. Such attempts are known as "efforts." They are meant to counteract the sleep of everyday life. Those who persist in this practice find that some of the "maleficent consequences of the properties of the organ kundabuffer" are, if not destroyed, at least interrupted, for these efforts help to dissipate daydreaming, absent-mindedness, and the hazy stupor in which we stumble through our lives.

These efforts of attention tie into other aspects of the teaching as well. Gurdjieff defined attention as "the direction of the think-ing center's activity."[24] Self-remembering, at least in the early stages, directs the "thinking center" toward the body, which is gov-erned by the "moving-instinctive center." Self-remembering thus tends to bring these two centers closer together; when the mind is paying attention to the body, they are working a bit more in har-mony, and the practitioner is slightly closer to becoming a unified being. (Because of its overpowering nature, the emotional center tends to be brought in last.)

Gurdjieff further explains that "making a conscious effort at the moment an impression is received" enables the organism to absorb more of certain subtle energies than it ordinarily does. These energies are used to create "higher being-bodies" that can withstand the shock of death.[25] Thus self-remembering, a practice as rich and multileveled as meditation itself, is meant not only to counteract the sleep and disunity of man, but to help one attain the immortality that, Gurdjieff says, usually exists for us as nothing more than a possibility.

A second, closely related practice is *self-observation,* whereby one tries to see as much as possible of one's own immediate state, including thoughts, moods, emotions, reactions, and physical pos-tures. Self-observation attempts to fulfill the injunction attributed to the ancient oracle at Delphi: "Know thyself." All true teachings must work toward this goal in some way. The Gurdjieffian technique is to observe ourselves in the course of daily life, to see ourselves as others see us, in all our moments of awkwardness, irrationality, and sleep.

This process not only helps students accumulate material for understanding themselves better, including the subtle organism of the "centers," but it enacts certain changes in its own right. "Many psychic processes can take place only in the dark," says Gurdjieff. "Even a feeble light of consciousness is enough to change completely the character of a process, while it makes many of them altogether impossible."[26]

## THE DARK MAGICIAN

The forces of sleep are overwhelming, and, Gurdjieff says, "one man can do nothing."[27] Thus working in a group is central to awakening, and indeed, much of Gurdjieff's public career from 1914 to his death in 1949 centered on work with groups. During these years he surrounded himself with a fascinating collection of people, including some of the most influential thinkers and artists of the day.

Ouspensky worked directly with Gurdjieff from their meeting in 1915 until breaking with him in 1924, whereupon Ouspensky carried on his own version of the teaching independently in London until his death in 1947.[28] But there were many others: Thomas de Hartmann, a Russian composer who collaborated with Gurdjieff on a number of haunting melodies evocative of the Middle East; de Hartmann's wife, Olga, who took much of the dictation for Gurdjieff's voluminous writings; A. R. Orage, hailed by T. S. Eliot as "the best literary critic of that time in London"; Jane Heap and Margaret Anderson, founders of *The Little Review*, one of the most influential journals in twentieth-century literature; and the writers Katherine Mansfield, Jean Toomer, and René Daumal.

Equally striking are the stories of the groups he formed around himself: the Petersburg group described in *In Search of the Miraculous*, composed of members of the prerevolutionary Russian intelligentsia; the "Institute for the Harmonious Development of Man," established by Gurdjieff at the Prieuré, an old abbey in Fontainebleau, forty miles from Paris, where he held court in the 1920s after fleeing Bolshevik Russia; "the Rope," the nickname for a group of women, mostly lesbians, with whom he worked in Paris in the 1930s; and the numerous people who flocked around him in his last years to be toasted as "idiots" at his legendary banquets.

What drew these people to Gurdjieff was his unquestionable charisma, which is in the forefront of every memoir of him. His pupil Georgette Leblanc provides one account:

> Great emotion. When I arrived at his apartment, he opened the door himself. . . . The light coming from the little salon shone on him brightly. Instead of concealing himself, he abruptly stepped back and leaned against the wall. For the first time, he allowed me to see what he really was . . . as if he had suddenly stripped away the masks behind which it is his duty to hide. His face was imprinted with a charity that embraced the entire world. Standing rigidly before him, I saw him with all my strength and I experienced a gratitude so deep, so painful, that he felt the need to quiet me. With an unforgettable look, he uttered, "God helps me."[29]

But Gurdjieff was never easy to work with—a fact he ascribed to his own sworn enmity to the "sleep" of all those he encountered. He confessed at one point that he had lived under a twenty-one-year vow to intensify his "inner benevolence" while externally "to-quarrel-ruthlessly-with-all-manifestations-dictated-in-people-by-the-evil-factor-of-vanity-present-in-their-being."[30]

If this was Gurdjieff's aim, he accomplished it masterfully. The memoirs of his pupils are peppered with strange stories: the aristocratic Olga de Hartmann was commanded to sell silk thread on the street during the Russian Revolution to overcome her "class pride";[31] Orage, working in the Prieuré garden, was ordered to dig a long ditch and then immediately told to fill it up again; Katherine Mansfield, dying of tuberculosis, was placed on a specially built balcony in the Prieuré cowshed, presumably to help her regain contact with the earth.[32]

Yet there is a darker side to the accounts of Gurdjieff that cannot be entirely explained by this merciless enmity to all that was false and weak in his pupils. Olga de Hartmann reported that "one evening Mr. Gurdjieff asked me to do something I felt I could not do."[33] She does not say that he asked her for sexual favors, although he may have done so; his liaisons with female pupils produced a number of illegitimate children (eight by one count). Gurdjieff's thirst for money was legendary—Orage once wished he had a million dollars to give him, just to see if he could go through it in a month—and Ouspensky says that he left because in the end he sensed "many destructive elements" in Gurdjieff's organization.

Given the enigma surrounding Gurdjieff and his avowed intention "never [to] do as others do,"[34] it is harder than usual to pass judgment on these actions. J. G. Bennett, one of his leading pupils, once observed, "All his strange and often repellent behavior was a screen to hide him from people who would otherwise have idolized his person instead of working for themselves."[35] Some even believe he was a follower of the "way of blame," a Sufi path whose practitioners make it a practice to conceal their goodness; seeming impious on the exterior, they in fact, according to the Sufi philosopher Ibn 'Arabi, "constitute the most elevated group" of adepts.[36] Even the choice of Beelzebub as narrator for Gurdjieff's epic account of the human race would seem to reflect this impulse, though Beelzebub is portrayed not as a devil but as a respected senior member of the cosmic hierarchy.

In some cases Gurdjieff's apparent cynicism certainly concealed kindnesses; while he prided himself on his ability to extract money from his followers, it is also true that he single-handedly supported dozens of Russian refugees in the 1920s. And however

eccentrically he may have treated Katherine Mansfield, most accounts of her stay at the Prieuré agree that she arrived in despair
and died in serenity.[37]

Even the "way of blame," however, fails to account completely
for the stark chiaroscuro in Gurdjieff's behavior, and the only way
to gain a fuller understanding of this quality is to look at his own
teachings. It is true that he made light of morality ("What is moral
in Petersburg is immoral in the Caucasus. And what is moral in
the Caucasus is immoral in Petersburg")[38] in favor of "conscience," a higher perception of objective good and evil that, he
said, is all but completely occluded in modern man. But another
clue to Gurdjieff's own understanding of his actions lies in a frag-
mentary ballet of his entitled *Struggle of the Magicians*.

Though Gurdjieff wrote music, choreographed dances, and
even made sets and costumes for this composition over a period
spanning more than thirty years, he never completed it, and it has
never been performed.[39] As its title suggests, it was supposed to
have depicted two schools, one of a black magician, the other of a
white. The same dancers would have to portray both schools; their
movements would have to be "attractive and beautiful" in one
scene and "ugly and discordant" in the next. "You understand that
in this way they will see and study all sides of themselves," Gurdjieff explained.[40]

This oddity points to a central feature of Gurdjieff's teaching. The contemporary Gurdjieffian Jacob Needleman explains:
"There are two directions of consciousness. There's an ascending
and a descending movement. A movement toward unity and a
movement toward multiplicity—what Gurdjieff calls an involu-
tionary, creative movement and an evolutionary movement."[41] In
the ballet the white magician would symbolize evolution and the
black, involution.

Unlike most esoteric teachings, which focus almost exclusively
on "evolution"—understood not in Darwinian terms but as an ascent toward God—Gurdjieff's teaching insists on both the movement up and the movement down. Like the dancers in the ballet,
those who take part in the Work must see both sides of them-

selves, the dark as well as the light. It is consciousness that reconciles them.

In this Gurdjieff's teaching resembles those of Jung and other twentieth-century explorers of the human mind. We have come to understand that too much emphasis on goodness has its dangers: to use Gurdjieff's language, we create "buffers" between our awareness and the sides of ourselves we don't want to see. These dark aspects can wreak havoc if we remain oblivious to them. Exposing them to the light of consciousness, on the other hand, not only renders them more manageable but brings us closer to having a "real, permanent I" that Gurdjieff says is our birthright.

Gurdjieff's followers have tended to push his darker side into the background, and one occasionally senses a desire to create a hagiography around him. Yet one can take what is of value from Gurdjieff's teaching without having to justify everything he did. If there is a regrettable side to Gurdjieff's legacy, it is that various pseudo-gurus, practitioners of "crazy wisdom," and their ilk use him as a model for their own sexual, emotional, and financial abuse of their students.[42] One even comes across Gurdjieff imitators of one stripe or another—obviously an absurd response to a man whose ideas call us to be more fully ourselves.

Yet Gurdjieff's behavior brings up a fundamental issue in the teacher-pupil relationship. It is illustrated by an old Hasidic story about a master whose students are crowding around him.

"What are you doing?" a bypasser asks.

One of the students turns and replies, "We want to see how he ties his shoes."

Usually this is taken to mean that a saintly man reveals his nature in even his most inconsequential actions. But the story has a double edge. It reminds us that the human mind has a tendency to mimic what it sees. We often unconsciously imitate friends, family, co-workers, even enemies. When someone approaches a spiritual teacher, it's natural to replicate his or her behavior in all details, including trivial or negative ones. But it's well to resist this temptation and remember that no human being, no matter how apparently enlightened, is worth imitating in all respects.

## GURDJIEFF AND HIS SOURCES

Where did Gurdjieff's ideas come from? His own pupils asked him over and over again and never got a satisfactory answer—or if they did, they have guarded the secret carefully.

Some of the most concerted efforts to unearth the sources of Gurdjieff's teachings have linked them with the esoteric traditions of Orthodox Christianity.[43] There is some validity to this view: Gurdjieff was raised in the Russian Orthodox Church, and he himself once remarked that his system was "esoteric Christianity."[44] Ouspensky's friend Boris Mouravieff (who, by his own account, helped precipitate the break between Gurdjieff and Ouspensky) claims that Gurdjieff was not only presenting esoteric Christianity, but was presenting an incomplete and unauthorized version of it. Mouravieff's own three-volume work *Gnosis* is his effort to set the record straight; as valuable as it is, however, it differs from Gurdjieff's ideas on so many different points that it is best understood as a completely separate system.

In the end, it is hard to accept Gurdjieff's teaching as esoteric Christianity in anything but the most general sense. One reason is that, as we have seen, one of the central practices of Christianity, esoteric and otherwise, is prayer, including the "Prayer of the Heart." Although Gurdjieff does not condemn prayer and even offered instructions about it to his disciples, it is not a central practice for him. This is because Gurdjieff says the "man-machine" cannot *do* anything, even pray. He is much better off attempting to unify his own being, which can then accomplish much of what he prays to God for.[45]

Similarly Christ himself, although always regarded with the greatest respect, is to Gurdjieff one (and not necessarily the most successful) of a number of "Messengers from Above" that have been sent to free humanity from the malign effects of the organ kundabuffer. According to Gurdjieff, contemporary Christianity has had much mixed in that "not only had nothing in common with the teaching of Jesus, but which sometimes even flatly con-

tradicted the truths this Divine Teacher taught."[46] (A similar lot
has befallen Islam and Buddhism, Gurdjieff believed.)

It is true that there are elements in common between Gurdjieff's ideas and Christianity: Gurdjieff's teaching about "higher
being-bodies" bears some resemblances, even in terminology, to
those set out by St. Paul. But ultimately trying to depict Gurdjieff's teaching as esoteric Christianity requires doing excessive violence to the ideas of both.

Other possible sources have suggested themselves, including
Sufism, Tibetan Buddhism, Kabbalah, and even alchemy. The contemporary Caucasian teacher Murat Yagan claims that Gurdjieff's
teaching is nothing more than Ahmusta Kebzeh, a 26,000-year-
old mystical tradition belonging to the Abkhazians of the Caucasus region,[47] while the idiosyncratic Bolivian magus Oscar Ichazo
says Gurdjieff was a Stoic like Epictetus and Marcus Aurelius.[48]
Despite intriguing similarities, however, the evidence fails to support any of these ideas conclusively. In the end we are left with
Gurdjieff's own version of his story: that he encountered a
monastery of the "World Brotherhood" in Central Asia, and that
he received much of his knowledge there. Though, as James
Moore points out, "Gurdjieff's provocative claim to have found
and entered 'the chief Sarmoung Monastery' is in effect a litmus
test, differentiating literal minds from those preferring allegory,"[49]
there is nothing inherently absurd about the idea. It is at least as
plausible as any of the other theories and prevents us from having
to fit Gurdjieff into the Procrustean bed of an alien system.

We must also admit that there is a great deal in Gurdjieff that is
unquestionably his own. No one else could have concocted the
strange terms like "Being-Partkdolg-duty" and "Surp-otheos" that
pepper his writings, particularly *Beelzebub*; insofar as people have
been able to tease out their roots, they have found them to be
portmanteau words, cobbled together from scraps of dozens of
languages like those in James Joyce's *Finnegans Wake*.[50]

The same is true of some aspects of Gurdjieff's thought. The
notion of the "man-machine" seems to owe as much to the Age of

Steel as it does to mystical schools in Turkestan, while his references to subtle energies as "carbon," "nitrogen," and "oxygen" can hardly antedate the nineteenth century.[51] In the end the best conclusion one can draw is that Gurdjieff had access to some sources of ancient wisdom and that he took upon himself—or was given—the task of reformulating it for the consciousness of modern humanity. At times he hinted at the scale of the task; as he said in a rare moment of humility, "I am small man compared to those who sent me."[52]

## THE WORK TODAY

To anyone familiar with the strange stories about Gurdjieff's antics, the present-day reality of the Work may come as a shock. Few of Gurdjieff's disciples who have carried on his legacy have shown much proclivity for "crazy wisdom" or other unorthodox means of precipitating enlightenment. In its seriousness and sobriety, the typical Work group today bears more resemblance to a Quaker meeting than to the master's vodka-laced banquets.

Most groups focus on the practices of self-remembering and self-observation; people also take part in various forms of physical labor and craftwork as a means of seeing different aspects of themselves. There are even some who continue an interesting facet of his teaching known as the Gurdjieff Movements.

We have already seen Gurdjieff as the composer of a ballet, and at the outset of *Beelzebub*, he describes himself as "a Teacher of Dancing."[53] In fact it was in this capacity that he first appeared in the United States: In early 1924, he and various disciples came to New York and put on an exhibition of the Movements at Carnegie Hall, causing a certain sensation in the novelty-hungry city and laying the foundation for the Work in America.

The Movements do not really resemble any other type of dance. Their origins form part of Gurdjieff's legend, for most people in the Work connect them with the "sacred dances" he describes in his account of the Sarmoung Brotherhood. These dances, which Gurdjieff claims are over 4,500 years old, "correspond precisely to our books. Just as is now done on paper, so, once, certain information about long past events was recorded in dances and transmitted from century to century to people of subsequent generations."[54] Each posture forms a letter in an alphabet of gestures; understanding this code, one can read the information therein.

Although the Movements, accompanied by music written by Gurdjieff and Thomas de Hartmann, are still taught in some Gurdjieffian schools, it is not clear that the means of "reading" them has been passed down as well. If Gurdjieff did impart the secret to some of his pupils, it has been well hidden. It is rarely possible even to see a performance of the Movements; the best way of glimpsing them is in the 1977 film of *Meetings with Remarkable Men*, directed by Peter Brook under the supervision of Gurdjieff's pupil Jeanne de Salzmann, which shows the performance of some of these dances toward the end.[55]

Anyone who does see them can understand how the Movements fit in with Gurdjieff's teaching. They require the performer to maintain two or three different rhythms with different parts of the body, say, the head, arms, and feet, often while executing complicated dance steps. The difficulty of these "sacred dances" is obvious, but they accord with Gurdjieff's goal of integrating the "three centers" so that a new, higher "I" can be created. As for the difficulty, Gurdjieff himself insisted that "only super-efforts count."[56]

What possibilities does the Work offer for the seeker today? Its hardships rarely take the peculiar forms they did under the direction of Gurdjieff himself, but much of the master's rigor remains. It is not a path for those who crave conviviality or emotional warmth; many who encounter the Work complain of its coldness. On the other hand, this very characteristic tends to weed out dilettantes, so the caliber of people one encounters is probably higher than in many traditions. There are of course dubious entities that lay claim to Gurdjieff's heritage, but most of them can be avoided if one keeps clear of groups that aggressively proselytize or demand exorbitant sums of money. Here as in most traditions, the best don't advertise.

For a sense of the possibilities offered by the Gurdjieff Work, one might take a clue from *Beelzebub*, whose hero at one point remarks that of all the creatures in our solar system, "Personally I liked best of all the three-brained beings breeding on the planet bearing the name Saturn."[57] Traditional astrology portrays Saturn as the cold, remote planet that creeps slowly through the sky. As such it has always been associated with slow, unstinting labor (which is why in the old rhyme "Saturday's child works hard for a living") as well as with authority and depth. Hence the "super-efforts" required by the Work may seem to lack glamour and fun, but they may also confer knowledge that cannot be won by easier means.

## THE ENNEAGRAM

One aspect of Gurdjieff's teaching deserves particular attention because of its great popularity. This is the enneagram, a nine-pointed figure that Gurdjieff introduced to his pupils in St. Petersburg; Ouspensky's record of it in *In Search of the Miraculous* is the first reference to this mystical diagram in written form.[58] "For the man who is able to make use of it," says Gurdjieff, "the enneagram makes books and libraries entirely unnecessary. *Everything* can be included and read in the enneagram." But Gurdjieff also added that he was presenting it in an "incomplete and theoretical form of which nobody could make any practical use without instruction from a man who knows."[59]

Again the secret is well hidden. The enneagram's dynamics can be represented in the Movements (one of these appears in the film of *Meetings with Remarkable Men*), but it is not clear how these ideas can be taken further into practical application. Of Gurdjieff's pupils, J. G. Bennett took the most active interest in this subject; his book *Enneagram Studies* is one of very few attempts to apply the dynamics of this diagram to processes in ordinary life, such as cooking a meal.[60]

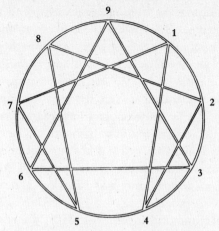

*Figure 4. The enneagram. For Gurdjieff, the en-neagram was a mystical symbol that encompassed all esoteric knowledge. The system of the "ennea-gram of personality" is a later innovation.*

But when people today talk about the enneagram, they are not using it in this sense. In fact the enneagram has attracted popular attention in a form that was alien to Gurdjieff himself. It is usually called the "enneagram of personality." It assigns everyone to one of nine different personality types, each of which is associated with a point on the enneagram.

There are of course innumerable systems for sorting people into a few broad and easily recognized categories. Gurdjieff had his own view of types, but it is not so easily summarized; in fact he insisted that "types and their differences cannot be defined in or-dinary language."[61] But he did try to pass on the art of types in his customarily unorthodox fashion. In Gurdjieff's late years, pupils who came to the dinners at his Paris flat were assigned to various categories of "idiots"—idiots could be "ordinary," "round," "zig-zag," "compassionate," even "enlightened"; there were twenty-one types in all, the last and highest being the "Unique Idiot," God himself.[62] Gurdjieff would order toasts to each type of the idiot in turn, and each person would have to stand up when his own type was called. In doing this Gurdjieff probably intended to teach his students about types by showing them living examples in themselves and each other. We do not know whether they retained this knowledge in any systematic form; at any rate Gurdjieffians no longer toast "idiots."

There is no evidence that Gurdjieff used the enneagram in his system of types. The contemporary "enneagram of personality" comes not from Gurdjieff but from the work of Oscar Ichazo. Ichazo's background, like Gurdjieff's, is obscure, but he began to publicly teach his own intricate esoteric system in Arica, Chile, in 1970 (the school is now known as Arica but is headquartered in New York).

The Arica training includes work with "the enneagon of the fixations," in which the nine points of the enneagram (which Ichazo calls the "enneagon") are attributed to defense mechanisms adopted by the ego in early life. Ichazo assigned each of these a nickname: point three is the "go," the ceaseless overachiever; point four is the "melan," the self-pitying melancholic; point five is the "stinge," the remote observer cut off from feelings.[63] Ichazo himself assigned his pupils to each fixation by personally analyzing their patterns of facial tension; only in recent years have Arican teachers been trained in the art of identifying fixations themselves.

A pupil of Ichazo's, the Chilean psychiatrist Claudio Naranjo, expanded upon this system further and began to teach it in the San Francisco Bay Area in the early 1970s. The enneagram of personality, as it became known in this form, spread rapidly in several circles, including among psychotherapists and Jesuits. In 1988, Helen Palmer, a teacher of intuitive techniques in Berkeley, California, who had learned the system from some of Naranjo's pupils, published the most successful book about it, entitled simply *The Enneagram*.[64]

The fundamental idea behind the enneagram of types is that each person has a core fixation around which the "false personality" or "ego" is constellated. These fixations or "passions" (associated with the Christian seven deadly sins, with deceit and fear added to make nine) are the fundamental means by which we deaden and impair ourselves. Palmer's view of the enneagram points, shared by most proponents of the system, can be summarized as follows:

**1. The Perfectionist.** Critical of self and others, Ones tend to believe there is a single right way to do something. They often feel ethically superior and may procrastinate for fear of making a mistake. Their passion is anger.

**2. The Giver.** Demanding affection and approval, the Giver seeks to be loved and appreciated by becoming indispensable to others. Devoted to meeting others' needs, Twos can be manipulative and can show a different side to each person. Their passion is pride.

**3. The Performer.** The classic Type A personality, Threes seek to be loved for achievement. Masters at appearance, they tend to confuse the real self with job identity. They can seem more productive than they actually are. Their passion is deceit.

**4. The Tragic Romantic.** This type is attracted to the unavailable or to that which is absent or lost. They tend to be melancholic, sensitive, and artistic. Passion: envy.

**5. The Observer.** Fives are concerned with keeping their own space. Distant and preoccupied with privacy, they prefer to do without rather than become involved. They feel drained by commitment to others. Passion: greed.

**6. The Devil's Advocate.** Sixes are dutiful and plagued by doubt. Procrastination is often evident. They identify with the underdog and are often antiauthoritarian, self-sacrificing, and loyal to a cause. Some may feel perpetually cornered and therefore confront terror in an aggressive way. Passion: fear.

**7. The Epicure.** This is the type of the *puer aeternus,* the eternal youth. Sevens are superficial, adventurous, and have trouble with commitment. Often happy and lively, they may start things without seeing them through. Passion: gluttony.

**8. The Boss.** This type has to be in control. Eights are productive and love a good fight. They like open displays of anger and force and respect opponents who will stand and fight. They tend to excess: too much, too loud, too late at night. Passion: lust.

**9. The Mediator.** Nines are obsessively ambivalent. They see all points of view and readily replace their own wishes with those of others. They may narcotize themselves with food, drink, or television. Passion: sloth.

Although Palmer profusely acknowledged her debt to Ichazo, he was displeased with her promotion of what he regarded as a bastardized version of his own teaching, and he sued her for copyright infringement in August 1990. His suit, though widely publicized, was unsuccessful. The judge ruled in Palmer's favor on all counts, and Ichazo's appeal was later denied. Though Ichazo and, more recently, Naranjo have denounced the superficiality of much of today's enneagram work, it remains firmly in the public domain.

In recent years the enneagram has grown enormously in popularity among both laymen and professionals: the first International Enneagram Conference, held in 1994, was sponsored by the Department of Psychiatry at Stanford University; a second was held in Maryland in 1997. Innumerable books discuss the enneagram of personality from almost every conceivable angle: one recent volume explains children's enneagram types to parents, and another, entitled *Getting Your Boss's Number*, is intended to help workers figure out their employers. Discussions of enneagram types may even be overheard at parties in the 1990s, much as astrological signs formed the subject of small talk back in the 1970s.

Whatever its value to psychologists and party conversationalists, the enneagram of personality is not really part of Gurdjieff's teaching, not only because it makes no mention of "idiots" but also because it confuses two similar but distinct ideas in his thought.

To understand how, we must return to a common theme in esotericism: the sharp distinction between nature and nurture. Gurdjieff's terms for these are *essence* and *personality* respectively. Essence is all that is inborn in us, the result of a number of influences including heredity and astrological influences. Personality, on the other hand, includes all that is acquired through upbringing, education, and environment. "Essence is the truth in man; personality is the false," according to Gurdjieff.[65] But the abnormal conditions of modern life reinforce personality at the expense of essence, so that the latter is often stunted at an infantile level.

Yet the growth of essence is central to the inner development of which Gurdjieff speaks; essence is in fact the seed of "real I." Esoteric development, in his view, runs against the current of ordinary life by nourishing essence and weakening personality.

In a discussion of fate, Gurdjieff also makes it clear that type has to do with essence rather than personality. "Fate is the result of planetary influences which correspond to a man's type. . . . A man can have the fate which corresponds to his type but he practically never does have it. This arises because fate has relation to only one part of man, namely to his *essence*."[66]

The proponents of the enneagram, however, have confused Gurdjieff's idea of type with a similar idea: *chief feature,* which he associates with personality: "Every man has a certain feature in his character which is central. It is like an axle round which all his 'false personality' revolves."[67] Gurdjieff went on to say that this "chief feature" or "chief fault" was quite individual and idiosyncratic. Pointing to one of his students, he said, "His feature is that he is never at home." Another pupil, told that his chief feature was arguing with everybody, burst out, *"But then I never argue!"*[68]

Many of today's writers on the enneagram err on this fundamental point when they speak of "personality types," which is, in Gurdjieffian terms, a confusion of levels. This is not to insist that Gurdjieff was the final authority on the makeup of the human character, but those who invoke Gurdjieff's legacy should at least understand what he is trying to say.

Despite this confusion, and despite the trivialization to which it has frequently been subjected, there is obviously a great deal of value in the enneagram of personality. Many people have found it of real help in understanding themselves and others. And in a larger sense both Gurdjieff and the proponents of the "enneagram of personality types" offer the same lesson: that ingrained and automatic ways of being are ultimately forms of enslavement. The difficult but crucial task is not only to recognize one's own habitual stance in the world but to overcome it. As Gurdjieff said, "The study of the chief fault and the struggle against it constitute, as it were, each man's individual path."[69]

## SUGGESTED READING

De Hartmann, Thomas and Olga. *Our Life with Mr. Gurdjieff*. Rev. ed. New York: Penguin Arkana, 1992.

Probably the most intimate and revealing of the memoirs by Gurdjieff's pupils.

Gurdjieff, G. I. *Meetings with Remarkable Men*. New York: E. P. Dutton, 1963.

Gurdjieff's engaging and profound autobiography is the most readable of his writings. The haunting 1977 film version by Peter Brook was undertaken as a Work project; it is not a Hollywood trivialization. Gurdjieff's magnum opus, *Beelzebub's Tales to His Grandson* (New York: E. P. Dutton, 1950), is a masterpiece but is probably better read after *Meetings with Remarkable Men* and Ouspensky's *In Search of the Miraculous. Views from the Real World* (New York: Penguin Arkana, 1984) is a collection of Gurdjieff's early talks.

Moore, James. *Gurdjieff: The Anatomy of a Myth*. Rockport, Mass.: Element, 1991.

A witty but highly sympathetic portrait.

Needleman, Jacob, and George Baker, eds. *Gurdjieff: Essays and Reflections on the Man and His Teaching*. New York: Continuum, 1997.

A collection of essays and memoirs written from a number of perspectives, mostly by participants in the Work.

Ouspensky, P. D. *In Search of the Miraculous: Fragments of a Forgotten Teaching*. New York: Harcourt, Brace, & Co.: 1949.

The most celebrated—and in many ways the best—summation of Gurdjieff's teaching, published posthumously. Gurdjieff, shown the book after Ouspensky's death, endorsed it himself. *The Psychology of Man's Possible Evolution* (New York: Alfred A. Knopf, 1954) is a collection of lectures by Ouspensky on Gurdjieff's teaching as it relates to human development.

Tart, Charles T. *Waking Up: Overcoming the Obstacles to Human Potential.* Boston: Shambhala, 1986.

A examination of Gurdjieff's teaching from the perspective of modern psychology.

Webb, James. *The Harmonious Circle: The Lives and Work of G. I. Gurdjieff, P. D. Ouspensky, and Their Followers.* New York: G. P. Putnam's Sons, 1980.

Wildly speculative about Gurdjieff's early years, but still overall the best account of the lives and impact of Gurdjieff and Ouspensky.

*Ten*

# SUFISM:
# THE POLES OF LOVE AND
# KNOWLEDGE

Sufism is an enigma for most people in the English-speaking world. The origin of the word Sufi itself is enigmatic. Some say it comes from the Persian word for "pure," others claim it is derived from the Arabic word for "wool," a reference to the simple woolen garments worn by early Sufis. Many people have witnessed "Sufi dancing," or read some of the poetry of Rumi, the great Sufi mystic, or come across the numerous books of Idries Shah, but such fleeting contacts often leave us with more questions than answers. Certain authorities insist that all true Sufis are Muslims; others insist that Sufism teaches the fundamental unity of the world's religions.

Even if one has actually encountered students of Sufism, things may be no less confusing. Members of different Sufi lineages or orders have wildly varying customs of dress, behavior, and outlook. Some seem like hippie survivors of the sixties; others seem as if they would be more at home in seventeenth-century Baghdad. Most are indistinguishable from the average person on the street. All this leaves one wondering whether there is a common thread that ties all Sufis together. Are Western followers of Sufism just caught up in a love of the exotic? Or is Sufism a spiritual path that can speak to the concerns of our everyday lives?

234

## THE ROOTS OF SUFISM

Whether Sufism is a strictly Islamic approach to mysticism or not is a point of debate among Western scholars. Less debatable is that the first historical traces of Sufism as a mystical path appeared within two centuries of the founding of Islam in the seventh century A.D.[1] The Prophet Muhammad was a profound mystic, and it is said that the Prophet instructed his son-in-law, Hazrati Ali, in the techniques and inner truths of his mysticism. Ali in turn personally instructed other early Muslims before he was killed in one of the power struggles that overtook Islam in the decades after the Prophet's death. Today nearly every Sufi order traces its lineage back to Ali and the circle of Muhammad's closest intimates.[2]

The earliest known Sufis were solitary mystics who attracted followers on the strength of their personal saintliness. These illumined beings taught their students the techniques they had employed to become "friends of God," and those who attained spiritual realization in turn taught others. By the ninth century, what had originally been informal teacher-student relationships formalized with the founding of *tariqahs,* or orders, each originating from a different Sufi saint.[3] Thus the Qadiri order descends from Abd al Qadir Jilani, the Rifai order descends from Ahmad Rifai, and so on.

Significantly, Sufis were generally accepted and respected within their surrounding communities. Thus their mysticism was seen as an extension and deepening of Islamic practice. Although individual Sufis were punished within Islam for statements and teachings that challenged the religious authorities, Sufism as a whole was allowed to flourish, and in many cases traveling Sufis were influential in introducing Islam to new cultures.[4]

## WHAT ABOUT ISLAM?

Despite the enthusiasm with which Westerners have embraced various "foreign" religions in recent decades, there is still something threatening about Islam. The Crusaders fought with Muslims over the Holy Land, and a defining moment in European culture was the victory over Ottoman forces on the outskirts of Vienna in 1683.

For a millennium Europe's great rival was Islamic civilization, ruled over by a succession of sultans and caliphs, who were at various times Arab, Persian, and Turkish. Even today we hear echoes of its challenge to the West in the militant voices of Khomeini, Hezbollah, and other radical Islamists. Yet the inner essence of Islam, like the inner essence of Christianity or Judaism, has little to do with the clamoring of those who jockey for power in the name of religion. This heart of Islam, which is perhaps best exemplified by the Sufis, transcends categories of East and West as well as cultural idiosyncrasies. Nevertheless, in order to understand Sufism and the essence of Islam, we must first examine the religious context in which Sufism developed.

"There is no god but God, and Muhammad is his Messenger" (*La ilaha ill Allah, Muhammadar rasul Allah*) is the fundamental statement of Islamic belief. The Prophet affirmed, above all else, the oneness of God and the unity of all life. He saw himself as the renewer of the monotheistic faith that the Prophet Abraham had taught and from which Judaism and Christianity had evolved. According to the Qur'an, the poetic scripture that Muhammad recited in installments over a twenty-three-year span, God (*Allah* in Arabic) sent 124,000 prophets to humanity over the course of history. Interpreted liberally, this statement implies that the founders and maintainers of the numerous religions worldwide share their roots in the same God. But Muhammad is called the "Seal of the Prophets," that is, the crowning advocate of this primordial tradition.

Unique among the world's scriptures, the Qur'an was memorized by those in the Prophet's circle as each new portion was recited aloud, resulting in an unaltered text as the Qur'an was written down. Even today, there are literally hundreds of thousands of Muslims who have committed the whole Qur'an to memory, still pristine in its seventh-century Arabic.

So what? we might be tempted to ask. Isn't this a recipe for fanaticism? The "final prophet" delivers an unaltered scripture and his followers ever after are ripe to transmogrify into what Eric Hoffer called "true believers," defenders of a single truth. To be sure, many Muslims are given to rigid and literal readings of Qur'anic verses, just as Christian fundamentalists do with the Bible, resulting in a monolithic approach to religion. Yet an antidote to this tendency is embedded within Islamic tradition, and it is the Sufis who provide this.

## LAYERS OF MEANING

Arabic is a poetic language whose alphabet consists of twenty-two consonants supplemented by diacritical markings that serve the function of vowels. Most Arabic words stem from roots that consist of three or four consonants. Thus the meaning of any one word is related at its root to many other words. Even taken alone, an Arabic word can have multiple meanings.

For instance, *qalb,* the word for "heart," can be read as the root word QLB in the original Arabic. Other variants on QLB include *taqallab* ("to be restless"), *munqallab* ("one who transforms") and *qalab* ("to extract the marrow of a palm tree"). Thus, in the original Arabic, the human heart implies both the core and something changeable or changing.[5]

In this way, the Qur'an has multiple implications built into every verse, including the literal meaning in the Arabic of the Prophet's era; a literal meaning as understood by Arabic speakers today; metaphors that suggest themselves to the poetic imagination; mystical readings that unveil themselves in quiet contemplation; and rhythmic shadings that come forth as the verses are sung. It is no coincidence that many of the greatest Sufis have also been great poets—Rumi, Attar, Saadi, and Hafiz come to mind—and it is often through the vehicle of inspired poem and song that Sufism has captured the essence of Islam and spoken to Muslims and non-Muslims alike across the centuries. However, the mystical interpretation of the Qur'an is but one facet of mystical Sufism, and for Westerners it is frequently far from the most appealing.

## SUFISM COMES WEST

Sympathetic interaction between Westerners and the Islamic world was scarce prior to the twentieth century. Moorish Spain may have represented the height of Spanish culture, but the expulsion of Muslims and Jews from Spain by the end of the fifteenth century was a cause for celebration among Catholic Europeans. The British encountered Islam as the British Empire expanded into Egypt, India, and Asia, but their interaction with it often consisted of manipulating various religious groups and nationalities as a means of dividing and conquering. An adventurous few such as Richard Burton, translator of the *Arabian Nights*, delved into Islamic culture. Burton himself was initiated as a Qadiri Sufi during a stay in India. But it wasn't until the arrival of Hazrat Inayat Khan in Europe in 1910 that Sufism began to attract attention in the West.

Inayat Khan, a talented musician, had been sent to Europe by his Master in the Chisti order of Sufism in order to introduce Sufism to the West. In view of the generally negative feelings of Europeans toward Islam, Khan strategically downplayed the Islamic roots of Sufism and emphasized its universalistic elements instead. He was in a good position to do so, since the Chisti order had flourished in multicultural India by avoiding Islamic sectarianism and embracing sincere mystics of various faiths. The Sufi custom of a close relationship between teacher (*sheikh* or *murshid*) and student (*murid*) was very close to that of the yogic guru and *chela* (disciple), and seekers in India were often attracted to great mystics regardless of their religious affiliations.

Thus the Sufism that Inayat Khan brought West accepted the love of God expressed by non-Muslims as a valid point of departure for studying Sufism. Khan was a great exponent of what Aldous Huxley called "the perennial philosophy," and went so far as to create a Universal Worship service that acknowledged the unity behind the great world religions. In his view,

> There is one religion and there are many covers. Each of these covers has a name: Christianity, Buddhism, Judaism, Islam, etc., and when you take off these covers, you will find that there is one religion, and it is that religion which is the religion of the Sufi.[6]

In addition to his Chisti background, Khan had also been trained in the three other major Sufi orders of northern India, the Naqshbandi, Qadiri, and Suhrawardi. Perhaps because of his multiple lineages, Khan dispensed with the usual Sufi practice of identifying with one primary order and gave his expanding circle the generic designation "The Sufi Order in the West." After his death in 1927, his followers continued to spread his message of Sufism as the "religion of the heart."

This was the Sufism that most Westerners knew of—with the exception of some Sufi poetry translated by R. A. Nicholson and A. J. Arberry—until the arrival of Idries Shah in the sixties. Shah, whose father, Ikbal Ali Shah, had immigrated to England from northern India in the twenties, first achieved some notoriety when he announced himself as a representative of "the People of the Tradition," a remote top echelon of Sufism supposedly located in the inaccessible Hindu Kush of Afghanistan.

Like Inayat Khan, Shah presented Sufism as a path transcending specific religions and adapted it to Western ways. In distinct contrast with Khan, however, he downplayed any religious or spiritual trappings and instead emphasized Sufism as a psychological technology leading to self-realization. This approach seemed especially pitched to followers of Gurdjieff, human-potential movement students, and intellectuals well versed in modern psychology. For instance, Shah wrote:

> Sufism . . . states that man may become objective, and that objectivity enables the individual to grasp "higher" facts. Man is therefore invited to push his evolution ahead towards what is sometimes called in Sufism "real intellect."[7]

Shah dismissed other forms of Sufism in both the East and West as "watered-down, generalized or partial,"[8] including not only Khan's version but the overtly Muslim Sufism found in most Islamic countries. A prolific author, Shah popularized Sufi teaching stories and jokes as primary ways of imparting wisdom, and oversaw the publication of numerous reprints of translations of classic Sufi texts in English. His associates also produced a number of books that included passages implying that Shah was the "Grand Sheikh of the Sufis," an exalted position of authority that was undercut by the failure of any other Sufis to acknowledge its existence.[9]

In the early 1970s, Sufism entered a new phase in the West. Where previously the followers of Inayat Khan and Idries Shah had the field pretty much to themselves, now a stream of *sheikhs* and teachers from Turkey, North Africa, the Middle East, and even Sri Lanka began to visit or move to Europe and North America. Each formed by the Sufism of their own particular culture, these Sufis tended to promulgate teachings and practices that were more traditionally Islamic.

## THE POINT OF SUFISM

The point of Sufism was not, and is not, the promulgation of organizations or of theological positions, or even of mystical poetry, no matter how universal. Rather, as in Gnosticism, at the heart of Sufism lies the cultivation of gnosis. *Marifah* in Arabic (or *irfan* in Persian), a term often translated as "gnosis," is the culmination of the Sufi's quest.

Unity is the preeminent principle of Islam, and this is often interpreted as referring to the monotheistic Oneness of God or, in a slightly broader scope, the intimate relationship between God and Creation at all levels. However, for the Sufi, unity (*tawhid* in Arabic) is the fundamental mystical experience of reality: beneath all appearances to the contrary, the Being of God and our own being are one. We arise from God and return to God, and this truth can be experienced and "known."

Sufi practices, which can include chanting, singing, group movement or dance, or more interior meditations, are all intended to lead the student toward the experience of annihilation (*fana*) of the ego in God. Unlike some Eastern paths where this bliss is often an end unto itself, however, Sufism teaches that the ideal state of realization is in the descent from this exalted state into one of "subsistence" (*baqa*), wherein the mystic maintains consciousness of this unity and of individual identity simultaneously. *Baqa* is often associated with "sobriety"—meaning the ability to function unobtrusively in daily life while maintaining the ecstatic connection with the Infinite.

Neither *fana* nor *baqa* can be forced; they are ultimately given to some and not to others, by the grace of God. However, Sufism preserves a body of techniques and practices that help purify the consciousness of the seeker, leading to a state of receptivity and "nearness" to God, where the spark has, perhaps, a better chance to make the leap.

Within an ongoing teacher-student relationship, a *sheikh* will likely give his students such individualized practices as specific numbers of prayers or Names of God to chant; meditations on subtle energy centers within the body; and tasks of service within the community. Through the students' reports of dreams and of colors and sounds experienced within meditation, as well as by personal observation, a skilled *sheikh* is able to track his students' progress.

Over the centuries, a system of temporary inner states or more permanent "stations" on the path of illumination has been delineated, and here too the skill of the *sheikh* may prove crucial. Since the student's original personality and habit patterns are progressively destabilized, psychological crises are likely to arise, calling for sensitivity and a sure-handed response. Sufism teaches that God's grace or blessing (*baraka*) may flow through the teacher, if the spiritual bond between teacher and student is strong, helping to energize and guide the process.

Since Sufism presumes a long-term commitment on the part of its followers, with no guarantee of gnosis, part of the wisdom the student must acquire is accepting the spiritual path regardless of outcome. God is often referred to as "the Beloved" in Sufi poetry, and the seeker is encouraged to experience a love of God, as if Allah Himself were one's ravishing lover. The remembrance of God from moment to moment becomes its own reward.

## Two Great Sheikhs

According to Sufi tradition, there is at any given moment on Earth one highly spiritual person (known as "the Pole" or *Qutb*) who anchors the spiritual affairs of humanity. Although the disciples of the various Sufi orders and circles through the centuries have commonly considered their own master to be the *Qutb* of the age, still it is possible to identify certain great *sheikhs* as extraordinary mystics and teachers.

Jelalludin Rumi (commonly referred to as *Mevlana* or "Master"), sometimes called the "Pole of Love," was born in Balkh in 1207, in what is now Afghanistan. He traveled west across the Islamic world and eventually settled in the Anatolian city of Konya, now in central Turkey, which was at that time the capitol of the Seljuk Dynasty. Rumi is arguably the greatest Sufi poet, and his works in English translation have become immensely popular over the last twenty years.

> *Friends, don't be discouraged.*
> *Compassion comes after trouble.*
> *Don't put on any dress but Love.*
> *Don't cover yourself with any garment but Love. . . .*
>
> *The day I met my Beloved,*
> *I screamed, I lost my mind.*
> *My trials to avoid guilt all disappeared.*
> *But this is Absence inside of Presence.*
> *This is eternal blessing.*

*If Love slips out of your hand*
*Don't fall into despair. Keep searching.*
*Fight to find it.*
*Until you reach Him, see Him,*
*Don't sleep, don't eat, don't relax.*[10]

In verses such as these, Rumi shows a generosity of spirit and encouragement that crosses cultural boundaries and centuries. His paeans to the Beloved work both as great love poems and as descriptions of the mystical state of annihilation.

Rumi's mentor and master was a remarkable dervish known as Shems-i Tabriz (named for Tabriz, a great city in Persia). Shems was something of a *melami* (literally someone on "the path of blame," a category of Sufis usually operating outside of formal orders who often courted criticism from others as a way to diminish their own egos). Rumi's followers were aghast when their teacher found Shems' company more irresistible than their own. Shems provoked Rumi to new heights of mystical love, inspiring some of Rumi's greatest poetry.

*A soul which is not clothed*
*with the inner garment of Love*
*should be ashamed of its existence.*

*Be drunk with Love,*
*for Love is all that exists.*
*Where is intimacy found*
*if not in the give and take of Love.*

*If they ask what Love is,*
*say: the sacrifice of will.*
*If you have not left your will behind,*
*you have no will at all.*[11]

Tradition has it that Rumi's jealous followers eventually murdered Shems, but the intensity of Rumi's love for the Beloved (both as

God and in the guise of Shems) has been immortalized in his works. The whirling "turn" that Rumi prescribed to his students as a form of moving meditation became one of the central practices of the Mevlevi order that was founded soon after Rumi's death. The "whirling dervishes" of Turkey have gone on to become possibly the most famous Sufis in the West, although, at this late date, not all public practitioners of the "turn" are in fact active Sufis.

Muyhiddin Ibn al-Arabi (Ibn 'Arabi for short) followed a path quite different from Rumi's. Born in twelfth-century Moorish Spain, he traveled eastward across North Africa, eventually settling in Damascus in Syria. If Rumi, the "Pole of Love," exemplifies what is called in yoga the *bhakti* (devotional) approach, Ibn 'Arabi is Sufism's greatest exponent of the way of knowledge or pure consciousness and he has been called the "Pole of Knowledge" or, more commonly, "Sheikh al-'Akbar" ("The Greatest Sheikh").

Ibn 'Arabi, who wrote over two hundred works, had an enormous impact on the development of Sufism. He was an exponent of the philosophy known as "the Unity of Being," an all-encompassing perspective that holds that Allah is the Being from which everything manifests and that the countless qualities (or "Names") of God are the root of all created things. The human being, as the reflection of the divine, has the capacity to experience the Names and trace his or her own consciousness back to the Source.

In Ibn 'Arabi's system, God's Being is both transcendent and immanent, and we are born with this innate knowledge whether we realize it or not. To truly know one's self, then, is to know God and vice versa. The whole of the universe can be found within ourselves, as Ibn 'Arabi indicates in his typically dense prose: "Every time that an intuitive person contemplates a form which communicates to him new knowledge which he had not been able previously to comprehend, this form will be an expression of his own essence and nothing unknown to him."[12]

One of Ibn 'Arabi's most important teachings was that of the "Perfect Man" (or "Complete Human"). ("Perfect" is used here in the sense of "perfected" or "complete," not in the sense of "flaw-less.") Existing both as a primordial template for the human being (akin to Adam Kadmon in Jewish mysticism) and as the potential destiny of each of us, the Perfect Man has realized all of Allah's Names, or qualities, within himself. The Prophet Muhammad is perhaps the quintessential example of the Perfect Man. He repre-sents the model of nobility, generosity, and mercy that Sufis (and all Muslims, for that matter) are urged to emulate.

In contrast to Rumi, whose forte was poetry and story, Ibn 'Arabi set out his rather complicated system in a series of demand-ing philosophical works and commentaries on the prophets, the Qur'an, and *shariah,* the Islamic law. Although Ibn 'Arabi did not found a formal *tariqah,* or order, his ideas and realization had a seminal influence on the early masters of the Naqshbandi order, on the Shadhili and Qadari orders, and on numerous others. In addition, lines of "Akbari" teaching (a name derived from Ibn 'Arabi's title "Sheikh Al-Akbar") and oral traditions survived the centuries.

## THE STATUS OF WOMEN

Interestingly. Sufism has attracted as many women as men in the West, if not more. At first glance this might not seem to make sense, since the Islamic matrix within which Sufism operates is popularly considered to be male-dominated. Yet if we look be-neath the surface, there is a logic to its attractiveness for women.

In emphasizing Sufism's universal aspects and downplaying its Islamic roots, Hazrat Inayat Khan and Idries Shah successfully dis-engaged their versions of Sufism from the cultural restraints that had previously shaped Sufism in traditional Islamic cultures. While Islam as originally promulgated by the Prophet actually widened women's options in Arabic society and brought them far more re-spect than they had enjoyed before, this liberating impulse was in-creasingly reined in over succeeding generations as cultural norms reasserted themselves. Thus exoteric Islam tended to support traditional gender roles and a strong family life as stabilizing forces within Islamic civilization.

Freed of those restraints in the modern West, Sufism was able to unfold as a path equally open to men or women. Sufism had always had its share of women saints, *"sheikhahs,"* and disciples—two of Ibn 'Arabi's most important teachers were women, for instance—although they tended to be segregated within the sphere of women, out of the public eye. Western Sufism has significantly altered that custom.[13]

Thus, after Inayat Khan's death, his North American successor was a woman, Rabia Martin, and Idries Shah's sister, Amina Shah, achieved some prominence as an anthologizer of Sufi stories and folk tales. Irina Tweedie emerged as a teacher in the "Golden" Sufi tradition, and exponents of the Mevlevi way in North America have pioneered the practice of male and female dervishes performing the whirling "turn" together. Samuel L. Lewis ("Sufi Sam") created what have become known as the Dances of Universal Peace (sometimes labeled "Sufi dancing"), which were open to both men and women. In a sense, as it had in other cultures, such as Turkey or India, Sufism in the West accommodated itself to the local norms.

Moreover, with its emphasis on the heart and God as the Beloved, Sufism has always fostered qualities that have traditionally been considered feminine. As such, it helped balance the more overtly masculine qualities within Muslim cultures. (This pattern has been shared by other esoteric and mystical currents in relation to their surrounding cultures.) However, it may only be in modern times that this aspect of Sufism has reached its fullest potential.

## IN DEFENSE OF TRADITION

No survey of contemporary Sufism is complete without a mention of one of the most influential currents in esoteric spiritual studies: Traditionalism. Here we mean not just the general idea of defending or preserving traditions, but a specific metaphysical outlook that was first delineated by a Frenchman named René Guénon.

Guénon was born in 1886 and raised a Catholic. Early in life he developed an aversion to both the West and modernism. In 1911, in the midst of a period of delving into Theosophy, Masonry, and other esoteric and occult teachings, he was initiated into a Sufi *tariqah* under the leadership of an Egyptian *sheikh*, Abder Rahman Elish El-Kebir, who had been trained in the teachings of Ibn 'Arabi.[14]

Guénon moved to Egypt in 1930 and formally embraced Islam. But well before this, he had already begun to develop an outlook based on pure metaphysics, independent of any single religious system. This outlook has come to be known as Traditionalism.

The Traditionalist perspective holds that all revealed religions are relatively true, united beneath their cultural differences by universal metaphysical truths.[15] This may sound similar to Hazrat Inayat Khan's teachings; Guénon, however, held that it was necessary for the seeker to align with one of the revealed religions and channel his or her efforts within its laws and rituals. This has come to be distilled in the Traditionalist slogan "No esotericism without exotericism."

The rigor of Guénon's thought attracted other thinkers such as Ananda K. Coomaraswamy, Frithjof Schuon, Titus Burckhardt, and Marco Pallis, who expanded on Guénon's perspective in their own writings, both before and after Guénon's death in 1951. In due course, Martin Lings and Seyyed Hossein Nasr joined the Traditionalist camp and came to prominence as exponents of Sufism to Western readers.

The impact of Traditionalism has been felt most strongly in academic circles, with Nasr in particular influencing the course of Islamic studies in the West. Huston Smith's works, such as *Forgotten Truth*, reflect Traditionalist ideas and in many ways are the most accessible presentation of that perspective.[16]

## SEEKING GUIDANCE

The seeker who feels inclined to undertake further investigation into Sufism or Islam has several options, none of them entirely satisfactory. First, we would suggest reading a selection of books about Sufism and the mystics of Islam, to acquaint oneself with the vocabulary and conceptual framework within which Sufism operates. The universal poetry of love and devotion is a good starting place, but behind this accessible exterior one soon discovers Arabic names, Qur'anic verses, and anecdotes from other times and cultures that will probably be unfamiliar and require a bit of study.

Recent years have seen a proliferation of local groups across North America attached to various Sufi orders. In any large American city, there are likely several different orders that can be visited in a spirit of sincere inquiry. We would suggest seeking out at least two or three in order to taste the different approaches and styles. There is no need to make a hasty decision to join or affiliate with one particular group, although some eager initiates might encourage you to do so.

A far better approach than diving in headfirst is to strike up a friendship with a student of Sufism who seems both approachable and knowledgeable. If he or she in turn can refer you to another friend who works with a different order or teacher, so much the better. Despite what some enthusiasts will say, no one order is the best for everyone, and it is not necessary to affiliate oneself with any order during initial investigations. It is far more important to discover a teacher or friend who exhibits those qualities that one would like to foster in oneself. The interaction with such a mentor is the best basis for studying Sufism.

Special care needs to be taken in "taking hand" (undergoing initiation and pledging allegiance) with a *sheikh*. Sadly, many *sheikhs* seem more interested in building organizations and perpetuating the ethnocentric idiosyncrasies with which they grew up than in encouraging the spiritual growth of individual students. If you feel a special affinity with Turkish or Persian or Arabic culture, then immersing yourself in that culture might be an attractive point of departure. However, it is easy to get lost in the minutiae of an adopted culture only to wake up years later with the realization that the work of Sufism has barely begun.

Some Sufi teachers, themselves the product of training within the traditions of particular *tariqahs,* have come to the conclusion that the era of the orders is rapidly passing. They point to the phenomenon of self-aggrandizing *sheikhs* with hundreds or thousands of followers—many of whom are lucky to spend ten minutes a year in the personal company of their master—as evidence of the degeneration of Sufism. In their view, the organizational hierarchy that such groups perpetuate nearly eliminates the possibility for the subtle interplay and guidance between teacher and student which is the crucial component of Sufi instruction. They suggest that it is better to forgo the formal role of *sheikh* and student altogether, to be replaced by the synergy between "friends," than to build more institutional castles in the sky.

This is a controversial view, but the would-be student of Sufism would do well to give it serious consideration. There is still vital work being done within orders, to be sure, but the way of the formal Sufi order is not the only option.

Must one become a Muslim in order to pursue Sufism? Historically, it is an acknowledged fact that some *sheikhs* living in areas shared by several religions had Christian and Jewish students who maintained the religions into which they were born. Similarly, as mentioned before, some *sheikhs* in multicultural India had Hindu disciples. Islam counsels respect for all "religions of the book," that is, revealed religions with sacred scriptures that ultimately point to one God. This allows for a fair amount of latitude if a teacher is so inclined.

Yet the fact remains that the vocabulary and theological underpinnings of Sufism are Islamic. The Prophet Muhammad is regarded as the exemplar *par excellence* of the Sufi path, and the founding *sheikh* of every Sufi order was a Muslim. Sufi teachings commonly interweave sayings of the Prophet, Qur'anic verses, and Islamic prayers in Arabic amidst the haunting poetry and mischievous anecdotes and teaching tales. Unless one feels at least some basic resonance with Islam, the pursuit of Sufism may not be a good idea.

Above all else, Sufis prize sincerity, and one approaching a teacher with an open heart and sincere intent is not likely to be turned away. On the other hand, if one's participation in a group *zhikr* (a series of chanted prayers) is to be anything more than the mere mouthing of Arabic words, the heartfelt chanting of "*La ilaha ill Allah*" (common to most *zhikrs*) means that one has internalized the most basic declaration of Islamic faith.

Whether embracing Islam in this simple fashion implies the necessity of following every jot and title of *shariah* (Islamic law) remains a matter of some dispute. Some sheikhs view strict adherence to *shariah* as a crucial building block for spiritual growth, while others take local cultural norms and individual students' circumstances into account and try to discern what aspects of *shariah* are most relevant to each stage of spiritual growth.[17]

## THE PRESENT CHALLENGE

A truly Western approach to Sufism remains embryonic. The sheer variety of the orders and groups that have come West is testimony to the way in which Sufism has accommodated itself to those cultures in the past. However, to advocate the slavish reproduction of particular Sufi centers—Turkish *tekkes,* Iranian *khaniqahs,* or Moroccan *zawiyas*—in North America or Western Europe betrays the dynamic creativity that has always characterized the essence of Sufism.

While Sufism is rightfully proud of the unbroken chain of saints and masters through whom its teachings and methods have been passed, every worthwhile teacher has met the challenge of finding new ways to present that heritage within the context of their time and place. To their credit, both Hazrat Inayat Khan and Idries Shah confronted this challenge and developed unique responses to it. But if Sufism is to survive today as a living tradition of mysticism in the West, it will further require the spiritual "opening" of homegrown Sufis who have scaled its heights and returned to daily life in this culture, able to convey to a skeptical world the reality of illumination and gnosis.

## SUGGESTED READING

Yasar Nuri Öztürk. *The Eye of the Heart.* Istanbul: Redhouse, 1988.

This fine little book provides authoritative information on the "northern" Sufi orders of Turkey and the Balkans; has numerous historical plates, many in color; and is translated into good clear English. It is available from Threshold Books in Putney, Vermont, or from the Sufi Book Club.

Inayat Khan and Coleman Barks. *The Hand of Poetry: Five Mystic Poets of Persia.* New Lebanon, N.Y.: Omega Publications, 1993.

A new collection of poems from five of the most eloquent poetic voices of Sufi mysticism. Saadi, Rumi, Hafiz, Attar, and Sanai, all represented in contemporary translations that read quite nicely. The accompanying talks by Inayat Khan provide an introduction both to the poets and to Khan's own style of poetic discourse.

Feild, Reshad. *The Last Barrier* and *The Invisible Way.* Rockport, Mass.: Element, 1993.

Slightly fictionalized and quite romantic, these two autobiographical books are delightful accounts of the author's encounter with Sufism. *The Last Barrier* in particular can arouse a strong desire to fly off to a Turkey that is rapidly disappearing.

Hilmi, Ahmet. *Awakened Dreams.* Translated by Refik Algan and Camille Helminski. Putney, Vt.: Threshold Books, 1993.

This book is a modern classic Sufi teaching text written in Turkey at the turn of the century. Marvelous allegorical stories trace the seeker's quest. The translation is extremely elegant and flowing.

Arasteh, A. Reza. *Growth to Selfhood.* New York: Arkana, 1990.

This short book lucidly relates Sufi teachings about the psyche to the concepts of modern psychotherapy. The author writes both as a psychiatrist and a student of Sufism, combining personal anecdotes with historical background and observations on human creativity.

Helminski, Kabir. *Living Presence*. New York: J. P. Tarcher/Perigee, 1992.

In careful, measured prose, Helminski leads the reader into the practice of self-observation and heightened awareness associated with the Sufi path. There is some overlap with Fourth Way work, with which Helminski is also familiar.

Idries Shah. *The Sufis*. Garden City, N.Y.: Anchor/Doubleday, 1971. This is an extremely readable and wide-ranging introduction to Sufism. Shah's own slant is evident throughout, and some historical assertions are debatable (none are footnoted), but no other book is as successful as this one in provoking interest in Sufism for the general reader.

Shah's *Learning How to Learn* (New York: Penguin Arkana, 1996), is a collection of interviews, talks, and short writings. It is one of his best and provides a solid orientation to his "psychological" approach to the Sufi work. At his best Shah provides insights that inoculate the student against much of the nonsense in the spiritual marketplace.

Schimmel, Annemarie. *Mystical Dimensions of Islam*. Chapel Hill: University of North Carolina Press, 1975.

An authoritative and wide-ranging investigation of the history and teachings of Sufism. If one were to read only one in-depth book providing an overview of Sufism, this would be the leading candidate. Schimmel writes as both a scholar and a sympathizer who resonates with the Sufi work.

Nasr, Seyyed Hossein. *Islamic Spirituality*. 2 vols. New York: Crossroad, 1987, 1991.

These two hefty collections of scholarly essays are truly encyclopedic in their coverage of the doctrines and details of Islamic Sufism. The writing is generally clear and authoritative, and the selection of contributors is salutary.

Ibn 'Arabi, Muhyiddin. *The Kernel of the Kernel*. Interpreted by Ismail Hakki Bursevi. Sherborne, Gloucestershire, England: Beshara Publications, n.d.

Possibly the most profound mystic and philosopher to ever walk the path of Sufism, Ibn 'Arabi is also the most distinguished proponent of the metaphysics of "the Unity of Being." Considerable familiarity with Sufi and Islamic concepts and vocabulary is crucial to penetrating his message. This book represents the most concise presentation of his mystical teachings.

Schuon, Frithjof. *The Essential Writings of Frithjof Schuon*. Edited by Seyyed Hossein Nasr. Rockport, Mass.: Element Books, 1991.

The most prominent traditionalist since Guénon, Schuon delivers metaphysical declarations as if from on high. Once past that stylistic challenge, however, there is much to gained from acquainting oneself with his wide-ranging writings, which cover everything from the nature of religion to aesthetics and epistemology.

Schuon's *Understanding Islam* (London: George Allen & Unwin, 1981) is one of his most readable books, full of startling insights into Islam from an esoteric perspective.

*Eleven*

# The Rumor of the Brotherhood: Secret Societies and Hidden Masters

Esotericism rarely occupies the center stage of history. Even its best-known figures are hardly household names, while most have been relegated to that special room in the attic of memory that is reserved for eccentrics.

This is not to say that esoteric currents have never touched great personages or events. If the Renaissance magicians and alchemists who made their way into the courts of monarchs were often welcomed as mere entertainers, there have always been members of royalty who have taken a serious interest in these subjects. Britain's Prince Charles is one example in our own day. His counterparts in an earlier era included Rudolf II, Holy Roman Emperor and King of Bohemia, and Frederick V, Elector Palatine of the Rhine, both of whom lived in the early seventeenth century.

Rudolf moved his imperial capital to Prague in 1583, making it a center for Kabbalists, alchemists, and magicians. Under Rudolf, Prague was a remarkably tolerant place, especially considering that the religious strife of the Reformation and Counter-Reformation was at its peak throughout Europe. Soon after Rudolf died in 1612, the hopes and dreams of those sympathetic to esotericism devolved upon Frederick, who ruled over a patchwork state in western and central Germany known as the Palatinate. His capital at Heidelberg became a treasure trove of wonders: a statue that resounded when struck by the rays of the sun, a water-organ, and singing fountains.

At this time two strange documents were published, the *Fama Fraternitatis* ("The Rumor of the Brotherhood") and the *Confessio Fraternitatis* ("The Confession of the Brotherhood"), together known as the Rosicrucian manifestos.[1] The *Fama* appeared in 1614, the *Confessio* in 1615, though they had been circulating in manuscript form possibly as early as 1610. They caused a great uproar throughout Europe.

The "brotherhood" of the title was what we would today call a secret society. It claimed to have "knowledge of Jesus Christ," and asserted, "Our Philosophy also is not a new invention, but as Adam after his fall hath received it, and as Moses and Solomon used it."

The brothers had sharp words for the powers of their day. "We do condemn the East and West (meaning the Pope and Mahomet) blasphemers against our Lord Jesus Christ," they said. "In *Politia* we acknowledge the [Holy] Roman Empire . . . albeit," they added darkly, "we know what alterations be at hand."[2] They also mocked "the accursed and ungodly gold-making, which hath so much gotten the upper hand," and said that true philosophers esteem "but little the making of gold."

Their order, known as the Fraternity of the Rosy Cross, was founded by a savant named "C. R." or "C. R. C."—usually understood as "Christian Rosenkreutz" or "Christian Rosy Cross." The pamphlets tell of C.R.'s journey to the Middle East in search of occult knowledge. Upon returning to Europe, he attempted to acquaint the scholars of various countries with his findings, "but it was to them a laughing matter."[3] Finally C. R. found eight sympathetic men in his native Germany and with them established his fraternity:

Their agreement was this: First, That none of them should profess any thing but to cure the sick, and that *gratis*. 2. None of the posterity should be required to wear any certain kind of habit, but therein to follow the custom of the country. 3. That every year upon the day C. they should meet together in the house *S. Spiritus,* or write the cause of his absence. 4. Every brother should look about for a worthy person, who, after his decease, should succeed him. 5. The word C.R. should be their seal, mark, and character. 6. The Fraternity should remain secret one hundred years.[4]

The pamphlets say it is possible to join the fraternity, but they do not say how. In the ensuing years many men tried to make contact with the brothers, even publishing essays stating their interest; one of these aspirants was the great French philosopher René Descartes. But no one we know of, including Descartes, ever made contact with the elusive brotherhood, or admitted that he had.

As the British scholar Frances A. Yates has shown, the Rosicrucian enthusiasm was entangled with political hopes held out for the Elector Palatine. These expectations ran especially high in Bohemia (today's Czech Republic). Several years after Rudolf's death the Bohemian crown had passed to the Archduke Ferdinand of Styria, a Catholic and a rabid enemy of heresy. Many Bohemians were Protestants, members of the Bohemian Church, started by the reformer Jan Hus over a hundred years before Luther. Unhappy with Ferdinand's plans for suppressing their faith, they offered their country's throne to Frederick in 1619.

This move provoked the Catholic Hapsburgs to drive Frederick out of Bohemia after he had reigned for only a winter; the Bohemian Church was wiped out soon thereafter. These events are not merely obscure footnotes to history: they triggered the Thirty Years' War, which ravaged Europe for a generation and from which Germany, the principal battleground, took a century to recover.

In the wake of these events people soon lost their interest in the Rosicrucians. In 1633 the Hermeticist Robert Fludd wrote, "Those who were formerly called Brothers of the Rosy Cross are today called the Wise, the name (of Rose Cross) being so odious to contemporaries that it is already buried away from the memory of man."[5]

Yet the Rosicrucian myth refuses to die. In the four centuries since the manifestos appeared, innumerable groups and individuals have claimed the name "Rosicrucian," including the Gold- und Rosenkreuz, a Prussian esoteric order of the eighteenth century;[6] Paschal Beverly Randolph, a nineteenth-century black American occultist;[7] and most famously, the Ancient and Mystical Order of Rosae Crucis (AMORC), founded in 1915 by a businessman named H. Spencer Lewis and familiar to generations of Americans for its magazine advertisements promising "the mastery of life."

The fascination seems inexplicable. Why should these obscure pamphlets promoting a failed German princeling continue to inspire anyone? Does the apparent persistence of the Rosicrucians mean there was any truth to the stories about them?

## ADEPTS AND HISTORY

The manifestos mark the first appearance in the modern West of a central esoteric theme: that there is a secret brotherhood of adepts, usually possessed of powers far beyond those of ordinary humans, who in some unseen way help shape the course of history.

If we regard the manifestos as setting out a political program, we can see that it failed. The Elector Palatine lost the throne of Bohemia, and the hoped-for flowering of a Hermetic enlightenment was drowned in religious warfare. The Rosy Cross brothers, for all their knowledge, did not seem capable of seeing very far into the future. Yet they may have seen further than they are given credit for. To see why, we must look for a larger import in the manifestos.

Esotericists do not often occupy themselves with current events. This is not because they are above it all (though some may feel they are), nor is it because they do not care about humanity. Rather they operate with a different sense of scale.

The basic principle is obvious. Historians know that events do not erupt suddenly out of nowhere, but have roots stretching back for generations. We know that today's strife in Northern Ireland, the Balkans, and the Middle East are all fueled by hatreds hundreds of years old. The same is true of the more beneficent parts of our heritage: democracy and religious toleration did not drop out of the sky but were won by generations of struggle and martyrdom.

To these considerations must be added another idea. A subtle impetus in the present can have enormous impact on the future if it is correctly placed. (It is like the familiar metaphor from chaos theory in which a butterfly flapping its wings in Brazil causes a rainstorm in China.) Historians continue to be amazed that an itinerant Jewish preacher whose career probably lasted three years has had more of an effect on world civilization than any number of kings and tyrants.

The Rosicrucian manifestos are best understood in this light. No matter how they were read at the time, their authors were probably not thinking of the transient fortunes of the Elector Palatine when they wrote them; indeed a careful reading reveals a much more comprehensive program. The beginning of the *Fama* sets it out: "So that man might . . . understand his own nobleness and worth, and why he is called Microcosmus, and how far his knowledge extendeth into Nature."[8]

This passage contains two themes that sound the dominant note of the modern age. First is the idea that man might "understand his own nobleness and worth, and why he is called Microcosmus" (a microcosm of the greater universe). Second is the goal of extending human knowledge of nature. Neither of these concepts was particularly important to medieval civilization: Christianity emphasized the wretched state of fallen man, while philosophers of the Middle Ages preferred to see the physical world as a rational, harmonious, but somewhat overschematic system, "esteeming Popery, Aristotle, and Galen . . . more than the clear and manifested light of truth," as the *Fama* goes on to say. There was little experimental science as we know it today.

The Rosicrucian manifestos announce a different program. Human dignity will be exalted, not abased, and humanity will read directly from the "book of Nature" rather than trusting to second-hand views handed down from the old philosophers. The modern era has begun.

Who were the seventeenth-century Rosicrucians? The most plausible guess is that they were a small collection of philosophers, devoutly Protestant, who studied the Hermetic, Kabbalistic, and magical teachings that enjoyed such popularity during the Renaissance. "Christian Rosenkreutz" is usually understood as a symbolic rather than as a historical figure, sometimes taken as representing the spirit of the order as a whole.

There is little if any direct evidence that the Rosicrucian order managed to survive and propagate itself. However, this is not to say that it perished. Secret societies are like underground streams, and may run invisibly for centuries.[9] When they are needed to play a particular role on the public scene, they surface, do their work, and afterward disappear. They may emerge again centuries later, or they may not. Gurdjieff described the work of the Fourth Way in similar terms:

> The fourth way is never without some *work* of a definite significance, is never without some *undertaking* around which and in connection with which it can alone exist. When this work is finished, that is to say, when the aim set before it has been accomplished, the fourth way disappears, that is, it disappears from the given place, disappears in its given form, continuing perhaps in another place in another form.[10]

Thus it is wise to avoid drawing too hasty a conclusion about the demise of the Rosicrucians. Many modern groups who style themselves "Rosicrucian" trace their heritage back to the brotherhood of the seventeenth century (H. Spencer Lewis of AMORC traced it back further still to ancient Egypt).[11] It is true that there is no proof of this link. But the lack of evidence does not prove there *was* no connection, especially in the case of societies that were trying to keep their existence secret.

## MASONS AND TEMPLARS

The Rosicrucian impulse was brought into the modern era by another formerly secret society that in recent centuries has been very public indeed. The origins of Freemasonry, also known as Masonry or sometimes "the Craft,"[12] are obscure and controversial. The most common view is that Masonry is descended from the old stonemasons' guilds of the Middle Ages, which often included moral and religious teachings along with practical instruction. When the medieval order began to break down, these guilds survived by taking in members who did not belong to the masons' trade. These newcomers often included gentlemen who were interested in learning the philosophical doctrines couched in the terms of the masons' craft. Eventually this "speculative Masonry" displaced the earlier "operative Masonry" of the lodges, and modern Freemasonry was born.

This theory faces at least two major problems. It does not explain why the European elite, who were obsessed with avoiding anything that smattered of manual labor, should have deigned to accept instruction from tradesmen. Nor does it say why the earliest evidence for the existence of Freemasonry can be found in Scotland, where there were few, if any, stonemasons' guilds, rather than on the European continent, where there were many.[13]

A second theory is considerably more romantic—but should not be dismissed on that account. It holds that Freemasonry is a continuation of the vanished medieval order known as the Knights Templar.[14]

Founded in 1118 to protect pilgrims journeying to the Holy Land, the Templars soon became a major force in the Crusades, helping to reconquer Palestine from the Saracens and keep it in Christian hands. The Templars soon outstripped their original purpose and grew into the most powerful military and economic force in Christendom. But by the end of the thirteenth century, their wealth and prestige had made them suspect to many of the sacred and secular powers. When the Holy Land fell back into

Muslim hands in 1291, the Templars seemed to have lost their reason for existence.

Not long thereafter, King Philip the Fair of France determined to lay his hands on the Templars' wealth. With the connivance of Pope Clement V, Philip contrived to have the order suppressed and its properties confiscated. On Friday, October 13, 1307 (a date which some believe gave rise to the popular fear of Friday the thirteenth), mass arrests were carried out on the Templars in France. In 1312 the order was dissolved, and in 1314 Jacques de Molay, the last Templar Grand Master, was burned at the stake in Paris.

The charges against the Templars were extremely peculiar. They were accused of both sodomy and heresy, and it was said that they required initiates to spit on the crucifix and worshiped an idol named Baphomet. These charges were almost certainly trumped up; in true medieval fashion, they were extracted by torture. Given that the Templars' courage in defending Christendom during the Crusades was never in dispute, the charges of disloyalty to the faith are hard to believe.

There is evidence that not all the Templars were arrested. Some were forewarned and managed to make their way to Scotland, which was at the time under excommunication by Rome (and hence was not bound by the papal suppression) and which was fighting to keep its independence from England (and hence needed good soldiers). Taking refuge there, the Templars hid their identity and perpetuated their esoteric teaching under the guise of a stonemasons' guild.

If this theory is true, the Templar tradition went underground for some three hundred years before resurfacing in the guise of Masonry. At any rate the first solid evidence for Masonic lodges as we know them comes from Scotland around the turn of the seventeenth century, just before the time of the Rosicrucian manifestos. Soon afterward Masonry began to spread to England, where it encountered esotericists who had fled from the Thirty Years' War then raging in Germany. These two currents, the old Templar tradition preserved in Scotland and the Rosicrucian ideas that had been brought from the Continent, may have produced modern Freemasonry as we know it.

The first man we can point to as having been initiated as a Mason is an Englishman named Elias Ashmole, who joined a lodge in 1646. A scholar and an antiquarian (his collection formed the nucleus of Oxford's Ashmolean Museum), Ashmole was also a part of a circle of intellectuals attempting to promote scientific inquiry. In 1660 they would form the Royal Society, which today is one of the most prestigious scientific bodies in the world. But intriguingly, while they were still meeting informally they called themselves the "Invisible College"—a phrase that clearly alludes to the Rosicrucians, who were nicknamed the "Invisibles" because no one could find them.[15]

This brief account is based on Frances Yates's *Rosicrucian Enlightenment*, which argues that many of the most famous figures associated with the birth of modern science in the seventeenth century, including Francis Bacon, Descartes, Robert Boyle, and Ashmole, were part of this Rosicrucian-Masonic current. If this is so, then science, with its mandate of extending human knowledge of nature, took at least part of its inspiration from an esoteric impulse.[16]

Even better known is the Masonic influence on political trends. Simplistic notions of a "Masonic conspiracy" aside, the role of the Masons in the American and French revolutions as well as in the unification of Italy in the nineteenth century has been well documented. In each case the Masons promoted liberal, representative government of the sort we now take for granted as modern democracy—again reflecting the goal of helping man "understand his own nobleness and worth" as set out in the manifestos.

With whatever foresight they possessed, it is unlikely that the Brothers of the Rosy Cross, clearly imagined the modern era, with all the benefits and problems of science and democracy. But they probably did have a clear sense of the crisis that their civilization was facing, for in the seventeenth century Europe was groaning under a rigid social system, the idea of the divine right of kings, and an ossified theology that was choking off any real quest for knowledge. They also probably glimpsed a way out; and they may have launched a subtle impulse at precisely the right time to bring about their goals over a span of two or three centuries.

## THE ROSE AND THE CROSS

It is not easy to summarize the teachings of the Rosicrucians, for the moment one tries to do so, one confronts the issue of who they were or are. Any number of groups have laid claim to the name "Rosicrucian" since the days of the manifestos. Many of these organizations have different and even conflicting doctrines, so to try to say what "the Rosicrucians" taught, or teach, requires passing some kind of judgment on what an authentic Rosicrucian is.

The Rosicrucians who produced the manifestos probably espoused a teaching that resembled Hermeticism, probably with some elements of Kabbalah mixed in. *The Chemical Wedding of Christian Rosenkreuz*, a small book that followed closely upon the manifestos, is obviously an alchemical allegory. And the writings of Michael Maier and Robert Fludd, two esotericists who may have been associated with the original Brothers of the Rosy Cross, also reveal Hermetic and Kabbalistic influences.

Beyond that it becomes difficult to say, but Rosicrucian threads wrap themselves around many esoteric groups that arose later. The ten degrees of the Golden Dawn initiation, for example, originated with the eighteenth-century Prussian order known as the Gold- und Rosenkreuz.[17] Nor is this surprising: the Golden Dawn was founded by members of a group of high-degree Freemasons who called themselves the Societas Rosicruciana in Anglia (Rosicrucian Society in England).

The issue becomes more complicated the closer we come to modern times. In the early twentieth century R. Swinburne Clymer, head of the Fraternitas Rosae Crucis, traced his lineage back to the American occultist Paschal Beverly Randolph, who espoused Rosicrucianism but frankly admitted, "Very nearly *all* that I have given as Rosicrucianism originated in my own soul."[18] Nonetheless Clymer entered into a long feud with H. Spencer Lewis of AMORC, each claiming legitimate roots in European Rosicrucianism.[19] Both Clymer's group and another small organization, the Rosicrucian Fellowship of Max Heindel, continue to exist today.[20] But in terms of practical success neither has been able to compete with AMORC, whose correspondence courses have provided what appears to be a solid method of esoteric instruction for nearly three generations.

The teachings of AMORC feature many occult concepts that we have already discussed. One important theme is the vibratory nature of all things; matter is ultimately seen as being reducible to energy in a manner similar to that expounded by modern physics. Since thought is also a vibration, thoughts can cause physical effects. Hence the art of mental concentration is given strong emphasis.[21]

Another recurring theme in many Rosicrucian teachings has to do with the use of sexual energy for higher transformation.[22] Though this idea does not appear in the manifestos, it is common to many of the modern Rosicrucian groups we have mentioned. Even so it is not well understood. The overall idea is that a great deal of subtle energy is lost in orgasm; by postponing or avoiding orgasm, one can retain most of this energy and use it for building higher subtle bodies. This is the apparent purpose of many Taoist and Tantric practices, which usually entail consciously directing sexual energy from the genitals upward toward the heart and the head.[23] Though many books give specific instructions for this process, one still has the impression that some essential part of the teaching has been lost or omitted.

At any rate some version of this technique was very likely taught in many of the groups who laid claim to the Rosicrucian heritage. But because this subject has been a matter of the utmost delicacy until very recently, it is not always possible to specify what sexual teachings were vouchsafed to initiates.

The leading Rosicrucian groups have not fared well in recent years. Most of the smaller ones seem to be fading away, and even AMORC, despite its size and wealth—its headquarters, Rosicrucian Park, occupies an entire block of downtown San Jose, California—has faced schisms and declining membership. H. Spencer Lewis said that the Rosicrucian Order alternated between public and private activity in 108-year cycles, and his organization may, intentionally or not, have fulfilled his prophecy by the time the order reaches the beginning of its next era in 2023.

## SMOOTHING THE ASHLAR

Freemasonry is a system of morality, veiled in allegory, illustrated by symbols. Not a religion but religious in character, it is a philosophy of ethical conduct which imparts moral and social virtues and fosters brotherly love. Its tenets have endured since man turned the first pages of civilization. They embody the understanding by which man can transcend ordinary experience and build "a house not made with hands" in harmony with the Great Architect of the universe.[24]

Masonry began its public life at the end of a long period of religious warfare in Europe, when people laid down their lives for theological issues that today seem trivial. It is thus not surprising that the Masons would have tried to create a clearing where members of different religions and political factions could meet in fellowship.

Hence there is no official Masonic doctrine as such. To be admitted to a lodge, a man is required only to state his belief in a Supreme Being, "Grand Architect of the Universe." Masonic teaching itself, "veiled in allegory, illustrated by symbols," is imparted by rituals. Though innumerable books explicate the meaning of these rites, no interpretation is regarded as definitive, and no Mason is required to agree with any of them.

To return to a point made elsewhere about ritual, there are

parts of the human mind that do not respond to words and do not understand them. To speak to the subconscious, to persuade it to accept a "system of morality," one must address it in language it can understand—that is, in pictures and physical movements. This method has another advantage: Because it has little verbal content, it leaves nothing to argue about. This helps explain not only the tremendous success of Masonry but also the fact that Masons have created much of the impetus for religious toleration over the past few centuries.

Masonic rites are numerous and intricate, and we will not be able to discuss them in any but the most basic way. Americans begin their Masonic affiliation in what are called "Blue Lodges" (a term not used in Britain or other countries). Initiation into the three first degrees—known as Entered Apprentice, Fellowcraft, and Master Mason—takes place here. Each of these has its own rite and symbols.

Anyone interested in Masonic affiliation must ask to join rather than being invited; this is to signify that one is willing to take responsibility for one's own inner development rather than being impelled by outward events. In the Entered Apprentice rite, the candidate goes in "slipshod": wearing slippers, loose clothing with one trouser leg rolled up, wearing a mask and with a noose around his neck—dressed, as some sources suggest, in the medieval garb for a convict en route to execution. This may be understood as meaning that whatever one's worldly achievements, one is, in the words of the ritual, "a poor candidate in a state of darkness." After passing through a number of tests and ordeals, the candidate is given a lambskin apron with Masonic emblems on it—a symbol of purity and renewal.[25]

The candidate at the outset is likened to the "rough ashlar"—in the language of the mason's trade, a roughhewn stone from the quarry. By being worked on with the tools of the Craft, he will be transformed into the "smooth ashlar"—symbolically, a perfect cube that is fit to be used in construction of the Temple.

The next grade, the Fellowcraft, is a rite of integration. Its central symbol is a winding staircase with a sequence of three, five, and seven stairs. The three stairs allude to the Three Great Lights of Masonry: Scripture, Square, and Compass. These are regarded as the "furniture" of the lodge and must be present during all workings. The Compass represents, among other things, the capacity to circumscribe desires and urges, while the Square represents an external standard of rectitude that enables the Mason to "square" his life. The Scripture represents the divine guidance that enables one to carry out this work. The set of five stairs represents the five orders of architecture, as well as the five senses; the seven stairs represent the seven liberal arts: grammar, logic, rhetoric, arithmetic, geometry, music, astronomy, as well as seven levels of consciousness possible within the psyche.[26]

But the most compelling of the Masonic initiations is the Master Mason degree. Here the candidate is taken through the symbolic death of Hiram Abiff. Hiram, in Masonic legend the architect of King Solomon's Temple, knows the "Master's Word" that enables him to direct the Temple's construction.[27] Three "ruffians" conspire to extract this secret from him.

One day as Hiram is leaving the site of the Temple, he is accosted by the ruffians. But Hiram refuses the secret to each of them in turn, and each one strikes him with one of the tools of the mason's trade. The third blow, struck with a heavy stone maul, slays him. The ruffians bury him "in the rubbish of the Temple," later moving him to a more remote spot under an acacia tree.

There Hiram's body is found by the workers of King Solomon and those of Solomon's colleague, another Hiram, king of Tyre; the two monarchs give Hiram Abiff his third and final interment "as near to the Sanctum Sanctorum as the Israelitish law would permit; there in a grave, from the centre three feet east and three feet west, three feet between north and south and five feet or more perpendicular."[28] They then erect a memorial of the loss of "the genuine secrets of a Master Mason."

What could this strange ritual possibly mean? It clearly has no literal meaning, for according to the biblical account Solomon's Temple was in fact finished; besides, what kind of "word" would be needed to complete it?

As we have already said, a definitive interpretation is not possible and perhaps not desirable. But Masonic writer W. L. Wilmshurst points toward one possible answer:

> Where, Brethren, do you imagine that grave to be? . . . Probably you have never thought of the matter as other than an ordinary burial outside the walls of a geographical Jerusalem. But the grave of Hiram is *ourselves*. . . . *We* are the grave of the Master. The lost guiding light is buried at the centre of ourselves. High as your hand may reach upwards or downwards from the centre of your own body—i.e., 3 feet between N. and S.—far as it can reach to right or left of the middle of your person—i.e., 3 feet between W. and E.—and 5 feet or more perpendicular—the height of the human body—these are the indications by which our cryptic ritual describes the tomb of Hiram Abiff at the centre of ourselves.[29]

In other words, Hiram Abiff is consciousness, specifically the higher consciousness that can build the Temple—the complete, integrated Self. Hiram has been slain by the three "ruffians," the three ordinary functions of the human mind known as thinking, feeling, and sensation. There are higher capacities in us as well, symbolized by Solomon and Hiram of Tyre, and though they can remind us of what has been lost, they cannot supply the missing "Word" of consciousness either.

As Wilmshurst goes on to say, Masonry "indicates whence we are come and whither we may return. . . . Its first purpose is to show that man has fallen away from a high and holy centre to the circumference or externalized condition in which we now live. . . . The second purpose . . . is to declare the way by which that centre may be found within ourselves, and this teaching is embodied in the discipline and ordeals delineated in the three degrees."[30]

Of the higher degrees of Masonry, the most familiar line in the United States is the Scottish Rite, which imparts degrees from the fourth through the thirty-third; the York Rite follows a parallel course, though with a total of only seven degrees beyond the first three (Masons may be initiated into both lines). Advanced or "fringe" Masonry goes further, the Order of Memphis and Misraim, with Egyptian-style rites that go back to the eighteenth-century magus Cagliostro, has as many as ninety-five. Mainstream Masonry does not initiate women, though an auxiliary group, the Order of the Eastern Star, is designed specifically for women. Co-Masonry, a more modern development, includes both men and women.

Although few other traditions have a more distinguished lineage, American lodges today complain of a dwindling and aging membership, and it may be that Masonry will soon become a little-used repository of esoteric knowledge. If so, its history points to one of the dangers of transmitting knowledge through ritual, for the subconscious, the part of the mind that ritual addresses, is also the part that is most given to automatic behavior. Hence one can go through the motions of a rite detached from any sense of the inner meaning, leaving it in the end an empty observance.

Even if Masonry dies out, however, most likely the knowledge itself will not perish but simply lie dormant, as it probably has for centuries in the past, until the time comes for it to be revived and reformulated for a new era.

## THE MADAME AND THE MASTERS

The Rosicrucian manifestos mark the beginning of the idea of the secret brotherhood in Western literature, but the notion of hidden masters who govern the spiritual evolution of humanity did not enter the popular consciousness until the advent of a remarkable woman named Helena Petrovna Blavatsky (1831–91).

If Blavatsky's life were written up as a novel, it would seem improbably romantic. Born to the Russian gentry, to escape her family she impetuously married an aged official when she was seventeen. The marriage soon ended in separation, though the amiable Nikifor Blavatsky continued to provide financial support for his absent wife for years thereafter.[31]

Blavatsky, or HPB, as she came to be known, devoted the rest of her life to the search for occult knowledge. Her exploits were impressive by any standard, and astonishing given the social constraints upon a woman in her day. She traveled to many countries, including Egypt, India, and the United States, but the decisive encounter in her life came in August 1851, when she encountered "the Master of my dreams" who was visiting London with an Indian delegation. The tall Hindu asked her cooperation in a work that he was about to undertake. In order to help him accomplish it, Blavatsky would have to spend three years in Tibet.[32]

There is some dispute about whether HPB actually visited Tibet, which was closed to Westerners at the time. At any rate this meeting began her work, which was to launch one of the most powerful religious impulses of the modern period. It was also to mark her initial encounter with a series of mysterious masters whose guidance and authority she claimed throughout her career.

We do not know who these masters were. Blavatsky and her disciples referred to the two principal ones as Morya and Koot Hoomi (or Kuthumi). The modern scholar K. Paul Johnson has connected them with Indian political and spiritual leaders Blavatsky was acquainted with; although questions remain even about Johnson's thesis, it remains the most plausible one.[33] The issue is complicated by the fact that to protect the masters' identities, Blavatsky altered certain details about them. They may also be composite figures, with features taken from several individuals.

Of course there is nothing innately unbelievable about the idea of Blavatsky meeting teachers from the mystic East; however, great controversy—both at the time and ever since—was provoked by the occult phenomena reported in connection with these figures.

Blavatsky herself was fond of producing such phenomena. In one famous episode, she caused a teacup and saucer to materialize at a picnic.[34] Accusations of trickery hovered around her, and in 1884 the British Society for Psychical Research sent an investigator to examine her claims; he pronounced her a fraud, though his findings have since been called into question.[35] If nothing else, these episodes serve as a reminder that the line between occult and stage magic is sometimes thin.

Blavatsky did not have to be present for strange incidents to occur. Her associate Henry Steel Olcott reported that one night, having retired to his room, he saw "towering above me in his great stature an Oriental clad in white garments," who advised Olcott that "a great work was to be done for humanity," and that Olcott could share in it if he wished. Despite his awe, Olcott wondered silently if Blavatsky had not cast some kind of "hypnotic glamour" over him. As if in response, the majestic personage removed his headcloth and left it behind as a souvenir before vanishing.[36]

Even assuming that these incidents cannot be explained away as prodigious feats of sleight-of-hand, one is tempted to ask, what is the point? Most esoteric writers warn against producing paranormal phenomena. In that case, why did these supposedly high adepts go through the rigmarole of producing occult parlor tricks? Morya himself warned of "the hankering after phenomena."[37]

The answer is best seen in the esoteric teaching that Blavatsky, with the help of her friends like Olcott, would propound as the culmination of her life's work. She would come to call it Theosophy—a proper noun that must be distinguished from theosophy in the general sense (theorizing about the nature of the divine). In the specific sense Theosophy refers to Blavatsky's own system of esoteric knowledge. It is propounded by the Theosophical Society, which she, Olcott, and a few others founded in New York in 1875, and which still operates today.

For most of her early career Blavatsky had focused on the Western esoteric tradition, and she had a deep familiarity with Hermeticism, Kabbalah, and Masonry; her first book, *Isis Unveiled*, published in 1877, is a long and discursive study of these themes. But after *Isis* appeared, Blavatsky and Olcott were drawn to India, where they arrived early in 1879.

Those were the days of the British Raj, when the morale of Indian civilization was probably at its lowest ebb. The great edifices of Hinduism and Buddhism were under assault not only from

Christian missionaries but from scientific materialism. If there were hidden masters directing the course of Blavatsky and her cohorts, it was evidently their aim to counteract this trend and to restore some measure of dignity to the great religions of the East. When asked by one of Blavatsky's pupils what good it did to pay attention to occultism, Koot Hoomi replied:

> When the natives see that an interest is taken by the English . . . in their ancestral science and philosophies, they will themselves take openly to their study. And when they come to realize that the old "divine" phenomena were not miracles, but scientific effects, superstition will abate. Thus, the greatest evil that now oppresses and retards the revival of Indian civilization will in time disappear.[38]

Theosophy was not meant solely to revive the flagging morale of Hinduism and Buddhism, however. The West was undergoing a spiritual crisis of its own: conventional Christianity found itself unable to confront new scientific findings that were challenging the Bible-based view of creation. Thinking people were left to choose between a rigidly materialistic science, which was telling them that the earth was millions of years old, and Christian theology, which insisted that the world had been created in 4004 B.C.

Blavatsky's perspective, set out most famously in her magnum opus, *The Secret Doctrine*, published in 1888, gave a third choice. Not only is our earth many millions of years old, it said, but the universe we know is only one of countless universes that are ceaselessly generated out of the Absolute. Moreover these facts were known to the sages of antiquity; in fact much of *The Secret Doctrine* consists of an extended commentary on a cryptic text called *The Stanzas of Dzyan*. Some scholars say this work forms part of the Kanjur, the immense canon of Tibetan Buddhist scripture, though skeptics assert that there is no evidence of this.[39]

*The Secret Doctrine* was the first book widely disseminated in the West to suggest "the Eternity of the Universe *in toto* as a boundless plane . . . 'the playground of numberless Universes incessantly manifesting and disappearing'," as Blavatsky put it.[40] As such it has influenced not only esotericists of every stripe but scientists as well: Einstein apparently kept a copy of it on his desk.[41] It is important not only because of the immeasurable scale on which it portrayed the universe, but because this scale was rooted in a spiritual perspective. The book teaches that behind the generation of numberless worlds lies the Absolute, "an Omnipresent, Eternal, Boundless, and Immutable Principle," which manifests in dual form, as "Spirit" and "Matter"; the interplay of these two forces causes all things to be.

Furthermore, all souls are fundamentally one with a cosmic Oversoul, which is itself but an aspect of the Absolute; hence the "Esoteric philosophy admits no privileges or special gifts in man, save those won by his own Ego through personal effort and merit throughout a long series of . . . reincarnations."[42]

Blavatsky here is alluding to another central idea in Theosophy: the doctrine of involution and evolution. But this teaching is far more comprehensive than Darwinian theory, for, in the words of one of Blavatsky's explicators, "the progressive development of everything, EVEN ATOMS, is taught."[43] That is, all of existence is taking part in an enormous cycle of the descent of Spirit into Matter and its eventual return to the bosom of the Absolute. Evolution is not a blind or mechanical process, but is guided by conscious forces, personified as the seven Dhyan-Chohans, "Cosmic Gods" who rule over nature.[44]

*The Secret Doctrine* also teaches human evolution, but again it is not the familiar kind. It speaks of "seven Root-Races" of humanity, of which ours is the fifth. The first race, known as "the Lords of the Moon," had only begun the descent into matter; they did not have a solid physical form as we know it but were composed only of subtle matter (Blavatsky jocularly called them "pudding-bags"). They were followed by the somewhat more palpable Hyperboreans, named after the country in ancient Greek myth located beyond the North Pole. The third race was the Lemurians; the fourth, the race of Atlantis; the fifth, ours, the "Aryans" (though this does not apply to any one ethnic group but to the whole of humanity of our period, having begun a million years ago). We are the race most firmly embedded in materiality, and we will in turn be followed by two more Root-Races, who will again become less material and more spiritual in substance.[45] Eventually we will all reach the stage of Dhyan-Chohans ourselves.

In *The Secret Doctrine*, then, there is a subtle dynamic between collective and individual evolution; throughout the gestation of universes and the cycles of races, each being, indeed each atom, is given the chance to attain consciousness. Evolution takes place through *karma* as played out in *reincarnation*. Although these two concepts have become deeply embedded in the popular consciousness, they still need to be clarified a bit.

Karma is often defined as the law of cause and effect. While this is true, it is not quite like ordinary mechanical causation, whereby, for example, my turning the key in the ignition causes the car to start. With karma, like causes produce like effects, but there may not be any obvious link between the two. Karma is registered in the astral light as upon photographic film,[46] and may lie dormant for years or even lifetimes before it becomes manifest. Moreover karma has a moral implication: good will yield good, and evil, evil. In the words of St. Paul, "Whatsoever a man soweth, that shall he also reap" (Gal. 6:7).

Hence reincarnation. The belief that we may live more than one life on earth has long been known in the West—the Greek philosopher Pythagoras probably taught a version of this doctrine in the sixth century B.C.,[47] and a reincarnation myth forms the culmination of Plato's *Republic*—but it has always been a minority view. The pagan Greeks and Romans tended to view the afterlife as a shadowy and dismal existence in Hades, while Christians have been suspicious of reincarnation as casting doubt on the sufficiency of Christ's atonement; the doctrine is also generally rejected by Muslims and Sufis. But in other esoteric circles the idea has found a congenial home. Many Neopagans, magicians, and New Agers believe in it (largely through the influence of Theosophy), and the Kabbalah speaks of reincarnation as the *sod hagilgulim,* or the "mystery of the cycles."

It is not hard to see why reincarnation has proved so popular in these quarters. Esoteric knowledge can hardly be seen as a requirement for salvation over the course of a single life: the way is too difficult and obscure, and too many people would be damned. Thus many attracted to esoteric ideas argue that gnosis is a matter of development: some people are ready for it and some are not. The latter will have the chance to learn again in another life.

Reading in Hindu and Buddhist literature will reveal that there reincarnation is often regarded as a bleak repetition of birth, death, and suffering; indeed the whole aim of Buddhism is to end this vicious cycle. But compared to the familiar Christian afterlife, where sinners endure eternal torments for their errors during a few years on earth, the concept of reincarnation is positively optimistic. It is not surprising that current polls show that it has gained a considerable following among Americans today.[48]

Most people think of reincarnation as a succession of lives upon earth, but according to Theosophy this is not necessarily the case. Just as humanity as a whole will evolve to the point where it transcends the material plane, so individuals will eventually develop to the point where they live on subtler planes than the one we know on this planet. It is here that many of the Masters and adepts live.

Blavatsky believed she was in contact with such people. Sometimes they made their appearance known to others. Her pupil Archibald Keightley reported once seeing "a distinguished Hindu, in full panoply of turban and dress" sitting on Blavatsky's sofa. As the room began to fill up, another guest walked up and sat down right in the middle of the distinguished Hindu—who promptly vanished.[49]

Even more than the other teachings we have examined, Theosophy comprises many intricate networks of systems, and this is also true of the hierarchy of masters and adepts. "The whole Kosmos is guided, controlled, and animated by an almost endless series of Hierarchies of sentient Beings, each having a mission to perform." Moreover "each of these Beings either *was,* or prepares to become a man, if not in the present, then in a past or a coming cycle."[50]

Blavatsky's own Masters were not disembodied entities; she portrayed them as human beings, living in Tibet, who were capable of making contact with chosen disciples on the astral plane or even materializing objects from afar. As we have seen, the Masters' ostensible aims lay in proving the validity of occult phenomena as well as promoting Indian civilization and combatting dogmatic Christianity and materialism in the West.[51]

The skeptic may look upon these high-minded goals with disdain, combined as they were with occult parlor tricks like materializing teacups and letters from the astral light. But a hundred years later, the Theosophical agenda appears to have succeeded remarkably well. India gained independence; the rigid dogmas of conventional Christianity have lost their hold on much of the populace—even more so in Europe than in America—and many once-esoteric ideas such as reincarnation and karma are now part of popular culture. It would be absurd to say that Blavatsky and her followers accomplished these things on their own.[52] But it is considerably less absurd to claim that, like the R. C. Brothers in their very different context, the Theosophists launched a subtle impetus that was to bear fruit over the next century.

To take one example, in 1893, two years after Blavatsky's death, the World Parliament of Religions in Chicago invited the first representatives of Asian religions to speak on equal terms with those of the Jewish and Christian faiths. As one delegate reported, the "seriousness, earnestness, devoutness, and spirituality" of the Asian representatives—several of whom were connected to Theosophy—"precluded any thought that the Oriental religions would 'fall or melt into mist' before a triumphant Christianity."[53]

One of the participants, the Hindu Swami Vivekananda, received such an enthusiastic reception that he stayed in the U.S. to teach; the next year marked the beginning of the Vedanta Society, the first large-scale Hindu movement in the West. By the late 1980s there were over seventy active groups in the U.S. promoting

Hinduism to Westerners.[54] Buddhism, particularly in its Zen and Tibetan forms, has had an even wider appeal, and prominent Buddhists such as the Dalai Lama and the Vietnamese monk Thich Nhat Hanh have achieved celebrity status.

After Blavatsky's death in 1891, the Theosophical Society was riven with conflict, producing several splinter groups, including a community at Point Loma, California, now headquartered in Altadena, California. There is also a smaller United Lodge of Theosophists, founded in 1909, which, like the Point Loma community, has served as a refuge for Theosophists who are dissatisfied with the main organization.

The Theosophical Society, based in Adyar, near Madras, India (with American headquarters in Wheaton, Illinois), remains the largest and most visible of Theosophical organizations. It was led by Olcott until his death in 1907; thereafter he was succeeded by Annie Besant, a former freethinker and political activist who had been converted to Theosophy by Blavatsky. Besant and C. W. Leadbeater, a former Anglican priest, guided the Theosophical Society into the 1930s.[55]

Theosophy today remains faithful to its "Three Declared Objects" as originally formulated:

1. To form a nucleus of the Universal Brotherhood of Humanity, without distinction of race, creed, sex, caste, or color.
2. To encourage the study of Comparative Religion, Philosophy, and Science.
3. To investigate unexplained laws of Nature and the powers inherent in man.[56]

What is striking about these objects is that they require no belief in Blavatsky's Masters, Theosophical teachings, or *The Secret Doctrine*. And no such demands are made of members, although in practice most Theosophists probably accept Blavatsky's ideas. The Theosophical Society remains a viable path for many, and it is likely to continue to do so for the foreseeable future, although like

Masonry and Rosicrucianism, it has probably seen its heyday, eclipsed in part by its direct descendant, the New Age movement.

## KRISHNAMURTI AND STEINER

Undoubtedly the strangest episode in Theosophical history after Blavatsky's death centered on Jiddu Krishnamurti (1895–1986), a Hindu Brahmin boy proclaimed by Leadbeater in 1909 to be the new World Teacher. Under the auspices of Leadbeater and Besant, the Theosophical Society adopted Krishnamurti and his brother, raised them, and educated them in England. The Theosophists also formed a subgroup called the Order of the Star to further his work.

The role of World Teacher never sat well with Krishnamurti, however, and in 1929 he surprised everyone by abruptly dissolving the Order of the Star and dissociating himself from Theosophy. In a famous address, he declared, "Truth is a pathless land. . . . The moment you follow someone you cease to follow Truth."[57]

For the rest of his life, this Brahmin raised by Theosophists was a profound but paradoxical figure: a teacher who disdained authority, a messiah who renounced salvation. His method of teaching was a relentless inquiry cutting away all intellectual concepts and appeals to authority, leaving the student only with his or her own naked consciousness, divorced from all preconceptions. Krishnamurti did not claim to belong to any lineage, but his teaching probably most resembles Advaita Vedanta, a Hindu tradition that teaches the essential unity of each human Self with universal consciousness. Illumination consists of recognizing the truth of this identity.[58]

Even early on, a number of Theosophists were doubtful about promoting Krishnamurti as World Teacher. One of these was the general secretary of the society's German branch, an Austrian named Rudolf Steiner (1861–1925). Steiner broke with the Theosophists over Krishnamurti in 1909, but he had already begun to differ with HPB's teachings on a number of points, notably her valuation of what Steiner called "the Christ event."[59] Blavatsky, who had little patience with Christian dogma, was inclined to see Christianity as in many ways inferior to the wisdom of the East. Nor did she ascribe any particular importance to the death and resurrection of Christ. Steiner disagreed.

Steiner was something of an esoteric Renaissance man who began his career by editing the scientific writings of Goethe. A natural clairvoyant, he became more and more drawn to unseen realities; later on, these insights would enable him to make his own contributions to fields as diverse as theater, dance, medicine, education, and agriculture. He eventually met a spiritual teacher whom he never identified but who assigned him the formidable task of reversing the trend toward materialism and of restoring to the West the concepts of karma and rebirth.[60]

Since these goals so strongly resembled those of the Theosophists, it is understandable that Steiner would work with them for a number of years. The complex esoteric system he described has much in common with Theosophy: their basic views of the Root Races, for example, are quite similar.[61]

Broadly outlined, Steiner's cosmology also corresponds to the Theosophical view, with its aeons-long perspective on the enfoldment of spirit into matter.[62] Steiner gives more emphasis, though, to the role of superhuman evil in this process. He stresses that long before human incarnation on this planet, the Godhead decided that "humanity certainly could have developed well, but could become even stronger if obstacles were put in its way."[63]

These obstacles have primarily taken the form of two cosmic beings called Lucifer and Ahriman. Lucifer is of course the traditional name for the "morning star," the angel who became the Devil after he fell from heaven; Ahriman is the name of the evil principle as portrayed in Zoroastrianism.

For Steiner, Lucifer is the source of pride, of self-will, and also of an underestimation of the physical world that we need to experience at this stage in our development. Ahriman, by contrast, is an overestimation of the physical; if Lucifer would have us detach ourselves from this plane too quickly, Ahriman would bind us to it. It is he that is responsible for mechanical ingenuity and for technical inventions that we develop before we have the moral capacity to handle them.

Neither of these entities is wholly adverse in his influence, for Lucifer is responsible also for our self-esteem, our desire for freedom, and our love of beauty and art, while Ahriman enables us to live grounded in physical reality. But in the course of human development, these entities began to engulf the core of our essence, which Steiner calls the "I," manifesting as lower desires of all sorts. Humanity would long have been entirely overcome by these forces had not certain angels and archangels chosen to incarnate in great world teachers.

The situation changed entirely when a certain high cosmic being chose to incarnate in the person of Jesus of Nazareth. Christ's death and resurrection not only released the "I" from its bondage to the forces of evil, but made it possible for us to redeem those forces. "Human beings will redeem Lucifer if they receive the Christ-power in the appropriate way," says Steiner. "As a result, human beings will grow stronger than they would have been otherwise."[64]

Steiner's cosmology arose not from reading or theorizing but from his "supersensible perception," that is, what he regarded as his clairvoyant capacity to read the Akashic Records, the images of past events that have been recorded on the astral light. For all his voluminousness (his lectures and writings fill three hundred volumes in German), Steiner was not a dogmatist: he did not insist on the correctness of his views, but said he was merely reporting on his clairvoyant observations.

The essence of Steiner's teaching, known as Anthroposophy or Spiritual Science, has to do not with learning Steiner's ideas, but with developing one's own supersensible capacities. An overview of this method appears in his book *How to Know Higher Worlds*.[65] Yet Steiner's followers have often been content with believing what he said rather than finding out for themselves—a fate that has in various forms often overtaken the legacies of Blavatsky, Gurdjieff, Jung, Krishnamurti, and indeed most spiritual teachers past and present: the ideas of these restless geniuses settle down into a comfortable slumber in the minds of followers.

## THE CONSCIOUS CIRCLE

We know nothing of Steiner's teacher. It is entirely possible that he was part of a Rosicrucian line that continued in Germany into the nineteenth century (Steiner believed Christian Rosenkreutz to have been "a high initiate" who had actually lived),[66] but this is speculation. We know little more about Blavatsky's Masters, Gurdjieff's teachers, or the shadowy adepts behind the Rosicrucian manifestos. And we are thus thrown back to the question of what this secret brotherhood is. Does it really exist?

In recent years conspiracy theories seem to have replaced baseball statistics as objects of popular fascination, and various esoteric or quasi-esoteric groups are frequently thought to be part of such cabals. The Freemasons are common targets, but probably the favorite object of suspicion is the Illuminati, another Rosicrucian-type order that flourished in Bavaria in the late eighteenth century. The Illuminati, a secret society designed to foment revolution, became an object of widespread fear in those days, when the French Revolution and its Reign of Terror darkly hinted to the powers of Europe what fate might lie before them. There is no reason to believe that the actual Order of the Illuminati outlasted the eighteenth century, but rumors of its persistence continue to fascinate many.

Allegations of global conspiracies involving the Freemasons, Illuminati, and other such organizations may form an entertaining pastime, but in the end they are hard to credit. It is certainly true that global wealth and power reside in the hands of comparatively few people, but from all evidence this exclusive club consists of the customary mix of those who have inherited their position and those crafty and willful enough to have fought their way to the top. Personal contacts of course form a crucial part of this network, but there is no reason to believe that admission to any mystical order confers these benefits on anyone.

Then there is the more elusive question of the "Secret Chiefs," the masters in embodied or disembodied form who hold their conclaves in the fastnesses of the Himalayas and constitute the hidden government of mankind. In one sense such claims are impossible to refute: no one could possibly delve into every inaccessible corner of the world and prove that no such groups meet there. But we have no way of knowing of them.

Gurdjieff spoke of the existence of a "conscious circle" of humanity. He regarded it not as an organization but as a level of understanding. Those who possess this level of understanding can have no discord among them. Moreover "their activity is entirely co-ordinated and leads to one common aim without any kind of compulsion." It is difficult to speculate about this aim, although Gurdjieff suggested that it has to do with human evolution.[67]

If our glimpses of the workings of this "conscious circle" have been correct, it is clear that its aims necessarily change over the course of time. In the seventeenth century, a time of religious bigotry and strife, the R.C. Brothers urged man to see "how far his knowledge extendeth into Nature." In the nineteenth century, with the very triumph of this "knowledge of Nature" in the form of scientific inquiry, and its consequent materialism, Blavatsky's Masters were urging the rediscovery of the spiritual realms. Obviously this is not ambivalence or opportunism: a given current inevitably produces its own excesses and follies, and a new current is needed to counteract them.

But what do these grand perspectives mean for the individual? Is one supposed to seek out the hidden brotherhood, wherever it may be, and petition for membership?

Admittance to this brotherhood—which is of course also a sisterhood—is not a matter of degrees or titles. For some it may well be marked by admission to various secret societies (and none of those we have named in this chapter can be reckoned among them; rather they are *formerly* secret societies that have for various reasons gone public). But ultimately, as Gurdjieff said, it is a matter of understanding. And this is not a matter of comprehension of mere facts and theories, but a level of consciousness. At its core it can be said to be marked by one salient characteristic: those who possess it recognize that, however it is grasped, *the work is worth doing for its own sake* apart from any reward that it may produce.

A seemingly obvious point, but it is not so obvious in practice. Nearly everyone undertakes the spiritual search for some personal gain. To judge by the books published on these topics, many people come to the path hoping it will win them money or love or personal fulfillment. Others view the benefits in more elevated terms, as gnosis, enlightenment, or salvation.

In a sense there is nothing wrong with these goals, for we must all begin at street level. And for a long time, no matter what path one chooses, personal development will be the focus of effort. But at a certain stage one must realize that the work of human evolution is worth doing in its own right, apart from any personal advantage that may accrue. Ironically, if one does not realize this truth after a certain point, personal growth will most likely stop or even reverse course.

Attainment of this understanding, which may or may not be marked by some formal ceremony, can be considered the first degree of initiation into the "conscious circle" of humanity. Having reached this understanding, one naturally concludes that each of us has a unique part to play in this work, and that one's own task is to find it or at least recognize it when it appears.

Beyond this it is difficult to speak in general terms. One's task may require participation in current events, or it may not; as we have seen, esoteric work operates on a larger scale than ordinary life.

## SUGGESTED READING

Blavatsky, H. P. *The Secret Doctrine*. London: Theosophical Publishing Co., 1888.

Few will be able to read this massive and often frustrating work straight through. But it is still worth approaching as a source of esoteric ideas. It has been reprinted frequently since its first appearance.

Case, Paul Foster. *The True and Invisible Rosicrucian Order*. York Beach, Maine: Samuel Weiser, 1985.

Much of this book discusses Tarot symbolism, but it also contains texts of the Rosicrucian manifestos and a profound discussion of "the inner school."

Ellwood, Robert. *Theosophy*. Wheaton, Ill.: Quest Books, 1986.

A sincere, thoughtful, and clear introduction to the basic ideas and aspirations of Theosophy.

Godwin, Joscelyn. *The Theosophical Enlightenment*. Albany: State University of New York Press, 1994.

A superb discussion of the occult and Enlightenment currents that joined to produce Theosophy.

Hall, Manly P. *The Lost Keys of Freemasonry*. 1923. Reprint. Los Angeles: Philosophical Research Society, 1976.

A concise guide to some of the hidden teachings that may be concealed in the first three Masonic initiations.

Hindes, James H. *Renewing Christianity*. Hudson, N.Y.: Anthroposophic Press, 1996.

This brief work focuses on the Christian Community, an esoteric Christian movement based on Rudolf Steiner's teachings, but it also offers an accessible overview of Steiner's ideas.

MacNulty, W. Kirk. *Freemasonry: A Journey through Ritual and Symbol*. London: Thames & Hudson, 1991.

A lavishly illustrated approach to the esoteric ideas buried in Masonic symbolism.

McIntosh, Christopher. *The Rosicrucians*. 1980. Reprint. York Beach, Maine: Samuel Weiser, 1997.

Originally published under the title *The Rosy Cross Unveiled*, this work contains a lucid history of the Rosicrucian movements and currents up to the present.

Steiner, Rudolf. *How to Know Higher Worlds*. Translated by Christopher Bamford. Hudson, N.Y.: Anthroposophic Press, 1994.

All in all the best of Steiner's writings to begin with. *An Outline of Esoteric Science* (Hudson, N.Y.: Anthroposophic Press, 1997) contains his cosmological views.

Yates, Frances A. *The Rosicrucian Enlightenment*. 1972. Reprint. London: Ark, 1986.

The single most important account of the milieu of the Rosicrucian manifestos and their influence on the early modern period.

*Twelve*

# THE ETERNAL NEW AGE

The New Age. By now we have come to associate it with innumerable fads, with Mayan calendars and crystals and messages from extraterrestrials, with celebrities telling of their previous incarnations and their dialogues with various forms of vegetable life. Few are more eager to distance themselves from this potpourri of crazes than many disciples of the Western esoteric traditions. The ritual magician, the Kabbalist meditating upon the names of God, and the Gurdjieffian soberly endeavoring to remember himself are often chagrined to learn that from the mainstream point of view they are as much a part of the New Age as those pursuing the most ephemeral of fads.

The popular imagination does not discriminate when it comes to alternative spirituality. Most people would see nearly all of the teachings discussed in this book as part of the New Age. Is there any reason, then, to consider the New Age as a separate category? There is, for although the New Age encompasses many of the themes we have already discussed, it has its own twist on them.

Moreover, this movement has become a large social force. Scholar Paul Heelas estimates that "considerably more than ten million in the USA draw on what the New Age has to offer." One study conducted in 1990 concluded that $4 billion a year is spent on "New Age consultants" by businesses alone (out of a total of $30 billion spent on business training). This, of course, does not include the enormous amount spent by individuals on New Age seminars, workshops, courses, and treatments ranging from Rolfing to aromatherapy, or on books and magazines.[1]

The heart of the New Age impulse consists of two fundamental ideas:

1. Spirituality is a matter of individual experience, growth, and authority; it cannot be dictated by dogmas and creeds. (Obviously this resembles the idea of gnosis.)
2. Humanity is at present undergoing a collective awakening of consciousness. When this is complete, society—and, some say, the consciousness of the planet itself—will have been restructured on more spiritual terms.

These ideas do not necessarily contradict each other, yet they cut across each other in certain ways. The resulting conflicts have helped cause much of the confusion surrounding the New Age. But before we can adequately examine these, it would be helpful to have some idea of the movement's background.

The New Age has always been with us. Throughout history people have always been proclaiming the imminent arrival of a new dispensation. Zoroastrianism, one of the oldest extant religions, founded sometime between 1500 and 500 B.C., preached the coming of a series of cosmic redeemers called the Saoshyants.[2] The prophets of the Old Testament envisioned a day when "the glory of the Lord shall be revealed, and all flesh shall see it together" (Isa. 40:5). Christianity's proclamation of a New Age formed part of the threat it posed to the authorities during the faith's infancy.

Each era in Western history contains forecasts of an epoch when all wrongs will be remedied and the sufferings of humanity assuaged. In more recent times, the eighteenth-century visionary Emanuel Swedenborg said that the Last Judgment had taken place on the heavenly planes in the year 1757, an event that would inaugurate a "New Jerusalem" for humanity on earth.[3] (A Sweden-borgian named Warren Felt Evans published a book entitled *The New Age and Its Message* in 1864.)[4] The Great Seal of the United States, reproduced on the back of the dollar bill, includes the phrase *Novus Ordo Seclorum*—a "new order of the ages."

Today this "new order" is often associated with the Age of Aquarius, a term that filtered into popular consciousness in the 1960s, and which actually refers to an astrological phenomenon. By most accounts, for the last two millennia we have been living in the Age of Pisces. This means that each year at the vernal equinox, the sun rises with the constellation Pisces in the background. Because of a phenomenon called the precession of the equinoxes (caused by a slight wobble in the earth's axis), this background constellation shifts over a long period of time: the equinox spends some 2,160 years in each of the twelve constellations in the zodiac. Thus the whole cycle takes approximately 25,900 years, known as a Great Year.

At some point the sun will rise with Aquarius in the background, and this will mark the dawn of the new era. Unfortunately, because there is no clear demarcation in the skies between one constellation and another, astrologers do not agree about precisely when the vernal equinox enters Aquarius. Estimates vary from those that say it happened as early as 1762 to those reckoning it at around 3000 A.D., with the majority expecting it between 2100 and 2300.[5]

Some astrologers associate the beginning of the Aquarian Age with a remarkable stellium, or conglomeration of planets, that took place on February 5, 1962, when the sun, moon, Mercury, Venus, Mars, Jupiter, and Saturn were all in the sign of Aquarius. There is a poetic truth to this timing, for Aquarius has to do with idealism, utopianism, and a love of freedom that often verges on eccentricity—precisely the traits that distinguished the 1960s worldwide. Moreover 1962 was the year of the Cuban missile crisis, the closest humanity has yet come to full-scale nuclear war. Did the shock of this event help create the surge of peace activism in that decade?

It is impossible to say for sure, but there is something arresting in the thought. At any rate many people involved in the New Age believe that we are on the cusp between two eras, and that many of the dislocations and discomforts of our time arise from this transition.

## ALICE BAILEY AND THE TIBETAN

One of the first people to speak of the New Age as it is understood today was Alice Bailey (1880–1949), an Englishwoman who, like Blavatsky, believed she had been contacted by a Master. She was fifteen at the time, and was staying at her aunt's house in Scotland. One Sunday morning she was home alone when a man wearing a turban and well-cut European clothes entered the room. He met with her briefly and said she would have some work to do in the future. Not wanting to be accused of religious hysteria, she kept the incident to herself, but she recognized the man years later in a portrait of a Master at a Theosophical lodge in California.[6]

In 1919, Bailey was telepathically contacted by "D.K." or "Djwhal Kul," a Theosophical Master who described himself as living in a physical body and serving as an abbot in a Tibetan lamasery. (D.K. seems to have been a different man from the one that walked into her aunt's house in Scotland.) For the next thirty years, Bailey would serve as D.K.'s amanuensis, transcribing works he was dictating telepathically from the Himalayas thousands of miles away.

Bailey's collaboration with D.K. was a form of *channeling.* Channeled material is believed to be transmitted through a living human being from another being—usually a disembodied spirit, though other entities, such as extraterrestrials, are occasionally involved; Bailey believed her source was a living human on the other side of the world.

In some respects channeling resembles possession as experienced by Spiritualist mediums or by devotees of Voudoun or Santería except that the "channel," the human being through whom the material is transmitted, is not always in a trance. Frequently, as with Bailey or Helen Schucman, the channel of *A Course in Miracles*, the recipient is completely conscious but simply hears the material as an inner voice. He or she may even be able to stop and start the dictation as necessary.

The import of channeled messages also differs from those in Spiritualism or the African traditions. Whereas mediums generally invoke spirits to satisfy the personal wishes of their clients and the gods of the African diaspora inhabit the bodies of their human devotees to experience physicality, channeling usually has a much more universal message. The comments of Mary-Margaret Moore, who channels an "energy" called Bartholomew, are representative:

> The energy has a spiritual flavor, rather than a karmic one. Questions like, "Will I ever have any money?" or "Will I marry Joe?" are best left to others in this field.
>
> This energy's concerns are with giving us tools to awaken from the illusion of our separateness from the One.[7]

Even granting that channeled messages are genuinely coming from another realm, why should we assume these "energies" or "entities" are beneficent or sincere? Sacred literature from all eras is full of warnings about malign and deceitful spirits. In the end we have no criterion other than D.K. himself offers:

> The books that I have written are sent out with no claim for their acceptance. They may, or may not, be correct, true and useful. It is for you to ascertain their truth by right practice and by the exercise of the intuition. . . . If the teaching conveyed calls forth a response from the illumined mind of the worker in the world, and brings a flashing forth of his intuition, then let that teaching be accepted. But not otherwise.[8]

Here we find one of the central themes of the New Age: the sufficiency of the individual's own insight for guidance. No external source can override this authority.

Bailey naturally believed that her story would interest the Theosophists, but they were not entirely pleased to find a new-comer with independent access to a Master, and she was accused of falsely claiming to have contact with the Tibetan. Leadbeater did not criticize her, however, and there is some evidence that the material in his book *The Masters and the Path* is based on an early Bailey work entitled *Initiation, Human and Solar.*[9]

Undaunted by her reception, Bailey continued for the rest of her life to serve as "amanuensis" for the ponderous blue volumes that bear her name. With titles like *Discipleship in the New Age, A Treatise on White Magic*, and *The Externalization of the Hierarchy*, they fill thousands of pages. They are also extremely dense. Bailey's husband, Foster, once admitted that in the first edition of *A Treatise on White Magic*, the printers had inadvertently typeset twenty pages twice and included them in the published volume. It was two years before anyone noticed, including the Baileys themselves.[10]

Even so, the central theme of the "Alice Bailey materials" (as they are often called) is clear enough. It is "*the raising of the level of human consciousness* . . . so that intelligent thinking men and women will be consciously in touch with the world of ideas and the realm of intuitive perception." To this end a "New Group of World Servers" is emerging "who are building the new world order," a synthesis of hierarchy and democracy.[11]

Bailey actually spoke of a "new world order" decades before it was proclaimed by President Bush. It is unlikely, of course, that either the president or his speechwriters had read Alice Bailey's books or had even heard of her, but details of this sort have given rise to the idea of a "New Age conspiracy." One fundamentalist Christian writer, Constance Cumbey, even depicts Bailey as the sinister ringleader of this cabal.[12]

There is no evidence that Bailey or her organization, the Lucis Trust, masterminded the New Age. It is true that her works set out the movement's major themes in an unusually prescient fashion, but it is also true that many people, even many leaders, in the New Age movement know nothing of her works. Marilyn Ferguson, whose book *The Aquarian Conspiracy* remains the definitive self-portrait of the New Age, sent out a survey to 185 leaders in the movement asking, among other things, what figures had most influenced them. Those most frequently named included Pierre Teilhard de Chardin, the French Jesuit anthropologist whose writings attempted to reconcile Christianity with the theory of evolution; C. G. Jung; psychologists Abraham Maslow and Carl Rogers; and Aldous Huxley. Bailey's name did not even appear.[13]

Nor, for that matter, did any one person or group mastermind the New Age. As most intelligent observers recognize, it is a broad social phenomenon with many roots and precursors, including New England Transcendentalism, the utopianism of the nineteenth century, Jungian psychology, the humanistic psychology of Maslow and Rogers, and the psychedelic revolution of the 1960s.[14]

One major inspiration for the Aquarian movement comes from the Eastern traditions, which began to be imported to the West at the end of the eighteenth century as texts like the *Bhagavad Gita* were translated into European languages. Sometimes this influence has come directly from Hindu and Buddhist teachers like Paramahansa Yogananda, author of the popular *Autobiography of a Yogi*, or the noted Zen Buddhist author D. T. Suzuki. In other cases, Eastern ideas made their way to the New Age through Westernized forms like Theosophy, which, for example, popularized the notion of the *chakras*, subtle energy centers in the human body that extend from the perineum to the crown of the head. The maverick Anglican priest Alan Watts and the Beat poets of the fifties also helped create a widespread audience for Buddhism.

The New Age has often turned to science for metaphors as well. One of the most common comes from Thomas Kuhn, whose classic *Structure of Scientific Revolutions* spoke of a "paradigm shift" that occurs when a new scientific model replaces an older one. Many New Agers believe society as a whole is undergoing a comparable shift today, when old models of thought and social structure are being replaced by a newer, more universal and inclusive vision.[15]

Science has also provided a conceptual framework for the UFO mythos. We have already discussed this intricate subject in the chapter on Jung, and in one sense it is impossible to add more, for any sober examination of the subject suggests that all the current explanations—whether advanced by believers or by debunkers—are extremely tenuous. It is as absurd to write all these sightings off as swamp gas or jetliners as it is to claim they come from far-off planets. As Jung said, we are left only with the conclusion that something is happening, but we don't know what it is.

But we also know that when the human mind encounters something unfamiliar, it attempts to explain this in terms of what it already knows. The "myth of things seen in the skies" has been with us for thousands of years; we can see evidence of it in Sumerian texts and in the famous chariot vision in the first chapter of Ezekiel. In the past people conceived of these "things seen in the skies" as gods or other supernatural beings. Today, thanks to our own explorations of the heavens, we are more likely to picture them in scientific or technological terms: the apparitions are not deities or angels, but humanoid figures in highly advanced spaceships.

There is also the bewildering phenomenon of people who believe they have been contacted or abducted by aliens for what often seem to be scientific experiments. It would be tempting to dismiss these accounts as sheer insanity, but there is often much consistency in detail among different accounts, even when the subjects had not been in contact with each other and had no previous knowledge of the phenomenon.[16] There are also people who regard themselves as "walk-ins"—extraterrestrials who have somehow inserted themselves into human bodies and now live among us.

If in fact they happen, are these occurrences new or have they always existed among us? Were the alien abductions of today described in ancient myths as seduction or rape by the gods? It is fascinating to speculate on these matters, but the answers still elude us. Perhaps we are not yet ready to learn the truth.[17]

## EDGAR CAYCE AND EARTH CHANGES

The prolix writings of Alice Bailey have never enjoyed a mass readership. A much better-known herald of the New Age is Edgar Cayce (1877–1945), the "sleeping prophet" from Kentucky who delivered over 14,000 "readings" in a trance state over a period of forty-three years. (Cayce was not conscious during these trances; he had no recollection of them afterward and was sometimes disturbed by what they said.) Many of these readings were for individuals and contain personal predictions and recommendations for healing. But Cayce (whose name is pronounced "Casey") also made many forecasts about the fate of humanity. Even more than the Alice Bailey materials, they have shaped the expectations of the New Age.

Bailey's books, though often sober and monitory in tone, do not stress any coming cataclysms; they mainly focus on the demands that will be made of the "New Group of World Servers." Cayce's readings give a different picture. They too speak of a New Age (which, according to Cayce, began in 1932)[18] and of the responsibilities that it lays upon people of our time. But they also contain forebodings of what Cayce calls "earth changes," or massive natural disasters in which present land masses will sink and others will rise from the ocean's depths.

Such prophecies have clearly been inspired by the story of Atlantis. The legend of this vanished country goes back at least as far as two dialogues of Plato, the *Timaeus* and the *Critias*, written around 355 B.C. They describe the lost continent beyond "the Pillars of Hercules"—the Straits of Gibraltar—and how it sank. Though it is not clear how literally Plato meant this story to be taken, the dialogues say this information came from the priests in Egypt, who had preserved it for nine thousand years.[19]

The priest quoted in the *Timaeus* also says, "There have been, and there will be again, many destructions of mankind arising out of many causes; the greatest have been brought about by the agencies of fire and water."[20] Clearly "earth changes" have been part of the legendary history of humankind for millennia.

Cayce's trance readings foretell similar tumults: Much of Japan, California, and the East Coast of the United States will sink, while "Poseidia" or Atlantis will rise again. Cayce's predicted date for this resurrection of the vanished continent was not correct—"Expect it in '68 or '69," he said, "not so far away!"[21]—but many still await "earth changes" that, Cayce says, are due in the imminent future.

As with the endless attempts to predict the date of Christ's return, the failure of past predictions does not forestall new ones; the date is simply pushed farther into the future (although it usually remains close enough to cause some anxiety). José Argüelles, making predictions based on a convoluted interpretation of the ancient Mayan calendar, insists that the present epoch will come to an end in 2012.[22] Difficult as they are to understand, Argüelles' theories inspired the Harmonic Convergence in 1987, the first New Age event to take place on a mass scale, when thousands of people gathered around the world to tune into a new, higher level of consciousness. Other New Age movements—many of a grassroots nature—proclaim similar events. At such junctures higher forces are said to be channeled to earth, "stepping up" the consciousness of the human race and sometimes of the earth itself, which is regarded as a living, evolving entity.

Obviously many of the predictions made for "earth changes" and similar catastrophes have been wrong. In the 1980s, Elizabeth Clare Prophet, the leader of a New Age sect who claims to channel Ascended Masters, advised her disciples to withdraw to mountain areas like Montana and stockpile food, as she predicted a likely nuclear war in early 1990. Many of her followers accompanied her to Montana; many also broke with her when the conflagration did not arrive.[23] "Ramtha," allegedly a 35,000-year-old entity channeled by JZ Knight, urged similar action upon his followers in the 1980s; predicting natural disasters in California, he encouraged his pupils to move to the Pacific Northwest. Since then he has toned down his warnings and today mostly concentrates upon presenting "Gnostic" teachings at Ramtha's School of Enlightenment in Yelm, Washington.[24]

In his book on channeling, the scholar Arthur Hastings concludes, "To my knowledge, in every case where prophecies of major disasters can be checked against real events, the channels do not stand up well. The events that are prophesied consistently do not occur."[25] Why, then, are people so drawn to them?

Most of us spend our time oppressed by worries about money, love, family, health, and a thousand other concerns great and petty; the quotidian hangs over us like a shroud. The dream of a new era that will sweep away these problems serves sometimes as an encouragement, sometimes as a narcotic. (Gurdjieff spoke of how the sacred function of hope had in modern man degenerated into a hideous disease called "tomorrow.")

Thus most New Age predictions of "earth changes" can be viewed as a twisted form of hope, since the forecasts usually also say that a small remnant (presumably including the prophet's audience) will be spared. But in another sense these messages also portray the collective fears of humankind. David Spangler, a leading New Age figure, offers this view, which he says was presented to him by a spirit guide he knows as John:

> There is a band of fear and psychic pain around your world, the psychic equivalent of the air pollution that surrounds your cities. It is here that the prophetic movies exist or can be constructed in the interaction between a psychic's personal fears and antipathies and those that resonate at this level. . . . There is a great deal of anger vibrating within this band of thought and feeling. Many prophecies that deal with the destruction and dismemberment of your civilization simply reflect and express that anger. They are not foretellings of the future, only revelations that anger exists and that people wish that that which angers and frustrates them would be destroyed.[26]

Even when cataclysms are forecast, they are frequently viewed as a prelude to the New Age itself, when "peace will guide the planets, and love will steer the stars," in the words of the sixties hit

"Aquarius." Nonetheless, whether the prophecies have emphasized disasters or coming felicity, their records for accuracy have not been good. Frustratingly, only in retrospect will we be able to know which ones were right.

## ACCELERATING EVOLUTION

Many dimensions of the New Age owe their existence to more conventional currents of thought. This is particularly the case with what has come to be called the *human potential movement,* which centers on the idea that by their own personal transformation, individuals can accelerate the evolution of humanity.

This idea is far removed from the standard Darwinian notion of natural selection. By the Darwinian view, an individual can do nothing to further the development of the species; one's genes will either prove advantageous to survival or not. Evolution as seen by the human potential movement is closer to the ideas of Jean-Baptiste de Lamarck (1744–1829), the great French naturalist who preceded Darwin by half a century.[27]

Unlike Darwin, Lamarck believed that acquired characteristics can be transmitted to one's progeny. In elementary texts this idea is sometimes derided by using the example of giraffes: by Lamarck's theory early giraffes would have stretched their necks to reach high foliage and would have somehow transmitted these stretched necks to their offspring. Nobody believes this nowadays, but many thinkers remain intrigued by the notion of creative evolution, the thought that we may further the progress of the species more actively than as mere sacs of genes. Versions of this idea can be found in Bernard Shaw; the French philosopher Henri Bergson (whose sister Moina was a leader of the Golden Dawn); the twentieth-century Indian philosopher Sri Aurobindo; and Teilhard de Chardin. But its most famous exponent was the great German thinker Friedrich Nietzsche (1844–1900), who wrote in *Thus Spake Zarathustra*:

*I teach you the overman.* Man is something that shall be overcome. What have you done to overcome him?

All beings so far have created something beyond themselves; and do you want to be the ebb of this great flood and even go back to the beasts rather than overcome man? What is the ape to man? A laughingstock or a painful embarrassment. And man shall be just that for the overman.[28]

This "overman"—or "superman" as he is more familiarly known—haunts the twentieth century. Even the dullest reader of Nietzsche must see that he would have been horrified by the Nazis and all they tried to do, but this did not prevent them from creating their own bizarre mutations of Nietzsche's thought. Hitler is said to have been obsessed by the idea of the superman or "new man": "The new man is living amongst us now! He is here!" he is rumored to have exclaimed to one of his deputies. "I have seen the new man. He is intrepid and cruel. I was afraid of him." Some contend that the whole Third Reich was nothing more than a twisted attempt to create such a "new man."[29]

Certain critics of the New Age, particularly fundamentalist Protestants, insist that today's human potential movement is trying to recreate the ideals of the Nazis.[30] It is true that the two movements agree in accepting the idea that humanity must "overcome" itself and serve as a bridge to something higher, but the human potential movement does not hold out the ideal of a "new man" who is "intrepid and cruel." Instead, in the words of Michael Murphy, cofounder of California's famous Esalen Institute and one of the movement's leading figures, "metanormal capacities . . . seem to develop best in conjunction with love for other living things." In his magnum opus, *The Future of the Body*, which exhaustively describes superhuman functioning in people ranging from Tibetan monks to baseball pitchers, Murphy includes such qualities as "love that transcends ordinary needs and reveals a fundamental unity with others."[31]

Murphy suggests that "a new evolutionary domain is tentatively rising in the human race, both spontaneously and by transformative practice."[32] Superhuman functioning, the harbinger of this new domain, is not limited to exceptional feats of physical prowess or paranormal abilities, but includes transcendent empathy and altruism.

By now it should be clear how the human potential movement both resembles and differs from the more mystical dimensions of the New Age. They agree in seeing a new era dawning for the human race, but where one sees this as the result of an outpouring of spiritual energy from higher planes (sometimes after various catastrophes and "earth changes"), the other sees it as arising from the creative edge of evolution itself. Moreover, says the human potential movement, we can speed up this process by our own transformative work, which may include anything from meditation to T'ai Chi to long-distance running. It is not clear, however, how this kind of development helps the species progress biologically, or why it is advantageous to survival. The details are left vague, which is why this version of evolution is in some ways closer to Lamarck than to Darwin.

## THE QUEST FOR THE TRANSPERSONAL

Accounts of exceptional functioning raise another question. Are those who display such powers harbingers of things to come for humanity, or are they manifesting capacities that already lie dormant within us?

Such issues are the domain of *transpersonal psychology*. Brant Cortright, a psychologist associated with this movement, describes it as a "melding of the world's wisdom traditions with the learning of modern psychology."[33] Like most forms of psychology including Freud's, it is concerned with human development. But as we have seen, Freudian analysis does not interest itself in spirituality and has often been hostile to it; Freud's chief goal was to restore his patients to a more or less normal life. Transpersonal psychology, while not necessarily denying Freudian theory, sees "transpersonal" or spiritual development as another phase of human growth beyond the level of ordinary personal concerns. To adherents of this movement, transpersonal work is intended not only to heal personal trauma, but to help people realize their fullest potential.

Transpersonal psychology is the child of *humanistic psychology,* which arose out of the work of Abraham Maslow among others. Maslow tried to alter the classic Freudian emphasis on dysfunction by studying individuals who were "self-actualized"—meaning that, in terms of inner wholeness and creativity, they were more fully developed than the ordinary run of people. From his work he concluded that

> We have, each of us, an essential biologically based inner nature. . . . This inner nature . . . seems not to be intrinsically or primarily or necessarily evil. The basic needs (for life, for safety and security, for belongingness and affection, for respect and self-respect, and for self-actualization) . . . are on their face either neutral, pre-moral or positively "good." Destructiveness, sadism, cruelty, malice, etc., seem so far not to be intrinsic but rather they seem to be violent reactions against frustration of our intrinsic needs.[34]

This notion of a core level of being appears in many esoteric teachings: it is what Jung knew as the Self, the Kabbalists as Tiferet, and Gurdjieff as "essence." And as all these authorities say, it is our task as human beings to develop this identity, which is "easily overcome by habit, cultural pressure, and wrong attitudes."[35]

Maslow did not use religious terminology, but many of those who were drawn to his ideas did. They chose to pursue "self-actualization" by means ranging from meditation to LSD use. They wanted not only to make closer contact with this "inner nature" and to help it to manifest in everyday life, but to push their explorations to the point where, as mystics of many ages have said, this inner nature is understood to be one with the source of all being.[36]

Taken at its broadest, transpersonal psychology encompasses all forms of psychology that regard the "transpersonal" or spiritual dimension to be an integral part of the psyche; it says that developing this dimension is part, perhaps even the core, of the purpose of human life. Jungian psychology itself is usually considered to be a transpersonal psychology; but there are other forms as well, including Roberto Assagioli's Psychosynthesis; Stanislav Grof's Holotropic Breathwork; and certain types of existential psychotherapy, which, rather than dealing with traumas from the past, focuses on the client's state in the here-and-now.

Transpersonal psychology has also promoted therapies that work with the body. The guiding genius behind this idea was Wilhelm Reich, a pupil of Freud's who contended that neuroses and other forms of psychological damage are expressed in habitual patterns of somatic tension; Reich called this "body armor." One method he used to break down this armor was to have patients hyperventilate, which, if done long enough, say for most of an hour-long session, can trigger deep emotional and somatic release.[37]

Reich's method is not used by many transpersonal psychologists today (though Grof's Holotropic Breathwork is similar),[38] but Reich's ideas have influenced any number of body-centered therapies, which employ techniques ranging from massage to movement as means of accomplishing similar ends. Some, like Rolfing, a form of deep-tissue manipulation, are notorious for being intense and often painful, but others, including most forms of massage, are usually gentle and pleasurable.[39]

These methods of increasing somatic relaxation and release are collectively known as *bodywork*. Practitioners range from the adept to the amateurish; certification is haphazard when it exists at all and is not much use as a guide for clients. Word of mouth is probably the best way to find a good bodyworker.

In some ways transpersonal psychology has not entirely lived up to its promise. Its advocates are fond of somewhat overschematic pictures of mystical experience, and, as Cortright remarks, the movement as a whole "has been marked by a paucity of critical examination."[40] But its chief difficulty is that it tends to regard the spiritual dimension as a developmental stage of growth.

Ken Wilber, for example, one of the movement's leading theorists, holds that one needs to pass through prepersonal and personal stages of development before attaining truly transpersonal states.[41] Similarly, both Jung and Michael Washburn, another major transpersonal theorist, often seem to regard spiritual concerns as surfacing usually only at midlife and later.

Many people today do tend to equate spiritual experience with psychological maturity. They seem to feel that if one has some contact with higher dimensions, one ought to be automatically at a higher stage of emotional development. Conversely, personal faults or immaturities seems to cast doubt on one's spiritual progress.

But the history of religious experience teaches a different lesson. Many mature, stable, and ethical people never show any interest in spirituality, whereas the universal tradition of the "holy fool" reminds us that a person can have profound and sustained mystical contact while being personally dysfunctional or even mentally ill.[42] (Sacred literature is also full of warnings of how mystical experience can *cause* madness.)

The truth seems to be closer to this: psychological and spiritual development run parallel and often independent courses; one can go far along one line and make no progress on the other. While obviously the ideal situation is to develop both, the fact that this does not always happen suggests that the connections between the two are weaker than we might think.

Nevertheless the transpersonal movement has made two major contributions to modern life. In the first place, it stresses that certain types of crisis are not forms of mental illness but natural by-products of spiritual growth. Such experiences may include "shamanic crises," "kundalini awakening" (whereby people may have profound but disruptive experiences of inner energy), and near-death and past-life experiences. Stanislav Grof and his wife Christina have coined the term "spiritual emergency" for such experiences.[43] Most transpersonal psychologists try to give support to people during such crises so that the issues can resolve themselves naturally; "curing" or suppressing these symptoms tends to be discouraged.[44]

Transpersonal psychology's second great contribution reaches further. Unlike many psychological approaches, which regard spirituality as a defense mechanism against ordinary problems, transpersonal psychology has made it much easier for therapists of all stripes to accept the spirit as a normal and indeed vital part of the human character. Transpersonalists have driven home the point that spiritual needs are not an aberration but need to be respected in their own right.

This raises the issue of the role of psychotherapy in spiritual work. A few esotericists—such as the magician Israel Regardie, who was himself a Reichian therapist—have urged aspirants to have therapy fairly early on in their esoteric development, though most regard it as a matter of personal discretion. Because psychotherapy has become so well accepted in modern American life, many people with spiritual aspirations will probably undergo it at some point in their lives. Generally speaking, it is best to find a therapist (of whatever approach) who respects the spiritual dimension rather than regarding it as a symptom of dysfunction. That such practitioners are becoming more common is largely thanks to the transpersonal movement.

## Truth in the Form of a Lie

Many speak about the New Age as if it had a creed like Roman Catholicism. But the New Age is more an atmosphere than an ideology. What unites it—to the extent that anything does—is the pair of ideas mentioned at the outset of this chapter: that spirituality is a matter of individual experience, and that humankind is presently undergoing a collective awakening. And these ideas are so broad that many mutually opposed groups and ideologies may share them.

For example, even though much New Age rhetoric claims to

go beyond the old political divisions of left and right, the movement is usually seen as heir to the 1960s Counterculture, with its call for peace, equality, and environmentalism. New Age people are often assumed to be political liberals, an impression that tends to be confirmed by reading popular New Age magazines.

Yet, perplexingly, the New Age also embraces figures like Elizabeth Clare Prophet, who espouses patriotic and anticommunist themes; she also holds that the global elite is dominated by "fallen angels" who have incarnated as human beings. David Icke, a former sportscaster in Britain, has gone on the lecture circuit with New Age conspiracy theories that resemble those of the extreme right.[45] Ramtha has warned about sinister global elites such as the "Graymen," whom he links with the House of Rothschild.[46]

Politics is a comparatively simple part of the equation. Theology, cosmology, human destiny are all subjects toward which one can find radically different approaches in the New Age. Indeed the New Age is marked by a radical eclecticism. It is the spiritual equivalent of cultural postmodernism, which draws upon the literary and artistic motifs of many generations in a manner that is sometimes refreshing, sometimes jarring.

This "postmodern spirituality" came to fruition in the 1960s; before then, esoteric and occult ideas were difficult to come by, the province of adepts and eccentrics. But the sixties carried a great revival of occultism in its wake; old texts were brought back into print, new ones written, and the Tarot, yoga, Zen, the Kabbalah, the *I Ching*, and *The Tibetan Book of the Dead* provided the content for myriads of LSD- and marijuana-fueled reveries.

Hence much of the vibrant if chaotic eclecticism of the Counterculture stamps the New Age. The typical New Age book may contain ideas from any of the Western esoteric traditions and will almost certainly include a number from the East as well. To take a typical example, Richard Dannelley's *Sedona: Beyond the Vortex* has chapters entitled "The Keys of Enoch," "Ascension Yoga," "The Antahkarana and the Pillar of Light," "Angels and Aloha," "Dolphin Breathing as Taught by Drunvalo Melchizedek," and "Relating the Flower of Life to the Mayan Calendar."[47]

It is tempting but mistaken to dismiss such efforts out of hand, for this often confused eclecticism has a positive side. Until very recently, it was *de rigueur* for religionists to automatically spurn other teachings; the more alien the faith, the more likely it was to be derided as barbaric or degenerate. The New Age often seems naïve in its enthusiasm for disparate teachings, but this enthusiasm is a great improvement over hatred and bigotry. And it seems entirely possible that out of this intermingling of ideas and traditions something newer, fresher, and more universal may emerge.

At the same time, much of New Age thought is shallow and vapid. Nor is it hard to understand why. As Gurdjieff explained:

> By reason of the many characteristics of man's being, particularly of the contemporary being, truth can only come to people *in the form of a lie*—only in this form are they able to accept it; only in this form are they able to digest and assimilate it. Truth undefiled would be, for them, indigestible food.[48]

In short, traditional esoteric systems may be too subtle or may demand too much effort to be accepted in their pure form at a mass level. As they are popularized, they are bound to be diluted and distorted. This does not mean that pop versions are to be dismissed completely, for they may be the only way people can begin to approach spirituality. Later on, with sustained interest and effort, one's knowledge may be refined.

Let us take one example of such a distortion: the New Age truism "You create your own reality."[49] This idea has a long lineage, particularly in the United States: it is nothing more than the latest version of the "positive thinking" gospel, which has been circulating since at least the nineteenth century and stems in part from the fundamental optimism of our national character. It is also rooted in New Thought and its various offshoots, including Christian Science and the Unity movement. Some view this concept in quasi-scientific terms. Today's physics suggests that at a submolecular level the observer affects the outcome of the observation; some New Agers believe this confirms their notion that "perception creates reality."

The idea that a positive outlook can change external reality has been promoted by figures like Norman Vincent Peale, Dale Carnegie, and, more recently, Deepak Chopra. Every generation seems to produce a new version of the positive thinking gospel. Yet however popular it may become, this idea does in fact have roots in more esoteric sources, such as the Kabbalah and ritual magic, which say that for something to manifest in the physical world, it must first exist in the world of images, the astral light, the Yetzirah of the Kabbalists. For most people most of the time, this is an automatic process that occurs unconsciously; the mixture of good and bad in our lives accurately reflects our conflicted thoughts and desires.

In order to consciously "create your own reality," you must first visualize it clearly and charge it with the force of your will. Peter Caddy, a founder of Scotland's Findhorn Community, one of the most celebrated New Age communities, says he learned this lesson from his teacher, Dr. Sullivan, a Rosicrucian who taught:

> *"All power and intelligence that I can use are already mine."* Constantly affirm this until it shall become part of your mental attitude and you unconsciously act from it. . . . Anything you desire, you will know is possible to you, and you will speak of it with the same certainty of its coming, as you now speak of the New Year's coming.[50]

This passage also stresses the importance of the subconscious, which, though inferior to the conscious mind in reason, far exceeds it in force. Imprinting such affirmations is a great deal of work, especially when (as is true for most of us) there is a great deal of unconscious negativity to be countered.

There is nothing wrong with such ideas; even mainstream psychology stresses the importance of a positive mental attitude. But in many corners of the New Age "You create your own reality" has decayed into an expectation that everything will drop into one's lap without the slightest effort. On other occasions, people will put tremendous work into "affirming" and "visualizing" without taking any more concrete steps to realize their desires. (And this is entirely apart from the question of knowing whether our desires are beneficial or not—sometimes the hardest thing of all.) In still other instances, people may use this idea to justify a certain callousness: others who are suffering "have created their own reality" and do not deserve compassion or help.

## CRYSTALS AND HOLISM

The crystal phenomenon, widely regarded as the epitome of New Age silliness, is another idea with esoteric origins, in this case from Hermeticism. This theory says that minerals possess a certain degree of intelligence, which can be cultivated and used by those with the right knowledge. Minerals with a crystalline structure, such as crystal quartz or amethyst, have often been regarded as particularly "intelligent"; they can retain certain types of subtle power. Shamans and other occultists have used them to absorb harmful energies; the crystals are then purified by such means as passing them through incense smoke or washing them in salt water.[51] There is even a body of lore setting out what mental and emotional ailments each type of stone can remedy.

Sometimes, on the other hand, the stones are imprinted with certain thoughts or images in a manner reminiscent of a computer chip; theoretically the knowledge can then be kept or imparted to somebody else. In some indigenous cultures, small crystals are said to be implanted in the body.

For most modern-day enthusiasts, crystals are jewelry. They are often strikingly beautiful, cheap, and have vaguely "spiritual" associations about them, and that is all. Indeed, if crystals can serve as a reminder of higher goals, they can be of real value, for after all, many religious symbols are nothing more than such reminders. The danger comes with believing that accumulating lumps of amethyst or rose quartz—or eagle feathers and Indian trinkets—

will in itself impart power and knowledge. Catholicism has even given a name to this trap: *simony*, after Simon Magus, a sorcerer who tried to buy the power of the Holy Spirit from St. Peter (Acts 8:9–24).

Another New Age idea with a mixed legacy has been the notion of holism. David Spangler even asserts, "Outwardly, the emergence of the New Age is primarily based on efforts to implement holistic and planetary values."[52] The central icon of the Aquarian Age itself is not a mystical symbol but the now nearly ubiquitous picture of the earth as photographed from space.

This is one type of holism, but there is another as well, drawn from any of the numerous esoteric systems, featuring hierarchies that extend unbroken from the visible to the invisible. The idea that these realms form one unbroken whole permeates New Age thought: holistic health offers the most obvious example. We have come to understand, however imperfectly, that the body cannot be detached from the mind and emotions and spirit, and that mental distress and emotional anguish are bound to affect physical health.

No doubt this truth was always understood to some degree, but the holistic health movement has helped bring it into focus as well as counteracting the coldness and heartlessness that have infected so much of mainstream medicine. It has also extended the range of holistic therapies. Many, like Rolfing and other forms of bodyworking, are new; others, like acupuncture and ayurveda (a traditional Indian system of medicine), are imports from other civilizations.

No one can deny that the environmental and holistic health movements have helped correct longstanding imbalances in our way of life. Yet they too are prone to abuses: as author Theodore Roszak has noted, many ecological activists "have shown little concern for the emotional toxic waste they have left behind."[53] Concern for the environment, however justifiable, has often become little more than another part of the background noise of anxiety that pervade modern life.

Holistic health has generated its own discontents. The esotericist Manly P. Hall once said that there is a type of person in whose mind God is always mixed up with vitamins. Richard Grossinger, author of *Planet Medicine*, puts it well:

> There are health and therapy junkies who go from treatment to treatment, looking for the one that has the insight to recognize them or the power to intercede in their behalf. Their earnest search for a cure becomes another symptom, and the longer the quest goes on, the less chance there is that they will regain their own priority. In flaunting their holism, they become solipsistic and righteous.

Grossinger adds, "It becomes crazy-making, because healing cannot be *instead of* living."[54]

Like much of the rest of the Counterculture's legacy, environmentalism and holistic health have fallen between two stools. Their advocates have been too dogmatic and partisan, while their detractors have often scorned even what is valuable in them. Fortunately this situation is changing. As both of these impulses become part of the mainstream, they are receiving more balanced scrutiny, and their insights may become integrated into our way of life without too much stridency and self-righteousness.

## WORK IN THE SINGULAR AND PLURAL

In many ways, the New Age ideas that have been most seriously distorted are the two central ideas, both aspects of a single theme, that we set out at the beginning of this chapter: the need for awakening that is both personal and collective. Much of what is worst in the New Age arises from an unwholesome dynamic between these two aspects. What is most true and powerful in one is frequently crippled by a debased understanding of the other.

The need for personal growth exhorts each of us to seek out our salvation with diligence. We cannot grow or evolve without dedicating considerable effort to the process. But in many New Age circles this truth is undercut by the expectation of a millennial future that is about to dawn, imagined sometimes as the aftermath of "earth changes," sometimes as the imminent gift of enlightened space brothers, a new World Teacher, or some inexplicable shift in mass consciousness. Thus "I do not need to awaken; tomorrow it will all be done for me."

On the other hand, the idea of collective awakening also implies that we will have to make some kind of collective effort to bring this about. This means occasionally setting aside one's own interests for the sake of the whole. But here the notion of personal growth is often invoked, consciously or unconsciously, to waylay this impulse. The seeker asked to work for goals beyond his or her own personal interests may shrug it off by asking, "What's in it for me?"

How can one escape this quagmire? The answer lies partly in disinterested service. Alice Bailey's writings make it clear that the "New Group of World Servers" is made up of those who embrace service apart from hopes of gain or advancement:

> It is only in a spirit of real *detachment* that the best work of a disciple is done. The disciple comes to realise that because of this detachment he is (for the remainder of his life) simply a worker— one of a great army of hierarchical workers with supposedly no personality inclinations, objectives, or wishes.[55]

Not many realize this ideal, nor, probably, is it completely desirable in a pure form, for each of us begins as raw material. We have our imperfections, and part of our work consists in refining them; otherwise we risk having them impede any larger good that we may want to serve. It is perhaps not a coincidence that the most dogmatic and sanctimonious New Age leaders are those who have to all appearances abandoned the work of self-perfection in favor of full-time service. They often head the most dysfunctional organizations and have the most trouble behaving decently to their own colleagues and subordinates.

At the same time, personal inner work in and of itself is not enough. If we forget that at the core we share a common life with other humans and indeed with all living things—and that this life asks our help in its own work of perfecting itself—we have missed an essential piece of knowledge.

The solution lies, then, in an artful balance of work for one's own sake and work for the sake of a larger whole—not only for one's own group or nation but for all humanity and indeed for all the universe insofar as we can conceive of it. Although we may be constantly tempted to ask "How am I doing?" it's also important to remember that esoteric work—particularly at the level of collective service, but often even in personal terms—must be pursued without an eye to apparent results. If the Rosicrucian Brothers of the seventeenth century had been forced to judge the results of their efforts at the end of their lives, they probably would have felt they had failed. Yet their achievements have endured. The work exists on a scale that is not always possible to understand in the course of a single lifetime, and focusing on the short term may blind one to real achievements and may even lead one off course. Indeed one contemporary esotericist has paradoxically remarked, "In this line your only credentials are your unseen results."

## THE POSSIBILITIES OF THE NEW AGE

What does the New Age offer to the serious seeker? That there are so many groups and trends lumped together under this rubric suggests that there is no simple answer. But there is something of benefit to be derived from many of these movements, assuming one follows the precautions we have already discussed.

In some senses the dangers are overrated, since the most sinister groups are likely to repel most normal people. How many, for example, would choose or endure life in the sect responsible for the 1997 Heaven's Gate mass suicide in Rancho Santa Fe, California? Its leaders' goal was to transcend all manifestations of humanness, even discouraging friendships and social contacts *within* the cult.[56] Such an atmosphere could hardly be appealing to many.

Nonetheless some caveats are in order. The chief one is to stay true to one of the central themes of the New Age: the sufficiency of one's own inner guidance and wisdom. Practically every teaching we have discussed in this book proclaims this ideal, yet remarkably few groups or individuals really honor it to the fullest.

Instead the seeker often slides down a slippery slope, which comes about like this: In the beginning you are drawn to a teaching because some of its insights resonate with your own experience. You explore the teaching further, read about it, perhaps join a group. Inevitably, however, some of the teaching's insights do *not* resonate with your experience; you may disagree with them, or may simply not have the knowledge to verify them (this is particularly true of elaborate cosmological and theological doctrines).

At this point you may be tempted, often completely unconsciously, to simply abandon your own judgment and embrace the teaching uncritically. (This sort of self-indoctrination occurs to a degree in all organizations built around some ideology, including mainstream churches and major political parties.)

If you can retain enough perspective at this point to be clear about what you know to be true, as opposed to what you are not sure of or flatly disagree with, you will avoid much of the dogmatism and claptrap to which people often fall prey. And, as we have seen, this advice is completely in harmony with the main theme, not only of the New Age, but with all that is best and truest in the Western inner traditions.

There is another danger that applies specifically to the New Age. Many of the teachings in this movement have a strong focus on the otherworldly, with a persistent fascination with such things as extraterrestrials, channeling, past lives, and contacts with Ascended Masters. Without disparaging these experiences as a whole, we can see that they tend to disengage the seeker from the ordinary world. It is not unusual to encounter people for whom

ETs or spirit guides are more real than their own friends and families. This infatuation with the otherworldly can be tremendously destabilizing, and there are many New Agers who seem to be walking around with their feet a few inches off the ground. The dangers of such disconnection is great; it can impede one's ability to cope with day-to-day realities and in the worst cases leads to mental disorder.

The answer to this problem lies in the "sobriety" of which Sufis speak. This sobriety, which follows illumination, enables one to feel connected with the higher worlds and with ordinary life at the same time. Such sobriety is itself part of the dimension of service, for, it is said, we humans are here to serve as the link between earth and heaven, between the visible and the invisible. No other creature that we know of can fulfill this function, and if we fail to do it, we are neglecting a cosmic responsibility.

One final question remains: Is a New Age really coming?

In one sense, yes; in fact it is already here. The New Age really cannot be understood except as a response to the horrors of the twentieth century, which have taught that the human race can no longer endure the petulance that its leaders and nations have displayed throughout history. The costs are now too great: the weapons are too powerful, and all parts of the globe are too closely intertwined. Our triumphs in communications, transportation, and the arts of war have brought us face to face with a new age whether we like it or not.

If humanity comes to its senses and copes well with these new responsibilities, an era may well dawn when many of today's customary sorrows will be mitigated. But as for the coming of a millennial epoch when history comes to an end, all woe vanishes, and the lion lies down with the lamb—that is wishful thinking, for the griefs and joys of the human condition seem likely to remain with us for as long as we are on earth.

Anton Chekhov put it well in his play *Three Sisters*, written in 1900. One character speculates about what life will be like in the future "after we're dead and buried." Another character replies:

When we're dead people will fly around in balloons, there will be a new style in men's jackets and a sixth sense may be discovered and developed, but life itself won't change, it will still be as difficult and full of mystery and happiness as it is now.[57]

## SUGGESTED READING

Cortright, Brant. *Psychotherapy and Spirit: Theory and Practice in Transpersonal Psychology*. Albany: State University of New York Press, 1997.

The best introduction to transpersonal psychology as a whole.

Crawford, Ina. *A Guide to the Mysteries: An Ageless Wisdom Digest for the New Age*. London: Lucis Press, 1990.

A clear and succinct guide to the Alice Bailey materials; probably the best entry point to her books.

Ferguson, Marilyn. *The Aquarian Conspiracy: Personal and Social Transformation in Our Time*. Second edition. Los Angeles: Jeremy P. Tarcher, 1987.

This influential overview has done much to shape how the New Age perceives itself.

Hanegraaff, Wouter J. *New Age Religion and Western Culture: Esotericism in the Mirror of Secular Thought*. Albany: State University of New York Press, 1998.

Ponderous and occasionally obtuse, this work is nonetheless probably the most comprehensive scholarly treatment of the New Age.

Hastings, Arthur. *With the Tongues of Men and Angels: A Study of Channeling*. Fort Worth, Texas: Holt, Rinehart, Winston, 1991.

Probably the best discussion of the channeling phenomenon; critical and insightful without being dismissive.

Melton, J. Gordon, Jerome Clark, and Aidan A. Kelly. *New Age Almanac*. New York: Visible Ink, 1991.

A comprehensive and readable reference guide to the major movements and characters of the New Age.

Murphy, Michael. *The Future of the Body: Explorations into the Further Evolution of Human Nature*. Los Angeles: Jeremy P. Tarcher, 1992.

A dense and voluminous work on exceptional functioning and the possibilities for human development. Digests a tremendous amount of research.

Spangler, David. *A Pilgrim in Aquarius*. Findhorn, Scotland: Findhorn Press, 1996.
A fresh look at the New Age from one of its seminal figures.

Teilhard de Chardin, Pierre. *The Phenomenon of Man*. Translated by Bernard Wall. New York: Harper & Row, 1961.
Perhaps the most sublime and powerful discussion of human evolution from a spiritual perspective.

## *Afterword*

In the introduction to this book we spoke of three basic requirements of the esoteric paths: discernment, decency, and hard work. As this book draws to a close, we would like to touch on a few other qualities that the sincere traveler will find of great benefit. Some of these have been implied earlier; now is a good time to make them explicit.

The first of these is groundedness. Just as electrical appliances which draw on heavy current require grounding wires, those who engage with the approaches we have discussed here require some form of grounding. Otherwise, the powerful spiritual currents expressed through these traditions can overpower or burn out the delicate wiring of our psyches.

Groundedness comes in many forms: resolute common sense, daily prayer or meditation, a regular job that keeps us engaged with material realities, physical exercise, or something as simple as family life. There is no single technique or stance that works best for everyone, but the end result will hopefully be the same: a sufficient engagement with the requirements of the so-called "real world" that we are less likely to fall prey to flights of fancy or become engulfed by archetypes, repressed complexes, or manias that make us lose our wits.

Though it is all too rarely spoken of in esoteric literature or at New Age workshops, the specter of madness haunts the spiritual search. To point this out should not be dismissed as mere pessimism or negativity.

A recurring motif of the esoteric traditions is the realm of the unseen—other dimensions, invisible entities, inner planes, etheric bodies, energy centers, planetary forces, hidden masters, the list goes on and on. While it may prove necessary to grant a provisional reality to such claims in the course of inner exploration, there lies a real danger in swallowing them wholesale and proceeding blithely onward. It is all too easy to project one's wishes or fears onto the twilight zone of the invisible, reading deep portents into chance occurrences and seeing connections where none actually exist.

Some people with a tendency toward paranoia are strongly attracted to the esoteric precisely because it mirrors their secret fears: unseen forces affect our lives, consensus reality is a sham, the universe is somehow converging on our personal slice of life. The spiritual landscape is littered with erstwhile magicians and addled mystics who jumped into esoteric belief systems that were more than their sanity could bear and—most significantly—more than their closely-watched personal experience had borne out.

Which leads us to the second skill that it would be wise to cultivate: the ability to maintain a simultaneous belief and disbelief in all matters esoteric until you have undeniably experienced them for yourself. Let us call this "faithful skepticism."

Exoteric religions encourage unquestioning belief in their tenets based on the authority of scripture or institutional leadership. For many of us, this is inadequate and unpersuasive. But by the same token, blind faith in esoteric traditions or the fascinating revelations of mystics and clairvoyants is no more advisable.

The kind of "knowing" that one finds in gnosis is personally verified. It isn't based on the hearsay of another's experience or revelation any more than it is based on theological dogma or belief. Even when you have experienced something that seems real, it is well to compare notes with an experienced teacher and keep room in your worldview for the possibility that it is all in your imagination.

The final quality worth cultivating has less to do with seeking than with finding. If one has safely piloted one's way through the hazards and joys of the spiritual journey and has reached the distant shore of gnosis, a nagging question remains: what is one to make of what one has found?

Illumination takes many forms—as many as there are individuals. Since each of us possesses a unique identity and a unique set of life experiences, chances are that the wholeness we achieve—our integration with the universe and its intelligence—will have a shape that suits us alone.

While the greatest mystics and esotericists have had the gift of expressing their experiences in ways that speak to many, few of us are so blessed. Your gnosis may be yours alone. In light of this, the final quality we suggest is simply keeping things in proportion.

No matter how shattering the truths revealed, how overwhelming the feelings unleashed, or how fascinating the manner in which "it all fits together," the fate of the universe does not hinge on convincing others of your truth. In fact, should you feel compelled to broadcast your revelations to the masses, it is a sure bet that the ego has seized hold of an insight and has inflated it into a life raft.

The paradox of gnosis is the realization that we are each simultaneously a speck of dust and Absolute Being. Esoteric work may lead us to this realization, but it remains for us to keep both sides of the equation in balance. If this book has provided even a small hint of ways in which one can work towards such inner equilibrium, we will be more than happy.

# Reference Notes

## INTRODUCTION

1. Sometimes the words *mystical* and *occult* are also used. Each of these terms has its own long and intricate history, but generally speaking *mysticism* is concerned with gnosis in a more or less direct, unmediated, and sometimes even unsystematic way. *Occultism,* on the other hand, a word that was once used in a neutral or even positive sense to refer to interactions with the unseen, has in the last fifty years become a derogatory term for dabbling in the supernatural.

2. A more detailed discussion of the key features of esotericism is available in Antoine Faivre's introduction to his *Modern Esoteric Spirituality*, coedited with Jacob Needleman (New York: Crossroad, 1992).

3. These two levels of attainment are described in Jean Borella, "René Guénon and the Traditionalist School," in Faivre and Needleman, pp. 346–47.

4. C. G. Jung, "Commentary," in *The Secret of the Golden Flower: A Chinese Book of Life*, trans. Richard Wilhelm (New York: Causeway Books, 1975), p. 82.

5. William G. Gray, *An Outlook on Our Inner Western Way* (New York: Samuel Weiser, 1980), p. 3.

## CHAPTER 1

1. C. G. Jung, *Memories, Dreams, Reflections*, trans. Richard and Clara Winston (New York: Vintage, 1961), pp. 106–7.

2. C. G. Jung, *Psychology of the Unconscious*, trans. Beatrice M. Hinkle (1912; reprint, Princeton: Princeton/Bollingen, 1991), pp. 93–94.

3. Richard Noll, in his book *The Jung Cult: The Origins of a Charismatic Move-

*ment* (Princeton: Princeton University Press, 1994), pp. 181–84, discusses various discrepancies in Jung's version of the story as it developed over the years. He also points out that the text, part of the Mithraic Liturgy, was published years before Jung said it was. On the other hand, Noll gives no evidence that the patient saw, or was likely to have seen, the text.

4.  Marie-Louise von Franz, "The Process of Individuation," in C. G. Jung and Marie-Louise von Franz, eds., *Man and His Symbols* (Garden City, N.Y.: Doubleday, 1964), p. 161.

5.  C. G. Jung, "Approaching the Unconscious," in Jung and von Franz, p. 49.

6.  The French phrase was coined by Jung's teacher, the psychologist Pierre Janet; cf. "The Transcendent Function," in Jung, *Structure and Dynamics of the Psyche*, trans. R. F. C. Hull, *Collected Works*, vol. 8, 2d ed. (Princeton: Princeton/Bollingen, 1969), p. 77.

7.  C. G. Jung, "The Psychological Aspects of the *Kore*," in *The Archetypes and the Collective Unconscious*, 2d ed., *Collected Works*, vol. 9,I (Princeton: Princeton/Bollingen, 1959), p. 190.

8.  C. G. Jung, "Commentary" in Richard Wilhelm, trans., *The Secret of the Golden Flower: A Chinese Book of Life* (1931; reprint, New York: Causeway Books, 1975), p. 82.

9.  C. G. Jung, "Conscious, Unconscious, and Individuation," in *The Archetypes and the Collective Unconscious*, p. 285.

10. C. G. Jung, "After the Catastrophe," in *Civilization in Transition, Collected Works*, vol. 10 (Princeton: Princeton/Bollingen, 1964), pp. 202–3. Emphasis here and in all other quotes is in the original unless otherwise noted.

11. C. G. Jung, "The Fight with the Shadow," in *Civilization in Transition*, p. 223.

12. Jung, "Conscious, Unconscious, and Individuation," p. 284.

13. Von Franz, pp. 196–204.

14. C. G. Jung, "Concerning Mandala Symbolism," in *The Archetypes and the Collective Unconscious*, p. 357.

15. Jung, "Approaching the Unconscious," in *Man and His Symbols*, p. 55.

16. Jung, *Memories, Dreams, Reflections*, p. 155.

17. Ibid., pp. 361–63.

18. C. G. Jung, "Flying Saucers: A Modern Myth of Things Seen in the Skies," in *Civilization in Transition*, p. 312. Emphasis Jung's.

19. Ibid., p. 414.

20. Ibid., p. 320.

21. Ibid., pp. 416–17.

22. *Oxford Classical Dictionary*, s.v. "Theophrastus."

23. C. G. Jung, "A Psychological Theory of Types," in *Modern Man in Search of a Soul*, trans. W. S. Dell and Cary F. Baynes (New York: Harcourt, Brace, & World, 1933), p. 91.

24. For a good summary of Jung's theory of types, see Robin Robertson, *Beginner's Guide to Jungian Psychology* (York Beach, Maine: Nicolas-Hays, 1992), pp. 71–104.

25. See Kendra Smith, "With Jungian Psychology, Do We Need Religion?" *Dialogue & Alliance*, vol. 5, no. 4 (Winter 1991–92), pp. 3ff.

26. Quoted in Edward F. Edinger, *The New God-Image* (Wilmette, Ill.: Chiron Publications, 1996), p. 27.

27. Ibid., p. 30.

28. Ibid., p. 31.

29. Ibid., p. 28.

30. For an overview of archetypal psychology, see Susan C. Roberts, "The Soul of the World: Exploring Archetypal Psychology," *Common Boundary*, Nov.–Dec. 1992, pp. 20–25. See also *A Blue Fire: Selected Writings of James Hillman*, ed. Thomas Moore (San Francisco: Harper & Row, 1989).

31. Reprinted in *Memories, Dreams, Reflections*, pp. 378–90.

32. *Memories, Dreams, Reflections*, p. 192.

33. Stephan A. Hoeller, *The Gnostic Jung and the Seven Sermons to the Dead* (Wheaton, Ill.: Quest Books, 1982), p. xxi.

## CHAPTER 2

1. Elaine Pagels, *The Gnostic Gospels* (New York: Random House, 1979), pp. xv–xvi.

2. Michael Allen Williams, in *Rethinking "Gnosticism"* (Princeton: Princeton University Press, 1996), makes a strong argument that the term *Gnosticism* is almost meaningless as a useful category for the variety of contradictory beliefs and myths that it usually encompasses. In a scholarly sense, this may be so. What we are attempting in this chapter is not an exacting scholastic analysis but a treatment of Gnosticism as it has caught the popular imagination.

3. Pagels, p. xx. Original quote conflated from *Gospel of Thomas* II, 35.4–7 and 50.28–30; see James M. Robinson, ed., *The Nag Hammadi Library in English*, 3d ed. (San Francisco: Harper & Row, 1988), pp. 127, 137.

4. Obviously the terms *Old Testament* and *New Testament* are Christian designations. We use them here for the sake of convenience, since the majority of our readers are likely to be familiar with them. The scriptures making up the "Old Testament," supplemented by the books of the Prophets and the Writings, are known to Jewish readers as the Torah.

5. *Gospel of Philip* 63:34–64:5; in James M. Robinson, ed., *The Nag Hammadi Library in English*, 3d ed. (San Francisco: Harper & Row, 1988), p. 148.

6. Christ as Logos or "Word" is present in the New Testament in the opening verse of the Gospel according to John, but the concept of Logos predates

Christianity. David Fideler notes that the early Christians appropriated the term from the Hellenistic cosmology of Philo and the Hermetic teachings. As Fideler says, "The Logos represents the first level of real manifestation or Being, for it encompasses within itself all the laws and relations which are later articulated in the phenomenal universe." In *Jesus Christ: Sun of God* (Wheaton, Ill.: Quest Books, 1993), p. 42.

7.  *The Gospel of Thomas* in Robinson, p. 126.

8.  *A Gnostic Book of Hours*, p. 79.

9.  *The Gnostic Jung and the Seven Sermons to the Dead*, p. 200.

10. Historically, the Virgin Mary has played this role for some in the Catholic Church, but contemporary feminism has usually seen Mary as a co-opted symbol commonly used to encourage women's submission.

11. The library amidst the ruins of Ephesus in modern-day Turkey features a still-standing statue of Sophia.

12. Margaret Starbird, "Imaging God as Partners," at WWWellness Web site: www.doubleclikd.com/Articles/imaging.html.

13. Pheme Perkins, *Gnosticism and the New Testament* (Minneapolis, Minn.: Fortress Press, 1993), p. 169.

14. *Gospel of Thomas*, 114; in Robinson, p. 138. See Jorunn J. Buckley, *Female Fault and Fulfillment in Gnosticism* (Chapel Hill: University of North Carolina Press, 1986), for further discussion of this.

15. *The Institute for Gnostic Studies: Introduction*, p. 3 (P.O. Box 492, Armidale NSWW 2350, Australia). See also the IGS Web site: http://www.ozemail. com.au/~pleroma.

16. Life Science Fellowship, "Unmasking the Grand Deception", *New Dawn Magazine* (G.P.O. Box 3126FF, Melbourne, VIC 2001, Australia) issue 36, May–June 1996, p. 53.

17. *Gospel of Philip*, 66:10–22; in Robinson, p. 149.

18. *Gospel of Philip*, 86:4–18, in Robinson, p. 160.

19. According to Church doctrine, ordinations and consecrations performed by a bishop are still held to be valid, even if the bishop has become a schismatic or left the organizational umbrella of the Roman Catholic Church or one of the many national churches within Eastern Orthodoxy. Most of the independent bishops in evidence today trace themselves back to Arnold Harris Matthews (1852–1919) and Joseph René Vilatte (1854–1929), who received orders from the Old Catholic Church of Holland, an independent church formed by a Catholic bishop in 1724, and from an independent South Indian church respectively. Not all independent bishops are of a gnostic orientation—in fact many are "more Catholic than the Pope" in their conservatism—but a good number are positively disposed towards Gnosticism or esotericism. See Stephan Hoeller, "Wandering Bishops: Not *All* Roads Lead to Rome," *Gnosis* 12 (Summer 1989), pp. 20–25.

**CHAPTER 3**

1. *The Cloud of Unknowing and Other Works*, trans. Clifton Wolters (Harmondsworth, Middlesex, England: Penguin, 1961), p. 69

2. See, for example, Kyriacos C. Markides, *The Magus of Strovolos: The Extraordinary World of a Spiritual Healer*. London: Arkana, 1985. More recently, however, Markides has repudiated his connection with Daskalos.

3. For an introduction to Boehme's thought, see Robin Waterfield, ed., *Jacob Boehme: Selected Readings* (Wellingborough, Northamptonshire, England: Crucible, 1989), esp. pp. 25–31.

4. Bible quotations, unless otherwise noted, are from the King James Version.

5. Boris Mouravieff, *Gnosis: Study and Commentaries on the Esoteric Tradition of Eastern Orthodoxy*, ed. Robin Amis (Newbury, Mass.: Praxis Institute Press, 1992), vol. 2, p. xxxiii.

6. Mouravieff, vol. 1, pp. 27–28. See also J.-M. Déchanet, *Christian Yoga* (New York: Harper & Row, 1960), pp. 63–72.

7. It is important to distinguish between this perspective and, for example, Jung's theory of types. Jung does not see any innate superiority in one type over the others; a feeling type is not better or worse than a thinking type. But esoteric Christianity definitely views the relation between these "types" in a hierarchical way; furthermore, it sees all of us as starting at the level of the "carnal."

8. Quoted in Richard Temple, *Icons and the Mystical Origins of Christianity* (Shaftesbury, Dorset, England: Element Books, 1990), p. 62.

9. The equivalent term in Judaism is *teshuvah,* meaning "turning" and having almost exactly the same connotation as *metanoia.*

10. Alan W. Watts, *Myth and Ritual in Christianity* (Boston: Beacon Press, 1968), p. 181.

11. *The Heart of Salvation: The Life and Teachings of St. Theophan the Recluse*, trans. Esther Williams (Newbury, Mass.: Praxis Institute Press, n.d.), p. 67.

12. Quoted in Stephan A. Hoeller, *The Mystery and Magic of the Eucharist* (Hollywood, Calif.: Gnostic Press, 1990), p. 9.

13. For a discussion of these metaphors, see Maurice Nicoll, *The New Man* (Boston: Shambhala, 1986) and *The Mark* (Boston: Shambhala, 1985).

14. C. W. Leadbeater, *The Science of the Sacraments* (Adyar, India: Theosophical Publishing House, 1920).

15. *The Philokalia of Origen*, quoted in Temple, p. 34.

16. Temple, p. 33; cf. Cynthia Bourgeault, "The Hidden Wisdom of Psalmody," *Gnosis* 37 (Fall 1995), p. 27.

17. For a Kabbalistic view of this story, see Z'ev ben Shimon Halevi, *Kabbalah and Exodus* (London: Rider & Co., 1980).

18. Richard Smoley, "Heroic Virtue: An Interview with Brother David Steindl-Rast," *Gnosis* 24 (Summer 1992), p. 40.

19. Bourgeault, ibid.

20. *The Rule of St. Benedict* (Collegeville, Minn.: The Liturgical Press, 1980), p. 215.

21. Robin Amis, *A Different Christianity: Early Christian Esotericism and Modern Thought* (Albany: State University of New York Press, 1995), p. 303.

22. *John Cassian: Conferences*, trans. Colin Luibheid (Mahwah, N.J.: Paulist Press, 1985), p. 133.

23. Gregorian chant, which goes back at least to the fourth or fifth century, vanished as a living tradition in medieval and modern times. Today's Gregorian chant is a nineteenth-century reconstruction. See Joseph Rowe, liner notes to *Alma Anima: Towards a New Gregorian Chant*, CD (Nanterre, France: Al Sur, 1996).

24. *Cloud of Unknowing*, ibid.

25. Mouravieff, vol. 2, pp. 214–19.

26. *Writings from the Philokalia on Prayer of the Heart*, trans. E. Kadloubovsky and G. E. H. Palmer (London: Faber & Faber, 1951), p. 253.

27. Robert K.C. Forman, *Meister Eckhart: Mystic as Theologian* (Rockport, Mass.: Element Books, 1991), p. 109.

28. Quoted in Amis, p. 255.

29. Wilson Van Dusen, *The Presence of Other Worlds* (New York: Swedenborg Foundation, 1974).

30. Mouravieff, vol. 1, p. 69; vol. 2, p. 108.

31. Kenneth Wapnick, *Absence from Felicity: The Story of Helen Schucman and Her Scribing of A Course in Miracles* (Roscoe, N.Y.: Foundation for *A Course in Miracles*, 1991); see also D. Patrick Miller, *The Complete Story of the Course* (Berkeley, Calif.: Fearless Books, 1997). Arthur Hastings, *With the Tongues of Men and Angels: A Study of Channeling* (Fort Worth, Texas: Holt, Rinehart, & Winston, 1991), chapter 10, discusses the *Course*. See also Mitchell B. Liester, "Inner Voices: Distinguishing Transcendent and Pathological Characteristics," *Journal of Transpersonal Psychology*, vol. 28, no. 1 (1996), pp. 1–30.

32. *A Course in Miracles* (Tiburon, Calif.: Foundation for Inner Peace, 1975), Workbook, p. 1.

33. Ibid., Text, p. 14.

34. Ibid., Teacher's Manual, p. 83.

35. Ibid., Teacher's Manual, p. 85.

36. Ibid., Text, pp. 1, 2.

37. Ibid., Workbook, p. 114.

38. Ibid., Text, p. 32.

39. Text, p. 47.

40. Pavel Florovsky, quoted in Christopher Bamford's foreword to Sergei Bulgakov, *Sophia: The Wisdom of God* (Hudson, N.Y.: Lindisfarne Press, 1993), p. xviii.

41. Stephan A. Hoeller, "The Divine Feminine in Recent World Events," *Gnosis* 25 (Fall 1992), pp. 10–11.

42. Daniel Andreev, *The Rose of the World*, trans. Jordan Roberts (Hudson, N.Y.: Lindisfrarne, 1997), p. 349.

43. [Valentin Tomberg], *Meditations on the Tarot: A Journey into Christian Hermeticism* (Warwick, N.Y.: Amity House, 1985).

44. Hoeller, pp. 20–25.

45. See also Lewis S. Keizer, *The Wandering Bishops* (N.p.: Academy of Arts and Humanities, 1976).

46. Dante, *Paradiso* 33.145.

## CHAPTER 4

1. *The Book of Legends: Sefer Ha-Aggadah*, ed. Hayim Nahman Bialik and Yehoshua Hana Ravnitzky, trans. William G. Braude (New York: Schocken, 1992), pp. 78–79.

2. Karl H. Schlesier, *The Wolves of Heaven: Cheyenne Shamanism, Ceremonies, and Prehistoric Origins* (Norman, Okla.: University of Oklahoma Press, 1987), p. 79 *et passim*.

3. Jung, *Memories, Dreams, Reflections*, p. 252.

4. The most detailed expression of the Noachide perspective can be found in the writings of a nineteenth-century Italian rabbi, Elijah Benamozegh. See his *Israel and Humanity*, trans. Maxwell Luria (Mahwah, N.J.: Paulist Press, 1995). For a view of the Noachide Movement by a participant, see Kimberly E. Hanke, *Turning to Torah: The Emerging Noachide Movement* (Northvale, N.J.: Jason Aronson, 1995). The Noachide Movement is thought to number about three to five thousand, chiefly in the U.S.

5. Bialik and Ravnitzky contains the most complete and accessible rendition of *aggadah*.

6. Z'ev ben Shimon Halevi, *Kabbalah and Exodus* (London: Rider & Co., 1980), pp. 15–16; cf. *The Zohar: Bereshith (Genesis)*, trans. Nurho de Manhar (San Diego, Calif.: Wizards Bookshelf, 1995), introduction, p. 3.

7. Because of the vagaries of transliterating Hebrew, the word is spelled a number of different ways in English. "Kabbalah" is generally preferred by writers with a Jewish orientation; those with a magical or occult perspective tend to like "Qabalah"; while those writers dealing with the Christian versions of the tradition popular during the Renaissance frequently spell it "Cabala." For simplicity's sake we will use the spelling "Kabbalah" in all contexts. Nearly all Hebrew terms in this chapter also have a number of different spellings.

8. Gershom Scholem, *Major Trends in Jewish Mysticism* (New York: Schocken, 1961), p. 20; cf. Z'ev ben Shimon Halevi, *Adam and the Kabbalistic Tree* (New York: Samuel Weiser, 1974), pp. 17–19.

9.  Scholem, p. 206. It is important to distinguish the generic term *theosophy* from the Theosophy which is specifically the esoteric teaching expounded by H. P. Blavatsky and which we will take up later. In this book we will distinguish the latter by capitalizing it.

10. Scholem, ibid.

11. *Sefer Yetzirah* 1:6, quoted in Halevi, p. 25.

12. Dion Fortune, *The Mystical Qabalah* (London: Ernest Benn Ltd., 1935), p. 139.

13. Quoted in Daniel C. Matt, *The Essential Kabbalah* (San Francisco: Harper-SanFrancisco, 1994), p. 45.

14. Matt, ibid. By "aliens" Cordovero means evil spirits.

15. Adin Steinsaltz, *The Thirteen-Petalled Rose*, trans. Yehuda Hanegbi (New York: Basic Books, 1980), pp. 24–31. The term *kelipot* is sometimes spelled *Qliphoth* or *Qelipot*.

16. Jung himself explicitly made this equation; see "Flying Saucers: A Modern Myth," in *Civilization in Transition*, p. 410.

17. Francis Brown, S.R. Driver, and Charles A. Briggs, *A Hebrew and English Lexicon of the Old Testament*, revised ed. (Oxford: Oxford at the Clarendon Press, 1953), entry under נצח (*netzach*).

18. Brown, Driver, and Briggs, entry under הוד (*hod*).

19. Hayyim Schauss, *The Jewish Festivals: A Guide to Their History and Observance*, trans. Samuel Jaffe (New York: Schocken, 1962), pp. 20–21.

20. Moshe Chaim Luzzatto, *The Way of God*, trans. Aryeh Kaplan (Jerusalem: Feldheim, 1988), p. 321.

21. Halevi, *Kabbalah and Exodus*, p. 129.

22. See for example S. L. MacGregor Mathers, *The Kabbalah Unveiled* (1887; reprint, New York: Samuel Weiser, 1974), chart inset facing p. 51.

23. See Halevi, *Adam and the Kabbalistic Tree*, p. 324.

24. See Dion Fortune for one system; an even more exhaustive series of lists can be found in Aleister Crowley, *777 and Other Qabalistic Writings of Aleister Crowley*, ed. Israel Regardie (New York: Samuel Weiser, 1977).

25. Cf. Cordovero, in Matt, p. 47 and Fortune, pp. 139, 161.

26. Cf. Cordovero, in Matt, p. 39, and Z'ev ben Shimon Halevi, *A Kabbalistic Universe* (London: Rider & Co., 1977), p. 18.

27. The early Kabbalistic text *Sefer Ha-Bahir* ("The Book of Brilliance") takes this form. See *The Bahir*, trans. Aryeh Kaplan (New York: Samuel Weiser, 1979).

28. Gershom Scholem, *Kabbalah* (1974; reprint, New York: Dorset Press, 1987), p. 172.

29. Scholem, *Kabbalah*, p. 337. Scholem also says there are other, more intricate, forms of *gematria*, some of which involve anagrams, others using letter substitutions in the manner of a code or cipher.

30. Aryeh Kaplan, *Sefer Yetzirah: The Book of Creation* (York Beach, Maine: Samuel Weiser, 1990), p. 64.

31. *Sefer Ha-Aggadah*, p. 376.

32. See Brown, Driver, & Briggs, entry under יהוה (YHWH), pp. 217–19.

33. Ira Robinson, ed., *Moses Cordovero's Introduction to Kabbalah: An Annotated Translation of His Or Ne'erav* (Hoboken, N.J.: KTAV Publishing, 1994), p. 113. Bracketed words are Robinson's. *Eyn Sof* is an alternate transliteration of *Ain Sof.*

34. Other examples include *El Hai Shaddai,* "The Living God Almighty," with Yesod; *Adonai,* "Lord," with Malkut; *Ehyeh Asher Ehyeh,* "I Am That I Am" (or, better, "I Will Be What I Will Be") with Keter. See Matt, pp. 39–40.

35. Matt, copyright page.

36. For one system, attributed to Isaac Luria, see Aryeh Kaplan, *Meditation and Kabbalah* (York Beach, Maine: Samuel Weiser, 1982), p. 257. A similar version appears in Robinson, ibid.

37. Kaplan, *Meditation and Kabbalah*, p. 11.

38. A contemporary version of the *merkavah* ascent is described in Z'ev ben Shimon Halevi, *The Work of the Kabbalist* (York Beach, Maine: Samuel Weiser, 1986), pp. 155–60.

39. *Sefer Ha-Aggadah*, p. 235. For a treatment of falling into the Abyss in modern fiction, see Malcolm Lowry's novel *Under the Volcano*; also Perle Epstein, *The Private Labyrinth of Malcolm Lowry: Under the Volcano and the Cabbala* (New York: Holt, Rinehart, & Winston, 1969).

40. Partial instructions for creating a *golem* can be found in Kaplan, *Sefer Yetzirah*, pp. 126–28.

41. Ivan Mackerle, "Who Was Prague's Golem?" *Fate*, Nov. 1996, pp. 22–26, contains a recent discussion of the evidence for the *golem*.

42. Kaplan, ibid.

43. Kaplan, *Sefer Yetzirah*, p. 51.

44. Matt, pp. 1–2.

45. Quoted in Scholem, *Kabbalah*, p. 12.

46. Scholem, *Major Trends in Jewish Mysticism*, p. 37.

47. Raphael Patai, *The Hebrew Goddess* (Detroit, Mich.: Wayne State University Press, 1990), contains a comprehensive discussion of the feminine in Hebrew mysticism.

48. Robinson, p. 56.

49. Scholem, *Kabbalah*, pp. 401, 409, 420–22.

50. Jay Kinney and Richard Smoley, "The *Gnosis* Interview with Ram Dass," *Gnosis* 26 (Winter 1993), p. 50. An account of this meeting can be found in Rodger Kamenetz, *The Jew in the Lotus* (San Francisco: HarperSanFrancisco, 1994).

51. Lawrence Sutin, "Messianism's Past, Present, Future," in *Gnosis* 39 (Spring

1996), pp. 68–69. A profile of this controversial figure can be found in Michael Specter, "Rabbi Menachem Schneerson: The Oracle of Crown Heights," in *The New York Times Magazine*, March 15, 1992, pp. 35ff. For a view of Schneerson's teachings, see Simon Jacobson, ed., *Toward a Meaningful Life: The Wisdom of the Rebbe Menachem Mendel Schneerson* (New York: William Morrow, 1995).

52. For *devekut,* see Shefa Gold, "Cleaving to God: A Jewish Way of Prayer" *Gnosis* 37 (Fall 1995), pp. 44–47. For *hitbodedut* or *hisbod'dus,* see Herbert Weiner, *Nine and One-Half Mystics: The Kabbala Today* (New York: Macmillan, 1969), pp. 245–49.

## CHAPTER 5

1. Richard Cavendish, *The Black Arts* (New York: G.P. Putnam's Sons, 1967), p. 17.

2. Henry Cornelius Agrippa of Nettesheim, *The Three Books of Occult Philosophy*, trans. James Freake, ed. Donald Tyson (1651; reprint, St. Paul, Minn.: Llewellyn, 1993), pp. li, liii.

3. The best account of Lévi's life and work can be found in Christopher McIntosh, *Éliphas Lévi and the French Occult Revival* (New York: Samuel Weiser, 1972).

4. Éliphas Lévi, *Transcendental Magic: Its Doctrine and Ritual*, trans. A. E. Waite (1896; reprint, London: Bracken Books, 1995).

5. The most comprehensive collection is in Israel Regardie, *The Complete Golden Dawn System of Magic* (Phoenix, Ariz.: New Falcon, 1994). Other materials can be found in S. L. MacGregor Mathers et al., *Astral Projection, Ritual Magic, and Alchemy*, ed. Francis King (Rochester, Vt.: Destiny Books, 1987).

6. See Charles Fielding and Carr Collins, *The Story of Dion Fortune* (Dallas, Texas: Star & Cross Publications, 1985).

7. For the life of Moina Mathers and her associates, see Mary K. Greer, *Women of the Golden Dawn* (Rochester, Vt.: Park Street Press, 1995).

8. Dion Fortune, *Psychic Self-Defence* (Wellingborough, Northamptonshire, England: Aquarian, 1957).

9. J.G. Frazer, *The Golden Bough* (New York: Macmillan, 1922), p. 13.

10. Aleister Crowley, *Magick in Theory and Practice* (1929; reprint, New York: Castle Books, n.d.), pp. xii–xiii. Crowley uses the spelling "magick," a practice continued by his disciples of various stripes.

11. Lévi, p. 36.

12. Lévi, p. 15.

13. Ibid.

14. See Michael Loewe and Carmen Blacker, *Oracles and Divination* (Boulder, Colo.: Shambhala, 1981), for an overview of the subject.

15. John Blofeld, *I Ching: The Book of Change* (London: George Allen & Unwin, 1965), introduction, p. 15. The most popular and respected version is *The I Ching or Book of Changes*, trans. Richard Wilhelm and Cary Baynes (Princeton, N.J.: Princeton University Press, 1967).

16. For a discussion of this distinction between the two types of divination, cf. Plato, *Phaedrus*, 244.

17. Cavendish, pp. 132–52.

18. Crowley, p. 129. Emphasis in original.

19. Ibid., pp. 92–93.

20. Crowley alludes to this process somewhat cryptically in pp. 95–96n.

21. *Religion Watch*, vol. 10, no. 1 (Nov. 1994), p. 7. There was, however, some evidence of lone perpetrators and couples claiming involvement with Satan. See also Debbie Nathan and Michael Snedeker, *Satan's Silence: Ritual Abuse and the Making of a Modern American Witch Hunt* (New York: Basic Books, 1995) and Chas S. Clifton, "The Three Faces of Satan: A Close Look at the 'Satanism Scare,'" *Gnosis* 12 (Summer 1989), pp. 8–18, and Donald Michael Kraig, "The 'Satanic Panic' in America, Part I" *Mezlim*, Lughnasadh (Summer) 1993, pp. 21–29.

22. For a discussion of this question from a Jungian perspective, see Alfred Ribi, *Demons of the Inner World: Understanding Our Hidden Complexes* (Boston: Shambhala, 1990).

23. Crowley, p. 136.

24. Alexandra David-Neel, *Magic and Mystery in Tibet* (1932; reprint, New York: Dover, 1971), pp. 162–63.

25. Crowley, p. 101.

26. Lévi, p. 317.

27. Crowley, p. 63.

28. Lévi, p. 253.

29. Siobhán Houston, "Chaos Magic," *Gnosis* 36 (Summer 1995), p. 55.

30. Peter J. Carroll, *Liber Null and Psychonaut* (York Beach, Maine: Samuel Weiser, 1987), pp. 47ff.

31. Associations for the outer planets are more speculative, since they were not known when this system was first formulated. Lead is ascribed to both Earth and Saturn. The colors for Malkut are often given as citrine, olive, russet, and black, associated with the four elements.

32. The most ambitious list of these correspondences can be found in Aleister Crowley, *777 and Other Qabalistic Writings*, ed. Israel Regardie (New York: Samuel Weiser, 1977). Dion Fortune's *Mystical Qabalah* contains others.

33. Dolores Ashcroft-Nowicki, *First Steps in Ritual* (Wellingborough, Northamptonshire, England: Aquarian, 1990), pp. 17–24.

34. Cavendish, p. 25.

35. The verification of psychic phenomena—often "psi" for short—is another

matter. Here experiments conducted over the course of a century suggest that such psychic capacities as clairvoyance, telepathy, and psychokinesis are real. For the most intelligent and up-to-date discussion, see Dean Radin, *The Conscious Universe: The Scientific Truth of Psychic Phenomena* (San Francisco: HarperSanFrancisco, 1997).

36. For a good discussion of these issues, see Donald Tyson, *The New Magus: Ritual Magic as a Personal Process* (St. Paul, Minn.: Llewellyn, 1987), pp. 187–94.

37. Crowley, p. 11.

38. Some magicians with a more Christian orientation are careful to distinguish the Holy Guardian Angel from any aspect of the self. See Gareth Knight, *Experience of the Inner Worlds* (York Beach, Maine: Samuel Weiser, 1993), pp. 115–16.

39. *The Book of the Sacred Magic of Abramelin the Mage*, trans. S. L. MacGregor Mathers (1900; reprint, New York: Dover, 1975).

## CHAPTER 6

1. Quoted in Stewart Farrar, *What Witches Do* (New York: Coward, McCann & Geoghegan, 1971), p. 194.

2. Doreen Valiente, *The Rebirth of Witchcraft* (Custer, Wash.: Phoenix Publishing, 1989), pp. 10–12.

3. *Wicca* today is usually used as an abstract noun, and many witches seem to think it comes from an Old English word meaning "the religion of the witches." It does not; though the word *wicca* does appear in Old English, it means "male witch" (the feminine form is *wicce*); the Old English word for "witchcraft" is *wiccecraefte*. See *The Oxford English Dictionary*, s.v. "witch."

4. Gerald Gardner, *Witchcraft Today* (New York: Citadel Press, 1955).

5. Aidan A. Kelly, *Crafting the Art of Magic* (St. Paul, Minn.: Llewellyn, 1991). Some research suggests that Gardner may have also been inspired by Woodcraft, a lodge movement started by the Canadian writer Ernest Thompson Seton that attempted to introduce the ideals of American Indian spirituality to the modern West. See John Michael Greer and Gordon Cooper, "The Red God: Woodcraft and the Origins of Wicca," *Gnosis* 48 (Summer 1998), pp. 50–58.

6. Margot Adler, *Drawing Down the Moon* (Boston: Beacon Press, second ed., 1986), p. 85.

7. David Clarke and Andy Roberts, *Twilight of the Celtic Gods* (London: Blandford/Cassell, 1996), pp. 22, 24, 38.

8. Robert Graves, *The White Goddess* (1948; reprint, New York: Farrar, Straus, & Giroux, 1966), pp. 488–89.

9. Possibly from the Old French *s'esbattre,* "to frolic."

10. Quoted in Margaret Murray, *The God of the Witches* (Oxford: Oxford University Press, 1931), p. 65.

11. Murray, *The God of the Witches*, p. 79.

12. Murray, pp. 160–97.

13. Keith Thomas, *Religion and the Decline of Magic* (New York: Charles Scribner's Sons, 1971), pp. 514–17.

14. Robin Briggs, *Witches and Neighbors: The Social and Cultural Context of European Witchcraft* (New York: Viking, 1996), p. 292.

15. Jacobus Sprenger and Heinrich Kramer, *Malleus Maleficarum*, trans. Montague Summers (London: Folio Society, 1968), p. 5; cf. Thomas, pp. 438–49.

16. Briggs, pp. 327, 335–336.

17. Thomas, p. 516.

18. Thomas, p. 456.

19. *Myth, Religion, and Mother Right: Selected Writings of J. J. Bachofen*, trans. Ralph Manheim (Princeton: Princeton/Bollingen, 1967), p. 71.

20. Marija Gimbutas, *The Language of the Goddess* (San Francisco: Harper & Row, 1989), p. xx.

21. Gimbutas, p. xxi.

22. Walter Burkert, *Greek Religion*, trans. John Raffan (Cambridge, Mass.: Harvard University Press, 1985), pp. 11–12. Other scholars are doubtful even about Çatal Hüyük; see Ronald Hutton, *The Pagan Religions of the British Isles: Their Nature and Legacy* (Oxford: Blackwell, 1991), pp. 40–42.

23. Thomas, p. 517.

24. Briggs, p. 8. The nine million figure can be traced to Gerald Gardner; *Witchcraft Today*, p. 35 *et passim*. Cf. Starhawk, *The Spiral Dance* (San Francisco: Harper & Row, second ed., 1989), p. 20, and Raymond Buckland, *Buckland's Complete Book of Witchcraft* (St. Paul, Minn.: Llewellyn, 1986), p. 5.

25. Charles Godfrey Leland, *Aradia: The Gospel of the Witches* (1899; reprint, London: Pentacle Enterprises, 1989), p. 5.

26. Doreen Valiente, *Witchcraft for Tomorrow* (Custer, Wash.: Phoenix Publishing, 1978), p. 27.

27. It is interesting to note how the theology of Witchcraft offers a precise mirror to that of Jewish Kabbalah. In the latter, the primal source of all things is usually imagined (consciously or unconsciously) as male; the feminine principle is seen as arising out of it and giving rise to limitation and destruction. In Wicca, the primordial source is envisaged as female; the male aspect is seen as secondary and destructive. Naturally this suggests that the dichotomy between "life-giving" and "destructive" cannot be exclusively identified with either sex.

28. Starhawk, *The Spiral Dance*, pp. 108–09.

29. Farrar, p. 42.

30. Starhawk, p. 143.

31. Valiente, *The Rebirth of Witchcraft*, pp. 132–33; Hesiod, *Theogony*, 117.

32. Leland, p. 5.

33. Janet and Stewart Farrar and Gavin Bone, *The Pagan Path* (Custer, Wash.: Phoenix Publishing, 1995), p. 212.

34. "Robin," "Sunlight and Shadows: Some Perspectives on Hereditary and Old Crafte Practice," *The Cauldron* 82 (1996), p. 5.

35. Valiente, *The Rebirth of Witchcraft*, p. 45.

36. Isaac Bonewits, *Real Magic* (York Beach, Maine: Samuel Weiser, 1989), p. 250. Emphasis Bonewits's.

37. Francis King, *The Rites of Modern Occult Magic* (New York: Macmillan, 1970), pp. 178–79. A version of this story appears in Valiente, *The Rebirth of Witchcraft*, pp. 45–46.

38. Valiente, *Witchcraft for Tomorrow*, pp. 159–63.

39. Farrars and Bone, pp. 199–200.

40. There is good reason to think that, since Gardner himself was a Mason, these rites owe much of their inspiration and basic structure to Freemasonry. See Chas S. Clifton, "The Craft Meets the Craft," *Gnosis* 6 (Winter 1988), pp. 28–29. The Great Rite, however, is not a part of the Masonic tradition.

41. For the Gardnerian rites of the three initiations, see Janet and Stewart Farrar, *The Witches' Way*, pp. 9–39, published in Janet and Stewart Farrar, *A Witches' Bible* (Custer, Wash.: Phoenix Publishing, 1996).

42. Farrars, *The Witches' Way*, p. 33. Emphasis in the original.

43. "Adrienne," "The Great Rite," *PanThology*, vol. 1, no. 4 (n.d.), pp. 6–7.

44. The Farrars' survey indicates that 60 percent of their respondents called themselves Wiccans. The Farrars are reluctant to draw universal conclusions from these results, since they admit, "We ourselves know more Wiccans than any other path, and to this degree our distribution of questionnaires was biased." Farrars and Bone, pp. 196–97.

45. The best-known description of Alexandrian Wicca is in Farrar, *What Witches Do*.

46. Caitlín and John Matthews, *The Western Way* (New York: Penguin Arkana, 1994).

47. The information in this section is taken from Farrars and Bone, *The Pagan Path*, pp. 22–36, 157–64; also De-Anna Alba, "The Goddess Emerging," *Gnosis* 13 (Fall 1989), pp. 28–31.

48. Migene González-Wippler, *The Santería Experience* (Englewood Cliffs, N.J.: Prentice-Hall, 1982), p. 107.

49. Luisah Teish, *Jambalaya: The Natural Woman's Book of Personal Charms and Practical Rituals* (San Francisco: Harper & Row, 1985), pp. 106–7. The

names given here are as in Santería; the *orishas* in Brazil and Haiti have different names; for example, Ogun, in Voudoun, is Ogu; Oshun is Erzulie; Elegguá is Legba; Changó, Shango. *Orishas* in Haiti are known as *loas.*

50. Joseph M. Murphy, *Santería: An African Religion in America* (Boston: Beacon Press, 1988), pp. 7–8.

51. González-Wippler, p. 14.

52. Maya Deren, *Divine Horsemen: The Living Gods of Haiti* (New Paltz, N.Y.: DocumenText, 1970 [1953]), p. 31.

53. Migene González-Wippler, *Santería: The Religion* (New York: Harmony Books, 1989), p. 14.

54. González-Wippler, *The Santería Experience*, pp. 146–57.

55. Deren, pp. 26–27. For a subjective description of possession in a Voudoun context, see Deren, pp. 247–62.

56. González-Wippler, *Santería: The Religion*, pp. 205–6.

57. *The Church of Lukumi Babalú Ayé vs. Hialeah, Florida.* See Bruce Davis, "Animal Sacrifice: Why and Why Not?," *Paganet News*, Yule 1996, n.p.

58. Arthur Lyons, *Satan Wants You: The Cult of Devil Worship in America* (New York: The Mysterious Press, 1988), pp. 101–2.

59. See René Guénon, *L'Erreur spirite*, second ed. (Paris: Éditions Traditionelles, 1952), pp. 301–28.

60. Frazer, p. 62.

61. Anton Szandor LaVey, *The Satanic Bible* (New York: Avon Books, 1969), p. 25.

62. Massimo Introvigne, *Indagine sul satanismo* (Milan: Oscar Mondadori, 1994), p. 273.

63. Michael Aquino, *The Crystal Tablet of Set* (San Francisco: Temple of Set, 1983), pp. 9, 45.

64. Michael Aquino, *The Book of Coming Forth by Night* (San Francisco: self-published, 1985), commentary, p. 10.

65. Chas S. Clifton, "The Three Faces of Satanism," *Gnosis* 12 (Summer 1989), pp. 9–18.

66. Isaac Bonewits, "The Future of Neopagan Druidism," *Green Egg*, vol. 29, no. 117 (Jan.–Feb. 1997), p. 6.

## CHAPTER 7

1. Michael Winkelman, unpublished dissertation at the University of California, Irvine, 1984; discussed in Stanley Krippner and Patrick Welch, *Spiritual Dimensions of Healing* (New York: Irvington, 1992), pp. 7–9.

2. Mircea Eliade, *Shamanism: Archaic Techniques of Ecstasy*, trans. Willard R. Trask (Princeton: Princeton/Bollingen, 1972), pp. 4–5. See also *Oxford English Dictionary*, s.v. "shaman."

3. Michael Harner, *The Way of the Shaman* (New York: Bantam, 1982), p. 2.

4. Carlos Castaneda, *The Teachings of Don Juan: A Yaqui Way of Knowledge* (Berkeley: University of California Press, 1968), p. 5.

5. Eliade, pp. 4–5.

6. Telephone interview, September 1997.

7. Rosita Arvigo, "Jaguar Shamans and Mayan Spirits: My Apprenticeship with Don Eligio Panti," *Shaman's Drum* 30 (Winter 1993), p. 21.

8. A. P. Elkin, *Aboriginal Men of High Degree: Initiation and Sorcery in the World's Oldest Tradition* (1945; reprint, Rochester, Vt.: Inner Traditions, 1994), p. 151.

9. Eliade, pp. 62–64.

10. Burkert, pp. 199–203.

11. Deren, pp. 60–64. Deren believes the Rada deities were imported from Africa while the Petro gods were handed on to the Africans from the Indians of Hispaniola.

12. Harner, pp. 73–88.

13. Ibid., p. 88.

14. Doug Boyd, *Mad Bear: Spirit, Healing, and the Sacred in the Life of a Native American Medicine Man* (New York: Simon & Schuster, 1994), p. 234.

15. Castaneda, pp. 121–23.

16. Harner, pp. 21–23.

17. Gert Chesi, *Faith Healers in the Philippines*, trans. W. S. Reiter (Wörgl, Austria: Perlinger Verlag, 1981). For a personal account of an experience with a faith healer, see Blaize Clement, "Which Way to Siloam?" *The Sun* 259 (July 1997), pp. 10–17.

18. Eliade, p. 256.

19. Harner, pp. 64–65.

20. Eliade, pp. 168–69.

21. Harner, pp. 93–98.

22. The prevalent scholarly opinion equates *soma* with *Amanita muscaria*. See Richard Evans Schultes and Albert Hofmann, *Plants of the Gods: Their Sacred, Healing and Hallucinogenic Powers* (1979; reprint, Rochester, Vt.: Healing Arts Press, 1992), pp. 82–84.

23. Terence McKenna, *The Food of the Gods: A Radical History of Plants, Drugs, and Human Evolution* (New York: Bantam, 1992), pp. 97–137, 223–45.

24. Castaneda, p. 33. Emphasis Castaneda's.

25. For Huxley's own account of his experiences with these materials, see his book *The Doors of Perception* (London: Chatto & Windus, 1954).

26. One researcher who has studied these materials is the Czech psychiatrist Stanislav Grof; see his *LSD Psychotherapy* (Pomona, Calif.: Hunter House, 1980). See also Myron Stolaroff, "Using Psychedelics Wisely," *Gnosis* 26 (Winter 1993), pp. 26–30. In recent years, the Food and Drug Administra-

tion has permitted some limited use of materials such as MDMA in psychiatric research.

27. Timothy White, review of *Psychedelic Shamanism*, by Jim DeKorne, *Shaman's Drum* 37 (Winter 1995), p. 68.

28. Schultes and Hofmann, p. 89.

29. Ibid., p. 136.

30. Omer C. Stuart, *Peyote Religion: A History* (Norman, Okla.: University of Oklahoma Press, 1987), p. 31.

31. Schultes and Hofmann, p. 143. The original homeland of the Delawares—the Mohicans of Cooper's novel—was in the northeastern U.S., far from regions where peyote grows. The Delawares are unlikely to have encountered it until they were removed to Oklahoma in the nineteenth century.

32. Stuart, pp. 213–38.

33. Jaya Bear, "*Ayahuasca* Shamanism: An Interview with Don Agustín Rivas-Vasquez," *Shaman's Drum* 44 (March–May 1997), pp. 44–47.

34. There is a certain amount of awkwardness about what the indigenous peoples of the Americas should be called. The term *Indian,* although rooted in the geographical confusion of the first European visitors to this continent, seems to be preferred by the Native people themselves. Here we will use the terms *Native American, American Indian* and *Indian,* and *Native* more or less interchangeably.

35. C. G. Jung, "The Complications of American Psychology," in *Civilization in Transition,* p. 510.

36. Quoted in Richard Smoley, "A Non-Indian's Guide to Native American Spirituality," *Yoga Journal,* Jan.–Feb. 1992, p. 84.

37. Quoted in Ward Churchill, "Spiritual Hucksterism," in *From a Native Son: Selected Essays on Indigenism, 1985–95* (Boston: South End Press, 1996), p. 360.

38. Churchill, pp. 360–61.

39. Smoley, p. 104.

40. Corbin Harney, *The Way It Is* (Nevada City, Calif.: Blue Dolphin, 1995), pp. 56–57.

41. Smoley, p. 86.

42. Vine Deloria, Jr., preface to John G. Neihardt, *Black Elk Speaks* (1932; reprint, Lincoln, Neb.: University of Nebraska Press, 1988), p. xiv.

43. Michael F. Steltenkamp, *Black Elk: Holy Man of the Oglala* (Norman, Okla.: University of Oklahoma Press, 1993). It has also been argued that the "Two Roads Map" itself is a missionary adaptation of Native teachings.

44. Gladys A. Reichard, *Navaho Religion: A Study of Symbolism* (Princeton: Princeton/Bollingen, 1950), p. 7. Emphasis Reichard's.

45. James R. Walker, *Lakota Belief and Ritual* (Lincoln, Neb.: University of Nebraska Press, 1980), p. 102.

46. Clark Wissler and D. C. Duvall, *Mythology of the Blackfoot Indians* (1908; reprint, Lincoln, Neb.: University of Nebraska Press, 1995), p. 9.

47. Quoted in Smoley, ibid.

48. Harney, p. 33.

49. Reichard, p. 4.

50. Harney, p. 4.

51. Roger Annis, "Quebec Postpones Hydroelectric Project, But Cree Leaders Remain Vigilant," *Shaman's Drum* 37 (Winter 1995), p. 18.

52. Quoted in Smoley, ibid.

53. Neihardt, p. 2.

54. George A. Dorsey, *The Mythology of the Wichita* (1904; reprint, Norman, Okla.: University of Oklahoma Press, 1995), pp. 20–22.

55. Walker, pp. 109–12, 75–76.

56. Tom Flanders, "The Way of the Real People: Living on the Earth," in Richard G. Carlson, ed., *Rooted Like the Ash Trees: New England Indians and the Land* (Naugatuck, Conn.: Eagle Wing Press, 1987), p. 62.

57. Walker, pp. 132–34.

## CHAPTER 8

1. Richard Grossinger, *Alchemy: Pre-Egyptian Legacy, Millennial Promise* (Richmond, Calif.: North Atlantic Books, 1979), pp. 247–48.

2. Joseph Rowe, "The Quintessence of Alchemy: The *Gnosis* Interview with François Trojani," *Gnosis* 39 (Summer 1996), p. 39.

3. Pamela H. Smith, *The Business of Alchemy: Science and Culture in the Holy Roman Empire* (Princeton: Princeton University Press, 1994), p. 181.

4. C. G. Jung, "The Psychology of the Transference," quoted in *Jung on Alchemy*, ed. Nathan Schwartz Salant (Princeton: Princeton University Press, 1995), p. 69.

5. Grossinger, pp. 190–91.

6. Scholars sometimes distinguish between "Hermetism," the version of this tradition that was known in late antiquity, and "Hermeticism," applied to its revival in the Renaissance and later. But this distinction is more likely to confuse than enlighten the general reader, so we will use the term "Hermeticism" throughout.

7. Walter Scott, *Hermetica: The Ancient Greek and Latin Writings Which Contains Religious or Philosophical Teachings Ascribed to Hermes Trismegistus* (1924; reprint, Boston: Shambhala, 1985), vol. 1, p. 41.

8. For a view of these texts as continuing the Egyptian tradition, see Peter Kingsley, "Poimandres: The Etymology of the Name and the Origins of the *Hermetica*," *Journal of the Warburg and Courtauld Institutes*, vol. 56 (1993), pp. 1–24.

9. *Oxford English Dictionary*, s.v. "alchemy."

10. Plutarch, *De Iside et Osiride*, 65; quoted in G. R. S. Mead, *Thrice-Greatest Hermes: Studies in Hellenistic Theosophy and Gnosis* (1906; reprint, York Beach, Maine: Samuel Weiser, 1992), p. 240.

11. Ibid., p. 205.

12. Julius Evola, *The Hermetic Tradition: Symbols and Teachings of the Royal Art*, trans. E. E. Rehmus (Rochester, Vt.: Inner Traditions, 1995), p. 23.

13. Ibid., p. 25. Emphasis Evola's.

14. Ibid., pp. 36–37.

15. Annie Besant, *Thought Power* (Wheaton, Ill.: Theosophical Publishing House, 1966), p. 13. Besant does not, however, explicitly equate the Knower with alchemical *sol*.

16. For an exploration of these dimensions of reality written by a Tibetan lama, see Tarthang Tulku, *Time, Space, and Knowledge: A New Vision of Reality* (Emeryville, Calif.: Dharma Publishing, 1977).

17. Henry Corbin, *Spiritual Body and Celestial Earth: From Mazdean Iran to Shi'ite Iran*, trans. Nancy Pearson (Princeton: Princeton/Bollingen, 1977), p. 47.

18. For a symbolic representation of this idea, see Jolande Jacobi, ed., *Paracelsus: Selected Writings* (Princeton: Princeton/Bollingen, 1951), p. 147.

19. Evola, p. 140.

20. Ibid., p. 163.

21. Ibid., p. 173.

22. Corbin, ibid.

23. Maurice Aniane, "Notes on Alchemy, The Cosmological 'Yoga' of Medieval Christianity," *Material for Thought*, Spring 1976, pp. 83–92.

24. E. A. Wallis Budge, *The Gods of the Egyptians*, vol. 1 (1904; reprint, New York: Dover, 1969), p. 111.

25. Quoted in Normandi Ellis, "The Body Electric," *Gnosis* 29 (Fall 1993), p. 26.

26. See Robert Masters, *The Goddess Sekhmet: The Way of the Five Bodies* (Amity, N.Y.: Amity House, 1988) and *Neurospeak* (Wheaton, Ill.: Quest Books, 1994); also Jean Houston, *The Passion of Isis and Osiris* (New York: Ballantine, 1995).

27. Most of the alchemists whose names we know were men, but there have always been female alchemists as well. A shadowy figure named Maria the Hebrew was apparently one of the seminal alchemists of antiquity; Hypatia, a female philosopher of the fourth and fifth centuries A.D., is also said to have been an initiate in the art. In other cases, alchemy involved the combined efforts of a man and woman. Nicolas Flamel worked with his wife Pernelle, while one of the most revealing works on the subject was written by Mary Anne Atwood, an Englishwoman of the nineteenth century who studied the Hermetic art alongside her clergyman father. See Mary Anne

Atwood, *Hermetic Philosophy and Alchemy: A Suggestive Inquiry* (1850; reprint, New York: Julian Press, 1960).

28. Rowe, p. 38.

29. Quoted in Stanislas Klossowski de Rola, *Alchemy: The Secret Art* (London: Thames & Hudson, 1973), p. 10.

30. Quoted in Frater Albertus, *The Alchemist's Handbook* (New York: Samuel Weiser, 1960), p. 76.

31. Frater Albertus, p. 73.

32. Klossowski de Rola, p. 19.

33. Ibid., p. 10.

34. Ibid., p. 21.

35. Ibid., p. 10.

36. For a development of this idea see Alice Bailey, *The Consciousness of the Atom* (New York: Lucis Trust, 1924).

37. Aniane, p. 59.

38. Meister Eckhart, *Treatises and Sermons*, quoted in Aniane, p. 58.

39. Ibid., p. 59.

40. Hans Nintzel, "Alchemy Is Alive and Well," *Gnosis* 8 (Summer 1988), pp. 11–15. See also Christopher Farmer, "Practical Alchemy and Physical Immortality: An Interview with Art Kunkin," *Gnosis* 8, pp. 16–20.

41. Rowe, pp. 36–37.

42. Ronald Decker, Thierry Depaulis, and Michael Dummett, *A Wicked Pack of Cards: The Origins of the Occult Tarot* (New York: St. Martin's Press, 1996), pp. 57–60.

43. Michael Dummett, *The Game of Tarot* (London: Duckworth, 1990), sets out this view in detail; Decker, Depaulis, and Dummett continue Dummett's argument.

44. Decker, Depaulis, and Dummett, p. 74.

45. Stuart R. Kaplan, *The Encyclopedia of Tarot*, (New York: U.S. Games Systems, 1978), vol. 1, pp. 40–47.

46. Dana Lloyd Thomas, "A Modern Pythagorean," *Gnosis* 44 (Summer 1997), pp. 52–59.

47. Another possibility is that the trumps were created in imitation of the triumphal pageants of Renaissance Italy, which often embodied esoteric ideas under the guises of pagan gods and allegorical figures. For a description of these *trionfi,* see Jacob Burckhardt, *The Civilization of the Renaissance in Italy,* trans. S. G. C. Middlemore (Vienna: Phaidon Press, n.d.), pp. 208–21.

48. Kaplan, vol. 3, pp. 168–69, 473, 491, 512, 575, 649.

49. Lévi, *Transcendental Magic,* p. 462.

50. Ibid. These are not the associations most familiar today; usually swords are connected with air and coins or pentacles with earth.

51. Lévi, pp. 473–78.

52. Tomberg, p. 4.
53. Kaplan, vol. 3, pp. 31–32.
54. Decker et al., pp. 35–37.
55. Mary K. Greer and Rachel Pollack, quoted in Decker et al., p. 26.

**CHAPTER 9**

1. St. Augustine, *Confessions* X.viii.15 and X.xxxii.48, quoted in Peter Brown, *Religion and Society in the Age of St. Augustine* (New York: Harper & Row, 1972), pp. 28–29.
2. P. D. Ouspensky, *In Search of the Miraculous: Fragments of a Forgotten Teaching* (New York: Harcourt, Brace, & Co.: 1949), p. 66.
3. James Moore, *Gurdjieff: The Anatomy of a Myth* (Rockport, Mass.: Element Books, 1991), pp. 339–40. This passage also discusses the ambiguities behind Gurdjieff's surname.
4. G. I. Gurdjieff, *All and Everything: Beelzebub's Tales to His Grandson* (1950; reprint, Aurora, Ore.: Two Rivers Press, 1993), p. v.
5. G. I. Gurdjieff, *Meetings with Remarkable Men* (New York: E.P. Dutton, 1963), pp. 148–64, 238–46.
6. Ouspensky, p. 59.
7. Gurdjieff's view of the human makeup is somewhat more complex than this, and in the end he lists seven different centers. But because he and his followers use this tripartite system as a kind of shorthand, we will follow this usage here.
8. G. I. Gurdjieff, *The Herald of Coming Good* (1934; reprint, Edmonds, Wash.: Sure Fire Press, 1988), pp. 28–30.
9. Ouspensky, p. 220.
10. Gurdjieff, *All and Everything*, pp. 85–93 *et passim*.
11. Ouspensky, pp. 154–57.
12. Ibid., p. 31.
13. Ibid., p. 219, 220.
14. Ibid., pp. 82–89.
15. Ibid., p. 83.
16. Ibid., p. 85.
17. Gurdjieff, *All and Everything*, p. 1106.
18. Ibid., p. 88.
19. Ouspensky, p. 45.
20. Ibid., p. 50.
21. Ibid., p. 117.
22. Richard Smoley and Jay Kinney, "One Path or Many?": The *Gnosis* Interview with Charles Tart," *Gnosis* 28 (Summer 1993), p. 32.
23. Jean Vaysse, *Toward Awakening: An Approach to the Teaching Left by Gurdjieff* (New York: Penguin Arkana, 1989), p. 160.

24. Ouspensky, p. 110.

25. Ibid., pp. 188–98.

26. Ibid., p. 146.

27. Ibid., p. 221.

28. For accounts of the break between Gurdjieff and Ouspensky, see Ouspensky, p. 389; Moore, pp. 204–7; also Boris Mouravieff, "Ouspensky, Gurdjieff, et les fragments d'un enseignement inconnu," (N.p.: Centre d'études chrétiennes ésotériques, n.d., reprinted from [Brussels] *Synthèses* 138, Nov. 1957).

29. Quoted in Roger Lipsey, "Gurdjieff Observed," in Jacob Needleman and George Baker, eds., *Gurdjieff: Essays and Reflections on the Man and His Teaching* (New York: Continuum, 1997), p. 330.

30. Gurdjieff, *Herald of Coming Good*, p. 68. Punctuation Gurdjieff's.

31. Thomas and Olga de Hartmann, *Our Life with Mr. Gurdjieff*, ed. T. C. and T. A. G. Daly (1964; reprint, New York: Penguin Arkana, 1992), pp. 48–49.

32. James Webb, *The Harmonious Circle: The Lives and Work of G. I. Gurdjieff, P. D. Ouspensky, and Their Followers* (New York: G. P. Putnam's Sons, 1980), pp. 236–37, 250.

33. De Hartmanns, p. 255.

34. Gurdjieff, *Beelzebub*, p. 27.

35. J. G. Bennett, *Witness* (Charles Town, W.Va.: Claymont Communications, 1983), p. 243.

36. Michel Random, "The Men of Blame and the Fourth Way," in Needleman and Baker, p. 226.

37. Webb, pp. 252–53.

38. Ouspensky, p. 156.

39. Moore, p. 349.

40. Ouspensky, p. 17.

41. Richard Smoley and Jay Kinney, "The Essence of the Work": The *Gnosis* Interview with Jacob Needleman, *Gnosis* 20 (Summer 1991), p. 31.

42. The best discussion of this issue is probably Georg Feuerstein, *Holy Madness* (New York: Viking Penguin, 1992); Gurdjieff is discussed on pp. 54–59.

43. Robin Amis makes the most valiant effort in *A Different Christianity: Early Christian Esotericism and Modern Thought* (Albany: State University of New York Press, 1995), but valuable as his work is in its examination of Orthodox mysticism, it is unconvincing in its claim to have uncovered the source of the Fourth Way. See also Amis's "Mouravieff and the Secret of the Source," *Gnosis* 20 (Summer 1991), pp. 46–51, as well as Mouravieff's works already cited.

44. Ouspensky, p. 102.

45. For Gurdjieff's views on prayer, see Ouspensky, pp. 300–303.

46. Gurdjieff, *Beelzebub*, pp. 702–3. Curiously, Gurdjieff adds that Christianity has been preserved intact only by the Brotherhood of Essenes, which is, according to the conventional view, a mystical Jewish sect that vanished in the first century A.D.

47. Murat Yagan, "Sufism and the Source," *Gnosis* 30 (Winter 1994), pp. 40–47.

48. Oscar Ichazo, "Letter to the Transpersonal Community," in *The Arican: The Teachings of the Great Telesmatta* (New York: Arica Institute, n.d.), pp. 88–90.

49. Moore, p. 31.

50. *Finnegans Wake* and *Beelzebub* were, oddly enough, written in the same time and place—Paris in the twenties and thirties—and one can wonder if some unexamined influence passed between the two men. Certainly they knew of each other: Gurdjieff's pupil Jane Heap was one of the first to publish Joyce's writing, and apparently Joyce even paid a visit to the Prieuré in the spring of 1923; see Moore, p. 191.

51. Ouspensky, pp. 90, 170–73 *et passim*. Gurdjieff distinguishes these substances from the elements as understood by science.

52. Solita Solano, "The Kanari Papers," in the journal *Telos: Inquiries into Self-Transformation in the Contemporary World*, unnumbered (Fairfax, Calif.: 1996), p. 10.

53. Gurdjieff, *Beelzebub*, p. 50.

54. Gurdjieff, *Meetings with Remarkable Men*, pp. 162–63.

55. See also Kathleen Riordan Speeth, *The Gurdjieff Work* (1976; reprint, Los Angeles: Jeremy P. Tarcher, 1989), pp. 83–89.

56. Ouspensky, p. 232.

57. Gurdjieff, *Beelzebub*, p. 92.

58. For possible references to the enneagram in earlier manuscripts and art, see Idries Shah, *The Commanding Self* (London: Octagon Press, 1994), pp. 286–87.

59. Ouspensky, p. 294.

60. J. G. Bennett, *Enneagram Studies* (York Beach, Maine: Samuel Weiser, 1983), p. 22–34. See also *The Intelligent Enneagram* by Bennett's pupil A. G. E. Blake (Boston: Shambhala, 1996).

61. Ouspensky, p. 246.

62. Moore, p. 261. The word *idiotes,* in Gurdjieff's native Greek, originally meant "private individual." But he was also playing with its more familiar sense.

63. Ichazo, p. 80.

64. Helen Palmer, *The Enneagram* (San Francisco: Harper & Row, 1988).

65. Ouspensky, p. 162.

66. Ibid., p. 161.

67.   Ibid., p. 226.

68.   Ibid., pp. 267–68.

69.   Ibid., p. 226.

## CHAPTER 10

1.   The Islamic calendar dates from the migration of the Prophet Muhammad and his early followers to the Arabian city of Medina in 622 A.D. For the sake of simplicity, all dates in this chapter are pegged to the more familiar Western calendar.

2.   There are a few Sufi orders whose lineages do not descend from Ali. The Naqshbandi order traces itself back to Abu Bakr, the Prophet's uncle, the initial successor to the Prophet in the leadership of Islam. Uwaysi orders trace themselves back to Uways, a saint in Yemen whom the Prophet spoke of approvingly but never met face-to-face.

3.   It is difficult to specify an exact date for the development of *tariqahs* as institutions. Important Sufis such as al-Muhasibi and al-Junayd maintained schools in the ninth and tenth centuries. However, almost all of the present orders in Sufism date from the eleventh century and later.

4.   This is not to say that Sufism was consistently on good terms with the *Ulama,* the Islamic doctors of law. The implicit tension between a formalistic understanding of Islam and the looser mystical approach resulted in periodic cycles of conflict down through the centuries. However, in the balance, Islam as a religion made a more explicit niche for popular mysticism than did Catholic Christianity or Orthodox Judaism.

5.   Noted by Bob Darr in personal conversation.

6.   Hazrat Inayat Khan, *The Unity of Religious Ideals* (New Lebanon, N.Y.: Sufi Order Publications, 1979), p. 29. This viewpoint is echoed in some of the verses of the Sufi poet Rumi.

7.   Idries Shah, *The Way of the Sufi* (London: Penguin Arkana, 1974) p. 29.

8.   Ibid., p. 22.

9.   See "The Mystics Choose a King," by Martin Brackett in *The Diffusion of Sufi Ideas in the West: An Anthology of New Writings by and about Idries Shah,* edited by L. Lewin (Boulder, Colo.: Keysign Press, 1972), pg. 188. A purportedly eye-witness account of the meeting of 155 Sufi Sheikhs in Turkey to elect their "High Guide, the Magnetic Pole of the Age," it implies that Shah was the elected Grand Sheikh without quite naming him.

10.  Mevlana Celaleddin Rumi, *Divan-i Kebir, Meter 1,* trans. Nevit O. Ergin (Walla Walla, Wash.: Current, 1995), p. 302.

11.  Mevlana Jalauddin Rumi, *Love Is a Stranger,* trans. Kabir Helminski, (Putney, Vt.: Threshold Books, 1993), p. 69.

12.  From Ibn 'Arabi, "The Word of Seth," in *Fusus al-Hikam,* trans. Titus Burck-

hardt and Angela Culme-Seymour (Sherborne, Gloucestershire, England: Beshara Publications, 1975), p. 30.

13. It is worth noting that Turkish Sufism, especially within the Bektashi and Mevlevi orders, upheld a more liberal approach towards women. Haji Bektash, the founder of the Bektashis, was a strong proponent of education for women and both sexes have traditionally met together in Bektashi circles. The Mevlevis, who were historically strongest amongst the Turkish aristocracy (in contrast to the largely rural-based Bektashis) also held gatherings with both men and women.

14. Robin Waterfield, *René Guénon and the Future of the West* (Wellingborough, Northamptonshire, U.K.: Crucible Books, 1987) pg. 41.

15. Guénon included Judaism, Christianity, Islam, Hinduism, and Buddhism in his pantheon of revealed religions. Later Traditionalists such as Frithjof Schuon also considered Shintoism and Native American religions to represent facets of primordial Truth.

16. Huston Smith, *Forgotten Truth: The Common Vision of the World's Religions* (1976; Reprint. San Francisco: HarperSanFrancisco, 1992).

17. The wide variance of attitudes towards *shariah* is perhaps best illustrated by the Bektashi order, which even includes ceremonial wine-drinking among its rituals. The ritual, which has strict parameters and is done under the disciplined guidance of a Bektashi elder, is an example of taking a local folk custom and transforming it into a spiritual practice.

**CHAPTER 2**

1. English versions of the *Fama* and *Confessio* can be found in Frances A. Yates, *The Rosicrucian Enlightenment* (London: Ark, 1986 [1972]), pp. 238–60. A third work, an alchemical allegory called *The Chemical Wedding of Christian Rosenkreutz*, was published in 1616; it is generally acknowledged to be the work of a Lutheran divine named Johann Valentin Andreae, who probably did not write the other two. A recent edition of this work is *The Chemical Wedding of Christian Rosenkreutz*, trans. Joscelyn Godwin (Grand Rapids, Mich.: Phanes Press, 1991).

2. Yates, pp. 239, 249, 251.

3. Ibid., p. 241.

4. Ibid., p. 243.

5. Quoted in Yates, p. 102.

6. See Christopher McIntosh, *The Rose Cross and the Age of Reason* (Leiden: E. J. Brill, 1992).

7. See John Patrick Deveney, *Paschal Beverly Randolph: A Nineteenth-Century Black American Spiritualist, Rosicrucian, and Sex Magician* (Albany: State University of New York Press, 1996).

8.	Yates, p. 238.

9.	H. Spencer Lewis claimed that the Rosicrucian Order deliberately alternates public activity and secret operation in 108-year cycles; see H. Spencer Lewis, *Rosicrucian Questions and Answers, with Complete History of the Rosicrucian Order* (San Jose, Calif.: AMORC, 1929). pp. 162–63.

10.	Ouspensky, p. 312.

11.	Lewis, pp. 29–66.

12.	Some modern Witches also, confusingly, refer to their tradition as "the Craft." The coincidence is not as peculiar as it may seem, since Gerald Gardner, founder of modern Witchcraft, was himself a Co-Mason, a member of a Masonic offshoot that included both men and women; Valiente, *The Rebirth of Witchcraft*, p. 32.

13.	For the Scottish origins of Freemasonry, see David Stevenson, *The Origins of Freemasonry* (Cambridge: Cambridge University Press, 1988).

14.	For discussions of the connection between the Templars and Freemasonry, see John J. Robinson, *Born in Blood: The Lost Secrets of Freemasonry* (New York: M. Evans & Co., 1989) and Michael Baigent and Richard Leigh, *The Temple and the Lodge* (London: Jonathan Cape, 1989); a considerably more speculative work is Christopher Knight and Robert Lomas, *The Hiram Key: Pharaohs, Freemasonry, and the Discovery of the Secret Scrolls of Jesus* (Rockport, Mass.: Element, 1996).

15.	Yates, pp. 182–83. Yates emphasizes that many of the key figures of the "Invisible College" were from the Palatinate.

16.	Ibid., pp. 171–205.

17.	Christopher McIntosh, *The Rosy Cross Unveiled* (London: Aquarian, 1980), pp. 89, 109–10.

18.	Ibid., pp. 130, 135.

19.	Ibid., pp. 135–41.

20.	See Max Heindel, *The Rosicrucian Cosmo-Conception* (Oceanside, Calif.: Rosicrucian Fellowship, 1909). Heindel was a pupil of Rudolf Steiner, whose teachings Heindel follows closely.

21.	For an unauthorized account of AMORC teachings, see Reuben R. Isaac, *The Unveiling of the Teachings of the Rosicrucian Order: An Exposé* (Baltimore, Md.: Noble House, 1995). See also AMORC, Master Monograph, Neophyte Section, Private Mandamus no. 5 (San Jose, Calif., n.d.), pp. 6–7.

22.	McIntosh, pp. 80–81 *et passim*.

23.	See, for example, Stephen T. Chang, *The Tao of Sexology: The Book of Infinite Wisdom* (San Francisco: Tao Publishing, 1986).

24.	From the Web site of the Grand Lodge of Free and Accepted Masons of Ohio: www.freemason.com/secret.html.

25.	For a firsthand account of the three first Masonic initiations, see Knight and Lomas, pp. 1–18.

26. W. Kirk MacNulty, *Freemasonry: A Journey through Ritual and Symbol* (London: Thames & Hudson, 1991), pp. 23–24.

27. A Hiram (or Huram) is mentioned in the biblical accounts of the Temple's construction; see 1 Kings 7:13–45; 2 Chron. 2:13–4:18. But there he is a worker in brass, not an architect; there is also no reference to his murder.

28. The Third Degree ritual, as quoted by Knight and Lomas, pp. 15–16.

29. W. L. Wilmshurst, *The Meaning of Masonry* (1927; reprint, New York: Gramercy Books, 1995), p. 73.

30. Wilmshurst, pp. 74–75.

31. Sylvia Cranston, *H.P.B.: The Extraordinary Life and Influence of Helena Blavatsky, Founder of the Modern Theosophical Movement* (Los Angeles: Jeremy Tarcher/Putnam, 1993), pp. 35–42.

32. Cranston, pp. 45–47.

33. K. Paul Johnson, *In Search of the Masters: Behind the Occult Myth* (South Boston, Va.: self-published, 1990); *The Masters Revealed: Mme. Blavatsky and the Myth of the Great White Lodge* (Albany: State University of New York Press, 1994); *Initiates of Theosophical Masters* (State University of New York Press, 1996); "Imaginary Mahatmas," *Gnosis* 28 (Summer 1993), pp. 24–30.

34. Cranston, pp. 216–18.

35. Most recently in Vernon Harrison, *H.P. Blavatsky and the SPR: An Examination of the Hodgson Report of 1885* (Pasadena, Calif.: Theosophical University Press, 1997).

36. Cranston, pp. 179–80.

37. Quoted in Cranston, p. 224.

38. Cranston, p. 222. Certain of Blavatsky's pupils supposedly communicated with the Masters by letter; the one quoted here is to A. O. Hume. The most famous collection can be found in *The Mahatma Letters to A. P. Sinnett*, ed. A. T. Barker et al. (Adyar, India: Theosophical Publishing House, 1923). The originals of these letters reside in the British Museum.

39. Cranston, pp. 386–87; Tim Maroney, "Introduction to *The Book of Dzyan*," unpublished ms.

40. H. P. Blavatsky, *The Secret Doctrine* (London: Theosophical Publishing Co., 1888), vol. 1, p. 16.

41. Cranston, p. 434.

42. Blavatsky, vol. 1, pp. 14–17.

43. Geoffrey A. Barborka, *The Divine Plan* (Adyar: Theosophical Publishing House, 1961), p. 98. Capitalization in the original.

44. Blavatsky, vol. 1, pp. 48, 277–78.

45. For a summary of the doctrine of the races, see Barborka, pp. 262–338.

46. Blavatsky, vol. 1, p. 104. Blavatsky also refers to the astral light by the Sanskrit term *akasha*.

47. W. K. C. Guthrie, *A History of Greek Philosophy, Vol. 1: The Earlier Presocra-*

*tics and Pythagoreans* (Cambridge: Cambridge University Press, 1971), pp. 186–87.

48.   Cranston, p. 504–05, cites a 1981 Gallup poll saying that 23 percent of Americans believed in reincarnation; as she notes, it has risen considerably even since then.

49.   Ibid., p. 337.

50.   Blavatsky, vol. 1, pp. 274–75. By "man," Blavatsky does not necessarily mean a human living on our particular planet, but a being having our degree of consciousness and materiality.

51.   Johnson, "Imaginary Mahatmas," p. 26.

52.   Though Olcott did a great deal to revive Buddhism in Ceylon, today's Sri Lanka. See Stephen Prothero, *The White Buddhist: The Asian Odyssey of Henry Steel Olcott* (Bloomington, Ind.: Indiana University Press, 1996).

53.   Cranston, p. 428.

54.   Ihla F. Nation, "Face to Face: Confronting the Guru-Disciple Relationship," *Gnosis* 39 (Spring 1996), p. 29.

55.   Robert Ellwood, *Theosophy* (Wheaton, Ill.: Quest Books, 1986), pp. 213–16.

56.   Quoted in Ellwood, p. 21.

57.   The whole address can be found in *Total Freedom: The Essential Krishnamurti*, ed. Mary Cadogan et al. (San Francisco: HarperSanFrancisco, 1996), pp. 1–7. A good discussion of Krishnamurti's character and influence can be found in Cheryll Aimée Barron, "The Anti-Guru," *Buzz* magazine, May 1995, pp. 81–88.

58.   For a brief overview of Advaita Vedanta, see Ati Akarta (Igor Kungurtsev, "Nonduality and Western Seekers," *Gnosis* 39 (Spring 1996), pp. 16–24. The author does not, however, connect Krishnamurti with this teaching.

59.   Robert A. McDermott, "Rudolf Steiner and Anthroposophy," in Faivre and Needleman, p. 292.

60.   McDermott, p. 291.

61.   See James H. Hindes, *Renewing Christianity* (Hudson, N.Y.: Anthroposophic Press, 1996), pp. 32, 43–44.

62.   It is set out in Rudolf Steiner, *An Outline of Esoteric Science*, trans. Catherine E. Creeger (Hudson, N.Y.: Anthroposophic Press, 1997). Earlier editions of this work had the title *An Outline of Occult Science*.

63.   Rudolf Steiner, "The Christ," in *The Spiritual Hierarchies and the Physical World: Reality and Illusion*, trans. R.M. Querido and Jann Gates (Hudson, N.Y.: Anthroposophic Press, 1996), p. 154.

64.   Steiner, *Spiritual Hierarchies*, p. 162.

65.   Rudolf Steiner, *How to Know Higher Worlds*, trans. Christopher Bamford (Hudson, N.Y.: Anthroposophic Press, 1994). Earlier editions had the title *Knowledge of the Higher World and Its Attainment*.

66. Rudolf Steiner, "Christian Rosenkreutz and the Temple Legend," in Paul M. Allen, ed., *A Christian Rosenkreutz Anthology* (Blauvelt, N.Y.: Rudolf Steiner Publications, 1968), p. 447.
67. Ouspensky, pp. 309–10.

**CHAPTER 12**

1. Paul Heelas, *The New Age Movement* (Oxford: Blackwell, 1996), pp. 113–14.
2. Corbin, p. 18 *et passim*.
3. Emanuel Swedenborg, *The Last Judgment in Retrospect*, trans. George F. Dole (West Chester, Pa.: Swedenborg Foundation, 1996).
4. Heelas, p. 17.
5. Nicholas Campion, *The Practical Astrologer* (New York: Harry N. Abrams, 1987), pp. 142–43. This shift involves the *sidereal zodiac,* which moves with the constellations over the course of millennia, rather than the fixed or *tropical zodiac,* which remains stationary in the sky. The tropical zodiac is the one used by most Western astrologers for predictions and natal charts.
6. Sir John R. Sinclair, *The Alice Bailey Inheritance* (Wellingborough, Northamptonshire, England: Turnstone Press, 1984), p. 19.
7. Mary-Margaret Moore, introduction to Bartholomew, *"I Come as a Brother": A Remembrance of Illusions* (Taos, N.M.: High Mesa Press, 1986), p. iv.
8. "Extract from a Statement by the Tibetan," in Alice Bailey, *The Reappearance of the Christ* (New York: Lucis Publishing Co.: 1948), pp. 1–2. This extract appears as a preface to most of the Alice Bailey books.
9. Sinclair, pp. 19–20. See C. W. Leadbeater, *The Masters and the Path* (Adyar, India: Theosophical Publishing House, 1925). Bailey had sent the manuscript around 1920–21.
10. Sinclair, p. 22.
11. Sinclair, p. 131; Corinne McLaughlin and Gordon Davidson, *Spiritual Politics: Changing the World from Inside Out* (New York: Ballantine, 1994).
12. Constance Cumbey, *The Hidden Dangers of the Rainbow* (Shreveport, La.: Huntington House, 1983).
13. Marilyn Ferguson, *The Aquarian Conspiracy: Personal and Social Transformation in Our Time*, second ed. (Los Angeles: Jeremy Tarcher, 1987), p. 420.
14. Ibid., pp. 45–63.
15. Ibid., pp. 26–28.
16. John E. Mack's *Abduction: Human Encounters with Aliens* (New York: Charles Scribner's Sons, 1994) is a controversial study of these experiences.
17. Jay Kinney, "Wars in Heaven," *Gnosis* 38 (Winter 1996), pp. 45–49.
18. Mary Ellen Carter, *Edgar Cayce on Prophecy* (New York: Paperback Library, 1968), p. 197.
19. Plato, *Timaeus* 21e–23b.

20. Ibid., 22c; translated by Benjamin Jowett.

21. Carter, p. 61.

22. José Argüelles, *The Mayan Factor* (Santa Fe, N.M.: Bear & Co., 1987).

23. Jay Kinney and Richard Smoley, "War on High: The *Gnosis* Interview with Elizabeth Clare Prophet," *Gnosis* 21 (Fall 1991), p. 32.

24. Hastings, p. 62; see also J. Gordon Melton, "An Initial Encounter with Ramtha," *Gnosis* 41 (Fall 1996), pp. 12–18.

25. Hastings, p. 64.

26. David Spangler, *A Pilgrim in Aquarius* (Findhorn, Scotland: Findhorn Press, 1996), pp. 90–91.

27. For an overview of Lamarck's ideas, see L. J. Jordanova, *Lamarck* (Oxford: Oxford University Press, 1984).

28. Friedrich Nietzsche, *Thus Spoke Zarathustra*, trans. Walter Kaufmann (Harmondsworth, Middlesex, England: Penguin, 1978), p. 12.

29. Louis Pauwels and Jacques Bergier, *The Morning of the Magicians*, trans. Rollo Myers (New York: Avon, 1968), pp. 217, 219.

30. Another criticism leveled by fundamentalists is that Nazism had its roots in occultism. While some Nazi leaders were fascinated by the subject and had connections to quasi-occult secret societies, the sources of Nazism owe far more to racist and anti-Semitic ideologies that were popular in Germany in the nineteenth century. Esoteric groups like the Rosicrucians, Theosophists, and Freemasons were persecuted by the Third Reich. For the best discussion of this topic, see Nicholas Goodrick-Clarke, *The Occult Roots of Nazism* (Wellingborough, Northamptonshire, England: Aquarian Press, 1985).

31. Michael Murphy, *The Future of the Body: Explorations into the Further Reaches of Human Nature* (Los Angeles: Jeremy P. Tarcher, 1992), p. 28. For Murphy's views on Nietzsche and Nazism, see pp. 196–97.

32. Murphy, p. 27.

33. Brant Cortright, *Psychotherapy and Spirit: Theory and Practice in Transpersonal Psychotherapy* (Albany: State University of New York Press, 1997), p. 8.

34. Abraham H. Maslow, *Toward a Psychology of Being*, second ed. (New York: Van Nostrand Reinhold, 1968), p. 3.

35. Maslow, p. 4.

36. Cortright, pp. 37–39.

37. For an introduction to Reich and his ideas, see W. Edward Mann and Edward Hoffman, *The Man Who Dreamed of Tomorrow: The Life and Thought of Wilhelm Reich* (Los Angeles: Jeremy P. Tarcher, 1980); also Wilhelm Reich, *The Function of the Orgasm*, trans. Vincent R. Carfagno (New York: Simon & Schuster, 1973).

38. Grof, a Czech psychiatrist now living in the United States, originally ad-

ministered LSD as a means of regressing patients to the experience of the birth trauma, which he regards as the source of many psychological problems. For his insights into this process, see his book *Beyond the Brain: Birth, Death, and Transcendence in Psychotherapy* (Albany: State University of New York Press, 1985). After LSD was banned in the 1960s, Grof began to use deep breathing as a method of regressing patients.

39. Cortright, pp. 115–20.

40. Ibid., p. 2.

41. Ibid., pp. 76–78.

42. Ibid., pp. 77–89.

43. Christina and Stanislav Grof, *The Stormy Search for the Self* (Los Angeles: Jeremy P. Tarcher, 1992).

44. Cortright, p. 183.

45. David Icke, *The Robots' Rebellion* (Bath, England: Gateway Books, 1994); *". . . And the Truth Shall Set You Free"* (Newark, Nottinghamshire, England: Bridge of Love, 1996).

46. "Ramtha," *Last Waltz of the Tyrants: The Prophecy*, ed. Judi Pope Koteen (Hillsboro, Ore.: Beyond Words Publishing, 1989), pp. 14–15 *et passim*.

47. Richard Dannelley, *Sedona: Beyond the Vortex; Activating the Planetary Ascension Program with Sacred Geometry, the Vortex, and the Merkaba* (Sedona, Ariz.: Vortex Society, 1995), table of contents. The Antahkarana is a term for a subtle vehicle linking the personal with the impersonal as described by Blavatsky and Alice Bailey. See Sinclair, pp. 61–63.

48. Ouspensky, p. 314.

49. The most influential version of this teaching probably comes from the Seth material channeled by Jane Roberts. See, for example, her book *The Nature of Personal Reality* (1974; reprint, San Rafael, Calif.: New World Library, 1994).

50. Peter Caddy, *In Perfect Timing: Memoirs of a Man for the New Millennium* (Findhorn, Scotland: Findhorn Press, 1996), pp. 33–34.

51. Uma Silbey, *The Complete Crystal Guidebook* (San Francisco: U-Read Publications, 1986), pp. 16–19, 192–99.

52. David Spangler, "Defining the New Age," in Paul Zuromski, ed., *The New Age Almanac* (New York: Doubleday, 1988), p. xii.

53. Address to the conference of the Association for Transpersonal Psychology, August 1993.

54. Richard Grossinger, "Beyond the Ideology of Healing," *Gnosis* 34 (Winter 1995), pp. 51, 53.

55. Alice A. Bailey, *Discipleship in the New Age* (New York: Lucis Publishing Co., 1944), p. 55.

56. See Robert W. Balch, "Waiting for the Ships: Disillusionment and Revital-

ization of Faith in Bo and Peep's UFO Cult," in James R. Lewis, ed., *The Gods Have Landed: New Religions from Other Worlds* (Albany: State University of New York Press, 1995).

57. *Three Sisters*, Act Two; in Anton Chekhov, *Five Major Plays*, trans. Ronald Hingley (New York: Oxford University Press, 1977), p. 224.

# Bibliography

Adler, Margot. *Drawing Down the Moon: Witches, Druids, Goddess-Worshippers, and Other Pagans in America Today*. Rev. ed. Boston: Beacon Press, 1986.

"Adrienne," "The Great Rite." *PanThology* 1, no. 4 (n.d.).

Agrippa, Henry Cornelius of Nettesheim. *Three Books of Occult Philosophy*. Translated by James Freake. Edited by Donald Tyson. St. Paul, Minn.: Llewellyn, 1993.

Aïvanhov, Omraam Mikhaël. *The Fruits of the Tree of Life: The Cabalistic Tradition*. Fréjus, France: Editions Prosveta, 1989.

———. *The Splendour of Tiphareth*. Fréjus: Editions Prosveta, 1987.

Alba, De-Anna. "The Goddess Emerging." *Gnosis* 13 (Fall 1989).

Allen, Paul M., ed. *A Christian Rosenkreutz Anthology*. Blauvelt, N.Y.: Rudolf Steiner Publications, 1968.

Amis, Robin. *A Different Christianity: Early Christian Esotericism and Modern Thought*. Albany: State University of New York Press, 1995.

———. "Mouravieff and the Secret of the Source." *Gnosis* 20 (Summer 1991).

AMORC [Ancient and Mystical Order of Rosae Crucis]. Master Monograph, Neophyte Section, Private Mandamus no. 5. San Jose, Calif.: AMORC, n.d.

Anderson, Margaret. *The Unknowable Gurdjieff*. London: Routledge & Kegan Paul, 1962.

Andreev, Daniel. *The Rose of the World*. Translated by Jordan Roberts. Hudson, N.Y.: Lindisfarne Press, 1997.

Aniane, Maurice. "Notes on Alchemy, The Cosmological 'Yoga' of Medieval Christianity." *Material for Thought* (Spring 1976).

Annis, Roger. "Quebec Postpones Hydroelectric Project, but Cree Leaders Remain Vigilant." *Shaman's Drum* 37 (Winter 1995).

Anonymous. "Unmasking the Grand Deception." *New Dawn* 36 (May–June 1996).

———. *The Institute for Gnostic Studies: Introduction*. Armidale, Australia: Institute for Gnostic Studies, n.d.

———. *The Way of a Pilgrim and The Pilgrim Continues His Way*. Translated by Helen Bacovcin. Garden City, N.Y.: Doubleday Image, 1978.

Aquino, Michael. *The Book of Coming Forth by Night*. San Francisco: self-published, 1985.

———. *The Crystal Tablet of Set*. San Francisco: Temple of Set, 1983.

Arasteh, A. Reza. *Growth to Selfhood*. New York: Arkana, 1990.

Archer, N.P., ed. *The Sufi Mystery*. London: Octagon Press, 1980.

Argüelles, José. *The Mayan Factor*. Santa Fe, N.M.: Bear & Co., 1987.

Arvigo, Rosita. "Jaguar Shamans and Mayan Spirits: My Apprenticeship with Don Eligio Panti." *Shaman's Drum* 30 (Winter 1993).

Ashcroft-Nowicki, Dolores. *First Steps in Ritual*. Wellingborough, Northampton-shire, England: Aquarian, 1990.

Ashlag, Yehuda. *Kabbalah: Ten Luminous Emanations*. Translated by Levi I. Krakovsky. 2 vols. Jerusalem: Research Center of Kabbalah, 1969.

Ati Akarta (Igor Kungurtsev). "Nonduality and Western Seekers." *Gnosis* 39 (Spring 1996).

Atwood, Mary Anne. *Hermetic Philosophy and Alchemy: A Suggestive Inquiry*. New York: Julian Press, 1960. Originally published in 1850 as *A Suggestive Inquiry into the Hermetic Mystery*.

Bachofen, J. J. *Myth, Religion, and Mother Right: Selected Writings of J. J. Bachofen*. Translated by Ralph Manheim. Princeton: Princeton/Bollingen, 1967.

*The Bahir*. Translated by Aryeh Kaplan. New York: Samuel Weiser, 1979.

Baigent, Michael, and Richard Leigh. *The Temple and the Lodge*. London: Jonathan Cape, 1989.

Bailey, Alice A. *The Consciousness of the Atom*. New York: Lucis Trust, 1924.

———. *Discipleship in the New Age*. New York: Lucis Publishing Co., 1944.

———. *The Reappearance of the Christ*. New York: Lucis Publishing Co., 1948.

Bamford, Christopher, ed. *Homage to Pythagoras: Rediscovering Sacred Science*. Hudson, N.Y.: Lindisfarne Press, 1994.

Barborka, Geoffrey A. *The Divine Plan*. Adyar, India: Theosophical Publishing House, 1961.

Bardon, Franz. *Initiation into Hermetics*. Translated by A. Radspieler. Wuppertal, Germany: Rüggeberg-Verlag, 1993.

Barron, Cheryll Aimée. "The Anti-Guru." *Buzz* (May 1995).

Bartholomew, *"I Come as a Brother": A Remembrance of Illusions*. Taos, N.M.: High Mesa Press, 1986.

Bear, Jaya. "*Ayahuasca* Shamanism: An Interview with Don Agustín Rivas-Vasquez." *Shaman's Drum* 44 (March–May 1997).

Benamozegh. Elijah. *Israel and Humanity*. Translated by Maxwell Luria. Mahwah, N.J.: Paulist Press, 1995.

Bennett, J. G. *Enneagram Studies*. York Beach, Maine: Samuel Weiser, 1983.

———. *Witness*. Charles Town, W.Va.: Claymont Communications, 1983.

Besant, Annie. *Thought Power*. Wheaton, Ill.: Theosophical Publishing House, 1966.

Bialik, Hayim Nahman, and Yehoshua Hana Ravnitzky, eds. *The Book of Legends: Sefer Ha-Aggadah*. Translated by William G. Braude. New York: Schocken, 1992.

Blake, A. G. E. *The Intelligent Enneagram*. Boston: Shambhala, 1996.

Blavatsky, H. P. *The Secret Doctrine*. London: Theosophical Publishing Co., 1888.

Bonewits, Isaac. "The Future of Neopagan Druidism." *Green Egg* 29, no. 117 (Jan.–Feb. 1997).

———. *Real Magic*. York Beach, Maine: Samuel Weiser, 1989.

Bourgeault, Cynthia. "The Hidden Wisdom of Psalmody." *Gnosis* 37 (Fall 1995).

Boyd, Doug. *Mad Bear: Spirit, Healing, and the Sacred in the Life of a Native American Medicine Man*. New York: Simon & Schuster, 1994.

Brianchaninov, Ignatius. *On the Prayer of Jesus*. Translated by "Father Lazarus." London: J. M. Watkins, 1952.

Briggs, Robin. *Witches and Neighbors: The Social and Cultural Context of European Witchcraft*. New York: Viking, 1996.

Brown, Francis, S. R. Driver, and Charles A. Briggs. *A Hebrew and English Lexicon of the Old Testament*. Rev. ed. Oxford: Oxford at the Clarendon Press, 1953.

Brown, Peter. *Religion and Society in the Age of St. Augustine*. New York: Harper & Row, 1972.

Buber, Martin. *The Legend of the Baal-Shem*. Translated by Maurice Friedman. 1955. Reprint. Princeton: Princeton University Press, 1995.

Buckland, Raymond. *Buckland's Complete Book of Witchcraft*. St. Paul, Minn.: Llewellyn, 1986.

Buckley, Jorunn J. *Female Fault and Fulfillment in Gnosticism*. Chapel Hill: University of North Carolina Press, 1986.

Bulgakov, Sergei. *Sophia: The Wisdom of God*. Hudson, N.Y.: Lindisfarne Press, 1993.

Burckhardt, Jacob. *The Civilization of the Renaissance in Italy*. Translated by S. G. C. Middlemore. Vienna: Phaidon Press, n.d.

Burckhardt, Titus. *Alchemy*. Baltimore, Md.: Penguin, 1971.

Burkert, Walter. *Greek Religion*. Translated by John Raffan. Cambridge, Mass.: Harvard University Press, 1985.

Butler, W. E. *Apprenticed to Magic and Magic and the Qabalah*. Aquarian Press, 1990.

———. *Lords of Light: The Path of Initiation in the Western Mysteries*. Rochester, Vt.: Destiny Books, 1990.

———. *Practical Magic and the Western Mystery Tradition*. Edited by Dolores

Ashcroft-Nowicki. Wellingborough, Northamptonshire, England: Aquarian Press, 1986.

Caddy, Peter. *In Perfect Timing: Memoirs of a Man for the New Millennium.* Findhorn, Scotland: Findhorn Press, 1996.

Cadogan, Mary, et al., eds. *Total Freedom: The Essential Krishnamurti,* San Francisco: HarperSanFrancisco, 1996.

Campbell, Joseph. *The Hero with a Thousand Faces.* Princeton: Princeton/ Bollingen, 1968.

Campion, Nicholas. *The Practical Astrologer.* New York: Harry N. Abrams, 1987.

Carlson, Richard G., ed. *Rooted Like the Ash Trees: New England Indians and the Land.* Naugatuck, Conn.: Eagle Wing Press, 1987.

Carroll, Peter J. *Liber Null and Psychonaut.* York Beach, Maine: Samuel Weiser, 1987.

Carter, Mary Ellen. *Edgar Cayce on Prophecy.* New York: Paperback Library, 1968.

Case, Paul Foster. *The True and Invisible Rosicrucian Order.* York Beach, Maine: Samuel Weiser, 1985.

Castaneda, Carlos. *The Teachings of Don Juan: A Yaqui Way of Knowledge.* Berkeley: University of California Press, 1968.

————. *The Art of Dreaming.* New York: HarperCollins, 1993.

Cavendish, Richard. *The Black Arts.* New York: G. P. Putnam's Sons, 1967.

Chang, Stephen T. *The Tao of Sexology: The Book of Infinite Wisdom.* San Francisco: Tao Publishing, 1986.

Chekhov, Anton. *Five Major Plays.* Translated by Ronald Hingley. New York: Oxford University Press, 1977.

*The Chemical Wedding of Christian Rosenkreutz.* Translated by Joscelyn Godwin. Grand Rapids, Mich.: Phanes Press, 1991.

Chesi, Gert. *Faith Healers in the Philippines.* Translated by W. S. Reiter. Wörgl, Austria: Perlinger Verlag, 1981.

Churchill, Ward. *From a Native Son: Selected Essays on Indigenism, 1985–95.* Boston: South End Press, 1996.

Clarke, David, and Andy Roberts. *Twilight of the Celtic Gods.* London: Blandford/ Cassell, 1996.

Clement, Blaize. "Which Way to Siloam?" *The Sun* 259 (July 1997).

Clifton, Chas S. "The Craft Meets the Craft." *Gnosis* 6 (Winter 1988).

————. "The Three Faces of Satan: A Close Look at the 'Satanism Scare'." *Gnosis* 12 (Summer 1989).

————, ed. *Witchcraft Today.* 3 vols. St. Paul, Minn.: Llewellyn, 1992–95.

*The Cloud of Unknowing and Other Works.* Translated by Clifton Wolters. Harmondsworth, Middlesex, England: Penguin, 1978.

Copenhaver, Brian P. *Hermetica: The Greek Hermetica and the Latin Asclepius in a New English Translation with Notes and Introduction.* Cambridge: Cambridge University Press, 1992.

*A Course in Miracles*. 3 vols. Tiburon, Calif.: Foundation for Inner Peace, 1975.

Corbin, Henry. *Spiritual Body and Celestial Earth: From Mazdean Iran to Shi'ite Iran*. Translated by Nancy Pearson. Princeton: Princeton/Bollingen, 1977.

Cordovero, Moses. *The Palm Tree of Deborah*. Translated by Louis Jacobs. New York: Sepher-Hermon Press, 1974.

Cortright, Brant. *Psychotherapy and Spirit: Theory and Practice in Transpersonal Psychology*. Albany: State University of New York Press, 1997.

Cranston, Sylvia. *H. P. B.: The Extraordinary Life and Influence of Helena Blavatsky, Founder of the Modern Theosophical Movement*. Los Angeles: Jeremy Tarcher/Putnam, 1993.

Crawford, Ina. *A Guide to the Mysteries: An Ageless Wisdom Digest for the New Age*. London: Lucis Press, 1990.

Crowley, Aleister. *Magick in Theory and Practice*. New York: Castle Books, n.d. (1929).

———. *777 and Other Qabalistic Writings of Aleister Crowley*. Edited by Israel Regardie. New York: Samuel Weiser, 1977.

Cumbey, Constance. *The Hidden Dangers of the Rainbow* Shreveport, La.: Huntington House, 1983.

Dannelley, Richard. *Sedona: Beyond the Vortex: Activating the Planetary Ascension Program with Sacred Geometry, the Vortex, and the Merkaba*. Sedona, Ariz.: Vortex Society, 1995.

David-Neel, Alexandra. *Magic and Mystery in Tibet*. 1932. Reprint. New York: Dover, 1971.

Davies, W. G. *The Phoenician Letters*. Manchester, England: Mowat, 1979.

Davis, Bruce. "Animal Sacrifice: Why and Why Not?" *Paganet News* (Yule 1996).

Déchanet, J.-M. *Christian Yoga*. New York: Harper & Row, 1960.

Decker, Ronald, Thierry Depaulis, and Michael Dummett. *A Wicked Pack of Cards: The Origins of the Occult Tarot*. New York: St. Martin's Press, 1996.

De Hartmann, Thomas and Olga. *Our Life with Mr. Gurdjieff*. 1964. Reprint. Edited by T. C. Daly and T. A. G. Daly. New York: Penguin Arkana, 1992.

Deren, Maya. *Divine Horsemen: The Living Gods of Haiti*. 1953. Reprint. New Paltz, N.Y.: DocumenText, 1970.

Deveney, John Patrick. *Paschal Beverly Randolph: A Nineteenth-Century Black American Spiritualist, Rosicrucian, and Sex Magician*. Albany: State University of New York Press, 1996.

Donnelly, Ignatius. *Atlantis: The Antediluvian World*. 1882. Reprint. Edited by Egerton Sykes. New York: Harper & Bros., 1949.

Dorsey, George A. *The Mythology of the Wichita*. 1904. Reprint. Norman: University of Oklahoma Press, 1995.

Dummett, Michael. *The Game of Tarot*. London: Duckworth, 1990.

Edinger, Edward F. *Ego and Archetype*. Boston: Shambhala, 1992.

———. *The New God-Image*. Wilmette, Ill.: Chiron Publications, 1996.

Eliade, Mircea. *Occultism, Witchcraft, and Cultural Fashions*. Chicago: University of Chicago Press, 1976.

———. *Shamanism: Archaic Techniques of Ecstasy*. Translated by Willard R. Trask. Princeton: Princeton/Bollingen, 1972.

Elkin, A.P. *Aboriginal Men of High Degree*. 1945. Reprint. Rochester, Vt.: Inner Traditions, 1994.

Ellis, Normandi. "The Body Electric." *Gnosis* 29 (Fall 1993).

Ellwood, Robert. *Theosophy*. Wheaton, Ill.: Quest Books, 1986.

Epstein, Perle. *Kabbalah: The Way of the Jewish Mystic*. Garden City, N.Y.: Doubleday, 1978.

———. *The Private Labyrinth of Malcolm Lowry: Under the Volcano and the Cabbala*. New York: Holt, Rinehart, & Winston, 1969.

Evola, Julius. *The Hermetic Tradition: Symbols and Teachings of the Royal Art*. Translated by E. E. Rehmus. Rochester, Vt.: Inner Traditions, 1995.

———. *The Mystery of the Grail*. Translated by Guido Stucco. Rochester, Vt.: Inner Traditions International, 1997.

Faivre, Antoine, and Jacob Needleman, eds. *Modern Esoteric Spirituality*. New York: Crossroad, 1992.

Farmer, Christopher. "Practical Alchemy and Physical Immortality: An Interview with Art Kunkin." *Gnosis* 8 (Summer 1988).

Farrar, Janet and Stewart. *A Witches' Bible*. Custer, Wash.: Phoenix Publishing, 1996.

Farrar, Janet, Stewart Farrar, and Gavin Bone. *The Pagan Path*. Custer, Wash.: Phoenix Publishing, 1995.

Farrar, Stewart. *What Witches Do*. New York: Coward, McCann, & Geoghegan, 1971.

Feild, Reshad. *The Invisible Way*. Rockport, Mass.: Element, 1993.

———. *The Last Barrier*. Rockport, Mass.: Element, 1993.

Ferguson, Marilyn. *The Aquarian Conspiracy: Personal and Social Transformation in Our Time*. 2d ed. Los Angeles: Jeremy P. Tarcher, 1987.

Feuerstein, Georg. *Holy Madness*. New York: Penguin, 1992.

Fideler, David. *Jesus Christ: Sun of God*. Wheaton, Ill.: Quest Books, 1993.

Fielding, Charles, and Carr Collins. *The Story of Dion Fortune*. Dallas, Texas: Star & Cross Publications, 1985.

Forman, Robert K. C. *Meister Eckhart: Mystic as Theologian*. Rockport, Mass.: Element Books, 1991.

Fortune, Dion. *The Mystical Qabalah*. London: Ernest Benn, 1935.

———. *Psychic Self-Defence*. Wellingborough, Northamptonshire, England: Aquarian Press, 1957.

"Frater Albertus." *The Alchemist's Handbook*. New York: Samuel Weiser, 1960.

Frazer, J. G. *The Golden Bough*. New York: Macmillan, 1953.

Gaer, Joseph. *The Lore of the New Testament.* 1952. Reprint. New York: Grosset & Dunlap, 1966.

————. *The Lore of the Old Testament.* 1951. Reprint. New York: Grosset & Dunlap, 1966.

Gardner, Gerald. *Witchcraft Today.* New York: Citadel Press, 1955.

Gikatilla, Joseph. *Gates of Light: Sha'are Orah.* Translated by Avi Weinstein. San Francisco: HarperSanFrancisco, 1994.

Gilbert, R. A. *The Golden Dawn: Twilight of the Magicians.* Wellingborough, Northamptonshire, England: Aquarian Press, 1983.

Gilchrist, Cherry. *The Elements of Alchemy.* Rockport, Mass.: Element Books, 1991.

————. *Theosophy: The Wisdom of the Ages.* San Francisco: HarperSanFrancisco, 1996.

Gimbutas, Marija. *The Language of the Goddess.* San Francisco: Harper & Row, 1989.

Godwin, Joscelyn. *The Theosophical Enlightenment.* Albany: State University of New York Press, 1994.

Gold, Shefa. "Cleaving to God: A Jewish Way of Prayer." *Gnosis* 37 (Fall 1995).

González-Wippler, Migene. *Santería: African Religion in Latin America.* New York: Doubleday Anchor, 1975.

————. *The Santería Experience.* Englewood Cliffs, N.J.: Prentice-Hall, 1982.

————. *Santería: The Religion.* New York: Harmony Books, 1989.

Goodrick-Clarke, Nicholas. *The Occult Roots of Nazism.* Wellingborough, Northamptonshire, England: Aquarian Press, 1985.

Graves, Robert. *The White Goddess.* 1948. Reprint. New York: Farrar, Straus, & Giroux, 1966.

Gray, William G. *An Outlook on Our Inner Western Way.* New York: Samuel Weiser, 1980.

————. *Inner Traditions of Magic.* New York: Samuel Weiser, 1970.

————. *The Talking Tree.* New York: Samuel Weiser, 1977.

Greer, John Michael. *Circles of Power: Ritual Magic in the Western Tradition.* St. Paul, Minn.: Llewellyn, 1997.

Greer, John Michael, and Gordon Cooper. "The Red God: Woodcraft and the Origins of Wicca." *Gnosis* 48 (Summer 1998).

Greer, Mary K. *Women of the Golden Dawn.* Rochester, Vt.: Park Street Press, 1995.

Grof, Christina and Stanislav. *The Stormy Search for the Self.* Los Angeles: Jeremy P. Tarcher, 1992.

Grof, Stanislav. *Beyond the Brain: Birth, Death, and Transcendence in Psychotherapy.* Albany: State University of New York Press, 1985.

————. *LSD Psychotherapy.* Pomona, Calif.: Hunter House, 1980.

Grossinger, Richard. *Alchemy: Pre-Egyptian Legacy, Millennial Promise*. Richmond, Calif.: North Atlantic Books, 1979.

———. "Beyond the Ideology of Healing." *Gnosis* 34 (Winter 1995).

Guénon, René. *L'Erreur spirite*. Paris: Editions Traditionelles, 1952.

———. *The Esoterism of Dante*. Translated by C. B. Bethell. Ghent, N.Y.: Sophia Perennis et Universalis, 1996.

———. *The Great Triad*. Translated by Peter Kingsley. Cambridge, England: Quinta Essentia, 1991.

———. *Introduction to the Study of the Hindu Doctrines*. Translated by Marco Pallis. 1945. Reprint. New Delhi: Munshiram Manoharlal Publishers, 1993.

———. *Man and His Becoming According to the Vedanta*. Translated by Richard C. Nicholson. New Delhi: Oriental Book Reprint Corp.: 1981.

———. *The Multiple States of Being*. Translated by Joscelyn Godwin. Burdett, N.Y.: Larson Publications, 1984.

———. *The Reign of Quantity and the Signs of the Times*. Translated by Lord Northbourne. Baltimore, Md.: Penguin, 1972.

———. *Symbolism of the Cross*. Translated by Angus MacNab. London: Luzac, 1958.

Gurdjieff, G. I. *All and Everything: Beelzebub's Tales to His Grandson*. New York: E. P. Dutton, 1950.

———. *The Herald of Coming Good*. 1934. Reprint. Edmonds, Wash.: Sure Fire Press, 1988.

———. *Life Is Real Only Then, When "I Am,"* New York: Viking Arkana, 1991.

———. *Meetings with Remarkable Men*. New York: E. P. Dutton, 1963.

———. *Views from the Real World*. New York: Penguin Arkana, 1984.

Guthrie, W. K. C. *A History of Greek Philosophy, Volume 1: The Earlier Presocratics and Pythagoreans*. Cambridge: Cambridge University Press, 1971.

Halevi, Z'ev ben Shimon. *Adam and the Kabbalistic Tree*. New York: Samuel Weiser, 1974.

———. *Kabbalah and Exodus*. London: Rider & Co., 1980.

———. *Kabbalah: Tradition of Hidden Knowledge*. London: Thames & Hudson, 1979.

———. *A Kabbalistic Universe*. London: Rider & Co., 1977.

———. *School of Kabbalah*. York Beach, Maine: Samuel Weiser, 1985. [Later editions have been retitled *School of the Soul*.]

———. *Tree of Life: An Introduction to the Cabala*. London: Rider & Co., 1972.

———. *The Way of Kabbalah*. London: Rider & Co., 1976.

———. *The Work of the Kabbalist*. York Beach, Maine: Samuel Weiser, 1986.

Hall, Manly P. *The Lost Keys of Freemasonry*. 1923. Reprint. Los Angeles: Philosophical Research Society, 1976.

———. *Man: Grand Symbol of the Mysteries*. Los Angeles: Philosophical Research Society, 1972.

————. *The Secret Teachings of All Ages*. Los Angeles: Philosophical Research Society, 1988.

Hanegraaff, Wouter J. *New Age Religion and Western Culture: Esotericism in the Mirror of Secular Thought*. Albany: State University of New York Press, 1998.

Hanke, Kimberly E. *Turning to Torah: The Emerging Noachide Movement*. Northvale, N.J.: Jason Aronson, 1995.

Harner, Michael. *The Way of the Shaman*. New York: Bantam, 1982.

Harney, Corbin. *The Way It Is*. Nevada City, Calif.: Blue Dolphin, 1995.

Harrison, Vernon. *H. P. Blavatsky and the SPR: An Examination of the Hodgson Report of 1885*. Pasadena, Calif.: Theosophical University Press, 1997.

Hastings, Arthur. *With the Tongues of Men and Angels: A Study of Channeling*. Fort Worth, Texas: Holt, Rinehart, & Winston, 1991.

Heelas, Paul. *The New Age Movement*. Oxford: Blackwell, 1996.

Heindel, Max. *The Rosicrucian Cosmo-Conception*. Oceanside, Calif.: Rosicrucian Fellowship, 1909.

Helminski, Kabir. *Living Presence*. New York: Jeremy Tarcher/Perigee, 1992.

Hillman, James. *A Blue Fire: Selected Writings of James Hillman*, Edited by Thomas Moore. San Francisco: Harper & Row, 1989.

Hilmi, Ahmet. *Awakened Dreams*. Translated by Refik Algan and Camille Helminski. Putney, Vt.: Threshold Books, 1993.

Hilton, Walter. *The Scale of Perfection*. Edited by Evelyn Underhill. London: J. M. Watkins, 1948.

Hindes, James H. *Renewing Christianity*. Hudson, N.Y.: Anthroposophic Press, 1996.

Hoeller, Stephan A. "The Divine Feminine in Recent World Events." *Gnosis* 25 (Fall 1992).

————. *The Gnostic Jung and the Seven Sermons to the Dead*. Wheaton, Ill.: Quest Books, 1982.

————. *Jung and the Lost Gospels*. Wheaton, Ill.: Quest Books, 1989.

————. *The Mystery and Magic of the Eucharist*. Hollywood, Calif.: Gnostic Press, 1990.

————. "Wandering Bishops." *Gnosis* 12 (Summer 1989).

Hopman, Ellen Evert, and Lawrence Bond. *People of the Earth: The New Pagans Speak Out*. Rochester, Vt.: Destiny Books, 1996.

Houston, Jean. *The Passion of Isis and Osiris*. New York: Ballantine, 1995.

Houston, Siobhán. "Chaos Magic." *Gnosis* 36 (Summer 1995).

Hutton, Ronald. *The Pagan Religions of the British Isles: Their Nature and Legacy*. Oxford: Blackwell, 1991.

Huxley, Aldous. *The Doors of Perception*. London: Chatto & Windus, 1954.

Ibn 'Arabi, Muhyiddin. *Fusus al-Hikam*. Translated by Titus Burckhardt and Angela Culme-Seymour. Sherborne, Gloucestershire, England: Beshara Publications, 1975.

————. *The Kernel of the Kernel*. Translated by Ismail Hakki Bursevi. Sherborne, Gloucestershire, England: Beshara Publications, n.d.

Ichazo, Oscar. "Letter to the Transpersonal Community." *The Arican: The Teachings of the Great Telesmatta* (New York: Arica Institute, n.d.).

*I Ching: The Book of Change*. Translated by John Blofeld. London: George Allen & Unwin, 1965.

*The I Ching or Book of Changes*. Translated by Richard Wilhelm and Cary Baynes. Princeton: Princeton University Press, 1967.

Icke, David. ". . . *And the Truth Shall Set You Free.*" Newark, Nottinghamshire, England: Bridge of Love, 1996.

————. *The Robots' Rebellion*. Bath, England: Gateway Books, 1994.

Idel, Moshe. *Kabbalah: New Perspectives*. New Haven, Conn.: Yale University Press, 1988.

Inayat Khan, Hazrat. *The Unity of Religious Ideals*. New Lebanon, N.Y.: Sufi Order Publications, 1979.

Inayat Khan, Hazrat, and Coleman Barks. *The Hand of Poetry: Five Mystic Poets of Persia*. New Lebanon, N.Y.: Omega Publications, 1993.

Introvigne, Massimo. *Indagine sul satanismo*. Milan: Oscar Mondadori, 1994.

Isaac, Reuben R. *The Unveiling of the Teachings of the Rosicrucian Order: An Exposé*. Baltimore, Md.: Noble House, 1995.

Jacobson, Simon, ed. *Toward a Meaningful Life: The Wisdom of the Rebbe Menachem Mendel Schneerson*. New York: William Morrow, 1995.

John Cassian. *Conferences*. Translated by Colin Luibheid Mahwah, N.J.: Paulist Press, 1985.

St. John of the Cross. *Dark Night of the Soul*. Translated by E. Allison Peers. New York: Doubleday/Image, 1959.

Johnson, K. Paul. "Imaginary Mahatmas." *Gnosis* 28 (Summer 1993).

————. *Initiates of Theosophical Masters*. Albany: State University of New York Press, 1996.

————. *In Search of the Masters: Behind the Occult Myth*. South Boston, Va.: self-published, 1990.

————. *The Masters Revealed: Mme. Blavatsky and the Myth of the Great White Lodge*. Albany: State University of New York Press, 1994.

Jonas, Hans. *The Gnostic Religion*. Boston: Beacon, 1963.

Jordanova, L. J. *Lamarck*. Oxford: Oxford University Press, 1984.

Jung, C. G. *Aion: Researches into the Phenomenology of Self. Collected Works*, vol. 9,ii. Translated by R. F. C. Hull. Princeton: Princeton/Bollingen, 1959.

————. *The Archetypes and the Collective Unconscious*, second edition. *Collected Works*, vol. 9,I. Princeton: Princeton/Bollingen, 1959.

————. *Civilization in Transition. Collected Works*, vol. 10. Princeton: Princeton/Bollingen, 1964.

————. *Memories, Dreams, Reflections.* Translated by Richard and Clara Winston. New York: Vintage, 1961.

————. *Modern Man in Search of a Soul.* Translated by W. S. Dell and Cary F. Baynes. New York: Harcourt, Brace, & World, 1933.

————. *Psychology of the Unconscious.* Translated by Beatrice M. Hinkle. 1912. Reprint. Princeton: Princeton/Bollingen, 1991.

————. *The Structure and Dynamics of the Psyche.* Translated by R. F. C. Hull. In C. G. Jung, *Collected Works,* vol. 8, second ed. Princeton: Princeton/Bollingen, 1969.

Kamenetz, Rodger. *The Jew in the Lotus.* San Francisco: HarperSanFrancisco, 1994.

Kaplan, Aryeh. *Jewish Meditation.* New York: Schocken, 1985.

————. *Meditation and Kabbalah.* York Beach, Maine: Samuel Weiser, 1982.

————. *Sefer Yetzirah: The Book of Creation.* York Beach, Maine: Samuel Weiser, 1990.

Kaplan, Stuart R. *The Encyclopedia of Tarot.* 3 vols. New York: U.S. Games Systems, 1978.

Keating, Thomas. *Open Mind, Open Heart: The Contemplative Dimension of the Gospel.* Rockport, Mass.: Element Books, 1986.

Keizer, Lewis S. *The Wandering Bishops.* N.p.: Academy of Arts and Humanities, 1976.

Kelly, Aidan A. *Crafting the Art of Magic.* St. Paul, Minn.: Llewellyn, 1991.

King, Francis. *The Rites of Modern Occult Magic.* New York: Macmillan, 1970.

Kingsley, Peter. "Poimandres: The Etymology of the Name and the Origins of the *Hermetica.*" *Journal of the Warburg and Courtauld Institutes,* vol. 56 (1993).

Kinney, Jay. "Déjà Vu: The Hidden History of the New Age." In Ted Schultz, ed., *The Fringes of Reason: A Whole Earth Catalog.* New York: Harmony Books, 1989.

————. "Wars in Heaven." *Gnosis* 38 (Winter 1996).

Kinney, Jay, and Richard Smoley. "War on High: The *Gnosis* Interview with Elizabeth Clare Prophet." *Gnosis* 21 (Fall 1991).

Klossowski de Rola, Stanislas. *Alchemy: The Secret Art.* London: Thames & Hudson, 1973.

Knight, Christopher, and Robert Lomas. *The Hiram Key: Pharaohs, Freemasonry, and the Discovery of the Secret Scrolls of Jesus.* Rockport, Mass.: Element, 1996.

Knight, Gareth. *Experience of the Inner Worlds.* York Beach, Maine: Samuel Weiser, 1993.

Kovalevsky, Eugraph. *A Method of Prayer for Modern Times.* Newburyport, Mass.: Praxis Institute Press, 1993.

Kraig, Donald Michael. "The 'Satanic Panic' in America, Part One." *Mezlim,* Lughnasadh [Summer] 1993.

Krakovsky, Levi Isaac. *Kabbalah: The Light of Redemption*. Jerusalem: Research Center of Kabbalah, 1970.

Krippner, Stanley, and Patrick Welch. *Spiritual Dimensions of Healing*. New York: Irvington, 1992.

*The Kybalion*. By "Three Initiates." 1908. Reprint. Clayton, Ga.: Tri-State Press, 1988.

LaVey, Anton Szandor. *The Satanic Bible*. New York: Avon Books, 1969.

Lawlor, Robert. *Sacred Geometry*. London: Thames & Hudson, 1982.

Layton, Bentley. *The Gnostic Scriptures*. Garden City, N.Y.: Doubleday, 1987.

Leadbeater, C. W. *The Masters and the Path*. Adyar, India: Theosophical Publishing House, 1925.

———. *The Science of the Sacraments*. Adyar, India: Theosophical Publishing House, 1920.

Leland, Charles Godfrey. *Aradia: The Gospel of the Witches*. 1899. Reprint. London: Pentacle Enterprises, 1989.

Le Mée, Katharine. *Chant: The Origins, Form, Practice, and Healing Power of Gregorian Chant*. New York: Bell Tower, 1994.

Lévi, Éliphas. *Histoire de la magie*. 1859. Reprint. Paris: Guy Trédaniel, 1986.

———. *Transcendental Magic: Its Doctrine and Ritual*. Translated by A.E. Waite. 1896. Reprint. London: Bracken Books, 1995.

Lévi-Strauss, Claude. *Tristes Tropiques*. Translated by John and Doreen Weightman. New York: Atheneum, 1974.

Lewin, L., ed. *The Diffusion of Sufi Ideas in the West: An Anthology of New Writings by and about Idries Shah*. Boulder, Colo.: Keysign Press, 1972.

Lewis, H. Spencer. *Rosicrucian Questions and Answers, with Complete History of the Rosicrucian Order*. San Jose, Calif.: AMORC, 1929.

Lewis, James R., ed. *The Gods Have Landed: New Religions from Other Worlds*. Albany: State University of New York Press, 1995.

Liester, Mitchell B. "Inner Voices: Distinguishing Transcendent and Pathological Characteristics." *Journal of Transpersonal Psychology*, vol. 28, no. 1 (1996).

Loewe, Michael, and Carmen Blacker. *Oracles and Divination* Boulder, Colo.: Shambhala, 1981.

Long, Max Freedom. *Mana*. Cape Girardeau, Mo.: Huna Research Inc., 1981.

———. *The Secret Science at Work*. Marina del Ray, Calif.: DeVorss & Co., 1953.

———. *The Secret Science behind Miracles*. Los Angeles: Kosmon Press, 1948.

Lossky, Vladimir. *The Mystical Theology of the Eastern Church*. Crestwood, N.Y.: St. Vladimir's Seminary Press, 1976.

Loyola. St. Ignatius. *The Spiritual Exercises of St. Ignatius*. Translated by Anthony Mottola. New York: Doubleday/Image, 1964.

Luhrmann, T. M. *Persuasions of the Witch's Craft*. Cambridge, Mass.: Harvard University Press, 1989.

Luzzatto, Moshe Chaim. *The Way of God.* Translated by Aryeh Kaplan. Jerusalem: Feldheim, 1988.

Lyons, Arthur. *Satan Wants You: The Cult of Devil Worship in America.* New York: The Mysterious Press, 1988.

Mack, John E. *Abduction: Human Encounters with Aliens.* New York: Charles Scribner's Sons, 1994.

Mackerle, Ivan. "Who Was Prague's Golem?" *Fate*, November 1996.

MacNulty, W. Kirk. *Freemasonry: A Journey through Ritual and Symbol.* London: Thames & Hudson, 1991.

Mann, W. Edward, and Edward Hoffman. *The Man Who Dreamed of Tomorrow: The Life and Thought of Wilhelm Reich.* Los Angeles: Jeremy P. Tarcher, 1980.

Markides, Kyriacos C. *The Magus of Strovolos: The Extraordinary World of a Spiritual Healer.* London: Arkana, 1985.

Maroney, Tim. "Introduction to *The Book of Dzyan.*" Unpublished ms., 1997.

Marrs, Jim. *Alien Agenda.* New York: HarperCollins, 1997.

Maslow, Abraham H. *Toward a Psychology of Being,* second edition. New York: Van Nostrand Reinhold, 1968.

Masters, Robert. *The Goddess Sekhmet: The Way of the Five Bodies.* Amity, N.Y.: Amity House, 1988.

———. *Neurospeak.* Wheaton, Ill.: Quest Books, 1994.

Mathers, S. L. MacGregor, trans. *The Book of the Sacred Magic of Abramelin the Mage.* 1900. Reprint. New York: Dover, 1975.

———. *The Kabbalah Unveiled.* 1887. Reprint. New York: Samuel Weiser, 1974.

Mathers, S. L. MacGregor, et al. *Astral Projection, Ritual Magic, and Alchemy.* Edited by Francis King. Rochester, Vt.: Destiny Books, 1987.

Matt, Daniel C. *The Essential Kabbalah.* San Francisco: HarperSanFrancisco, 1994.

———. *Zohar: The Book of Enlightenment.* Mahwah, N.J.: Paulist Press, 1983.

Matthews, Caitlín and John. *The Western Way.* New York: Penguin Arkana, 1994.

Matus, Thomas. *Yoga and the Jesus Prayer Tradition.* Ramsey, N.J.: Paulist Press, 1984.

McIntosh, Christopher. *Éliphas Lévi and the French Occult Revival.* New York: Samuel Weiser, 1972.

———. *The Rose Cross and the Age of Reason.* Leiden: E. J. Brill, 1992.

———. *The Rosicrucians.* 1980. Reprint. York Beach, Maine: Samuel Weiser, 1997.

———. *The Rosy Cross Unveiled.* London: Aquarian, 1980.

McKenna, Terence. *The Food of the Gods: A Radical History of Plants, Drugs, and Human Evolution.* New York: Bantam, 1992.

Mead, G. R. S. *Thrice-Greatest Hermes: Studies in Hellenistic Theosophy and Gnosis.* 1906. Reprint. York Beach, Maine: Samuel Weiser, 1992.

McLaughlin, Corinne, and Gordon Davidson. *Spiritual Politics: Changing the World from Inside Out.* New York: Ballantine, 1994.

Melton, J. Gordon. "An Initial Encounter with Ramtha." *Gnosis* 41 (Fall 1996).

Melton, J. Gordon, Jerome Clark, and Aidan A. Kelly. *New Age Almanac*. New York: Visible Ink, 1991.

Meyer, Michael W., ed. *The Ancient Mysteries: A Sourcebook*. San Francisco: Harper & Row, 1987.

Miller, D. Patrick. *The Complete Story of the Course*. Berkeley, Calif.: Fearless Books, 1997.

Moore, James. *Gurdjieff: The Anatomy of a Myth*. Rockport, Mass.: Element, 1991.

Mouravieff, Boris. *Gnôsis; Étude et commentaires sur la tradition ésoterique de l'orthodoxie orientale*. 3 vols. Neuchatel, Switzerland: Éditions à la Baconnière, 1969–72.

———. *Gnosis: Study and Commentaries on the Esoteric Tradition of Eastern Orthodoxy*. 3 vols. Edited by Robin Amis. Newbury, Mass.: Praxis Institute Press, 1989–93. A translation of the work listed above.

———. "Ouspensky, Gurdjieff, et les fragments d'un enseignement inconnu." N.p.: Centre d'études chrétiennes ésotériques, n.d., reprinted from *Synthèses* 138 (Brussels; Nov. 1957).

Murphy, Joseph M. *Santería: An African Religion in America*. Boston: Beacon Press, 1988.

Murphy, Michael. *The Future of the Body: Explorations into the Further Evolution of Human Nature*. Los Angeles: Jeremy P. Tarcher, 1992.

Murphy, Michael, and Steven Donovan. *The Physical and Psychological Effects of Meditation*. Big Sur, Calif.: Esalen Institute, 1988.

Murray, Margaret A. *The God of the Witches*. Oxford: Oxford University Press, 1931.

———. *The Witch Cult in Western Europe*. Oxford: Oxford University Press, 1921.

Myer, Isaac. *Qabbalah: The Philosophical Writings of Avicebron*. 1888. Reprint. New York: Samuel Weiser, 1970.

Nahman of Bratslav. *The Tales*. Translated by Arnold J. Band. New York: Paulist Press, 1978.

Nasr, Seyyed Hossein, ed. *Islamic Spirituality*. 2 vols. New York: Crossroad, 1987, 1991.

Nathan, Debbie, and Michael Snedeker. *Satan's Silence: Ritual Abuse and the Making of a Modern American Witch Hunt*. New York: Basic Books, 1995.

Nation, Ihla F. "Face to Face: Confronting the Guru-Disciple Relationship." *Gnosis* 39 (Spring 1996).

Needleman, Jacob. *The Indestructible Question*. New York: Penguin Arkana, 1994.

———. *Lost Christianity*. San Francisco: Harper & Row, 1980.

———. *The New Religions*. New York: Pocket Books, 1972.

Needleman, Jacob, and George Baker, eds. *Gurdjieff: Essays and Reflections on the Man and His Teaching*. New York: Continuum, 1997.

Neihardt, John G. *Black Elk Speaks*. 1932. Reprint. Lincoln: University of Nebraska Press, 1988.

Nicoll, Maurice. *The Mark*. Boston: Shambhala, 1985.

———. *The New Man*. Boston: Shambhala, 1986.

Nietzsche, Friedrich. *Thus Spoke Zarathustra*. Translated by Walter Kaufmann. Harmondsworth, Middlesex, England: Penguin, 1978.

Nintzel, Hans. "Alchemy Is Alive and Well." *Gnosis* 8 (Summer 1988).

Noel, Daniel C. *The Soul of Shamanism*. New York: Continuum, 1997.

Noll, Richard. *The Jung Cult: The Origins of a Charismatic Movement*. Princeton: Princeton University Press, 1994.

Ouspensky, P. D. *In Search of the Miraculous: Fragments of a Forgotten Teaching*. New York: Harcourt, Brace, & Co., 1949.

———. *The Psychology of Man's Possible Evolution*. New York: Alfred A. Knopf, 1954.

Pagels, Elaine. *The Gnostic Gospels*. New York: Random House, 1979.

Palmer, Helen. *The Enneagram*. San Francisco: Harper & Row, 1988.

Papus [Gérard Encausse]. *The Tarot of the Bohemians*. Translated by A. P. Morton. London: Chapman & Hall, 1892.

*Paracelsus: Selected Writings*. Edited by Jolande Jacobi. Princeton: Princeton/Bollingen, 1951.

Pauwels, Louis, and Jacques Bergier. *The Morning of the Magicians*. Translated by Rollo Myers. New York: Avon, 1968.

Patai, Raphael. *The Hebrew Goddess*. Detroit, Mich.: Wayne State University Press, 1990.

Perkins, Pheme. *Gnosticism and the New Testament*. Minneapolis, Minn.: Fortress Press, 1993.

Pico della Mirandola. *Heptaplus, or, Discourse on the Seven Days of Creation*. Translated by Jessie Brewer McGaw. New York: Philosophical Library, 1977.

Plato. *The Collected Dialogues*. Edited by Edith Hamilton and Huntington Cairns. Princeton: Princeton/Bollingen, 1963.

Poncé, Charles. *Kabbalah*. Wheaton, Ill.: Quest Books, 1978.

Prothero, Stephen. *The White Buddhist: The Asian Odyssey of Henry Steel Olcott*. Bloomington: Indiana University Press, 1996.

Radin, Dean. *The Conscious Universe: The Scientific Truth of Psychic Phenomena*. San Francisco: HarperSanFrancisco, 1997.

"Ramtha." *Last Waltz of the Tyrants: The Prophecy*. Edited by Judi Pope Koteen. Hillsboro, Ore.: Beyond Words Publishing, 1989.

Redfield, James. *The Celestine Prophecy*. New York: Warner Books, 1993.

Regardie, Israel. *The Complete Golden Dawn System of Magic*. Phoenix, Ariz.: New Falcon, 1994.

———. *The Eye in the Triangle: An Interpretation of Aleister Crowley*. Phoenix, Ariz.: Falcon Press, 1970.

————. *The Golden Dawn*, St. Paul, Minn.: Llewellyn, 1982.

————. *The Tree of Life: A Study in Magic*. New York: Samuel Weiser, 1969.

Reich, Wilhelm. *The Function of the Orgasm*. Translated by Vincent R. Carfagno. New York: Simon & Schuster, 1973.

Reichard, Gladys A. *Navaho Religion: A Study of Symbolism* Princeton: Princeton/Bollingen, 1950.

Reuchlin, Johann. *On the Art of the Kabbalah: De arte cabalistica*. Translated by Martin and Sarah Goodman. Lincoln: University of Nebraska Press, 1993.

Ribi, Alfred. *Demons of the Inner World: Understanding Our Hidden Complexes*. Boston: Shambhala, 1990.

Roberts, Jane. *The Nature of Personal Reality*. 1974. Reprint. San Rafael, Calif.: New World Library, 1994.

Roberts, Susan C. "The Soul of the World: Exploring Archetypal Psychology." *Common Boundary*, Nov.–Dec. 1992.

Robertson, Robin. *Beginner's Guide to Jungian Psychology*. York Beach, Maine: Nicolas-Hays, 1992.

"Robin." "Sunlight and Shadows: Some Perspectives on Hereditary and Old Crafte Practice." *The Cauldron* 82 (1996).

Robinson, Ira, ed. *Moses Cordovero's Introduction to Kabbalah: An Annotated Translation of His Or Ne'erav*. Hoboken, N.J.: KTAV Publishing, 1994.

Robinson, James M., ed. *The Nag Hammadi Library in English*. San Francisco: Harper & Row, 1988.

Robinson, John J. *Born in Blood: The Lost Secrets of Freemasonry*. New York: M. Evans & Co., 1989.

Rose, Seraphim. *The Soul after Death*. Platina, Calif.: St. Herman of Alaska Brotherhood, 1980.

Rowe, Joseph. "The Quintessence of Alchemy: The *Gnosis* Interview with François Trojani." *Gnosis* 39 (Summer 1996).

*The Rule of St. Benedict*. Collegeville, Minn.: The Liturgical Press, 1980.

Rumi, Mevlana Celaleddin. *Divan-i Kebir, Meter 1*. Translated by Nevit O. Ergin. Walla Walla, Wash.: Current, 1995.

————. *Love Is a Stranger*. Translated by Kabir Helminski. Putney, Vt.: Threshold Books, 1993.

Salant, Nathan Schwartz, ed. *Jung on Alchemy*. Princeton: Princeton University Press, 1995.

Schauss, Hayyim. *The Jewish Festivals: A Guide to Their History and Observance*. Translated by Samuel Jaffe. New York: Schocken, 1962.

Schimmel, Annemarie. *Mystical Dimensions of Islam*. Chapel Hill: University of North Carolina Press, 1975.

Schlesier, Karl H. *The Wolves of Heaven: Cheyenne Shamanism, Ceremonies, and Prehistoric Origins*. Norman, Okla.: University of Oklahoma Press, 1987.

Schaya, Leo. *The Universal Meaning of the Kabbalah*. Translated by Nancy Pearson. London: George Allen & Unwin, 1971.

Scholem, Gershom. *Kabbalah*. 1974. Reprint. New York: Dorset Press, 1987.

———. *Major Trends in Jewish Mysticism*. New York: Schocken, 1961.

———. *On the Kabbalah and Its Symbolism*. Translated by Ralph Manheim. New York: Schocken, 1969.

———, ed. *The Zohar: Basic Readings from the Kabbalah*. New York: Schocken, 1963.

Schultes, Richard Evans, and Albert Hofmann. *Plants of the Gods: Their Sacred, Healing and Hallucinogenic Powers*. 1979. Reprint. Rochester, Vt.: Healing Arts Press, 1992.

Schuon, Frithjof. *The Essential Writings of Frithjof Schuon*. Edited by Seyyed Hossein Nasr. Rockport, Mass.: Element Books, 1991.

———. *Light on the Ancient Worlds*. Translated by Lord Northbourne. Bloomington, Ind.: World Wisdom Books, 1984.

———. *Understanding Islam*. London: George Allen & Unwin, 1981.

Scott, Walter. *Hermetica: The Ancient Greek and Latin Writings Which Contain Religious or Philosophical Teachings Ascribed to Hermes Trismegistus*. 1924. Reprint. Boston: Shambhala, 1985.

Shah, Idries. *The Commanding Self*. London: Octagon Press, 1994.

———. *Learning How to Learn*. London: Octagon Books, 1978.

———. *The Sufis*. Garden City, N.Y.: Anchor/Doubleday, 1971.

———. *The Way of the Sufi*. 1974. Reprint. London: Penguin Arkana, 1990.

Sharp, Daryl. *C. G. Jung Lexicon: A Primer of Terms and Concepts*. Toronto: Inner City Books, 1991.

Shumaker, Wayne R. *The Occult Sciences in the Renaissance*. Berkeley: University of California Press, 1972.

Silbey, Uma. *The Complete Crystal Guidebook*. San Francisco: U-Read Publications, 1986.

Sinclair, Sir John R. *The Alice Bailey Inheritance*. Wellingborough, Northamptonshire, England: Turnstone Press, 1984.

Singer, June. *A Gnostic Book of Hours: Keys to Inner Wisdom*. San Francisco: HarperSanFrancisco, 1992.

Sinnett, A. P. *The Mahatma Letters to A. P. Sinnett*. Edited by A. T. Barker, Christmas Humphreys, and Elsie Benjamin. Adyar, India: Theosophical Publishing House, 1923.

Smith, Huston. *Forgotten Truth: The Common Vision of the World's Religions*. 1976. Reprint. San Francisco: HarperSanFrancisco, 1992.

Smith, Kendra. "With Jungian Psychology, Do We Need Religion?" *Dialogue & Alliance*, vol. 5, no. 4 (Winter 1991–92).

Smith, Pamela H. *The Business of Alchemy: Science and Culture in the Holy Roman Empire*. Princeton: Princeton University Press, 1994.

Smoley, Richard. "Heroic Virtue: An Interview with Brother David Steindl-Rast." *Gnosis* 24 (Summer 1992).

———. "A Non-Indian's Guide to Native American Spirituality." *Yoga Journal*, Jan.–Feb. 1992.

Smoley, Richard, and Jay Kinney. "The Essence of the Work: The *Gnosis* Interview with Jacob Needleman. *Gnosis* 20 (Summer 1991).

———. "One Path or Many? The *Gnosis* Interview with Charles Tart." *Gnosis* 28 (Summer 1993).

Solano, Solita. "The Kanari Papers." *Telos: Inquiries into Self-Transformation in the Contemporary World*, unnumbered (Fairfax, Calif.), 1996.

Spangler, David. *A Pilgrim in Aquarius*. Findhorn, Scotland: Findhorn Press, 1996.

Specter, Michael. "Rabbi Menachem Schneerson: The Oracle of Crown Heights." *New York Times Magazine*, March 15, 1992.

Speeth, Kathleen Riordan. *The Gurdjieff Work*. Los Angeles: Jeremy P. Tarcher, 1989 (1976).

Sprenger, Jacobus, and Heinrich Kramer. *Malleus Maleficarum*. Translated by Montague Summers. London: Folio Society, 1968.

Starhawk. *The Spiral Dance: A Rebirth of the Ancient Religion of the Great Goddess*. Rev. ed. San Francisco: Harper & Row, 1989.

Steiner, Rudolf. *How to Know Higher Worlds*. Translated by Christopher Bamford. Hudson, N.Y.: Anthroposophic Press, 1994.

———. *An Outline of Esoteric Science*. Translated by Catherine E. Creeger. Hudson, N.Y.: Anthroposophic Press, 1997.

———. *The Spiritual Hierarchies and the Physical World: Reality and Illusion*. Translated by R. M. Querido and Jann Gates. Hudson, N.Y.: Anthroposophic Press, 1996.

Steinsaltz, Adin. *The Thirteen-Petalled Rose*. Translated by Yehuda Hanegbi. New York: Basic Books, 1980.

Steltenkamp, Michael F. *Black Elk: Holy Man of the Oglala* Norman: University of Oklahoma Press, 1993.

Stevenson, David. *The Origins of Freemasonry*. Cambridge: Cambridge University Press, 1988.

Stolaroff, Myron. "Using Psychedelics Wisely." *Gnosis* 26 (Winter 1993).

Strong, Mary. *Letters of the Scattered Brotherhood*. San Francisco: HarperSanFrancisco, 1991 (1948).

Stuart, Omer C. *Peyote Religion: A History*. Norman: University of Oklahoma Press, 1987.

Suarès, Carlo. *The Cipher of Genesis*. Boulder, Colo.: Shambhala, 1967.

Sutin, Lawrence. "Messianism's Past, Present, Future." *Gnosis* 39 (Spring 1996).

Swedenborg, Emanuel. *Heaven and Hell*. Translated by George F. Dole. New York: Swedenborg Foundation, 1976.

————. *The Last Judgment in Retrospect*. Translated by George F. Dole. West Chester, Pa.: Swedenborg Foundation, 1996.

Tart, Charles T. *Waking Up: Overcoming the Obstacles to Human Potential*. Boston: Shambhala, 1986.

Tarthang Tulku. *Time, Space, and Knowledge: A New Vision of Reality*. Emeryville, Calif.: Dharma Publishing, 1977.

Teilhard de Chardin, Pierre. *The Phenomenon of Man*. Translated by Bernard Wall. New York: Harper & Row, 1961.

Teish, Luisah. *Jambalaya: The Natural Woman's Book of Personal Charms and Practical Rituals*. San Francisco: Harper & Row, 1985.

Temple, Richard. *Icons and the Mystical Origins of Christianity*. Shaftesbury, Dorset, England: Element, 1990.

————. *Icons: A Sacred Art*. London: Temple Gallery, 1989.

Theophan the Recluse. *The Heart of Salvation: The Life and Teachings of St. Theophan the Recluse*. Translated by Esther Williams Newbury, Mass.: Praxis Institute Press, n.d.

St. Teresa of Avila. *Interior Castle*. Translated by E. Allison Peers. New York: Doubleday/Image, 1961.

Thomas, Dana Lloyd. "A Modern Pythagorean." *Gnosis* 44 (Summer 1997).

Thomas, Keith. *Religion and the Decline of Magic*. New York: Charles Scribner's Sons, 1971.

[Tomberg, Valentin.] *Meditations on the Tarot: A Journey into Christian Hermeticism*. Translated by Robert A. Powell. Warwick, N.Y.: Amity House, 1985.

Tyson, Donald. *The New Magus: Ritual Magic as a Personal Process*. St. Paul, Minn.: Llewellyn, 1988.

Valiente, Doreen. *The Rebirth of Witchcraft*. Custer, Wash.: Phoenix Publishing, 1989.

————. *Witchcraft for Tomorrow*. Custer, Wash.: Phoenix Publishing, 1978.

Van Dusen, Wilson. *The Presence of Other Worlds*. New York: Swedenborg Foundation, 1974.

Vaysse, Jean. *Toward Awakening: An Approach to the Teaching Left by Gurdjieff*. New York: Penguin Arkana, 1989.

Von Franz, Marie-Louise, and C. G. Jung. *Man and His Symbols*. Garden City, N.Y.: Doubleday, 1964.

Waite, A. E. *The Book of Ceremonial Magic*. New York: Bell, 1969.

————. *The Holy Kabbalah*. New York: University Books, n.d.

Walker, James R. *Lakota Belief and Ritual*. Lincoln: University of Nebraska Press, 1980.

Wallis Budge, E. A. *The Gods of the Egyptians*. 2 vols. 1904. Reprint. New York: Dover, 1969.

Walsh, Roger N. *The Spirit of Shamanism*. Los Angeles: Jeremy Tarcher & Co., 1990.

Wapnick, Kenneth. *Absence from Felicity: The Story of Helen Schucman and Her Scribing of A Course in Miracles.* Roscoe, N.Y.: Foundation for A Course in Miracles, 1991.

Waterfield, Robin, ed. *Jacob Boehme: Selected Readings.* Wellingborough, Northamptonshire, England: Crucible, 1989.

———. *René Guénon and the Future of the West.* Wellingborough, Northamptonshire, England: Crucible, 1987.

Watts, Alan W. *Myth and Ritual in Christianity.* Boston: Beacon Press, 1968.

Webb, James. *The Harmonious Circle: The Lives and Work of G. I. Gurdjieff, P. D. Ouspensky, and Their Followers.* New York: G. P. Putnam's Sons, 1980.

———. *The Occult Establishment.* La Salle, Ill.: Open Court, 1976.

———. *The Occult Underground.* La Salle, Ill.: Open Court, 1974.

Weiner, Herbert. *9½ Mystics: The Kabbala Today.* New York: Macmillan, 1969.

White, Timothy. Review of Jim DeKorne, *Psychedelic Shamanism.* In *Shaman's Drum* 37 (Winter 1995).

Wilber, Ken. *The Eye of Spirit.* Boston: Shambhala, 1997.

———. *Sex, Ecology, Spirituality.* Boston: Shambhala, 1995.

Wilhelm, Richard. *The Secret of the Golden Flower: A Chinese Book of Life.* 1931. Reprint. New York: Causeway Books, 1975.

Williams, Michael Allen. *Rethinking "Gnosticism."* Princeton: Princeton University Press, 1996.

Wilmshurst, W.L. *The Meaning of Masonry.* 1927. Reprint. New York: Gramercy Books, 1995.

Wilson, Colin. *The Occult: A History.* New York: Random House, 1971.

Wissler, Clark, and D. C. Duvall. *Mythology of the Blackfoot Indians.* 1908. Reprint. Lincoln: University of Nebraska Press, 1995.

*Writings from the Philokalia on Prayer of the Heart.* Translated by E. Kadloubovsky and G. E. H. palmer. London: Faber & Faber, 1951.

Yagan, Murat. "Sufism and the Source," *Gnosis* 30 (Winter 1994).

Yasar Nuri Öztürk. *The Eye of the Heart.* Istanbul: Redhouse, 1988.

Yates, Frances A. *The Rosicrucian Enlightenment.* 1972. Reprint. London: Ark, 1986.

*The Zohar: Bereshith (Genesis).* Translated by Nurho de Manhar. San Diego, Calif.: Wizards Bookshelf, 1995.

*The Zohar.* Translated by Harry Sperling and Maurice Simon. Five volumes. London: Soncino Press, 1934.

Zuromski, Paul, ed. *The New Age Almanac.* New York: Doubleday 1988.

# Index

# FOR THE BEST IN PAPERBACKS, LOOK FOR THE

In every corner of the world, on every subject under the sun, Penguin represents quality and variety—the very best in publishing today.

For complete information about books available from Penguin—including Puffins, Penguin Classics, and Arkana—and how to order them, write to us at the appropriate address below. Please note that for copyright reasons the selection of books varies from country to country.

**In the United Kingdom:** Please write to *Dept. EP, Penguin Books Ltd, Bath Road, Harmondsworth, West Drayton, Middlesex UB7 0DA.*

**In the United States:** Please write to *Penguin Putnam Inc., P.O. Box 12289 Dept. B, Newark, New Jersey 07101-5289* or call 1-800-788-6262.

**In Canada:** Please write to *Penguin Books Canada Ltd, 10 Alcorn Avenue, Suite 300, Toronto, Ontario M4V 3B2.*

**In Australia:** Please write to *Penguin Books Australia Ltd, P.O. Box 257, Ringwood, Victoria 3134.*

**In New Zealand:** Please write to *Penguin Books (NZ) Ltd, Private Bag 102902, North Shore Mail Centre, Auckland 10.*

**In India:** Please write to *Penguin Books India Pvt Ltd, 11 Panchsheel Shopping Centre, Panchsheel Park, New Delhi 110 017.*

**In the Netherlands:** Please write to *Penguin Books Netherlands bv, Postbus 3507, NL-1001 AH Amsterdam.*

**In Germany:** Please write to *Penguin Books Deutschland GmbH, Metzlerstrasse 26, 60594 Frankfurt am Main.*

**In Spain:** Please write to *Penguin Books S. A., Bravo Murillo 19, 1° B, 28015 Madrid.*

**In Italy:** Please write to *Penguin Italia s.r.l., Via Benedetto Croce 2, 20094 Corsico, Milano.*

**In France:** Please write to *Penguin France, Le Carré Wilson, 62 rue Benjamin Baillaud, 31500 Toulouse.*

**In Japan:** Please write to *Penguin Books Japan Ltd, Kaneko Building, 2-3-25 Koraku, Bunkyo-Ku, Tokyo 112.*

**In South Africa:** Please write to *Penguin Books South Africa (Pty) Ltd, Private Bag X14, Parkview, 2122 Johannesburg.*